SCIENCES OF THE FLESH

REPRESENTING BODY AND SUBJECT
IN PSYCHOANALYSIS

WRITING SCIENCE

EDITORS   Timothy Lenoir and Hans Ulrich Gumbrecht

SCIENCES OF THE FLESH

Representing Body and

Subject in Psychoanalysis

Dianne F. Sadoff

STANFORD UNIVERSITY PRESS

STANFORD, CALIFORNIA 1998

Stanford University Press
Stanford, California
© 1998 by the Board of Trustees of the
Leland Stanford Junior University
Printed in the United States of America

CIP data appear at the end of the book

Acknowledgments

This book has been a long time in the writing, and I have been privileged to receive much professional and financial support during those years. I thank, above all, the John Simon Guggenheim Foundation for a fellowship that allowed me a year off from teaching during 1990–91. I would also like to thank my colleagues at Colby College and at the University of Southern Maine. At Colby, Robert P. McArthur, dean of the faculty and vice president for academic affairs, provided several years of leave during which this project took shape and concluded; Suanne Muehlner administered three research grants that allowed me to travel to libraries in California; the Interdisciplinary Studies Committee provided travel money for a research trip to London. At the University of Southern Maine, Richard Stebbins, dean of the College of Arts and Sciences, provided a semester's leave during which I made the final push to finish the manuscript; the Department of English supported that leave during my first semester of employment at the university. Secretarial help from Rosina Menna, at the University of Southern Maine, and Alexandra Peary, at Colby College, made last-minute research checking possible. My editors at Stanford University Press—Helen Tartar, Xavier Callahan, and Peter Dreyer—have been patient and dedicated. For all this support, I am extremely grateful.

Many librarians and library staff have helped me do research, much of it long distance. Nancy Zinn, director of the archival collections at the University of California at San Francisco Library, helped me gain access to nineteenth-century sources and facilitated the archival photography; the staff at the Wellcome Institute for the History of Medicine aided my work at their library; Ellen Wolfe and the staff of the Rare Books Collection at Harvard University's Countway Medical Library have been extremely helpful. Kate Ruddon at the American College of Obstetricians and Gynecologists sent me bibliographical information and materials. Most important, Sunny Pomerleau, interlibrary loan specialist at Colby College, made my research life as easy as it could be. How she persuaded other librarians to send off their rare volumes and to make microfilms and microfiches of archival holdings, I shall never know, but without her care and dedication, this project would not have been possible.

Many friends and colleagues have supported my work during the writing of this book, and I would like to thank, in particular, several individuals who helped in significant ways. During summer conversations on the Maple porch at the Bread Loaf School of English, Isobel Armstrong helped me position the book's discourse toward questions of representation; John Kucich read the entire manuscript and helped me reframe the argument as I began the last revision; Diana Long introduced me to Bruno Latour's work at a crucial moment during revision, and Cathy Siebold to Otto Kernberg's. I am grateful, as well, to other colleagues who read parts or all of this manuscript or offered crucial advice and assistance while I worked. They include Elizabeth Abel, Laura C. Berry, William Cain, Carol P. Christ, Deirdre David, Martha Noel Evans, Diana Fuss, Toby Gelfand, Deborah Gorham, Susan S. Lanser, Susan Lurie, Jim Messerschmidt, Jessica Munns, Jack Pressman, George E. Smith, and Joan Tronto.

I must mention, in addition, three special debts of gratitude. J. Hillis Miller's 1977 National Endowment for the Humanities Summer Seminar at Yale University changed the course of my professional life. Miller's support during the years of my writing have shaped my sense of myself as an academic, a critic, and a Victorianist gone theoretical. As an example of intellectual dedication and integrity, moreover, Miller is without peer. And to the daily caretaking of Deborah Wertz Scott and Joan Tronto during the darkest days of this book's writing, I owe my emotional survival; without their love, I could not have started to write again, after crisis.

D.F.S.

Contents

A Note on Abbreviation

For in-text citations throughout this book, the 24-volume *Standard Edition of the Complete Psychological Works of Sigmund Freud* (Hogarth Press, 1955–74) is abbreviated *SE*, with volume and page numbers following.

Psycho-analysis may be said to have been born with the twentieth century; for the publication in which it emerged before the world as something new—my *Interpretation of Dreams*—bears the date "1900." But, as may well be supposed, it did not drop from the skies ready-made. It had its starting-point in older ideas, which it developed further; it sprang from earlier suggestions, which it elaborated. Any history of it must therefore begin with an account of the influence which determined its origin and should not over-look the times and circumstances that preceded its creation.

—SIGMUND FREUD, "A Short Account of Psycho-Analysis" (1924 [1923])

No science can exit from the network of its practice. . . . [E]very-thing happens by way of mediation, translation and networks, but this space does not exist, it has no place. It is the unthinkable, the unconscious of the moderns.

—BRUNO LATOUR, *We Have Never Been Modern* (1993 [1991])

SCIENCES OF THE FLESH

REPRESENTING BODY AND SUBJECT
IN PSYCHOANALYSIS

Introduction

Flesh, Ghost, and History

"On the evening of October 20, 1887, Ilma S., Hungarian, aged twenty-nine, single, merchant's daughter, was brought to the hospital by the police authorities of Graz."

So begins Richard von Krafft-Ebing's account of an experimental case study of hypnotism. Krafft-Ebing's study illustrates a problem psychoanalysis would seek to solve: how psyche and soma are linked in hysteria—in this case, through sexual transgression and transitivity. Ilma had been accused of theft by her landlady and, before that, by the nuns of the convent where she had boarded. She told the clinic's doctors that when she awakened from a strange "sleep," she discovered that she had stolen the Lady Superior's cash box. For two years, she suffered attacks of "nerves and fever," during which time she dressed and acted as a man and taught privately in an upper-middle-class family, only to flee when the children's mother fell in love with the handsome, youthful "tutor." While working in a railway office, the cross-dressed Ilma joined her colleagues in carousing with prostitutes. Exposed to male backstage sexual behavior, she had taken an "unconquerable dislike" to men's ways with women and had begun, she said, to enjoy women's "sympathy" and "intelligence."[1]

Later, ill, and acknowledging herself a woman again, Ilma entered a Budapest clinic, where the staff subjected her to hypnotic experimentation, inducing contractures, hallucinations, insensibilities, and cataleptic body poses, Ilma said, as well as brandings inscribed by suggestion: "the five wounds of Christ" on her feet and "the letter J burnt on her right arm." They measured and graphed her states of insensibility, produced spots of bleeding, and magnetically transferred anesthesias from one side of her body to the other. Variously diagnosed as epileptic, hystero-epileptic, cataleptic-hysteric, and said to be afflicted with "congenital perverse sexual feeling," Ilma was a "genuine hysterical character," Krafft-Ebing pronounced (1896 [1889], 1–27). The emphasis in her treatment always fell on the obscure relationship between psychic dysfunction and somatic, indeed histrionic, enactment.

A year earlier, on November 26, 1886, overlooking the psyche-soma problem, which was central to an emergent psychoanalysis, the young Sigmund Freud had presented a male hysteric to the Vienna Society of Medicine. "The patient is a 29-year-old engraver, August P.," Freud began; "the patient's father died, at the age of 48, of Bright's disease; he was a cellar-man, a heavy drinker and a man of violent temper. His mother died, at the age of 46, of tuberculosis." In the write-up of his presentation, "Observation of a Severe Case of Hemi-Anaesthesia in a Hysterical Male," Freud described August's mother's headaches and his five brothers' troubled lives (the oldest had led "an irregular life" and died of syphilis, the second was a hysteric, the third had disappeared, and the other two had died young; Freud's patient was the youngest). August's hitherto uneventful childhood had ended at the age of 8, Freud continued, when he was run over in the street, suffered a ruptured eardrum, and sustained permanent hearing impairment. He thereafter fell ill with fits for two years. Apprenticed to a skilled engraver, the ambitious and hard-working August had sequestered himself, reading and drawing. Falling into reverie and reflection, he had begun to suffer palpitations and to worry about his mental health. His present illness, Freud said, had begun after a dispute with his "dissolute" brother, who, after refusing to pay back a loan, had threatened to kill him and subsequently attacked him with a knife. Fearful, his ears ringing, August had fallen unconscious in the street after this scene, and now suffered hemi-hyperesthesia and -anesthesia, agitation, fatigue, palpitations, tremors, and hallucinatory states.

After he had presented August P.'s family and medical history, hereditary predisposition to illness, and traumatic disease onset, Freud went on to demonstrate to his skeptical audience of physicians his physical examination procedures. He pressed August's "mental nerves" to demonstrate neuralgic change; pricked, pinched, and twisted his ears and earlobes and inserted a small roll of paper into his nose to show cutaneous insensibility on the cranial and facial left side, and normal but anomalous sensibility on the right; introduced his fingers into his throat, producing retching on the sensible side, to show reflex dysfunction concomitant with anesthesia; asked the patient to touch specified anesthetic parts of his face to demonstrate his disordered sense of spatial location; bandaged his eyes, and made him move first his arms and then his fingers to display his disturbed mobility. Freud diagnosed hysterical hemi-anesthesia, with symptomatic hysterogenic zones, mock ovaralgia, and post-traumatic paralysis (*SE*, 1: 25–27).

Freud's presentation barely hints that he would become the renowned inventor of psychoanalysis. For both he and Krafft-Ebing diagnosed hysterical phenomena whose dysfunctions were conceptualized neurologically as motor and nervous incapacity. When differentially diagnosed in relation to functioning bodies, the neurological body in the discourses of neuropathology and psychopathology produced a conventionally framed, recounted, and analyzed account of physiological derangement. The subjectivity under scrutiny could, moreover, be assessed and classified as singular, as possessing a "character": the hysteric lacked secure self-awareness, coherent memory, consistent rationality, and smoothly functioning intentionality. Both Freud and Krafft-Ebing followed the scientific example of the French neuropathologist Jean-Martin Charcot. When Freud presented August P., he mimicked Charcot's modes of physical examination, anatomical mapping, medical interrogation, and pantomimic staging; he appropriated Charcot's demonstrational and diagnostic strategies. Indeed, word of the spectacularly dysfunctional bodies on view at the Salpêtrière Hospice in Paris, where Charcot worked, had been disseminated across Europe through the representational tactics of medical presentation, professional and iconographic publication, and coverage in the popular press. Freud's attempt to transport Charcot's research findings from the research-based Paris hospital to the society of Viennese physicians was only one such translation, although perhaps for my purposes the most notable. Charcot's laboratory experimentation offered researchers a model of and methodology for scientific investigation. Using modern medical technologies for measuring muscular fatigue, energy, and stress, his clinic at the Salpêtrière deployed new concepts developed from human and animal motion studies to produce cutting-edge research findings on physiological function and dysfunction.[2]

Yet the two hysterical patients whose stories I have summarized presented enigmatic somatic symptoms that physiology could not explain, and complex familial and sexual histories. Krafft-Ebing's patient, for example, had contravened a wide range of cultural codes and practices; had disobeyed the dictates of religious and paternal authority by openly carrying on a heterosexual liaison and, covertly, a homosexual one; had shown no reverence for personal property or the demands of institutional loyalty. The enigmatic disease of hysteria, characterized by somatic symptoms without clear organic cause, demanded new theories with which to link psyche and soma. Simultaneously, too, it provided the site on which to construct them.

My central argument is that shifts in nineteenth-century medical and scientific theories of psycho-physical correlation enabled Freud to reinvent, as a means of understanding hysteria's enigmatic symptoms and disordered subjectivities, "plausible bridges" between soma and psyche. I use the term "plausible bridges" to link a number of binary oppositions within which Freud worked to fashion psychoanalysis; for in seeking to produce a modern theory of subjectivity, Freud rejected the psycho-physical theories of concomitance (in which physiological substrata underlay behaviors) and of reflex action (in which behaviors were built of sets of reflexes). By surpassing physiological reductionism, Freudian psychoanalysis joined psyche and soma through a theory of representation (in which one realm stood for, indicated, or implied the other).[3] Pathological psychical structures were thus inscribed in and upon or represented to the organism; the body, in turn, represented these mental structures and registrations as disordered perception, cognition, and subjectivity. By refashioning psycho-physical correlation, psychoanalysis participated in the production of a multiple subjectivity rooted in, yet conceptually separable from, the body—one that complemented modern notions of subject formation emerging simultaneously in the discourses of philosophy, political theory, and the arts. Providing the site on which to construct these plausible bridges, the enigmatic disease of hysteria presented Freud with the perfect opportunity to participate in the production of a modern and multiple subjectivity. The plausible scientific bridges that I identify in this book, which are often constructed on the basis of undemonstrable logical propositions, allow me to highlight the structural power, and yet provisionality, of psychoanalysis's early theories of subjectivity and modes of representation.

By 1905, when Freud published *Three Essays on the Theory of Sexuality*, science had entirely rejected the research methodologies he and Krafft-Ebing had demonstrated in 1886 and 1887. We can witness the shift between 1889 and 1892 in Freud's work, as he invented a new case-historical mode for representing hysteria to medical audiences and the medical public. In 1889, Freud began his case history of Emmy von N.

with a sure sense of traditional diagnostic categories and techniques. "[A] lady of about forty years of age," Emmy "was a hysteric and could be put into a state of somnambulism with the greatest ease." While Freud here deployed Josef Breuer's "technique of investigation under hypnosis" rather than Charcot's tactics of hospital isolation, physiological testing, and medical surveillance, he nevertheless still understood what the medical community meant by diagnosing a patient, with certainty, as hysterical. Yet by 1892, Freud was treating patients who failed to meet the usual requirements for such diagnosis. Lucy R., English governess to a factory director's young children, suffered from "chronically recurrent suppurative rhinitis"; her physician, probably Wilhelm Fliess, could not attribute all her symptoms to "local affection" and referred her to Freud for treatment of olfactory insensitivity, low spirits, fatigue, heaviness in the head, diminished appetite, and loss of efficiency (*SE*, 2: 48, 106). Elisabeth von R., a young lady suffering from pains in her legs and difficulty walking, had been referred to Freud by a physician who thought the "case was one of hysteria," although the patient presented "no trace of the usual indications" of the disease. But Elisabeth's family and medical history, full, disappointingly enough, of "commonplace emotional upheavals" (her father's death, mother's subsequent illness, and sister's death; the patient's sick-nursing and social isolation), could not explain either why she'd fallen ill with hysteria or why her symptoms took the form of leg pain and muscular dysfunction (*SE*, 2: 135, 144). And Katharina, even more strangely, suffered hysterical attacks whose uncommon content was sexual anxiety. By 1905, however, Freud had conceptualized those contents not only physiologically but psychologically, calling Dora's "merely a case of '*petite hystérie*' with the commonest of all somatic and mental symptoms: dyspnoea, *tussis nervosa*, aphonia, and possibly migraines, together with depression, hysterical unsociability, and a *taedium vitae* which was probably not genuine" (*SE*, 7: 23–24; see 15, 55–56, 44–47). Once characterized by neurological and physiological disorder, common hysteria had become a psychical disease.[4]

Freud's neurological training had hardly prepared him to treat these uncommon hysterias. His early research on eel tissue, the anesthetic properties of cocaine, and aphasic cerebral localization prepared him to perform microscopic histological work and neurophysiological tissular investigation. By 1893, moreover, Charcot's example as neuropathology's spokesman no longer seemed to serve him, theoretically or clinically. When he encountered the enigmatic disease of hysteria repeatedly in his

Vienna consulting room, Freud developed new concepts and clinical treatments, new ways to represent these new theories to other medical practitioners. Hypnotic experimentation's physiological testing, observational sketching, and documentary graphing and photographing could not comprehend the patient's symptoms; laboratory reproduction of localized pain, experimentally deranged somatic sensation, and cataleptic paralysis presented symptoms as physiological. Charcot's amphitheatrical presentations of anatomical mapping and theatricalized disability, moreover, no longer properly represented the hysterical patient, nor did it solicit the right audience. Moreover, S. Weir Mitchell's, Joseph-Jules Dejerine's, and Paul Dubois's treatment technologies—rest cure, isolation, and hypnotic suggestion—had failed to cure Freud's hysterical patients. Engineering a new clinical practice and analytic theory, Freud appropriated and revised the concepts of a late-century neuropathology by rewriting existing psycho-physical correlation and causation theories. These rewritings occurred simultaneously and influenced one another in tangled discursive and representational ways; as rewritings, they necessitate that I view the nineteenth-century production of psychoanalysis as a series of theorizations of plausible bridges between soma and psyche, physiology and psychology. I shall therefore examine the psycho-physical theories and concomitant clinical practices of Charcot's neuropathology, Pierre Janet's psychology, Mitchell's rest cure, Dejerine's and Dubois's psychotherapies, and Krafft-Ebing's and Havelock Ellis's sexologies as discursive domains among and within which Freud worked to craft the discourse of psychoanalysis. For Freud innovated even as he borrowed from his teachers, mentors, and peers, recursively rewriting the rules for psycho-physical theorization as representational. Having trained in neurology and set out to treat common hysteria, Freud would end up, nevertheless, rewriting the traditional medical concepts of psycho-physical correlation and causation, patient presentation, and, as August P.'s case has already hinted, family milieu.

This book, then, is about the historical production of psychoanalysis as a modern science of subjectivity that is rooted in yet conceptually separable from the body, a science that linked the two through a particular theory of representation. I shall examine the historical conditions of the emergence of psychoanalysis, concentrating primarily on the 1880s and 1890s and paying particular attention to moments of theoretical formulation in Freud's career from 1885 to 1920. For psychoanalysis emerged out of complex debates in which a number of scientific discourses contested the concepts they shared; Freud's location within these discourses enabled him to move among them, as I have already suggested, and to translate terms and scientific practices from one research site to another. I discuss, too, psychoanalysis's postulations about individual case histories and their embeddedness in family and social circumstances, from the early studies of common and uncommon hysterias published in 1892–93, to the 1905 "Fragment of an Analysis of a Case of Hysteria" (which we know and I shall refer to as "Dora"), and, finally, the 1910–20 cases of fantasied sexual hysteria, homosexuality, and treatment by "wild" psychoanalysis. When Freud published his later texts on hysteria, however, he was no longer concerned with the central problem for hysteria research and treatment: organic as opposed to psychical dysfunction, the ways nerves transmitted bodily perceptual data to the mind and, then, the mind to periphery. He was concerned instead with the ways in which dreams were the "indirect method of representation in the mind," the ways "*symptomatic acts*" pantomimed psychical conflicts and fantasies, the ways memories and self-reflection mediated subjectivity (*SE*, 7: 77–78).

Leaving a neurological or reflex psycho-physical correlation behind, Freud had begun to conceptualize the ways pathological psychical structures were represented by the body in symptomatic acts and representative texts. For uncommon symptomatic contents, like Katharina's sexual anxiety, refused to disappear from Freud's consulting room, and he found that his hysterical patients' commonplace emotional upheavals signified their symptoms' embeddedness in their personal histories, family relations, and social circumstances. Altering Charles Féré's definition of the "neuropathic" family, Freud portrayed it as a unit of subject formation that supported and spawned fantasies, affects, and self- and other-representations. Hereditary predisposition had vanished from Freud's texts; a "*liability* to being ill" had been rewritten as a psychical "*motive* for being ill" (*SE*, 7: 42). Yet from the first, Freud's attention to mental representations adumbrated his later theories of psychical reality and unconscious fantasy, however suppressed and temporally mediated their emergence as concepts was. I view Freud's psychoanalytic invention of a new psycho-physical theory as itself embedded in the hysteria debate in the 1880s and 1890s, a debate in which psyche's relation to soma was being scientifically interrogated, scrutinized, and renegotiated.

In deploying the concepts of discursive emergence and historical embeddedness, I have found the opposed theories of both Jean Laplanche and Michel Foucault useful yet partial. For Laplanche, psychoanalysis represents an epistemic shift, since psychoanalytic emergence bears a "*foundational* import," as does the clinical and theoretical gesture that "creates the psychoanalytic situation." Founding thus "means founding anew," tracing the new science historically to "the founding act" and the "founder" who performed "an inaugural gesture." Laplanche argues that the "heterogeneous and exogenous foundations" some critics have proposed for psychoanalysis cannot explain its historical emergence. These "domains," Laplanche concedes, "have a place" in the "field opened up by psychoanalysis," but that place—both on the boundaries of and within the psychoanalytic field—does not imply a historically causal relationship between them. Thus Freud's physiological representation of the psychical apparatus misrecognized, Laplanche maintains, and indeed relied upon, not a true but "a *false* biology" (Laplanche, 45–46, 53–54, 16). Although the psychoanalytic domain modified neighboring knowledges, it neither emerged from, nor could be deduced from or reduced to, heterogeneous disciplinary fields. In Laplanche's portrait, psychoanalytic emergence is an epistemic rupture, produced by an originating act, and serves as a discursive break with other contemporary systems of knowledge. Foucault's analytics, on the contrary, debunks traditional historical values and institutions by theorizing its originating moments as historically fortuitous (Goldstein 1987, 3–5). Foucault's work is not based on the "attribution of influences, exchanges, transmitted information, or communications." It requires neither the speaking and self-knowing subject nor causal individual activities. "No one is responsible for an [interpretation's or discourse's] emergence; no one can glory in it, since it always occurs in the interstice" (Foucault 1972, 138; id. 1977, 150). Because Foucault empties historical and discursive categories of the subject, initiative and initiating acts become, as he says, interstitial, highly mediated in their contingency. Foucault thus analyzes the field of relations that obtain between discursive formations so as to produce a theory of discursive drift, an "analysis of *transformations*" that traces "phenomena of continuity, return, and repetition." Foucault's mapping of discursive formations, then, does not "found" a theory but "establish[es] a possibility" for discursive emergence.[5]

My notion of psychoanalytic emergence as embedded in a complex and interrelated set of discursive domains appropriates and revises these theories of epistemic shift and discursive drift. Foucault's archaeology formulates rules by which the analytic interpreter may describe the historical specificity of discursive formations to show how one acts upon another, how concepts are appropriated, translated, and rewritten from one field of knowledge to another. Although this idea of historical dissemination supports and sustains my work here, I view Freud's innovations within this matrix of discourses as significant. While I demonstrate that Freud shared terminologies and concepts with precursors and contemporaries, I also maintain that the conceptual space his theories occupied deviated from, even as they overlapped with, other such conceptual structures. My account of psychoanalytic emergence, then, attends to the historical translatability of concepts across discursive boundaries and among research settings; I analyze the complex, layered series of advances, retreats, negotiations, rewritings, suppressions, and returns that Freud undertook in response to other formulations of plausible bridges between hysterical psyche and soma, between the discourses of physiology and psychology.

Because I examine the ways in which psychoanalysis is both an innovation and a historically located emergent discourse, moreover, I must recount psychoanalysis's history from a nonteleological perspective, without a traditional plot that inevitably produces Freud as hero. In the chapters that follow, therefore, I shuttle between Freud's texts and the discourses he rewrote, moving nonteleologically within and among the discourses in play in the hysteria debates. Yet I also view Freud's conceptual innovations as a complex set of "revisions"—of other scientific concepts and, later, of his own early notions—that enabled him to institutionalize psychoanalytic theory and practice. I portray Freud's invention of psychoanalysis, then, as both dialogic and dynamic. From this perspective, as I have said, psychoanalysis innovatively revised even as it emerged from nineteenth-century psychiatric, neuropathological, and sexological theories of psycho-physical correlation, family relations, and sexual desire.

Since I view psychoanalytic theory as both revisionary and innovative, I seek neither to mythologize nor to demonize Freud, its "founder." Debunking Freud has become a facile scholarly activity. Yet I endeavor, too, not to replicate the honorific representation of Freud as "lonely genius."[6] Indeed, I view Freud's invention of this myth as serving to claim scientific distinction and credit for himself, to pose as theoretical originator and member of collegial networks. I seek, then, to avoid producing either of the competing myths of psychoanalytic founding that Arnold I. Davidson identifies: Freud as "triumphant revolutionary" or Freud as "demagogue, usurper, and megalomaniac" borrower of ideas.[7] Terry Eagleton provides, perhaps, a more balanced assessment of Freud's historical location and his status as founder. Eagleton's perspective, like my own, historicizes psychoanalysis neither to celebrate nor debunk Freud but to theorize psychoanalytic discourse as implicated in the production of modern subjectivity. For, he argues, Freud produced "a materialist theory of the making of the human subject." Eagleton also suggests the ways in which psychoanalysis can be viewed as socially or culturally significant, as theorizing the notion that subjects are related to yet different from objects, nature, and nonhuman beings. Despite its apparent elision of the social and cultural, he maintains, psychoanalysis makes it possible to imagine the development of the human individual in social and historical terms; although psychoanalysis functioned by applying late nineteenth-century concepts of social and sexual normativity, those norms are everywhere and always historically situated, by no means self-evident, and in no sense, as Eagleton says, "given by Nature" (Eagleton 1983, 162–64). Here, Eagleton touches on binary oppositions that I deploy throughout this book to argue that Freud interrogated even as he participated in the modern project to constitute a new subjectivity rooted in, yet different from, the body. Because, like Eagleton, I view psychoanalytic emergence as dialogic and its rewritings as innovative, I describe its inventions as negotiations of a historically produced, normative but not necessarily normalizing, subjectivity. That subjectivity, rooted in yet conceptually separate from the body, was produced by even as it helped fashion new psycho-physical theories of psyche and soma, and challenged even as it helped constitute the difference between physiology and psychology. Among and within such retheorizations, the modern notions of subject formation, the oedipalized family, and sexual normativity were being invented.

I have used the term "science" to describe Freud's new discourse, a term currently contested within and outside psychoanalytic theory. Adolf Grünbaum, for example, attacks psychoanalysis as epistemologically flawed and untestable because it provides a poverty of clinical confirmations (Grünbaum 1984, 124, 189); Frank J. Sulloway attempts to reduce psychoanalytic theory to evolutionary biologism to prove it unoriginal (Sulloway 1979, 498–99 et passim); Malcolm Macmillan argues that psychoanalysis is illogical and speculative, that it substitutes "plausible explanations" for facts (Macmillan 1991, 7, 195–96, 141–42, 117–19). Yet neither the accusation that psychoanalysis failed to produce experimental replications, nor that it deployed a natural theory of organisms, nor that it displaced the "real" with hypothesis comprehends Freud's use of the term "science." I use that term to mean that psychoanalysis is a knowledge-producing system based on observation; those observations, collected over sufficiently repeated trials, can be tested by comparison of cases, inductive reasoning, formulation of hypotheses, and logical production of generalized and generalizeable as well as systematic statements. I use the term "experiment," to refer to the procedures of laboratory-based research projects and to similar, although not biological or histological, testings performed in other locations that also undertake procedures based on scientific principles—locations such as the sexologist's office and the psychoanalytic consulting room. Although it theorizes natural or "hard" laboratory science, Bruno Latour's ethnography of science anchors and sustains my view that psychoanalysis can be described as a knowledge-producing set of practices that meet the requirements of a science. Claiming to reproduce natural events in the laboratory, Latour maintains, the experimental scientist fabricated the very laws of nature he presumed to "discover"; declaring objects and testable events as naturally occurring, he manufactured those events in the laboratory and through his research practices. Deploying the scientific networks to which he belonged, he translated his findings to other research locations. As Latour insists, "No science can exit from the network of its practice" (Latour 1993, 24).

Taking its cue from laboratory research, psychoanalysis, too, experimentally investigated the human organism. Although a different kind of research domain than the laboratory, Freud's consulting room was, I maintain throughout this book, no less a "laboratory" of sorts for producing scientific theories about the human subject. For in his early work on hysteria, Freud observed not natural organisms but the join between organism and subject. Observing and collecting data on the relationship between hysterical soma and psyche, reasoning inductively about the observations he had collected, Freud posited a plausible new bridge between material and mental life. This psycho-physical representation theory of body's link to psyche and psyche's to body created hypotheses about a natural yet social entity, a hybrid and highly mediated being. Produced by scientific networks, translatable from one research site to another, the hysteric was an experimental quasi-object, available for scrutiny, testing, and inductive reasoning. As figure or trope, she both sustained and flouted the modern project to isolate an essentialized subjectivity that was separated from natural objects through the mediatory work of social and discursive scientific practices. Seeking to breach them even as his theories sustained these oppositions, Freud participated in the scientific work of translating explanations and findings between research sites—and leveraging them into the cultural domain. For Freud so profitably mobilized his research results, I maintain in my conclusion, that he produced new scientific and institutional networks, new social groups of allies, adherents, and followers. Freud's psychoanalytic "laboratory" thus participated in what Latour calls "the modern critique," the project to separate the category of subjects from the social and natural domains and, at the same time, to disavow that very separation (Latour 1993, 23–39).

Fundamental to Freud's innovative rewritings of psycho-physical theories, I also argue here, was a revised theory of representation. Conceptualizing the hysterical body as a medium for the representation of symptoms that disobeyed organic laws and, instead, symbolized psychical dysfunctions or disabilities, Freud developed a diagnostic semiotic that could read symptoms as visible signs on the body of pathological mental structures. Hardly mimetic representations, however, these were psycho-physical expressions of illness always themselves mediated by certain structures of representation. Conceptualizing organic as opposed to psychical dysfunction, Freud traced the ways in which nerves transmitted somatic perceptual data to the mind and the ways in which the mind then represented those data to the body's periphery and so projected them as personality. The individual's cognitive sense of self, then, was produced by and embedded in a series of sensual and perceptual acts that produced, and were themselves forms of, self-representation. Only ascertainable in analysis through observation, interpretation, and reconstruction of the patient's recounted and enacted self-representations—her visualized scenes, erotic scenarios, and transference behavior—these representations were mediated by the signifying structures of words and images, the retrospective reinventions of memory, the deferred action of trauma, and the diphasic onset of sexuality. As analyst and case historian, Freud then represented appropriate cases to other medical and clinical practitioners; seeking to translate his research along scientific networks, Freud created a new form for patient presentation, a new representational text. Like the hysteric's representation of her body and subjectivity to herself, like her self-representations in the psychoanalytic situation, the Freudian case history was a special kind of representation; it necessarily recounted the layered representations and multiple identifications that the patient had recounted and the analyst had then interpreted. The patient could be said to recover because, although she had presented with a personal history disrupted by illness, she left treatment with a highly mediated and narratively constituted scenario, a reworked personal history, and a sense that her life story had been rewritten for the better. Because Freud's concept of representation was fundamental to his psycho-physical theorizations, I maintain here, it enabled his production of this new scientific genre.

The centrality of the subject to psychoanalysis disturbs or delights Freud's current critics. Mikkel Borch-Jacobsen argues that Freud presupposed what his theory sought to explain: the formation of the subject. By smuggling the concept of representation into the unconscious (*Vorstellung*), Borch-Jacobsen maintains, Freud reintroduced into theory the idea he was trying to banish, "a subject to which representations appear" (Borch-Jacobsen 1997, 211). In order to make this claim, however, Borch-Jacobsen reduces the Freudian unconscious to a Cartesian dualism, effectively denying Freud's dynamic and interactive model of consciousness, the unconscious, and identification. Seeking to complicate this dualism, Borch-Jacobsen argues that the primary emotional tie is to the mother and prior to any object relation or concept of sexual difference; thus original identification precedes and coincides with object relation and belies any notion of a preexistent subject. Indeed, he says, quoting Freud, the infant expresses identification by object relation: "'The breast is a part of me, I am the breast.' Only later: I have it, that is, 'I am not it'" (*SE*, 23: 299; Borch-Jacobsen 1994, 270). Psychoanalysis forecloses this identification, Borch-Jacobsen says, suppressing questions of mimetic desire, identification as implicated in desire, and the possibility of homosexuality. Making object-desire central to sexuality, then, psychoanalysis "reinstates [the] old but always new question of the subject." In analysis, as a result, the "structure of representation as autorepresentation" becomes the "true and ultimate subject" of psychoanalysis (Borch-Jacobsen 1988, 117–19; id. 1992b, 15–24). Paul Ricoeur argues, to the contrary, that psychoanalysis is an archeology of the subject. Its concepts dispossess consciousness of immediacy, identifying it as a topographical locality and undoing the old psychology of consciousness. Indeed, Ricoeur emphasizes, as did Freud, that subject formation is a mechanism and analytic work, a form of action. The activity of interpretation, Ricoeur insists, is performed on a field, not of the analyst's subjectivity, but of a semiotics, and the analytic work is a *"discipline of reflection."*[8] Yet both Borch-Jacobsen's and Ricoeur's portraits simplify psychoanalytic representation, the one as a naively produced autorepresentation, the other as a teleologized self-consciousness. Neither portrait views psychoanalytic representation as itself a multiple act of psycho-physical self-inscription.

Positing psychoanalysis as a dialogically produced and multiply embedded discourse, I view patient self-representation similarly, as a doubly
reflective practice of self-and-other spectatorship. That activity, a kind of
scenic reproduction, constituted and was reconstituted in a multiply embedded set of patient self-representations—dreams, fantasies, reveries,
memories, transferential pantomimes—in which the patient portrayed
herself as embodied subject. Watching those pictures of herself, she
viewed herself as herself, yet saw herself depicted as though she were another. The self-representation on which this subject reflected, moreover—
the reflected and reflected-upon representation of herself—made possible
identification with self and with other, with self-as-other; in a complex
activity of recognition and misrecognition, this dialectic stimulated both
identification and desire. Such scenic reproduction by the patient of and
to herself both enabled and defeated the mirroring of body and psyche;
as self-representation, it embodied and elided subjective formation. Prac-
titioner as well as object of self-spectatorship, this hybrid subject in
analysis recounted, reflected on, and reciprocally reinterpreted those narrativized self-and-other depictions. The psychoanalytic discipline thus
produced cure—the provisional and unstable effect enabled and elided
by self-reflection—through the semiotic work of multiply embedded acts
of discursive and scenic representation. Leaving analysis with this discipline as habit, the psychoanalyzed subject practiced reflection: watching
her self- and other-representations, cautioning herself about such representation when she saw them recursively repeat, reflecting on the scenarios imaginatively narrativized around those reflections. Not a singular or
univocal autorepresentation, as Borch-Jacobsen depicts it, psychoanalytic
representation was a highly mediated, multiply produced, and palimpsestically represented set of sensate, perceptual, and discursive acts. Not a
teleological temporal progression to self-knowledge, as Ricoeur portrays
it, psychoanalytic self-representation was a multiply plotted and diffusely
embedded practice of subject formation.

This theory of psychoanalytic representation likewise enables me to
view the concept of affect as central to, if elided in, Freud's early studies
on hysteria. Reducing the Freudian transference to hypnotic "rapport,"
Borch-Jacobsen theorizes affect as the force that informs the mimetic efficacy of cures for and through what he calls "trance" states. Yet Borch-
Jacobsen also retreats from that position, arguing instead that trance
states—which are paradoxically universal and culturally variant—
demonstrate in common a depersonalization (transgressing the boundaries

between self and other) that constitutes an "incommunicable *lived experience*." Hence, he maintains, trance states are closely connected with body and affect, and are disconcertingly linked with "memory, will, and self-consciousness." The physician cures by inducing a trance that is continuous with and mimes the patient's possession by speaking it as a publicly visible mimetic indifferentiation of self and other. For Borch-Jacobsen, as for Michel Henry, affect is acted, outside will and want, and without the mediation of representation.[9] Yet this position regards affect primarily and solely as passion in action, limiting its usefulness as a heuristic. I broaden the concept of affect here, drawing on Otto Kernberg's theorization of affects as psycho-physiological behavior patterns that include specific cognitive appraisals, facial expressions, subjective experiences of a pleasurable or painful nature, and a muscular and neurological discharge pattern (Kernberg 1991, 3–20). This theory of affect, which articulates acts, subjective experiences, cognitions, and representations of self and object relations as well as passions, enables me to theorize affects as psycho-physical plausible bridges and depict them as implicated with, rather than radically separate from, representation; it allows me, as well, to view Freud's earliest plausible bridges as adumbrating his later, more complexly representational ones. Using this conceptualization, I portray affect as bodily, emotive, cognitive, and communicative; as structuring and structured by the subject's fantasmatic wishes, desires, and hallucinations; as psycho-physical linkage within psychoanalytic theory of physiology and psychology. I also depict affect, then, as recursively reemergent in Freud's later theory; for his later notions of drive as internal self-representation recuperated the notion of affect implicit in abreaction and cathartic cure. The analytic tasks of scenic reproduction, self-spectatorship, narrative recounting, and collaborative interpretation could produce these affect-laden acts as meaningful or significant only because Freud placed psycho-physical representation squarely at the center of a theory of subject formation.

My notion of psychoanalytic representation likewise reveals Freud's theory of sexuality as a displacement from hysterical psycho-physical symptomatology. In "Dora," Freud began to investigate hysterical symptoms as highly mediated representative enactments of sexual dysfunction, self- and other-representations, and erotic scenarios. In *Three Essays on a Theory of Sexuality*, Freud suppressed psycho-physical representation as the mechanism that expressed the somatic symptoms and sustained cathartic abreaction; he replaced the early theories of seduction and actual neurosis (disease caused by real sexual dissatisfaction) with, he specified, a *theory* of sexuality, a physiology of permeable membranes and sensual pleasures. Indeed, sexuality proved to be the perfect psychophysical plausible bridge; both physiological and psychological, sensate and affective, sexuality as a concept could govern subject formation and structure the personal history in which it was embedded. When fashioned as the fundamental conceptual structure in a psychology of subjectivity rooted in the body, the theory of sexuality resolved the problems implicit in representation as plausible bridge between psyche and soma, problems I shall address later in this book. Both "Dora" and *Three Essays*, moreover, gendered and stratified the psychoanalytic investigation of sexuality, suppressing, on the one hand, the conceptualization of female homosexuality and, on the other, making the male subject central to psychoanalytic theoretical production. These 1905 theories, however, adumbrated the homosexual's replacement of the hysteric as central case-historical figure. For a *theory* of sexuality that interrogated even as it deployed sexual normativities paradoxically produced sexual transitivity, the ability to cross as well as mediate boundaries, as its privileged theoretical trope.

The gendering of sexuality has caused or facilitated the difficult relations between psychoanalysis and feminism, relations that have often been staged around the figure of Jacques Lacan. Seeking to reintroduce the hysteria diagnosis to French psychoanalytic practice, Lacan and his followers "praised" the disease, reducing its symptomatology to an always already available female sexuality and the hysterical transference to a demand for love, as distinct from need or desire (Safouan 1980, 55–60). Bernini's statue of St. Theresa, Lacan proclaims, makes hysteria immediately visible: "you only have to go and look" to see that she swoons, she is ecstatic, "she's coming, there is no doubt about it" (Mitchell and Rose 1982, 147). From this perspective, hysteria is watched by and produced for the knowing male analyst rather than the psychoanalytic patient: her symptomatology is *for* him; her (eroticized) histrionics produce his visual pleasure. His vision is unmediated, his observation unproblematic, his reasoning unquestionable. Despite its spectacular staging of hysteria in a domain of visibility, however, this aestheticization of a disease as female and necessarily sexual labels and so effectively trivializes an illness that deserves diagnosis and treatment rather than mythologizing. My representations of hysteria, my notions of representation as the privileged mechanism of hysterical symptom formation, seek instead to mediate and problematize the binarisms everywhere apparent in the hysteria discourse. I view the histrionic body's symptomatic action, pantomimic acts, and fantasmatic scenarios as necessarily locating the body as matter and image in space and time, in its history, as part of a matrix in which plausible bridges between physiology and psychology, female sexuality and a historically situated sociality, may be theorized.

This book is a result, at least in part, of my dissatisfactions with feminist theory's encounter with Freud. My perspective on psychoanalytic emergence, representation, and psycho-physical retheorization leads me to modify and displace either naive feminist or singularly psychoanalytic accounts of hysterical psycho-physical correlation. I argue, implicitly but with rigor, against feminist notions of hysterical symptomatology as a form of self-expression. The literary-critical move to generalize hysteria outside the field of psychology, to package it as an aesthetic or poetic category especially appropriate for describing, interpreting, and analyzing the cultural work of women, sentimentalizes a debilitating condition, essentializing and marginalizing female literary and artistic production. I reject strictly social constructivist feminist accounts of hysteria that portray the hysteric as a victim of power struggles with nineteenth-century doctors, as disfigured by the social roles available to women and by Victorian ideologies of womanhood. I view accounts of the hysteric as proto-feminist or subversive sorceress that depict the disease as an appropriate and available strategy for resisting such victimization as retrospectively reinterpreting real women's suffering, as making historically teleological and efficacious a symptomatology that disabled nineteenth-century patients. Feminist studies of discourse, this book argues, must carefully temper the claims of social constructivism (the "social roots" of disease) with an understanding of its explanatory limitations. For modes of resistance that enfeeble rather than empower the person who practices them bow to rather than challenge dominant social values and practices. My own account of hysteria seeks to mediate the dualisms of social constructivism and essentialism by deploying psycho-physical concepts of body, subject, and sexuality. Although it is historical rather than philosophical, my project resembles Elizabeth Grosz's attempt to refigure and place the body squarely within a theory of subjectivity.[10] Informed by feminist epistemology, this book nevertheless avoids a feminist program.

I have chosen to frame this book about Freud's theories and practice with his early case histories of women to demonstrate the centrality to psychoanalytic theory of female subjectivity and self-representation. I begin with *Studies on Hysteria* to sketch the terms and methodologies of Freud's new semiology; I end with "Dora" and "The Psychogenesis of a Case of Homosexuality in a Woman" (1919) as case historical inventions and argue that the latter rewrites the former with the homosexual at its center.[11] Freud's "rhetoric" of the hysterical body, I argue in Chapter 1, identified the organism as a medium through which the mind, via the nervous system, represented dysfunction. Receiving sensations and perceptions from the body periphery, the mind transmitted messages that caused voluntary and involuntary motor activity, cutaneous sensibility, and sensate function, but might have, in addition, sent messages of localized muscular immobility, pain, insensibility, or dysfunction. The mind produced articulated and bundled concepts of personality, self-presentation, and character, yet might, in addition, disarticulate or dissociate those concepts of self. I take as foundational "Some Points for a Comparative Study of Organic and Hysterical Motor Paralyses" (1888–93), in which Freud conceptualized psycho-physical correlation for his emergent clinical practice; in that essay, Freud described hysterical paralysis as representational, as an immobility that expressed itself somatically but disobeyed organic laws of muscular function and bodily localization. Representation, then, served as an early, and provisional, plausible bridge between psyche and soma in hysterical symptom formation. Freud's modes of interpretation mobilized rhetorical categories with which to read these symptoms that, disregarding organic rule, represented the body symbolically and as symbol. To read the psychic conflicts he soon saw as motivating somatic malfunction, Freud created a semiotic of pathological structures; these interpretive strategies unriddled symptoms as representing past, and now repressed and thus unconscious, events. By 1900, then, Freud had begun to conceptualize patient reproduction of scenes, the ways memory reworked and restructured their elements, and the notion of representability.

In Chapters 2 through 4, I examine three interrelated discursive domains as contextual sites for Freud's theories of psycho-physical representation. I identify those sites with the discourses of diagnosis, research description, and clinical treatment, and locate them within three dominant fields of nineteenth-century neuropathological and psychopathological discourse: the history of hysteria, the debates about experimental laboratory research, and the discourse of rest cures. Chapter 2 quickly sketches hysteria's medical history, from the Greeks to Freud, to demonstrate the discursive shift from anatomical to physiological models of the diseased body (see Roudinesco 1986, 1: 21–84). While the anatomical notions of location and proximity anchored Hippocratic and ancient gynecological propositions about wandering wombs, the nervous system and the con-comitant terminologies of transmission, circulation, and imitation had be-come central by the time of Sydenham; in the nineteenth century, the "nerves" and their functions grounded the debate about social-situational, somatic, or psychical causation (see King 1993 and Rousseau 1993). Be-cause I view psycho-physical theorization as central to Freud's invention of psychoanalysis, I argue that nineteenth-century neurological positings of disease seat, organic localization, and sympathetic nervous system transmission through reflex action competed in his early work with the emerging psychoanalytic concept of representation as the privileged mechanism of symptom formation. For cathartic therapy and abreactive acts depended, in part, on reflex theories of psycho-physical correlation, theories fundamental to Breuer's conceptualization of the talking cure. The sexed body also underwrites my look at hysteria's medical history. First known as the "disease of the mother" (or womb or "matrix"), hyste-ria took as its seat, early modern doctors assumed, the female reproduc-tive organs; their function and dysfunction, the female life-cycle changes they caused, the characterological functions they supported or deformed, all affected patient self-representation. Indeed, the breast as reproductive and sexual organ circulates through my own text, for its role in function-alizing females takes center stage in Freud's early "A Case of Successful Treatment by Hypnotism" (1892–93), a case in which Freud restored through suggestion the flow of a new mother's breast milk. The breast's sexual, social, and historical meanings proved useful, then, not only to early modern gynecologists but to nineteenth-century cultural anthro-pologists, sexologists, and hypnotists, as well as to nerve doctors.

In Chapter 3, I argue that Freud's translation of Charcot's experimen-tal laboratory research into his clinical practice enabled his theoretical production of psycho-physical representation. The Salpêtrière's sophisti-cated neuropathological work articulated clinical observation with basic scientific work in neurology, physiology, and pathological anatomy to produce groundbreaking research on nerve tissue morphology and physi-ology. Theorized by Charles Féré and Alfred Binet, performed by the staff on hypnotized research subjects, the clinic's research studied a wide range of somatic dysfunctions. In the laboratory, the staff provoked and reproduced somatic symptoms such as paralysis, fit, and catatonia; they applied electricity to nerves and muscles to test for muscular strength, neuronal sensitivity, and bodily mobility. Using new technology devel-oped by the physiologists Angelo Mosso (the ergograph) and E. J. Marey (chronophotography), the Salpêtrians tested physiological fatigue and observed the body immobilized or in motion over time, catatonic or facially disfigured, and invariably displaying physiological dysfunction.[12] Pierre Janet, who conceptualized the psychological aspects of the clinic's research, tested for deranged sensation and perception; he presented hypnotized research subjects situated in fictitious scenarios, whom he required to produce acts appropriate to the experimentally induced symptom he had created. Janet called hysteria a "malady through representation," and I have found his phrase useful throughout this book as both conceptual frame and rhetorical focus. Although he did not theorize the complex of psycho-physical, self and object representative, and affect-laden events that Freud studied as hysterical representation, Janet meant that, when presented with fictitious events and false outcomes, the hypnotized, will-less, and purposeless hysteric misrepresented the world to and for herself as profoundly as she did when not somnambulous.

Charcot has been demonized by twentieth-century critics for his notion of "hysteria major," a universalizing disease schema that aroused medical and scientific debate about the clinic's research methods in its own time, as it does now. Yet I argue that, despite his scientific commitment to reflex psycho-physical theories, Charcot's demonstrations adumbrated a rudimentary representational bridge between psyche and soma. His presentations mapped anatomical configurations and hysterogenic zones; demonstrated physiological dysfunctions (disturbed gaits, senses of spatial location, and muscular contortions); and modeled his methodologies for causing and stopping fits, swoons, and attacks. The clinic's staging of bodily contortions, cataleptically transfixed women, and hallucinatory tableaux made hysteria visible even as it paradoxically exoticized and naturalized the disease sufferer, soliciting spectatorship of female and male bodies. The clinic's photographic studios and the iconographies they produced collected, narrativized, and documented the clinic's research subjects as naturally subject to such experimentation, archeologizing and archiving even as it pictured them. Invoking the scientific terminology of John Hughlings Jackson, the clinic produced and documented "experiments made by nature." I pay particular attention to Charcot in this book because he has been misrepresented by feminist and Foucauldian critics of psychoanalysis (see Showalter 1985, 145–64; Didi-Huberman 1982). Freud learned from Charcot, I maintain, how to stage hysteria as a set of physiological dysfunctions available to scientific observation and analytic scrutiny; he learned from Janet, one of Charcot's star pupils, how to use and transmute the notion of scenarios. And by "staging" and "scenario," I mean the public showing of events that had been reproduced in the laboratory, the soliciting of an assembled public as potential interest group, as possible adherents and agitators outside the laboratory for the research's mission.[13] Adding Charcot's structures of spectatorship to his own notion of abreactive psycho-physical acts, Freud fashioned a clinical practice historically continuous and discursively contiguous with that of Charcot.[14]

In Chapter 4, I argue that hysteria treatments from rest cure to psychotherapy treated the reflex rather than the representational body and so failed to address the central problem of hysteria, the body's physical representation of psychical suffering. S. Weir Mitchell's rest cure, deployed by Freud and Breuer in their first clinical work with hysteria, produced and normalized the healthy body, seeking to functionalize and make productive the ill individual. Mitchell represented the hysterical body as in need of simple, natural remedy. To make fat and blood, he prescribed rest in bed, a milk diet, and gradual dietary addition of broths and beef tea; isolation, sequestration, and lack of excitation; massage and faradization to prevent muscular atrophy; and moral persuasion by an authoritative physician. Mitchell restored the wasted body to its proper plumpness through a rigorous economy of input and outcome. Corpulent again through dietary, somatic, and functional superintendence, the fattened body could return to regimes of social circulation, to circuits of exchange within and outside the domestic domain, and, to the proper fleshy female state, pregnancy. Claiming the status of the benevolent professional, Mitchell represented his female patients as reducible to infancy, as morally reeducable into nerve, willpower, belief in individual agency, and social-somatic productivity. Rest-cure therapeutics, then, served to shore up nineteenth-century ideologies associated with the bourgeois family's biological and moral imperatives, the valuing of the domestic as opposed to the public domain, and woman's (re)productive function within it. Rest cures sought to allay even as they exposed anxieties about middle-class domestic and economic arrangements in general. Synecdochally reading the body's symptoms as characterologically and socially determined, Mitchell seemed to conflate the natural and cultural domains. Yet I emphasize in this chapter that the naturalized notion of the body in rest-cure representations was homologous with but not reducible to social circulations. For these homologies produced and governed late-nineteenth-century thinking about bodies, motion, work, and sex and the scientific research that had theorized, documented, and functionalized each.[15]

The twin notions of functionalism and productivity also governed psychotherapeutic representations of patient and possible cure. In these treatment regimes, physicians portrayed patients as teachable and trainable, as needing to learn appropriate bodily and social functions. Mitchell's authoritative and benevolent moral reeducation belonged to this class of treatments. So, too, did Freud's early hypnotic cures and the persuasive and "rational" psychotherapies of Dubois and Dejerine. Whether practiced in Europe or the United States, these nineteenth-century psychotherapies depicted patients as physically ill because their diseased willpower, nerve, and sense of capability had malfunctioned. Like rest-cure physicians, psychotherapists practiced in part by isolating and sequestering patients; confinements ranging from disciplinary to surveillant moved out of the asylum or hospital ward and into the outpatient clinic or private practice to heal members of the middle class. Portrayed by physicians as sickened by the business and domestic regimens of civilized life, the middle-class patient often shopped for cures, as had Freud's Wolf-Man, going from doctor to doctor and seeking to relieve the malaise that ailed him. Functionalizing the dysfunctional body, persuasive psychical treatments restored individual patients to health, to a capacity for work and sexual satisfaction, to reproductive capability and a general sense, if not of well-being, at least of psychological betterment. Freud and Breuer's cathartic treatment, I argue, both appropriated and departed from these therapeutics. Deploying the concept of affects as psycho-physical bridge, the cathartic cure articulated neurological and emotive discharge, symbolic action, cognitive appraisal, self- and object-representation, bodily sensation, psychomotor behavior, and communicative storytelling into its clinical practice. While Freud's studies of hysteria broke with even as they rewrote Breuer's neurological reflex theories, the cathartic cure made possible Freud's invention of a science that, knowing its curative limits, did not seek to functionalize and make productive the ill individual.

In my final three chapters, I examine the dominant nineteenth-century sources of material for the construction of modernized plausible bridges, from sexology to psychiatric case study. In Chapter 5, I argue that scientific sexology, deploying the new physiology, represented the body as always already, or ready to be, aroused. Rather than map the body with nerves that transmitted messages, or portray it as an overwrought organism in need of rest, sexologists depicted the body as a fabric of mucous membranes, a tissue of sensation-producing boundaries, and a set of penetrable openings. The logic of sex, a term I borrow from

Foucault, sought to describe, analyze, and rationalize pleasure, to make it functional and place it in the service of (hetero)sexual and reproductive acts. Yet function inevitably suggested dysfunction. Or rather, patients who consulted physicians like Richard von Krafft-Ebing and Albert von Schrenck-Notzing suffered serious dysfunction and so focused sexual science on what it defined as aberrant or deviant acts, especially homosexuality and perversion. Marshaling the concept of instinct, the sexologists, like the moral medicators, sought to restore malfunctioning bodies to full physiological function and sexual satisfaction. Male patients—a large percentage of the sex doctors' clients—were thus restored to potent heterosexual intercourse, and women to fertility, maternity, and biologico-moral nurture. Like many of the physicians I write about here, Freud crossed the boundaries between and among these late-nineteenth-century functionalizing discourses. Yet while he treated his first patients for real sexual abuse or difficulty, and so fashioned the seduction and sexual theories, Freud disavowed his early sexological treatments in favor of a psychosexual therapeutics. Rewriting the sexologists' deployment of instinct as physiological functionalism, Freud theorized an always already dysfunctional sexuality. He translated the sexological pleasure body into the fantasmatic and erotogenic body that, inscribed with its desiring history, inevitably produced dissatisfaction (see David-Ménard 1989, 65–104). The infant body, moreover, situated in family, home, and nursery, had been stimulated into sensation from birth. The paths along which it developed, attached to objects, and altered or played out aims as the perverse body came under the sway of normative reproductivity, were fraught with danger and traversed with risk.

I return to hysteria in Chapter 6 to demonstrate its link with the late-century production of sexualities and to survey hysterical sexuality as continuous with it. For Freud's fascination with sexuality and his production of sexuality theory was stimulated, I argue, by his spectatorship of sexual dysfunction at Paris and Nancy. Even as his clinic disavowed sexuality at the level of theory, Charcot produced a living pathological theater of sexual acts, pantomimes, and tableaux. The Salpêtrians wrote up and tabulated patient stories of personal crisis, tragedy, seduction, and sexual abuse but denied them foundational conceptual status. They duly noted their patients' sexualized, often aggressive, acts and pantomimes; duly excoriated their eroticized relations with one another. Patient ovaries were palpated, pressured, and compressed; mapped in anatomical proximity to other hysterogenic zones; and demonstrated as strategic and manipulable spots on which to stop or initiate fits. While Charcot disavowed the uterine theory and criticized mid-century social-sexual notions of hysteria etiology, sexuality was everywhere visible, under observation, and on display at the Salpêtrière. Freud appropriated, translated, and rewrote this spectacular body into his own clinical practice. Here, Katharina serves me as specimen case. Her hallucinated symptoms, which stood for sexual acts, produced Freud's first sexual case of hysteria and enabled his articulation of narration with a transmuted structure of self-representational spectatorship. Katharina's spectatorship of herself as subject in reproduced visualizeable scenes and family scenarios created a decipherable case and a readable case history. It facilitated Freud's later production of sexuality as fundamental plausible bridge between psyche and soma, psychology and physiology, sex act and sociality.

In Chapter 7 I maintain that, representing sexuality as privileged site of psycho-physical representation, Freud rewrote the medical-psychiatric discourse of case study as case history. As Lawrence Rothfield argues, the epistemological and hermeneutic imperatives at work in both genres identify them as sharing a common dedication to teleologies, representations, and historiographies of embodied subjectivity (Rothfield 1992, 200). Yet while the case study characterized the patient as case, determined its protagonist's disease as inherited, and represented curative outcome as unproblematic, the case history represented the patient as individual sufferer, as retrospectively reconstructing a sense of subjectivity, as continually negotiating a sense of stability. Weaving together the patient's narrative, the doctor's story, the history of the illness, the history of the treatment, and case historical commentary, Freud's case history as genre rewrote a set of medical histories to produce a modern representation of patient care. Featuring these multiple narratives differently in each of his case histories, Freud nevertheless foregrounded the analytic work as the history of the treatment. As a result, patient presentation and the narrative teleology of case report shifted. The incommensurability of patient's and doctor's stories—an incommensurability central to medical diagnosis and treatment, Kathryn Montgomery Hunter argues—emerged as central to the new scientific genre, and the problem of analytic interpretation became visible as its primary representational difficulty (Hunter 1991, 123–47). I look quickly at "Dora" here, a case about which much has been written, only to show that the problem of interpretation defines the case history as case history. Yet "Dora" also suggested, and "The Psychogenesis of a Case of Homosexuality In a Woman" demonstrated, that sexual transitivity—cross-sex identification and same-sex desire—were central to a modernized concept of psycho-physical sexuality.

Hysteria, the enigmatic illness Freud first studied, proposed as the fundamental problem for psychoanalytic theory the ways in which the body represented the mind (or "soul" or "ego" as certain of Freud's contemporaries, such as Thomas Laycock, called it), the ways in which the doctor represented the patient and the ways in which the patient, in treatment, represented herself. Indeed, between 1850 and 1900, the hysteria discourse constituted scientific networks even as it helped produce distinct knowledges with which to theorize the plausible bridges between psyche and soma. Was hysteria "a true disease in the flesh, or its ghost?" the British surgeon F. C. Skey asked, figuring the basic question (Skey 1867, 37). If organic, where might the disease's seat be localized in the body: the nervous system, the brain, or the uterus? How did the body circulate the disease: via the (sympathetic) nerves, the menstrual blood, or the effluence of putrid organs? How did a group of sequestered bodies exchange illness symptoms? Was it "spread" among a population by contagion, imitation, or neuromimesis? Did constitutional predisposition, hereditary factors, or generationally determined degeneracy make individuals susceptible to the disease? What in the patient's personal history abetted disease etiology: her family constellation, her work situation, her class position, her religious or racial background? Finally, could men contract the disease, or was it primarily a plague of women? I argue in the early section of this book that Freud appropriated and rewrote psychophysical theories that addressed these questions of correlation and causation. Psychoanalysis thus emerged from a multiply constituted discursive field characterized by a certain diffusion of terminologies and concepts. The hysteric became visible in various discourses because, as trope, she was translatable across disciplinary boundaries and along scientific networks; she could therefore be appropriated for different discursive purposes. The disease from which she suffered gave Freud the perfect research entity with which to theorize his new science.[16] Freud's research thus translated the hysteric from hospital and laboratory settings in Paris and Nancy to his virtual laboratory, the consulting room; mobilizing his research on psycho-physical representation and sexuality, Freud invented a new scientific genre, the psychoanalytic case history, to represent, and so win allies for, his new science. After the emergence of psychoanalytic theory, an emergence marked by discursive shifts enacted around the translatable figure of the hysteric, Freud sought to stabilize and delimit the domain of analytic theory and clinical practice. Hoping to mythologize himself as founder and, in addition, to control the distribution of credit and distinction along the new scientific networks already in place, Freud recursively produced a coherent and centered set of revisions within psychoanalytic theory. Historicizing himself as founder and his new science as epistemic rupture, Freud "founded," as well, the history of psychoanalysis, a history in which this book participates.

CHAPTER 1

A Rhetoric of Hysteria

Elisabeth von R. consulted Freud in 1892, complaining that, for two years, she had suffered pains in her legs and difficulty walking. During physical examination, Elisabeth's legs demonstrated normal motor power and reflexes but were hypersensitive over their entire length and surface; the pain radiated from, focused on, and acquired its greatest intensity in her anterior right thigh; her muscles and skin were sensitive to pressure and pinching, although, Freud reported, the prick of a needle "met with a certain amount of unconcern." Yet Freud found that if he compressed or squeezed Elisabeth's symptomatic legs, her face "assumed a peculiar expression [of] pleasure rather than pain." She cried out, shut her eyes, and threw her head back; her face flushed and her body arched backward. Her physician interpreted these gestures as signs that a "voluptuous tickling sensation" traveled through and over her body. The patient's symptoms, her indefinite complaints, and the results of physical examination, Freud said, ruled out organic neuropathology. Physician observation produced, without doubt, a diagnosis of hysteria. And although Elisabeth presented standard hysterical symptoms, after undergoing the traditional somatic treatments, she would face a new medical regimen. For during four weeks of what Freud called "pretence" therapy—systematic massage and painful high-voltage electric shocks to limbs to prevent muscle atrophy—he had been preparing her to enter his first full-length "psychical treatment" (*SE*, 2: 135–38).

Although in subsequent chapters I historicize and contextualize Freud's "new psychoanalytic method," in this chapter I chart his efforts to theorize the symptom as representative of psyche to soma, his struggle to depict the symptomatic body in a new psychoanalytic discourse. Rethinking hysterical in relation to organic illness, Freud encountered and sought to solve the vexed problem of psyche's relation to soma in a disease that imitated organic symptoms. Freud's mentors, Jean-Martin Charcot and Josef Breuer, taught and practiced a medicine based on reflex theory, the dominant model of psycho-physical correlation; and as Freud transmuted Charcot's notions and contested Breuer's, he worked to rewrite reflex action as a representation theory of psycho-physical correlation for hysteria. But this psychically inscribed body demanded new modes of medical observation, diagnosis, and description. Indeed, to understand this psycho-physical entity, Freud invented a methodology that read symptom formations as structurally homologous with pathological mental structures; he mapped forgotten events and unconscious ideation as registrations in the organism that could be recaptured through the mechanism of affective memory. For each set of hysterical symptoms— motor paralysis or incapability, sensory dysfunction, or full-blown fit— Freud created a set of figures that linked mind and body, figures that, even as they enabled his rewriting of psycho-physical correlation, covered over the conceptual difficulty of constructing plausible theoretical bridges between psyche and soma. Indeed, he analyzed his hysterics' self-representational texts without having fully conceptualized representation at the level of theory, for throughout his career, Freud revised, refashioned, and reimagined the meaning of psycho-physical representation. *Studies on Hysteria* sought to introduce Freud's and Breuer's emergent theories of hysterical psycho-physical correlation, to claim scientific priority, and to assemble allies in Vienna for the new clinical practice. Indeed, representational and diagrammatic practices for and in science, according to Bruno Latour, serve the goal of transporting, transferring, or displacing other theoretical explanations; they mobilize scientific rewriting, make for easy transportation and rapid communication of conceptual formulation between research centers, and so enable theoretical production (Latour 1986, 1–26).

In this chapter, I sketch out arguments to which I return later in this book. I discuss at length elsewhere the join between spectatorship and storytelling, self-representation in the psychoanalytic situation, perversion's relation to "normal" sexuality, and twentieth-century debates about the seduction theory. Here, I trace Freud's interrogation of then available scientific theories of psycho-physical correlation, his move away from the theories and practices of neuroanatomy and physiology and toward the discourse of psychology. In particular, I seek to address the production and modes of representation of, and the conditions for representability in, Freud's early work on hysteria: the ways he described and depicted an enigmatic disease that, he said, had "never yet been represented."

I

Freud's and Breuer's contemporary Pierre Janet theorized hysteria as a "malad[y] through representation." In a quick overview of hysteria research, Janet said that the disease, characterized in ancient times in terms of a wandering womb and in the modern period by convulsive attacks, had, in the late nineteenth century, been psychologized. He credited Pierre Briquet with having initiated this shift, for Briquet had focused not on the body but (however fuzzily) on emotion, and, after 1859, hysteria could be assessed, not as a purely physical, but as a "moral" or mental disorder. The problem for Janet, as for Briquet, was the link between mind and body. Fixed or unconscious ideas, Janet maintained, could become independent of a subject's normal thoughts, forming a separate or doubled personality. The brain, then, produced psychological phenomena it could not always group in unified sets of perceptions, and a "field of consciousness" could shrink, narrow, or split. This tendency to dissociation determined, Janet said, the disturbances of movement and sensation, the hallucinations, and the forgetfulness or deliria of hysteria. The hysteric's transitory enthusiasms, exaggerated despairs, impulses and caprices— his or her "excessive and unstable disposition"—resulted from a *"special moral weakness,"* a *"lack of power . . . to gather, to condense, his psychological phenomena, and assimilate them to his personality."*[1] When Janet termed hysteria a "malady through representation," then, he addressed questions of perception, cognition, personality, and self-presentation. The body pictured or represented its images to the brain, which, in turn, succeeded or failed to organize those images, to make the body move, sense, and see. The ego, again in turn, organized those images as personality and so made a picture of the self to present to the external world.

Freud joined in the move that psychologized a physiological ailment. Still, he began his career in somatic medicine, and, in "Some Points for a Comparative Study of Organic and Hysterical Motor Paralyses" (1888– 93), he practiced neurology, analyzing the nervous structures that pictured immobilized body parts to and in the brain. In organic "projection paralysis," the spinal cord relayed or "projected" disabled elements of the body's periphery to the brain point by point, element for element. In cortical "representation paralyses," the nerve fibers strung from spine to brain failed to project a "faithful reproduction" of body part to brain and produced a "tendency to dissociation" of images. Hysterical paralyses, Freud claimed, simulated only representation, never projection, paralyses. The body's ability to picture itself as image in the cortex and the brain's inability, in turn, to successfully manage perception, movement, and personality, were thus central to the disease's somatic dysfunction. But how hysterical paralysis worked in the physiological body stymied Freud. Although it resembled organic cerebral paralysis, hysterical paralysis often failed to observe the fixed neurological rule that a distant body part (the hand, for example) was more seriously affected than a nearby one (the arm). Thus in hysterics, the shoulder or thigh might be more paralyzed than the hand or foot; fingers might move when hands could not. Research physicians like Charcot, moreover, could "artificially reproduc[e]" in the laboratory isolated hysterical paralyses of, for example, the thigh or leg. Subject to certain qualifications, Freud reasoned, hysterical immobility was a representation paralysis, but one "with a special kind of representation whose characteristics remain[ed] to be discovered."[2] To describe hysteria's special sort of representation, Freud left neurology behind and entered "the field of psychology." The symptomatology of organic paralyses was, he said, a "fact of anatomy." The "construction of the nervous system and the distribution of its vessels," the relations of these two series of facts to the circumstances of a lesion, could be explained by reference to the human organism's scientifically derived structures. Not the nature but the extent and localization of the lesion to the nervous system, then, determined the characteristics of organic paralysis. Hysterical lesions, however, left no trace in the body and could not be discerned at postmortem. These "dynamic" or "functional" lesions seemed independent of the nervous system's morphology: "*in its paralyses and other manifestations hysteria behave[d] as though anatomy did not exist or as though it had no knowledge of it.*" And although hysterical immobilities simulated organic paralyses, they presented extravagant symptomatic manifestations characterized by "*precise limitation*" on the body and "*excessive intensity*" of pain. Since hysterics were ignorant of the distribution of nerves in the body, their paralyses were based, not on neuroanatomy, but on everyday ideas of body part, structure, and joint articulation. Hysterics thus understood organs "in the ordinary, popular sense" of their names: "the leg is the leg as far up as its insertion into the hip, the arm is the upper limb as it is visible under the clothing." The observable and observed body, the arm and leg as constructed by "tactile" and "visual perceptions," provided the semantic field on which the body's parts were named, the whole body structured, and hysterical symptomatology produced. The hysteric's brain, then, represented the body apart from the physiological facts of the nervous system, its conductive fibers and cortical lesions; it relayed disordered bodily functions that inscribed paralytic symptoms in precisely limited areas or pain with excessive intensity. The dynamic lesion altered, not the body itself, but the hysteric's cortical conceptualization of, and its resulting depictions to, the body. The body's representability, its cognitive mode of being pictured to the brain and relayed to embodied and embodying subject, then, made hysteria a malady of representation. Comparing organic with hysterical paralyses, Freud freed hysteria from the facts of anatomy, he said, and located it securely in a "special sort of representation."[3]

Freud's notion of representation as necessarily opposed to the facts of anatomy was, of course, a convenient fiction. Nothing about anatomy is "pure fact" and, as Thomas Laqueur has shown, anatomy as a disciplinary and scientific discourse is itself based not on observation alone but on the social and cultural constraints that govern science. Anatomical drawings, Laqueur argues, themselves help constitute the bodies they represent. Mapping a wide variety of bodily parts, they focus on some topographical features and exclude others; they assume a point of view and so strip away some tissues while leaving others; they situate the body in relation to morbidity, pathology, and death. Anatomical illustrations "are representations of historically specific understandings of the human body and its place in creation and not only of a particular state of knowledge about its structures." But what Laqueur has discovered about anatomy—and what is important for my argument about Freud's shift from neurology to the field of psychology—is that nineteenth-century scientists themselves believed their claims that a biologically informed anatomy generated scientific knowledge about psychology, sexuality, and the like. Taking the synecdoches they had generated about personality from studying the body, moreover, scientists did produce new knowledge about the body's workings. Still, doctors and scientists like Freud maintained, at century's end, that biology and the anatomy that mapped it were not epistemological but factual (Laqueur 1990, 163–81, esp. 164). And Freud used that claim, not only to lend his hypotheses about body, psyche, and psychology scientific credibility, but, in addition, to make productive reconceptualizations of body and psyche possible.

When Freud moved the material body from anatomy to this special sort of representation, the mental apparatus acquired a status and function that, in turn, required to be represented. In describing these structures, previously unavailable to medical scrutiny, Freud parenthetically apologized for his metaphorical language. "I am making use here of a number of similes," he said, "all of which have only a very limited resemblance to my subject and which, moreover, are incompatible with one another. I am aware that this is so, and I am in no danger of over-estimating their value. But my purpose in using them is to throw light from different directions on a highly complicated topic which has never yet been represented." Attempting to represent that which had never been represented, Freud immediately encountered the problem of psycho-physical correlation and its link with disease causation. He called upon figuration to help him paint the disease's clinical picture (its classifiable and listable symptomatic occurrences) and the physiological dysfunctions that both caused and presented it. The pathogenic material was "like a foreign body"; consciousness, a "narrow defile" or "cleft"; memory retrieval, a cutting of isolated ideas into "pieces or strips" cut to fit into consciousness; the treatment, a failed surgical "removal" or "extirpation" of "infiltrate" from the pathogenic psyche. "Anyone who has a craving for further similes," Freud wryly concluded, "may think at this point of a Chinese puzzle" (*SE*, 2: 290–91).

Freud's jest about Chinese puzzles articulated the exceptional difficulty of conceptualizing the psyche-soma problem for hysteria. Neurologists and physiologists had, in fact, been attempting to solve this problem for brain localization research since the 1870s. Realizing that material and mental realms could not be conceptualized as simply existing side by side or as causing action in one another, Susan Leigh Star says, neurologists built "plausible bridges" between soma and psyche that allowed them to continue their work without, in fact, having solved the problems posed by correlation's complex connection with causation. Still, for neurologists, the nervous system seemed to offer an answer. John Hughlings Jackson's theory of psycho-physical parallelism posited that "states of consciousness" or mind were "utterly different from nervous states"; that for every mental state, a correlative nervous state existed; and that mental and nervous states occurred in parallel and did not interfere with one another. This doctrine arose out of scientific necessity and the working conditions of a new medical specialism; it set the stage for the creation of other plausible bridges. Concomitance theories, for example, viewed anatomical or physiological substrata as underlying functions or behaviors; psycho-physical correlation was therefore based on "temporal simultaneity." Thus in aphasia research, a lesion to brain tissue was thought to be concomitant with the mental inability to produce speech. Reflex theories, on the contrary, conceived of actions or behaviors as built of "particulate sets of reflexes." While reflex theory accounted for the basic units of mind or brain, Star says, it could not resolve the problems of how the material body stored nervous impulses or how it coordinated those basic units. Differing from either concomitance or reflex theories, "representation theories"—the most complex and fragile of plausible bridges—linked mind and body by positing that one realm symbolized or stood for the other. Representation theorists (including Janet) conceptualized the gap between psyche and soma as bridged by an "imaging" between mental and material realms, and explained problematic physiological actions in terms of consciousness and unconsciousness or, in some cases, symbolic interaction.[4]

In his early work, Freud tried on several psycho-physical theories before settling on representation to solve the psyche-soma problem in hysteria. He used concomitance notions of correlation between material substrata and ideation to solve the conceptual difficulties posed by sensory and motor dysfunction; used reflex action to resolve problems posed by a neurologized psychical apparatus; used symbolic models to address questions posed by unconscious ideation, by the dissociated imaging of body periphery to cortex. In his work on aphasia, in fact, Freud argued against Jackson's strictly neurological notion of "dependent concomitan[ce]" of psychical and physiological processes precisely because it failed sufficiently to address the problems of memory and unconscious ideation. Concomitance theory argued that physiological modification of nerve fibers (which accompanied sensory excitation) modified central nerve cells, which, in turn, produced the physiological correlate of a psychical "presentation" (or representation, or ideation). Yet, Freud maintained, concomitance theories said considerably more about presentations than modifications, "of which no physiological characterization ha[d] yet been reached." Strictly psychological theories, however, which said much about presentations, conceived of nerve-fiber excitation and brain localization too simplistically, thus confusing psychology with physiology. "What," Freud asked, "is the physiological correlate of a simple [or recurring] presentation? Clearly nothing static, but something in the nature of a process [that] admits of localization." Freud had himself occluded the problem of psycho-physical correlation by elliptically stating the link between ideation and its physiological alteration, its anatomical location. Substituting for nerve modification and localization the concept of mental apparatus and functions, Freud sought to sidestep this complex conceptual difficulty. In detailing disturbances of speech, for example, he sought to "keep the psychological and anatomical sides of the question as separate as possible," and, in doing so, to theorize the difference between "word-presentations" and "object-presentation[s]" (*SE*, 14: 206–9, 214). Yet Freud had no more resolved the problem of psycho-physical correlation for hysteria than had neurological or physiological theorists for brain localization research. For the problems of memory and the unconscious—of psychical (re)presentation, physiological alteration, and storage of registrations—would not go away.

Freud sought to overcome this problem by positing conversion as hysteria's primary mechanism of symptom formation. Whether hysterical symptoms were motor or sensory (that is, paralyses and fits or anesthesias and pain), their physiological presence, Freud said, necessarily implied a psychical correlate. What process or physiology linked these mental and material states? Freud could say only, at this point in his project, that psychical events were somehow converted into somatic symptoms, but that, using the doctrine of psycho-physical correlation, the physician could posit their symbolic relation one to the other. In hysteria, he said, "incompatible idea[s]" (or presentations) were "rendered innocuous" when their "*sum of excitation*" was "*transformed into something somatic.*" This transformation or conversion followed the line of motor or sensory innervation that was symbolically related, "whether intimately or more loosely," to the trauma that caused it. Although now free from an incompatible idea, the ego had become burdened with a memory trace, a "mnemic symbol" that lodged in consciousness "like a sort of parasite" or "foreign body," as an "unresolvable motor innervation" or a "recurring hallucinatory sensation." Displaying a special "*capacity for conversion,*" a "psycho-physical aptitude" for transposing sums of excitation into somatic innervation, the hysteric somehow produced the symptoms in which "something in the nature of a process" linked psyche and soma (*SE*, 3: 48–51; *SE*, 2: 165; *SE*, 14: 208; Freud's emphases). The body thus stored nervous alterations and the brain, inscriptions or presentations, that presented to the physician as the motor or sensory dysfunctions of hysteria symptomatology. Although he was conceptually unclear about the precise nature and functions of psycho-physical correlation, Freud's initial formulation sufficed in

1895 to move the study of hysteria from neurology to psychology, a move that would enable his continuing retheorization of representation as linking nerves and bodily periphery to brain, and psyche to soma.

When allied with Janet's notions of dissociation, for example, Freud's conceptualization of the hysterical body made it possible to theorize the unconscious. From a psychological perspective, Freud said, if the concept or idea "arm" could not enter into association with other ideas that constituted the self, or ego—of which "the subject's body form[ed] an important part"—the arm would be banished from the mind's play of associations. The hysterical lesion, therefore, could be defined as "*the abolition of the associative accessibility of the conception of the arm.*" The subject's notion of her arm might momentarily cease to exist, or her arm be rendered insensate or hypersensate, or be imagined immobile. But even if the conception of the arm were altered, and, indeed, lost, it could be "inaccessible without being destroyed" and without its "material substratum"—the nervous tissue—being damaged. It could become unavailable to consciousness, and so "subconscious." Because this banished, yet intact, idea of the arm was invested with a "quota of affect," it could also be isolated from other ideations and its functions thus lost. When the quota of affect was "wiped out," the conception would once more be accessible to "conscious associations and impulses." Freud drew his examples from tactile perception. In each instance, either the body part touching or object touched could never again be associated with other objects or other touchers: a loyal subject, having touched his sovereign, would not wash his hand; a couple broke the celebratory glass at their wedding; a savage tribe burned horse, weapons, and wives after their chief's death. The social ritual that situated such associations identified this refusal to touch as normal rather than pathological, as culturally symbolic rather than meaningless and maladaptive.[5] But these social acts nevertheless illustrated Freud's point, that dissociated or unconscious concepts informed, even governed, people's lives.

In his clinical practice, Freud observed this unconscious governance at work in patients' lives. But he had trouble linking unconscious material with memory, the twin concept that Hughlings Jackson's concomitance theories had failed to solve. Indeed, he warned, the physician could easily misinterpret unconscious texts. When he touched a "hysterogenic point," he might awaken a memory that could cause hysterical attack; if he knew nothing of "this psychical intermediate link," the doctor might imagine that "the operation of [his] touch" had caused the attack. For the unconscious presented its images cannily and so seemed difficult to decipher. "Let us take the instance," he suggested, "of a young girl who blames herself most frightfully for having allowed a boy to stroke her hand in secret, and who from that time on has been overtaken by a neurosis." She could seem "an abnormal, eccentrically disposed and oversensitive person," but analysis showed that "the touching of her hand reminded her of another, similar touching, which had happened very early in her childhood and which formed part of a less innocent whole, so that her self-reproaches were actually reproaches about that old occasion." Symbolically significant, this touch, like the socially performed ones Freud posed as examples of dissociation, articulated other, here earlier, touchings that had been pathologically excluded from consciousness. Meaningless until memory had been restored, these tactile attempts to broach the body's periphery resulted in symptomatic self-misrepresentation. Yet, Freud said, the hysteric's response to psychical stimuli only seemed exaggerated if the observer misrecognized the larger, memorial context that located her motives. The precipitating cause of attack, then, might seem innocuous or innocent, yet only because it invoked "*unconscious memories*" could a particular perception provoke fits (*SE*, 3: 217–18). Very early, then, Freud had discovered that "*hysterics suffer mainly from reminiscences*," although he did not yet know what that meant (*SE*, 2: 7; Freud's emphases).

Still, Freud's early representational theories of psyche's relation to soma, as I argue in the next sections of this chapter, were nevertheless highly dependent on reflex notions of neurological excitation and innervation. Indeed, metaphor, which figured the mental realm as somehow material, facilitated Freud's rewriting of reflex as representational psychophysical correlation and enabled him to sketch sensation's link to presentations, however naively and reductively. Mobilizing the energy of tropes, Freud generated theory, then used those concepts to seek allies for his notion that hysteria was a malady of representation. These ideas, which he had brought back to Vienna from the laboratories, hospitals, and clinics of Paris and Nancy, would provide the conceptual field for theoretical production. Later, as I argue in Chapters 2, 3, and 4, Freud would leverage psychoanalysis into culture, fashion a discursive institution around himself as founder, and institute psychoanalytic historiography in an effort to control the dissemination of his new science's theoretical concepts and clinical technologies. Sketching his ideas in letters, drafts, and two-dimensional diagrams, presenting them to medical men in theaters of proof, Freud prepared to translate his emergent psychoanalytic theories to other research sites and to create scientific networks.

II

While Freud struggled to create a rudimentary representation theory of correlation between material and mental realms, Breuer touted reflex theory as the talking cure's fundamental psycho-physical concept. And although the two physicians introduced a variety of tropes into the mind-body problematic, none proved more useful than the schema that pictured nervous fibers and electric circuitry as structurally homologous. This trope served both Breuer's reflex and Freud's emergent representation theories of psycho-physical correlation. In the one case, highly specialized nervous functions could be viewed as anchored in localized neurological tissue, and, in the other, as transmitting sensory images or ideas to a localized site in the cerebral cortex.[6] Freud justified using this figural nervous economy by invoking its utility: just as physicists hypothesized the flow of electrical current by analogy to other kinds of flowings, he said, psychologists used the nerves as analogy to correlate psychical states or conditions with physiological alterations (*SE*, 3: 60–61). This figure of speech, then, constructed a plausible bridge between psyche and soma by positing a process or function that linked them. Mapping a material space that could be traversed, these metaphors depicted a function played out on or across the diagrammatic space of electrical circuitry, depicting by analogy mental work in the material realm of objects. Indeed, this trope functioned to mobilize Freud's and Breuer's emergent theories of hysterical psycho-physical correlation, and their efforts to assemble allies in Vienna for their new clinical application of psycho-physical theories. Such deployments of metaphor for and in science, Bruno Latour says, displace other theoretical explanations; they energize scientific rewriting and so activate theoretical production. No matter that a mere image subtends powerful theoretical creation, Latour insists; metaphor invigorates the two-dimensional representations that make theory easily transportable between research centers, from laboratory setting to hospital, clinic, and consulting room.[7]

Breuer's electrical tropes suited his own notion of psycho-physical correlation, the reflex theory. "I shall scarcely be suspected of identifying nervous excitation with electricity," he said, "if I return once more to the comparison with an electrical system. If the tension in such a system becomes excessively high, there is danger of a break occurring at weak points in the insulation. Electrical phenomena then appear at abnormal points; or, if two wires lie close beside each other, there is a short circuit. Since a permanent change has been produced at these points, the disturbance thus brought about may constantly recur if the tension is sufficiently increased. An abnormal 'facilitation' has taken place." In the nervous system, as in an electrical one, Breuer said, excitations or currents might run into "resistances" when, "owing to excessively high tension, the insulation of the wires in a lighting system breaks down and a 'short circuit' occurs . . . [producing] overheating or sparking . . . , the lamp to which the wire leads fails to light. In just the same way, the affect fails to appear if the excitation flows away in an abnormal reflex and is converted into a somatic phenomenon." Along well-worn "paths of conduction," disease was likely. If a psychical reflex occurred during a traumatic experience, Breuer said, little excitation would be stored as recollection; if, however, the original affect was discharged in an abnormal reflex, excitation was converted into a somatic event, and frequent repetition of such anomalous reflexes caused suppression of affect, and, hence, hysterical symptom formation. For, Breuer maintained, that "old 'reflex theory'" should "not be completely rejected," since, reimagined as "nervous" theory, it accounted for hysteria's complex and enigmatic "empirical clinical picture" (*SE*, 2: 203–7, 242). Here, Breuer hypothesized the flow of electrical current by analogy, deploying the nerves to picture "nervous" psychical states that he had correlated with physiological alterations.

Freud's "Project for a Scientific Psychology" literalized his and Breuer's electrical trope, constructing a psychical apparatus by analogy to a physiological energistic model. This logical and rhetorical move enabled Freud to confront the theoretical problem that subtended Hughlings Jackson's concomitance theory: its failure conceptually to link physiological modification securely with presentation, or to what Freud variously termed representation, inscription, or registration. Permeable neurons, Freud posited, transmitted and so failed to retain perceptions, while impermeable neurons resisted transmission and so accumulated undischarged energy. Contact-barriers loaded resistances (and so "afforded a *possibility of representing memory*"), yet they also could conduct and facilitate transmission (offering the possibility that "*memory is represented by the differences in the facilitations*"). Although Freud recognized that no biological or histological evidence supported his supposition of two functionally differentiated systems of neurons, he claimed that mechanistic and genetic hypotheses supported his thesis. He assigned consciousness, more-over, to a third neuronal system, rejecting for the moment Hughlings Jackson's psycho-physical theory of consciousness (*SE*, 1: 295–315; Freud's emphases). The tripartite structure Freud invented resembled an electric circuit that facilitated, resisted, discharged, and stored various quantities of energy. It made more complex the conceptual framework for adequating localization and function in a mental apparatus even as it used neuro-logical fictions to produce a plausible theoretical bridge between psyche and soma. It sought to square the "information" of "reflex discharge" (by assuming the rise of additional excitations) with the concomitant emer-gence of a "*motor* [kinaesthetic] *image*" in the impermeable neuronal sys-tem. It sought to solve the problems of memory and unconscious ideation by positing physiological alteration as "facilitating" the inscription or reg-istration of "nervous" energy (*SE*, 1: 318, 299–302). In fact, Freud de-scribed his own process of writing this "Psychology for Neurologists," as—more metaphors—a falling away of veils and a lifting of barriers, as itself facilitating theoretical production and transportation. In the "Pro-ject" itself, a sudden meshing of gears manufactured a theoretical "ma-chine" that "shortly would function on its own" (Freud 1985, 127, 146).

Yet however apt an analogy, neither electric circuitry nor reflex arcs really explained psycho-physical correlation or the conversion theory de-pendent upon it. While the nervous circuitry relayed cortical images of dysfunction through neuronal resistances and facilitators, the nature, ori-gin, and quantity of such excitations remained mysterious. This trope seemed problematic in other contexts as well. Freud called heredity, for example, a "multiplier in an electric circuit"; it increased the "visible de-viation" of an instrumental "needle" but did not "determine its direc-tion." Here, a structural figure obscured questions of origin and quantity. Such electrical charges seemed always already produced and magically circulating through some already-in-place organic machinery. As Freud admitted about quotas of affect or sums of excitation, this quantity iden-tified "something" capable of increase, decrease, displacement, and dis-charge, but that something resisted measurement. While excitation flashed over memory traces "somewhat as an electric charge is spread over the surface of a body," its point of departure remained mysterious. Such elisions characterized Freud's early psycho-physical thinking and, while providing theoretical leverage, represented a conceptual danger. Freud sought, but sometimes failed, to both confront and acknowledge this risk. Breuer, who did acknowledge it, claimed that he had solved the problem by refusing to "drive" the analogy between electrical and nervous systems "to death" (*SE*, 3: 147, 49–50, 60–61; *SE*, 2: 207).

Indeed, the metaphorical link between psychical and physical functions, Breuer warned, meant the analyst's own figures of speech could "trick" him.

It is only too easy to fall into a habit of thought which assumes that every substantive has a substance behind it—which gradually comes to regard "consciousness" as standing for some actual thing; and when we have become accustomed to make use metaphorically of spatial relations, as in the term "sub-consciousness," we find as time goes on that we have actually formed an idea which has lost its metaphorical nature and which we can manipulate easily as though it was real. Our mythology is then complete. . . . We [think and] talk in spatial metaphors. Thus when we speak of [conscious and unconscious] ideas, we almost inevitably form pictures of a tree with its trunk in daylight and its roots in darkness, or of a building with its dark underground cellars. If, however, we constantly bear in mind that all such spatial relations are metaphorical and do not allow ourselves to be misled into supposing that these relations are literally present in the brain, we may nevertheless speak of a consciousness and a subconsciousness. But only on this condition. . . . We [must] always remember that after all it is in the same brain, and most probably in the same cerebral cortex, that conscious and unconscious ideas alike have their origin. How this is possible we cannot say. But then we know so little of the psychical activity of the cerebral cortex that one puzzling complication the more scarcely increases our limitless ignorance. (*SE*, 2: 227–28)

Aware of science's inability to formulate the link between psyche and physiology, Breuer cautioned against the easy reification of conceptual terminologies. While tropes encouraged researchers to "picture" spatial analogies, the scientist should not be seduced into thinking that the relation between consciousness and the unconscious was really anything like a tree with its roots in darkness or a building with cellars. If consciousness could be represented as a tree or house, it could in turn be mistaken for that (or an) actual "thing" and subconsciousness for something "real," even though neither was literally present—although produced and originating—in the brain. Dead metaphors were dangerous. While figures produced theory, Breuer cautioned, they could as well manufacture "mythologies," hypotheses that, masquerading as truth, naturalized figures from a reality to which they bore a specular, while pretending a substantive, relation. Once the physician forgot that to describe the psyche, he had invented a trope based on concepts borrowed from nature, he had also blinded himself to the possibility of scientific error.

Ignoring Breuer's warning, Freud used metaphor unsparingly throughout his early work, both to cover over conceptual difficulties and to energize theoretical production. Pictured by topographical differentiation, for example, the psychical material presented as a "structure in several dimensions": memories appeared in a retrospective linear and chronological structure; these "files" ("like a file of documents, a packet"), organized into "themes," stratified themselves "concentrically" around the disease's "pathogenic nucleus"; a "logical thread" linked nucleus and stratifications in an "irregular and twisting path," a "zig-zag line" much like the "Knight's Move problem" in chess (*SE*, 2: 288–89). The analytic work picked up and followed the logical thread so as to "penetrate to the interior," to open the "inner strata" to clinical observation. How "a camel like this got through the eye of the needle," Freud acknowledged, he did not know. Freud's diagram of this analytical work represented the pathogenic material as grounding a journey of zigs and zags through ever-deeper layers of the unconscious strata that organized scenes, fragments, and memories (*SE*, 2: 290–92; Freud 1985, 246–47). Having entered dark depths, analyst and analysand ascended and redescended. Or, figuring the infantile scenes reproduced by their patients in relation to the "rest of the case history," the therapists worked as though "putting together a child's picture-puzzle"; eventually certain "which piece belongs in the empty gap," they recognized that that particular piece—and the only available piece—"fill[ed] out the picture" and made edge meet edge so as "to leave no free space and to entail no overlapping" (*SE*, 3: 205).[8] Seeking to confront the conceptual problems of memory, consciousness, affect, and representation, Freud created his own Chinese puzzles.

Yet Freud had failed to resolve the primary conceptual problem of memory in psycho-physical correlation. In the dream book, Freud proposed a photographic apparatus or compound microscope to picture the psyche, a trope Breuer invoked in *Studies on Hysteria*. This metaphor allowed Freud to sidestep a problem central to his correlation theory: that the same physiological entities could not receive and transmit messages (*SE*, 2: 188–89). Standing in a regular spatial relation to one another, like systems of lenses, Freud said, the mental agencies were influenced in a temporal sequence; containing a sensory and a motor end, they produced innervations out of stimuli. Perceptions, which impinged on the psychical apparatus, left memory traces on it and, through association, an excitation was transmitted through facilitating paths and around resistances. Unconscious memories (innervations inscribed in, but outside, ideation) could become conscious; individuals described as their "character" the memory traces of their impressions. A critical agency directed waking life and determined voluntary, conscious actions; the preconscious distributed attention and held the key to voluntary movement. This schematic picture, as Freud called it, functionalized the faradic metaphors he had used just a few years earlier to portray the psyche by accounting for the order and sequence in which energy passed from one point to another in the mental apparatus (*SE*, 5: 536–41).

Freud proposed this trope, in addition, to address the problems of both functional differentiation and anatomical localization elided by his emergent representation theories. "I shall entirely disregard the fact," Freud said, "that the mental apparatus with which we are here concerned is also known to us in the form of an anatomical preparation, and I shall carefully avoid the temptation to determine psychical locality in any anatomical fashion. I shall remain upon psychological ground" (*SE*, 5: 536). Yet, as Jean Laplanche and J.-B. Pontalis suggest, the anatomical reference is far from absent in this schema. For Freud had recourse here to the reflex theory of psycho-physical correlation; he could not resolve the dilemma of how registrations from the perceptual system eventually produced motor acts—which possessed the same quota of energy—without conceptualizing mental agencies as building or simply impinging somehow on one another. Indeed, although Freud sought to limit his theory's indeterminacy by invoking reflex processes as the "model" of every "psychical function," those processes also retained, as Laplanche and Pontalis notice, their literal meaning. The facts of neurophysiology, facts with which Freud would have been professionally familiar, dictated that— as Breuer had proclaimed and Freud here reiterated—the same physiopsychological system could not both receive and transmit stimuli. This problem, which Freud's magical photographic microscope occluded, originated in his need to account for the retention and transmission of both external and internal stimuli, of perceptual information and, as Freud had earlier and would later call them, instincts (Laplanche and Pontalis 1973, 451–53).

The "Project for a Scientific Psychology," with its literalized neurological model for the psyche, uncovered and sought to confront these conceptual problems. Freud solved the problem of differing functions in neurological systems by positing the dual system of permeable and impermeable neurones; the problem of "qualities" of consciousness, a third system of neurons; the need for memories to be both forgotten and reproducible, a reflex discharge of excitation that created motor images; the causation and origin of sensations, a functionally differentiated set of perceptual, ideational, and motor representations. Yet he resolved these theoretical problems through hypothesis and supposition. Because remembering differed in quality from perception, Freud "summon[ed] up the courage to assume" the existence of a third system of neurons that, excited with perception but not reproduction, produced "qualities" or "*conscious sensations.*" "How is this contradiction to be explained?" he asked of the neurons' ability—whether permeable or impermeable—to recover resistance after excitation; by "assuming" it to be a characteristic of contact barriers, he answered. Because consciousness contained not only sensory qualities but "sensations of *pleasure* and *unpleasure* that "call[ed] for interpretation," he was "tempted to identify" pleasure with inertia; thus "pleasure would be the sensation of discharge," and, the "hypothesis would follow," that strong cathexis produced unpleasure (*SE*, 1: 309, 316, 312; Freud's emphases). Here and throughout the "Project," Freud argued circularly by assuming what he set out to prove.

Energized by its rhetorical tropes, however, the "Project"'s problematic logic enabled Freud initially to conceptualize emotions and affective states. It formulated representation as physiological registration or inscription even as it depended on reflex theories of psycho-physical correlation. For memory had still to *represent* something that had been resisted and stored, however separately, because it proved frightening or anxiety-producing for the person who had experienced it. Indeed, given the initial helplessness of human beings, Freud said, the discharge of energy as communication proved necessary to human morality. Specific actions that altered arrangements in the external world constituted human society. Acts of nurture and care, for instance, aroused in the individual reflex actions that, producing the "*experience of satisfaction,*" created bonds between people. Mnemic images stored in the impermeable neurons fashioned wishful states, hallucinations, and pain. Thus cognition, judgment, wishing, willpower, choice, intention, reality testing, dreaming—all normal states of consciousness or semi-consciousness—could be systematized, mapped, and located in a psychical apparatus characterized by uniformity of structure and functional localization (*SE*, 1: 317–22; Freud's emphases). Yet, as Freud acknowledged later when working with Dora, the "translation" of "psychical excitation into physical terms" was so problematic, so unstable, and so variable, that—another metaphor crept in—it resembled a current that, passed from a new source of excitation to the old point of discharge, flowed like "new wine into an old bottle" (*SE*, 7: 54). Metaphorical energy, as Breuer had intuited, could mobilize, even as it could subvert, theoretical production.

Although the neurological model in Part I of the "Project," with its literalized tropes for psycho-physical correlation, had failed fully to articulate the concepts that would structure a representation theory, Freud would solve that problem in Part II by rewriting the symptom precisely as symbol and self-representation. And I argue, in the next section of this chapter, that Freud solved the problems of psycho-physical correlation and causation specifically by retheorizing memory and consciousness. Positing the notion of "mnemic image," he created a conceptual category that linked the mental and material realms in hysteria. The mnemic image, then, was the mere registration of an event in the physiological material that constituted the psychical apparatus, while its presentations somehow revived, reinvigorated, and reproduced that image. The patient's re-presentation or "reproductive remembering," based on the "law of *association by simultaneity*" or contiguity, functioned through the rhetorical act of symbolization; her self-representation, which recounted that now visualizable and visualized mnemic image as scene or scenario, facilitated abreaction and so discharge in a cure that linked psyche and soma through catharsis (*SE*, 1: 319). The physician thus interpreted the patient's self-representations symbolically, representing, in turn, her psycho-physical representations to her and, later, to an audience of medical specialists. I return to medical re-presentations in Chapter 3; here, I argue that Freud had begun to discover, in his tropes for hysteria, that "scene" was the privileged mode of psychoanalytic (self-)representation.

III

The body was never absent from Freud's psychical theories, just as his earliest physiological concepts always implied the psychical realm. As he troped a neurologized psyche that was capable of both registration and presentation, Freud portrayed hysteria as operating through rhetorical structures capable of being both read and re-presented. His newly developing psycho-physical theory, moreover, deployed a different logos of temporal causality than did neuroanatomy. Seeking to posit psycho-physical causation alongside correlation, Freud invented trauma and sexuality as categories that explained how psyche affected soma, and soma psyche. Yet these concepts produced a logical problem, a psycho-physical dilemma: how could traumas, registered in the organism through reflex action, be forgotten by the mind? Here, "the old reflex theory," as Breuer called it, blocked Freud's rewriting of psyche's relation to soma. Because traumas were registered in both the material, physiological realm and the correlate mental realm, Freud surmised, traumas had to be understood as unconscious yet as somehow homologous with conscious ideation. Thus memory loaded certain presentations or images with anxiety and affect, making them symbols of earlier, forgotten events that, when constructed as contiguous, could be read as meaningful. While the patient reproduced newly remembered scenes, the analyst constructed a schema of psycho-physical correlation (the disease symptom and the patient's psychical structures) and causation (the traumatic, usually sexual, event that, registered in the body, had been stored as mnemic image and been reinvigorated through re-presentation). Analytic interpretation, then, became a psycho-physiological reading across spatio-temporal registers, registers that, through concepts such as "mnemic image," "mnemic symbol," and reproduced "scene," themselves articulated psyche and soma for psycho-analytic theory.

Yet Freud's first attempt to comprehend symptom formation produced a naive version of psycho-physical representation. Interpreting symbols as unmediated expressions written on the body, Freud collapsed the category of psyche with soma, literalizing symbolic figuration as material and real. Elisabeth von R.'s and Cäcilie M.'s cases serve as illustration. Cäcilie's stabbing angina equaled, Freud said, something that "stabbed [her] to the heart"; headache, "something's come into [her] head"; hysterical aura, she "shall have to swallow this." The hysteric did not take liberties with words, Freud maintained, flirting again with reflex theory, but revived the sensations to which verbal expression "owe[d] its justification"; the figure of speech, "swallowing something," thus originated in the pharyngeal "innervatory sensations" produced when someone refused to react to insults. Yet Cäcilie's body also symbolized her painful social and familial relations: her facial neuralgia, her husband's "bitter insults" as "like a slap in the face"; shooting pain in her heel when she walked, her "not 'finding herself on a right footing'" with strangers at a sanitarium; penetrating headaches, her grandmother's judgmental look, a look that "pierc[ed] right into her brain" (SE, 2: 177–81). Deploying similar logical reductions, Freud analyzed Elisabeth's painful legs as having accumulated her repressed cathexes and so made standing or walking difficult. She described one day a series of episodes in which the "fact of her 'standing alone'" had proved "painful"; another in which her "unsuccessful attempts to establish a new life for her family" provoked feelings of helplessness, fears "that she could not 'take a single step forward.'" Freud commented: her paralysis had provided a "somatic expression for her lack of an independent position" and her inability to alter her circumstances; phrases such as "not being able to take a single step forward" or "not having anything to lean upon" served, Freud said, as "bridge" for the conversion process in which mind made body symptomatic (SE, 2: 152–53, 176). Although Freud had failed to theorize this bridge's mediating mechanism, structure, or function, it was clearly a psycho-physical representation bridge to which he here referred. He also failed to state this bridge's etiological status: did symbolization cause, facilitate, or precipitate symptom-formation? "create" or "increase" somatic pain? It remained an "open question," Freud equivocated, whether sensations caused ideas or ideas sensations. He had not yet constructed a plausible bridge that could translate an emergent representation theory into clinical technology.

Yet this literalization of psyche to soma clearly stated the problem Freud needed to solve: how could a reflex act register a sum of excitation in the body and yet be unavailable to the mind? As answer, Freud traced disease origin back to infantile experiences, which seemed especially momentous precisely because they occurred during a time of "incomplete development" and so were "liable to have traumatic effects." Invoking the experimental results of embryology, Freud argued that whereas the prick of a needle might do no damage to a fully grown animal or larva, that same prick would result in severe developmental disturbances to an embryo (SE, 16: 361–70). Although Freud drew his example from biological science rather than psychology, he argued in effect that the traumas of childhood, whether materially or psychically wounding, had identical consequences for the patient who endured them. That trauma was sexual and visualizeable. One persistent patient, he told Fliess, had produced a scene that met the requirements for etiological causation: it was "sexual, innocent, natural, and the rest" (Freud 1985, 391). Experienced in his second year, this traumatic sexual event had been registered and stored in the boy's psyche, its appropriate affect undischarged.[9] Likewise, Frau P., haunted by hallucinatory sensations and images, reported scenes as disease origin. In treatment, she imagined that a housemaid's "improper idea" had caused a sensation in her own genitals, where she felt an almost continuous "heavy hand"; hallucinated visions of a hairy vulva and heard voices uttering threats and reproaches. She recounted a "series of [nursery] scenes" of brother and sister showing their naked bodies to one another; Frau P.'s unconscious thoughts and repressed memories, Freud said, symbolized a childhood affair. During the analytic "work of reproduction," moreover, the patient's genitals "joined in the conversation"; when she'd recounted each traumatic scene, her visions and vulval sensations disappeared (*SE*, 3: 175–83). In both E.'s and Frau P.'s cases, Freud had fashioned a psycho-physical account of symptom formation by deploying the concept of trauma. Yet he had also produced an emergent, although unformulated, representation theory of psycho-physical causation. For if the body participated in remembering, the clinical work necessarily aroused sensations and excitations that, although they had been forgotten by the psyche, could be recaptured during the patient's reproduction of traumatic scenes. Thus mnemic symbol and childhood scene somehow, Freud began to see, articulated soma and psyche, the first linking reflex with symptomatology, the second making ideation available to and for (re)presentation.

But what did Freud mean by "scene"? For although he'd told Fliess in 1897 that "everything goes back to the reproduction of scenes," he was not yet sure how to read them, how to use them to cure hysterical patients (Freud 1985, 239). In the dream book, a 40-year-old mother's hallucination helped him theorize the formal elements of scenes.

One morning she opened her eyes and saw her brother in the room, though, as she knew, he was in fact in an insane asylum. Her small son was sleeping in the bed beside her. To save the child from having a *fright* and *falling into convulsions* when he saw his *uncle*, she pulled the *sheet* over his face, whereupon the apparition vanished. This vision was a modified version of a memory from the lady's childhood; and, though it was conscious, it was intimately related to all the unconscious material in her mind. Her nurse had told her that her mother (who had died very young, when my patient was only eighteen months old) had suffered from epileptic or hysterical *convulsions*, which went back to a fright caused by her brother (my patient's *uncle*) appearing to her disguised as a ghost with a *sheet* over his head. (*SE*, 5: 545; Freud's emphases)

Freud's underscoring points out what he goes on to explain: that the vision "contained the same elements of the memory" (brother, sheet, fright and its results), but those elements "had been arranged in a different context and transferred on to other figures." The vision's motive was to replace the thoughts the woman had repressed: her concern that her son, who resembled his uncle, would "follow in [that uncle's] footsteps." Thus hysterical scenes, like hallucinations and dreams, transformed thoughts into images, thoughts "intimately linked" with suppressed or unconscious memories. Infantile experiences, fantasies based upon them, and scenes or their reproductions as fantasies articulated "*psychical* perceptual" visions, somatic excitations aroused by "*memory*," and the "*revival* of a visual [or sensory] excitation" (*SE*, 5: 544–46). Here, physiological notions of reflex excitation as material substratum anchored and sustained the psychophysical concept of re-presentation. Indeed, represented memory reproduced traumatic sensations, acts, or events because defense necessitated not only the revival of visual excitations but their rearrangement in the visual scene through condensation and displacement. Infantile scenes— which articulated memory fragments, physiological impulses, and protective fictions—were seen like hallucinations; they lost their sensory vividness only when recounted. In Freud's new theory, then, the scene served perfectly as the "form of representation" that joined psychic and somatic registers through the mechanisms of clinically based reproductive remembering (*SE*, 3: 154–55).

In the "Project for a Scientific Psychology," Freud fashioned a new mode of reading psycho-physical correlation and causation as inscribed across a set of scenes. The agoraphobic Emma, who could not shop alone, remembered during treatment having entered a shop (at age 12) in which the assistants laughed at her clothing and from which she had run away in fright; before that, she had entered a shop (at age 8) in which the grinning shopkeeper had twice touched her genitals through her clothing. Ignoring Breuer's caution that substantives did not suggest substance, Freud seemed to explain this traumatic mechanism neurologically: the memory aroused "a *sexual release*." Here, however, Freud conceptualized sexual trauma, not as accidental, as had Charcot, but as a psycho-physical category that could mobilize or paralyze the ill body. Because the postpubertal experience of laughter endowed the memory of a grin with pathogenic force, because memory thus operated as though it were a contemporary event or through "posthumous action," reminiscence and its release of unpleasure produced the first shopping trip as traumatic in the present although, because it had occurred before puberty, it had not been traumatic when it had happened. This present unpleasure also isolated the imagery from association and presentation to consciousness. Emma's agoraphobia portrayed her as a subject who knew but had refused to know that she had been subjected to inappropriate sexual touching. In recovering the memories of what Freud called "scene

I" (the laughing assistants) and "scene II" (the grinning shopkeeper), Emma provided Freud the texts with which to interpret her symptoms. That interpretation correlated psyche and soma, accounting for disease causation through the temporal mechanisms of memory and identifying the scene as key to clinical cure. For the shopkeeper's grin and shop assistants' laughter echoed one another in the same conceptual space despite their separation by years in Emma's experience. Scene II represented, or was representative of, scene I, and the structures linking them proved readable.[10] As a readable structure, Emma's scenes, like the mother's hallucination, contained the same elements, arranged in a different context and transferred onto other figures.

Freud's diagram of Emma's reproductive remembering sketched in two dimensions his plausible representation bridge between psyche and soma. The darkened circles at the picture's top represented events of scene I (the assistants' "laughing"); the undarkened ones, at center, the events of scene II (the shopkeeper's "assault"); the circles surrounded by lines (labeled "being alone," "shop," and "flight") represented the fearful events that brought Emma to Freud's consulting room (see Figure 16 in *SE*, 1: 354). Freud could interpret these scenes only when events in all three registers echoed or visually symbolized one another. Thus, in each, Emma entered or could not enter a shop; in scene I, the shop assistants' laughter resembled the shopkeeper's grin in scene II; in scenes I and II, clothes signified, somehow, both Emma's pleasure (one assistant "pleased her sexually") and the body beneath her clothing. Displacement and condensation constituted this structural picture of Emma's repressed memories as symbolic symptoms: assistants (scene I) became shopkeeper (scene II), laughter (scene I) became grin (scene II), and clothing stood in for the body (which both scenes conflated) (*SE*, 1: 354–55). Freud's diagram also represented Emma's symptoms (flight, agoraphobia) as temporally sequenced and narratively overdetermined. A series of linked traumas represented the unconscious chain of associations that articulated symptom with pathogenic event. Freud's teleological arrow, which designated narrative temporality in his picture, began with the shop assistants' laughter, moved by displacement through the shopkeeper's assault, on which converged the condensation of clothing, toward a bracket that stood for Emma's body, the figure's "nodal point"; from this "body," the arrow moved toward "sexual release" and, producing the symptom of "flight" by compromise, out into Emma's experiential world. Freud's remarkable diagram, then, portrayed symptoms as palimpsestically arranged to both expose and cover over the symptom's origin and significance. Here, Freud sketched a quadrature, correlating psyche and soma through the (apparently suppressed) mnemic symbol. Indeed, the figure depicted the visualized set of scenes as themselves articulating psychical perceptual visions, somatic excitations aroused by memory, and revived sensory excitation.

In fact, Freud had stumbled here on the concept of representability, the notion that neuroses appropriated language and pictures to both disguise and depict their structures. Thus in dreams, as in reproduced scenes and hallucinations, he would later say, the thoughts that "admit[ted] of visual representation," even if apparently "unadaptable," could be "recast" into a new visual and verbal form; "thing[s] that [were] pictorial" and so "*capable of being represented*" could "facilitate" representation and so relieve the "psychological pressure caused by constricted [or repressed] thinking." Mnemic symbols, reproduced scenes, and dreams fashioned a "new form of expression" that situated images of the "subject's own body" in a pictorial and verbalized space traversed by memories, fears, and desires. The hysterical fantasies on which scenes drew, however, could be conscious or unconscious; if unconscious, they became pathogenic and caused symptoms or attacks. Linked to the sexual life, fantasies were created out of "deprivation and longing," and, drawing on the "whole might of the person's need for love," the fantasy culminated in "auto-erotic gratification" at its imagined "climax," producing a "realization of the situation" of satisfaction. Once unconscious, this fantasy could "grow and spread," achieving expression as a "morbid symptom."[11] This structure or mechanism situated the imagined body within a scenario created specifically for the purpose of overcoming deprivation of love and achieving satisfaction; it produced auto-erotogenic pleasure of the widest possible sort; it fulfilled wishes, sustained sexual gratifications, and expressed the component parts of the hysteric's sexual instinct. Freud's conceptualization of this fantasmatic articulated his sudden sense that hysteria had a structure, suited his new mode of reading figuratively between the registers of psyche and soma, and theorized his hysterics' reproduced scenes as linked to the sexual life.

Freud's emergent representation theory, then, conceptualized bodily sensations, innervations, and excitations as inscribed in and structuring psychic symbols, memories, and scenes. Some infantile sexual traumas, which linked psyche and soma in a particularly privileged way, seemed especially representable. Embedded in family and social circumstances, these scenes, usually of seduction, reproduced self- and object-representations in an affective matrix of rage and regret. Fathers, as I discuss in Chapter 5, seemed especially representable for Freud's hysterical patients. The notion of representability, moreover, anchored and sustained Freud's theory that scene was the fundamental form of psycho-physical representation, and reproductive remembering its central clinical technology. For as a concept, representability and its clinical method, the reproduction of scenes, enabled Freud to move away from reflex and toward representation models of psycho-physical correlation and causation. Building a new plausible bridge between psyche and soma, Freud also sketched new scientific representations suitable for mobilizing theoretical production of a subjectivity that was rooted in, yet logically separable from, the body. In the next section of this chapter, however, I argue that, defining its mechanisms as displacement and condensation, Freud portrayed the scene's structuring of sexual transitivity and multiple identifications as fundamental to this subjectivity and its expression in patient self-representation.

IV

Freud's notion of psycho-physical representation raised another crucial problem for an emergent psychoanalytic theory: how did scene or fantasy represent the real? For sexual trauma as a psycho-physical category of causation, and scene as its privileged mode of representation, suggested that lived experience shaped subject formation. As Freud sought to address this problem, he discovered yet another, for the problem of the real could be conceptualized, he found, only through the mechanism of identification, a mechanism that intricated the real with the psychical. For identifying with others like herself, the hysteric represented herself to herself; identifying herself with ill others, she imitated their illness; identifying herself with others different from herself, she produced dysfunctional sexual desire. In this theory of identification, Freud posited subject formation as a sort of psycho-physical self-representation. In this way, Freud could more fully account for the embeddedness of his patients' symptoms and scenes in family and social circumstances. For hysterical scenes invariably depicted sexual acts with family members or others; these psycho-physical scenes, inscribed as excitations in the subject's body through the mechanism of identification, reproduced perverse subjectivities.

Indeed, Freud's attention to perverse sexuality displaced hysteria from its position of theoretical and clinical centrality and served to suppress the concept of affect. As I argue in Chapter 6, a theory of affect would artic-

ulate psycho-physiological behavior patterns with specific cognitive appraisals, facial expressions, subjective experiences of a pleasurable or
painful nature, and a muscular and neurological discharge pattern (Kernberg 1991, 3–20). This theory of affect, which articulates acts, subjective
experiences, cognitions, and representations of self and object relations,
enables me to portray psycho-physical plausible bridges as implicated
with, rather than radically separate from, representation. When Freud
fashioned psychoanalysis as a discourse about sexuality, however, hysteria—the malady through representation—no longer served him as specimen disease.

Freud's early observations conceptualized, however rudimentarily, the
hysteric's identifications as enabling her to represent herself in scenes of
pain and sensation. For in maladies through representation, Freud told
Fliess in February 1897, disease sufferers displayed symptoms that pantomimed bodily movements or paralyses the hysteric had seen, imagined,
or feared.

Somnambulism . . . has been correctly understood. The most recent result is
the unraveling of hysterical cataleptic fits: imitation of death with rigor mortis,
that is, identification with someone who is dead. If she has seen the dead person,
then glazed eyes and open mouth; if not, then she just lies there quietly and
peacefully.

Hysterical cold shivers = being taken out of a warm bed. Hysterical
headache with sensations of pressure on the top of the head, temples, and so
forth, is characteristic of the scenes where the head is held still for the purpose
of actions in the mouth. (Later reluctance at photographer's, who holds head in a
clamp.)

Unfortunately my own father was one of these perverts and is responsible
for the hysteria of my brother (all of whose symptoms are identifications) and
those of several younger sisters. The frequency of this circumstance often makes
me wonder.[12]

In this remarkable letter, Freud equated imitation with the mechanism of
identification and both with performative hysterical self-representation.
Cataleptic fits, then, reproduced the action of inaction, of corpselike stiff-
ness. Identification located the body in specific situations of risk—being
held down, deprived of warmth, dying—and simultaneously performed
and defended against such feared outcomes. These bodily imitations acted
out "scenes," and those scenes reproduced actions practiced on the body
that the hysteric symbolized as hypersensation or, here, pain. Moreover,
identification depended upon the mechanism of looking: if the hysteric

had seen a corpse, she might imitate its rigor; if not, she enacted her romanticized notion of corpseness. Thus witnessing or experiencing pain could, through the mechanism of identification, produce or reproduce that pain in a later time, another place. Hysterical identification thus bridged a hitherto untheorized gap in Freud's theory of representation by adding the concept of imitation to those of scene, reproductive remembering, and visual excitation. As a concept, it sought to account for what Freud had neglected: how the real was symbolized in and on the organism through psycho-physical representation.

This theory sought to revise the notion of hysterical imitation that Freud had inherited from his scientific predecessors. He asked in the dream book, "What is the meaning of hysterical identification?" and answered, a version of mimetic representation. Hysterical identification depended upon the "capacity of hysterics to imitate any symptoms in other people that may have struck their attention—sympathy, as it were, intensified to the point of reproduction." Here, Freud defined reproduction as the enactment of scenes that both performed and defended against pretended identifications. It thus articulated psycho-physical correlation through theatricality and described identification as the mechanism that enabled psychical, indeed unconscious, causation in the physiological realm. This notion, however, replicated aspects of earlier, logically reductive notions of hysterical identification. On a hospital ward, this "psychical infection" played itself out among multiple, usually female, subjects. Because the patients knew one another's symptoms better than the doctor did, they sympathized with another's attack and inferred that they would experience a similar fit; because the inference remained unconscious, it in fact produced attack. "Thus identification," Freud clarified, was "not simple imitation but *assimilation*"; it expressed a "resemblance" and was derived from a "common element," which remained unconscious. Indeed, hysterical identification most often seized upon a "common *sexual* element," for the hysteric symptomatically identified with people with whom she had experienced an erotic connection (*SE*, 4: 149–50). Hysterical fantasies, then, reproduced as scenes the hysteric's unconscious identifications with the same sexual others she desired in a fantasmatic scenario.

In December 1896, Freud reported to Fliess a case in which multiple identification linked scenic reproduction with the real.[13]

One of my patients, in whose history her highly perverse father plays the principal role, has a younger brother who is looked upon as a common scoundrel. One day the latter appears in my office to declare, with tears in his eyes, that he is not a scoundrel but is ill, with abnormal impulses and inhibition of will [and] what are surely nasal headaches. . . . That evening the sister calls me because she is in an agitated state. Next day I learn that after her brother had left [her lodgings], she had an attack of the most dreadful headaches—which she otherwise never suffers from. Reason: the brother told her that when he was 12 years old, his sexual activity consisted in kissing (licking) the feet of his sisters when they were undressing at night. In association, she recovered from her unconscious the memory of a scene in which (at the age of 4) she watched her papa, in the throes of sexual excitement, licking the feet of a wet nurse. In this way she surmised that the son's sexual preferences stemmed from the father; that the latter also was the seducer of the former. Now she allowed herself to identify with him and assume his headaches. She could do this, by the way, because during the same scene the raving father hit the child (hidden under the bed) on the head with his boot.

The brother abhors all perversity, whereas he suffers from compulsive impulses. . . . If he could be perverse, he would be healthy, like the father.[14]

The problem of the real, especially when conceptualized as paternal seduction, emerged here with special force. Still, Freud suggested, this hysterical self-representation did not invite naive interpretation. These two scenes, like the hysterical mother's, which I described in Section III, contained the same elements (sexually aroused male, female feet, licking and its consequence, seduction), but those elements had been arranged in a different context and transferred onto other figures: the wet nurse of the memory scene was replaced, in the brother's recounted scene, by the girl herself; the two scenes, joined through the symbol of licking, had repressed that perverse and fetishized sex through the symptom of headache. The patient's infantile experiences and reproduced scenes joined psychical perceptual visions, excitations aroused by memory, and revived visual sensations.

This group of reproduced scenes and memories, moreover, depicted the patient's identifications as the privileged mechanism of hysterical symptom formation. Her headache represented her identification with her victimized brother and with his position in the scene she had seen, a position she understood as resembling her own (as hidden and kicked witness) in the reproduced scenes in which her brother had seduced her. Thus father licking wet nurse, father seducing brother, and brother licking and seducing sisters, all functioned psychopathogically only because, like Emma's, the two scenes visually echoed one another and were representable. Freud here depicted hysterical subjectivity, moreover, as embedded in a perverse family scenario. Understanding that his hysterics' symptoms were thus embedded in family and social circumstances, Freud embarked on the psychoanalytic project: to describe the individual as constituted by and through affect-laden representations that articulated fantasy and the real. The psychoanalytic subject thus constituted itself in and through self- and other-representations that were always already inscribed with somatic excitations and sensations.

But Freud still had not fully articulated scenic reproduction with the sexual real. Indeed, as Freud produced sexuality as the fundamental category of psychoanalytic representation, he displaced other concepts of psycho-physical correlation. These depictions of hysterical representation drove logically toward the sexual life, with which, Freud asserted, hysterical unconscious fantasies demonstrated an "important connection." Identical with the patient's first masturbatory fantasies, such fantasies performed acts of auto-erotic wishing, self-pleasure, and sexual gratification. Freud here invoked multiple and cross-sexual identification, the mechanism by which he had earlier conceptualized hysterical psycho-physical representation, only to reduce its usefulness as heuristic. The fantasizing masturbator could "picture himself" as both man and woman in an imagined situation; a hysterical patient, playing both parts of the repressed fantasy behind a "plastically portrayed" attack, "pressed her dress to her body with one hand (as the woman) while trying to tear it off with the other (as the man)."[15] Freud here produced a theory of identification that accounted for sexually transitive subject formation, a theory increasingly suited to address modern fears about—and celebrations of—sexual insufficiency as defined through a functionalizing notion of sexual adequacy. He began, as well, to conceptualize a hybrid subject that would enable him to use the patient's recounted scene to link psyche and soma, fantasy and familial circumstances. He could thus build a larger plausible bridge for his emergent science.

Yet Freud here mobilized his theory of psycho-physical subjectivity by strategically allying his new science with sexology. The 1908–9 essays about hysterical attacks from which I have argued appeared in journals edited, not by analysts, but the prominent sexologists Magnus Hirschfeld and Albert Moll. Flushed with the success of his 1909 Clark Lectures— in which he had brought the psychoanalytic plague to North America— Freud returned to Europe, seeking to interest more physicians in his work, especially those who specialized in the established medical practice of sexual pathology. Indeed, having produced an emergent discourse around the figure of the hysteric, Freud was about to embark on a significant mid-career project that would marginalize her as trope. As he sought to control the dissemination of the new psychoanalytic concepts and clinical technologies, Freud insisted on the centrality of sexuality to psychoanalytic theory. His strategy identified sexologists as the new science's adherents, excoriated its enemies as inexpert, and added new allies from other specialisms to emerging groups of psychoanalytic professionals. As battle lines were drawn between true followers and quack practitioners, an internecine struggle erupted and, after 1910, ultimately produced the celebrated secessions and expulsions of Alfred Adler and C. G. Jung from the psychoanalytic fold. Although the figure of the hysteric had helped Freud begin a career in neuropathology, its usefulness for mobilizing theoretical production, gaining mentors and adherents, and creating new scientific networks had reached its historical limit.

Freud's early rhetoric of hysteria, however, effectively served his project to illuminate a highly complicated topic that had never yet been represented. To define the characteristics of hysteria's "special kind of representation," its modes of depicting psyche to soma and so enabling the patient to portray herself to herself and others, Freud rewrote dominant reflex theories of psycho-physical correlation as representation theory. He shifted his new science, in turn, from the discourses of neuroanatomy and physiology toward those of psychology. He retheorized memory and trauma as psycho-physical concepts, which enabled him to conceptualize identification as multiple and as the privileged mechanism of subject formation. Clinical practices deployed and helped shape these theories, and in his consulting room Freud fashioned the concepts of reproduced scene as psycho-physical self-representation and repetitive remembering as curative technology. Understanding that his hysterics' symptoms were embedded in family and social circumstances and recounted in their presenting stories, I argue in Chapter 7, Freud embarked on the psychoanalytic project: to describe and theorize the individual as constituted by and through affect-laden representations that articulated fantasy and the real. From this perspective, the subject constitutes itself in and through self- and other-representations that are always already inscribed with somatic excitations and sensations. Understood in the widest possible sense as a representation theory of psycho-physical correlation and psychopathological causation—as the scientific constitution of plausible bridges between psyche and soma, physiology and psychology, sexuality and sociality—

psychoanalysis is a theory of modern subjectivity as it is anchored in, represented through, yet conceptually separable from the body.

This book argues that by appropriating and transmuting the scientific practices in which he had been trained, Freud fashioned a modern science and its curative technologies. In the next chapter, I sketch hysteria's history to situate Freud within the larger hysteria debates. I trace the ways this discourse shifted, moving with scientific retheorizations from anatomical to physiological representations of the enigmatic disease that imitated physical illness but had no organic cause. This sketch serves me, however, primarily to locate and describe the nineteenth-century discourses from which Freud drew his primary materials. Thus I view as central to Freud's emergent psychoanalysis the discourses of neuropathology, sexology, and physiology. In Chapter 2, I argue that Charcot's neuropathology, his groundbreaking conceptualizations of functional lesions in hysterical neuroanatomy, enabled Freud to revise the contemporary medical practices of functionalization, especially the technologies of rest cure and sexological treatment. In Chapter 3, I argue that Freud learned the tactics of scientific debate at least in part from Charcot's amphitheatrical displays, his canny appropriation and transmutation of conventional medical presentation. Charcot's shows taught Freud how to stage hysteria for an emerging "medical public," the mass of interested and informed consumers who crowded the nervous doctors' consulting rooms. Freud won allies to the psychoanalytic cause, then, because he had translated from Paris and Nancy the tactics of scientific publicity and debate, strategies he later used in London, New York, Berlin, and Geneva, as well as in Worchester, Massachusetts. As Freud said in one of the historicizing documents that provide my epigraphs, psychoanalysis began in, developed, and elaborated earlier suggestions about psycho-physical correlation and psychopathological disease causation. "Any history of it must therefore begin with an account of the influences which determined its origin and should not overlook the times and circumstances that preceded its creation."[16]

"Toujours la chose génitale"

The status and functions of the female body had always been a problem for the hysteria discourse. Indeed, in his history of the psychoanalytic movement, Freud jokingly invoked the moment he learned this. At one of Charcot's receptions, he had overheard the great man gossiping to the gynecologist Paul Brouardel about a nervous sufferer whose symptoms her "impotent" or "awkward" husband had precipitated; Brouardel, "astonished," and Freud, "almost paralysed with amazement," listened, as Charcot, hugging himself and jumping up and down with glee, expostulated, "Mais, dans des cas pareils c'est toujours la chose génitale, toujours." The paralyzed Freud wondered why, if Charcot knew that, he never said so. Still, with brain anatomy and experimental induction of hysterical paralyses absorbing all his interest, Freud forgot—or repressed—this impression. By mid-career, however, Freud knew, too, the difference between a passing *aperçu* and theoretical production; repeating this tale as a parable of scientific knowledge transmission, he claimed responsibility for the sexual theory despite his bows to the "parentage" of Charcot, Rudolf Chrobak, and Breuer. For theoretical production resembled, Freud said, not a "casual flirtation" but a "legal marriage with all its duties and difficulties"; "*épouser les ideés de . . .* " was "no uncommon figure of speech, at any rate in French"![1] Likening himself to Charcot's paralyzed hysterics, Freud would wed himself, against his figurative parent's stated wishes, to the sexual theory, which would displace hysteria as investigative site of psycho-physical correlation.

For the hysteria discourse, of course, the psyche-soma link had always been a question of the genitals. In this chapter, I examine a series of moments in which discursive shifts enabled concepts about the female genitals to change, notions that eventually anchored Freud's emergent ideas about plausible bridges for psycho-physical correlation. Using the uterine theory as lens in Section I, I sketch the shifting discourses of the female body as governed by its reproductive organs, organs first described geographico-anatomically, and, later, physiologically. The gynecological texts of antiquity, for example, represented the female body through concepts of organic proximal location; those of the early modern period, through the locational and pathological refinements of the new anatomical science; those of the nineteenth century, through the discourses of physiology and neurology. As a result, the discourse of wandering wombs gradually but incompletely gave way to that of imbalanced humoral spirits, and, then, to nervous system transmission, sympathetic interaction, and reflex arcs. The uterine theory first served and then was abandoned by medicine as these scientific discourses emerged beside, contested, and delimited one another. The shift from anatomical to physiological formulations that occurred during the nineteenth century—but not in any evenly developing way—made it possible for Freud, I argue, to "espouse" a sexual theory. It enabled him, too, to put his precursors in their place, to dismiss Breuer in 1914 as antipathetic to sexuality and his theoretical concepts as merely "physiological" (*SE*, 14: 11). Seeking to construct plausible bridges between psyche and soma, Freud appropriated, criticized, and then rewrote the uterine theory as sexual theory, the mode of psycho-physical representation that would supplant hysteria's mimetic representations of organic, motor, and sensible dysfunction.

Theories of social functions also shifted as historically situated anatomical accounts of the hysterical body gave way to physiological ones. Read by synecdoche from nature or organism to social group, aggregate, or organism, social functions could be presumed to be natural; the concept of contiguity, which guaranteed synecdoche as a trope, also presumed that the natural and social realms, which included different objects of different statuses and kinds, were homologously structured. The ancients, sure of the female body's fecundity, thus viewed social functions as existing on the same explanatory level as physical or biological facts. These apparently natural functions became available for scrutiny, however, as the discourse of medical observation shifted.

By the nineteenth century, scientific observation had, through the discourses of pathological anatomy and neurophysiology, problematized the link between biological and social functions. The notions of organic lesion, disease seat, and anatomo-pathological localization altered the ways in which the female reproductive body was represented and its functions conceptualized, justified, and authorized. Submitted to physiology, the discourse of functions became a moral value, with the functionalized body serving to anchor discourses that were grounded on, and that in turn produced, theories of sexual difference, discourses such as sexology and psychopathology. By the nineteenth century, nature had also been invented as part of the nature/social binarism. No longer existing on the same level of explanation as biological and physical fact, no longer simply conceived of as a Nature created by a Being who controlled it, nature had become the scientific ground on which knowledge was produced and through which it was disseminated. As Bruno Latour suggests, science had produced the concept of nature as positivistically observable, as experimentally reproducible, as reliably representing and witnessing the truth of elemental forces. The mediation of the laboratory constituted and organized the binarism of nature/social, making it an unstable but structurally consistent mode of scientific representation. This "work of purification," which constructed nature and the social as distinct from each other, covered over, even as it abetted, the "work of mediation," the production by scientific practices of the hybrid research subject. The "work of translation," which guaranteed the transmission of knowledge along professional networks, likewise institutionalized scientific claims, created credibility for findings, and constituted hierarchies of merit and distinction (Latour 1993, 20–29). Nineteenth-century scientists appropriated these conceptual tools and work practices to attack and demolish the uterine theory. At century's end, Freud could thus criticize the old discourse of anatomy as inadequate to represent the hysterical body. For the modern body, produced by the representations and social work practices of science, was hardly natural, despite—perhaps because of—its apparently reliable testimony in the laboratory.

The relation of body to mind had always constituted a philosophical problem for science. By the nineteenth century, however, it had become a problem that scientists could submit to experimental observation and about which they could produce knowledge. Hysteria, a common and imitative disorder that had foregrounded the problematic link between the biological organism and mental life, had by midcentury become historically available for conceptualization through the mediation of the laboratory. And although he has been maligned by postmodern and feminist theorists, Charcot performed groundbreaking work, submitting hysteria to the work of the laboratory and making it possible to produce scientific findings about the sickened female body. Using clinical picturing and differential diagnosis, he assembled symptomatic events, reasoned inductively, and identified disease entities; mobilizing the realm of representation, he made hysteria visible in the medical theater of proof. He sketched dysfunctional sensate mappings to assert that, although it imitated organic disease, hysteria flouted the laws of anatomy. Indeed, Charcot produced a rudimentary representation theory of psycho-physical correlation from which Freud borrowed, and which he then revised. Embedded in the discursive shifts that made the psyche-soma problem visible in surgeries, in amphitheaters, and on grand rounds, medical observations of hysteria provided an opportunity to stage, debate, and so produce psycho-physical theory. Charcot's laboratory research enabled Freud to move hysteria from the discourse of anatomy to physiology and then to psychology; it facilitated his fashioning of a plausible representational bridge between psyche and soma. Indeed, Charcot made hysteria worthy of scientific interest.

In this chapter, I look at how the hysteria discourse, from the ancients to Charcot, represented the symptomatic female body, how discursive shifts placed Freud opportunely within the history of a common but enigmatic disease. I trace, in Section I, the historical production of "nature" as cause of hysteria. That nature, first produced in a binarism with supernature (whether demonic possession, witchcraft, or God), later with the social, cultural, or historical, came to govern the organic functions and dysfunctions imitated by the disease and represented on or in the body. Each historically situated theory posited a plausible bridge between psyche and soma, spirit and body; each differently articulated a psychophysical theory of correlation and disease causation. In Section II, I sketch the ways in which Charcot's groundbreaking neuropathology marshaled tropes to represent the hysterical body, mobilizing metaphor's energy to win allies to his physiologically based reflex theories, theories that nevertheless adumbrated the psycho-physical concepts that Freud would invent for an emergent psychoanalysis. In this chapter, I argue that the uterine theory, while undergoing change and revision, was historically sustained and sustainable within the hysteria discourse precisely because of its plasticity and flexibility. Because it was "toujours la chose génitale."

I

As Helen King has demonstrated, theories about the ancients' clinical and diagnostic practices with regard to hysteria have been retrospectively misread by historians. The Hippocratic gynecological texts did not present a clinical disease entity, hysteria, that resembled the diagnosis made so routinely in the nineteenth century but focused, rather, on describing the body's geography.[2] In the gynecological texts of Soranus of Ephesus (A.D. 98–138), for example, the body's structures are described in terms of their shapes, locations in the body, and proximity to other organic structures. The uterus is larger than the bladder and does not lie fully beneath it; thin membranes connect the uterus with other organs; six finger-breadths long and composed of nerves, veins, arteries, and flesh, the uterus can be described as sinewy (Soranus 1956, 9–11). In Soranus's two-dimensional map, the fundamental anatomical elements of spatialization and proximity describe the body's geography; anatomy localizes organs in space and configures their relation to one another.

Ancient classificatory medicine, moreover, linked portrayal of physiological spaces to the doctrine of sympathies between organic entities. The uterus could be distended, drawn into a different configuration, or shape itself differently. Uterine disease could anatomically redistribute itself through the body, whether by radiational diffusion, functional correspondence of organ dysfunction, or systematic (usually nervous) relay of inflammation. Anatomy thus represented the interplay between the spatializations of location and the flexibility of configuration as accounting for organic alteration and so for disease.[3] Soranus represents these sympathies as a rudimentary theory of functions. When postmortem proved that suckers—protuberances similar to breasts—did not exist in the uterus, for example, an emergent research technology had, he says, disproved an anatomical theory that had "no foundation in nature" (Soranus 1956, 13). Recourse to a material, rationally knowable, and naturalized reality thus informed the ancients' theories about the body.

But the body was not simply a blank and irreducible materiality. Although having a nature, and so natural states of relaxation or constriction, the female reproductive organs participated in a creativity, an instrumental making and producing of the fetus, for example, or of effluvia held in a vital economy, a functionalizing of health or dysfunctionalizing, disease. Soranus represents these alterations and functions as connected, however problematically, to the female life cycle, to menstruation, conception, and pregnancy. Because intercourse harms the body's economy, he maintains, permanent virginity benefits women; still, because consistent with the "general principle of nature" that causes humans to reproduce, defloration and intercourse may occur when menstruation begins—if the physician attends to the uterus's natural functions and spatializations (it should be roomy and ready to receive seed). This naturalized notion of the body's functions and its functionalizing creativity was matched by a discourse about conditions "contrary to nature" that specifically afflicted women. Soranus identified one such disease, hysterical suffocation (*hysterike pnix*), as differentiated from the related maladies of epilepsy, apoplexy, catalepsy, and lethargy; although hysterical suffocation resembled these illnesses because all presented with seizures, only in hysterical disease was the uterus inflamed and retracted. He criticized the Hippocratic theory of the wandering womb and ancient treatments designed to move the uterus with evil or sweet smells. [4]

By the second century A.D., then, theories of inflammation and sympathetic communication between spatialized and functionalized body parts supplemented and sought to displace the representation of wandering wombs. And although Soranus describes seizures and aphonia as central to hysteria, he does not include as symptoms the motor and sensory or the emotional disturbances by which nineteenth-century doctors would characterize the disease. Although Soranus had produced a theory of bodily functions as "naturally" related to female reproductive functions and life-cycle events, moreover, he did not have available the conceptual tools that would enable the historically later discourse of physiology to produce an experimentally verifiable theory of somatic functionalism, a theory that, through the concept of life-cycle events, could produce and naturalize a synecdochically readable concept of social and cultural functions from organic alterations.

In the seventeenth century, hysteria became a disease with a "naturall" rather than a supernatural cause. In 1603, Edward Jorden used the spatialized and functionalized body to argue against demonic possession as cause of uterine affliction. He pictured the female body as centered on a nervous, porous uterus capable of "distention and contraction" and tied by ligaments, nerves, veins, and arteries to virtually all other parts of the body. The animal, vital, and natural faculties became affected "by consent" with the diseased uterus or by proximity to it. In the disease he called "suffocation of the mother," symptoms affected vital functions, which were governed by the heart. Natural functions were governed by the liver, and animal functions by the brain. The symptoms of aphonia, coma, apoplexy, epilepsy, catalepsy, paralysis, insensibility, and deficiencies of judgment, reason, and memory were thus caused by the brain, not the uterus. Still, this womb or "matrix" traveled through the body, emitting evil vapors that caused ligaments to shorten and draw it up, contracting and rising toward the midriff to cause a choking or strangling sensation. The range of symptoms Jorden linked to "the mother" represented the disease as capable of producing multiple dysfunctions, including the classic attack with arched back (Jorden 1971 [1603], 5–16). While based in anatomical spatialization and proximity, however, his mode of representing the body systematically served to functionalize it. Localizing the uterus and configuring its spatialization, Jorden focused primarily on the sympathetic communications relayed and diffused through the body, on the functional correspondences that produced systematic dysfunction. Yet Jorden's anatomical representation sketched an aspect of functioning just beginning to be conceptualized: the mental. The mind could emerge as representable primarily because an increasingly functionalized body localized functions in organs and organic systems.

Thomas Sydenham foregrounded the mind–body problem in the hysteria debate by depicting mental functions, not only as localizeable, but as economically structured. Preaching the superiority of clinical observation to theory or speculation, Sydenham observed that hysteria simulated localized disease symptoms in organs throughout the body. He characterized the disease by the "multiformity of the shapes [it] puts on"; its symptoms were "not less numerous than varied, proteiform and chameleon-like," a "farrago of disorderly and irregular phenomena."[5] "Few of the maladies of miserable mortality," he maintained, "are not imitated by it." These numerous forms, moreover, could appear anywhere in the body and, because "whatever part of the body it attacks, it will create the proper symptoms of that part," the physician had to exercise judgment and sagacity to avoid being misled into thinking that the hysteric passion was an organ's essential disease. Symptomatic epileptic spasms, strangulation of the womb, head pain and vomiting, heart palpitations, coughing, iliac distress, muscular paralysis or cutaneous insensitivity, corpselike fits of coldness, and kidney and bladder dysfunction (and so excessive and limpid urine, which Sydenham viewed as pathognomic for diagnosis) all thus characterized this disease. Yet none of these symptoms signified that the organ so affected was itself diseased. A disorder of the "animal spirits" caused them to bear down on particular organs and excite spasm and pain where sensations were acute, to derange and pervert the functions of bodily parts as these spirits moved through the body. Characterized by transmission of disorder and dysfunction, this body's humoral economy suffered damage, its "irregularity" of sensate distribution standing opposed to nature. Moreover, not "*shaken* in body only," the doctor's unhappy patients also suffered in mind; despair, foreboding, melancholy, jealousy, fear, and anger all arose capriciously, without cause. The disease's mental manifestations, "commotions of the mind," emerged from "over-ordinate actions of the body." Sydenham conceptualized the body, then, as an economic system, characterized by the penetration of mental effects, although the notion of psycho-physical disease causation was not yet available for theorizing. And the "proper arrangement of the ,spirits" within that economy was restored, not by bleeding and purging, but the healing operations of rest and exercise.[6]

In the eighteenth century, the discourse of pathological anatomy questioned the brain's organic functions in mental disease. Philippe Pinel instituted large-scale observations, took detailed patient history, and compiled postmortem statistics at the Bicêtre and Salpêtrière hospices in Paris to identify and classify the lesions that would prove mental alienation an organic disease. As Stanley Joel Reiser maintains, organs were thus believed to consist of tissues that, during disease, became locally injured, inflamed, or impaired; by viewing diseased tissue, a visible biological substance, and the organ where it was located, the physician could read the indices of symptom and internal injury together so that observation correlated the two (Reiser 1978, 16–17, 18–19). Yet because he often found no such brain lesions, Pinel surmised that alienation could be moral or physical or a mixture of both, could be, that is, functional or organic. "Derangement of the understanding," he said, could not be traced to "organic lesion of the brain," for, in many cases, such theories proved "contrary to anatomical fact" (Pinel 1806, 46, quoted in Vieth 1965, 177). Deploying pathological anatomy to analyze the body, breaking the entity into its parts to discover their natures, proportions, functions, and interrelations, Pinel disconfirmed that a specific organic lesion caused mental disease. Rather than theorizing about the brain's proportions or nature, Pinel's moral treatment refunctionalized body and mind, returning supposed incurables to family, work, and social life. Anatomizing the body's structures and reading them by synecdoche into social relations and a potentially functionalized social space, Pinel reimagined the ill body's relation to mind and to a public domain, institutionalizing those homologies in his hospital's segregated work and treatment spaces.

As pathological anatomy more accurately localized organic disease, a new set of medical questions emerged. Did diseases exist without "lesional correlative"? Was pathological anatomy's disease seat a first cause of disorder or its effect? Largely because of Pinel's work, nineteenth-century doctors would come to believe that nervous diseases did not, or did not necessarily, present brain lesions at autopsy. Following Pinel's nosographical practice, René Laënnec (1781–1826) had classified diseases as those characterized by present organic lesions and those that, like nervous diseases, left no lesional alteration in the body to which the disease's origin could be attributed.[7] In the wake of Pinel, somaticist theories of inflammation, irritation, and reflex action sought to resolve the problem of disease seat by rethinking systematic functions. In the 1830s, for example, Marshall Hall transformed the doctrine of sympathy into the theory of reflex action. Identifying the reflex arc as produced in and by a spinal nervous system unrelated to but influenced by the brain, Hall identified the spinal cord as both controlling mechanism and site of relayed communications within the body. This view of the body as a system of reflex interrelations revised pathological anatomy's representation of the body as spatialized by localized lesions, replacing it with a model that privileged physiological functioning.[8] Although Hall did not conceptualize reflex theory as necessarily participating in the medical mind-body debate, he had provided the tools for building such plausible bridges between psyche and soma.

This functional perspective also reintroduced the debate about uterine theory into the hysteria discourse. No longer simply represented through anatomical configuration, the uterus was pictured as pathological-anatomical seat, a body part in which some power, function, or quality was thought to be localized. While the womb no longer wandered, it emitted signals and produced symptoms that affected other bodily organs by reflex action. In the 1840s, Moritz Romberg in Berlin and Thomas Laycock in England attributed the origin of reflex action to the uterus and the ovaries respectively. When irritated, especially during menstruation, uterus or ovaries relayed reflex irritation to other parts of the body, causing attacks, convulsions, insensibilities, and paralyses. In 1845, Laycock proposed that, although the nervous system served as seat of "nerve" disease, the brain, nerves, and membranes of the spine were linked to the ovaries by the sympathetic nervous system; brain, blood, glands, muscles—all organs of the body—could thus be affected by ovarian irritation. George Beard identified brain, stomach, and genitals as three centers of reflex action in the 1870s; when one center was "irritated by overuse or direct abuse," injury radiated in any or all directions, creating the nervous patients' multiple and various symptoms.[9]

Deploying the reflex theory in gynecology, Horatio R. Storer argued that the brain was the seat but not the cause of insanity in women. Such insanity, he said, could exist without structural changes in the brain, and structural changes in the brain could occur without insanity resulting. Because reflex action could account for insanity without positing brain lesions, and because in insanity the brain's *functions* might be deranged but not its material substratum, "THE BRAIN [WAS] ALWAYS THE SEAT OF INSANITY, BUT IT [WAS] NOT ALWAYS THE SEAT OF ITS CAUSE (Storer 1972 [1871], 36–62). Although Storer tried to unriddle the problem of disease causation and localization, he only managed to scramble the two. Still, the symptomatic body had become immensely more theoretically complex than it had been in 1603. For the nineteenth-century emergence of neurology as theory and as a medical specialism had made the concepts of disease seat, localization, and functional differentiation available for interrogation, clarification, and theorization.

Yet this discourse, especially when deployed by gynecology, could be used to reassign hysteria to women. The discourse of "nerves," proposed centuries earlier by Sydenham, had confirmed "a great similitude" between hypochondriac complaints and uterine disease. While women suffered from these disorders—or chronic diseases—more often than men, Sydenham argued, not the womb's easy indisposition but woman's "more fine and delicate habit of body" destined her for a "life of more refinement and care." In claiming that the female's social function was thus "endowed by Nature," Sydenham had submitted hysteria, the common and female disorder, to the dictates of what he viewed as a God-imbued force (Sydenham 1848–50, 2: 85, 91). Nineteenth-century scientists, however, explained the link between organic and social functions not as quasi-spiritual but as justifiable by virtue of experimentally reproducible facts, facts that could be read, as Latour suggests, as generalizable from natural forms to human discourses through the work of purification. Nervous functions thus were paradoxically naturalized even as natural bodies were differentiated from and justified by social conventions or constitutions, as Latour calls them (Latour 1993, 35–46). The discourse of neurologically posited functions and social functionalisms posed a problem, however; for the female reproductive system was periodically and continuously both functioning yet interrupting health, especially during the childbearing years. Because "pathological disturbances" arose more often in the female than the male reproductive organs, Storer argued, that somatic system served as seat of the body's sympathetic irritations. By synecdoche, Storer's "deranged" female function became "disorder," and, as he literalized his mobilized tropes, insanity. Breakdown and madness proliferated around the female life cycle's physiological crises: menstruation, puberty, pregnancy, childbirth, and menopause (Storer 1972 [1871], 62–87).

Female physiology thus both produced and mobilized notions of female character and duties. Women's susceptible and irritable nervous systems, Laycock said, caused both her feminine virtues (compassion, kindness, piety, honest sincerity, and constancy) *and* her frailties (religious enthusiasm, erotomania, nymphomania, monomania, rage and jealousy, craftiness and cunning) (Laycock 1840, 32, 76, 178, 227, 238, 353). Woman's mission as mother and sick-nurse necessitated the exercise of the female virtues Laycock had listed. The functionalized uterus, then, produced a new semiology that posited social productivities and read all deviations from the norm as pathological. And because the female body was, by definition, routinely pathologically disturbed, the norm for woman had become infected by pathology. Rhetorically and logically tautological, this valuing nevertheless permeated the mid-century medical models of female health: "What is woman?" Storer asked, and replied, "Disease, says Hippocrates" (Storer 1972 [1871], 152).

At midcentury, Pierre Briquet intervened in the uterine debate to point out the theory's illogical neurology. Finding himself by circumstance head of the hysteria ward at the Charité hospital in Paris, Briquet resigned himself to studying this female disease and, much to his surprise, his systematic and meticulous observation overturned the uterine theory. For the presence of male hysterics at the Charité meant that Briquet studied both men and women; because no evidence existed, Briquet said, that male genitals caused the disease, the same should logically be true of women. The disease's seat could therefore not be located in the uterus. Hysteria, he had come to believe, was a "neurosis of the brain" whose symptoms were physiological. Disease phenomena obeyed precise laws, presented as perturbation of vital actions, and manifested as affective sensation and behavioral passion whose effects might outlast their causes. Praising Charles Lepois and Nathaniel Willis for having replaced uterus with brain in hysteria etiology, Briquet criticized his nineteenth-century colleagues for reviving the genital theory. That the ovaries caused the disease, he said, was nothing but hypothesis.[10] Briquet's treatise, then, represented hysteria as an observable, coherent disease entity, with comprehensible phenomena and precise symptomatologies, with brain rather than womb as the hysterical body's functional center.

Briquet's brain-centered theory of hysteria exposed the social and cultural values that anchored a functionalizing physiology. His observations of impoverished and incarcerated charity patients, he said, disconfirmed that hysteria was a disease of the leisured upper-class lady, although idleness enlivened nervous susceptibility, and manual labor diminished sensibility. Briquet's observations disproved the notion that working-class women, being habituated to the privations of a hard life, never became nervous. Quite the contrary. Abusive treatment of infants by parents or of wives by husbands; the preoccupations, cares, and contrarieties of marriage and family; the inquietude of affairs of commerce, fortune, and social position; the difficulties of the domestic service undertaken by most country-dwellers who had migrated to the city; and the fears and anxieties of love all caused hysteria. Briquet also exposed as mythological the contemporary medical notion that sexual continence produced the disease. He found that nuns hardly ever became hysterical; that female servants fell ill because financial and sexual circumstances in the families they worked for put them at risk; that prostitutes got sick because of the "moral insensibilities" to which their profession submitted them; that widows stayed healthy because, living alone, they simply were not exposed to nervous disease. Briquet studied 197 prostitutes, aged 16–30, who had been registered by the Paris police and who lived and worked in brothels or operated from their own residences. More than half suffered the disease to some degree, Briquet said; misery, insomnia, alcoholism, abusive treatment by men, fear of the police, forced medical sequestrations, and the jealous and violent passions associated with sexual labor explained the frequency of the disease that he had observed among them. Neither sexual continence nor satisfaction protected working women from hysteria, for moral and physical suffering, not sex or sexlessness, caused hysteria. Still, Briquet supported in part the uterine theory's synecdochal rhetoric. Not her sexual organs but her tender, delicate brain and nervous tissue accounted for woman's disposition to and frequency of hysteria; this tissue endowed woman with a special and gendered moral sensibility guaranteed to aid her "noble" social "mission" of raising children and caring for the old and infirm.[11] Briquet thus challenged the uterine theory's class and sexual biases, but did not flout mid-century theories of sexual and social difference.

Robert Brudenell Carter, an ophthalmologist by training and profession, claimed in 1853 that not the brain but mental states caused hysteria. "Emotion," he said, "is a force adequate to the production of very serious

disorders in the human frame, acting upon the muscular, vascular, and secretory organs, and causing various derangements both of their structure
and function." The nervous system transmitted sensation via spinal and
sympathetic nerves throughout the organism. Although hysteria affected
the brain, neither brain lesion nor injury, but undischarged emotion
caused the disease. Emotions naturally tended toward discharge through
the nerves, which afforded "speedy and evident relief" from anguish; and
strong feelings deemed unacceptable or inappropriate for expression
could, if concealed or repressed, cause convulsive paroxysms. Fear, terror,
erotic passion, jealousy, envy, and selfishness, then, could all endanger
health. Civilized morality demanded the suppression of emotion, especially by women, yet the ability to judge which emotions to conceal operated independently of "moral excellence or depravity." The sufferer's
obsessive concentration on her illness produced her convulsions; secondary
somatic complications of forceful emotions (such as vomiting or coughing) had been misread by doctors as organic distress. "Acts of attention"
to the body largely "independent of the will"—in short, psychological
states—determined hysteria's onset.[12]

While Carter contradicted the uterine theory, he nevertheless suggested that sex caused hysteria. For the often symptomatic uterus attracted the patient's obsessive attention and could itself create secondary
complications (uterine congestion, repeated miscarriage, or immoral sexual reverie). Systems of sexual difference likewise underwrote Carter's
notions of the etiology of hysteria. Built differently, the sexes experienced
feelings differently: men reasoned, women felt. More prone to emotions
than men, women were nevertheless more frequently called on to "conceal" or "repress" them "in compliance with the usages of society"; emotions thus broke out violently or produced morbid effects. "When sexual
desire is taken into the account," Carter added, it intensified "the forces
bearing upon the female, who is often much under its dominion, and
who, if unmarried and chaste, is compelled to restrain every manifesta-
tion of its sway. Man, on the contrary, has such facilities for its gratification, that as a source of disease it is almost inert against him, and when
powerfully exercised, it is pretty sure to be speedily exhausted through
the proper channel" (Carter 1883 [1853], 19–23, 26, 31–34). Carter presented two case studies to prove that sexual life affected emotional health.
When Miss A., who had experienced anxiety over her own postponed
marriage, returned home from a trip to the country to find her sister engaged to be married and the sister's fiancé visiting, she fell into a parox-

ysm of crying. Sarah W., a hard-working and industrious domestic servant, experienced hysterical fits, catalepsy, and attacks of sleep; the doctor
discovered that she had found herself pregnant and had told her seducer—who had refused to marry her—on the night she had had her
first fit. Both these perfectly healthy women, Carter claimed, exhibited
no "especial proclivity" toward hysteria. Their fits had been provoked by
"strongly-excited feeling," and the paroxysms' violence was directly pro-
portional to the length of time they had kept their feelings secret (ibid.,
29–31). Carter's case studies mobilized rudimentary notions of repression,
catharsis and abreaction, involuntary ideation excluded from experience,
and the sexual life as etiological force. Yet the discursive field in which
Carter worked had not yet developed sufficiently to support his conceptualization of these psychological notions. Still, he saw quite clearly that
both the middle-class Miss A. and the hard-working Sarah W. experienced acute distress in their sexual lives, were forced through social constraint to repress their fears and terrors, and had fallen ill with fits. Carter
had joined the chorus of physicians disputing the uterine theory but had
unwittingly proposed its transmutation into what Freud would later call
"the sexual theory."

Although it continued to attract spokesmen, the uterine theory had
reached its discursive and historical limit. Retrospectively created by
anatomists rereading the classic gynecological and Hippocratic texts, the
uterine theory had functioned well in a representational system that
anatomized the body with the tools of spatialization. In ancient medicine,
physicians and patients had used the uterus to configure organic sites and
geographical proximities. It had functioned to explain morbidity, too, in
an eighteenth-century pathological anatomy that represented the living
body in relation to death. In these anatomical discourses, the body had
become a set of figures, of forms and deformations, bound together by a
geography that could be read spatially and temporally and could support
etiological interpretations at postmortem. The nineteenth-century neurologized body, however, criss-crossed by the nervous system, could be
analyzed, pathologized, and submitted to the concept of norms; its pain
located and localized; its disease traced to lesional sites that anchored illness. This neurologically functionalized body worked, if female, because
of and through its reproductive organs; its periodic and routine, but nevertheless functional, dysfunctions (such as menstruation) could be read
synecdochically to justify or generate femininities and womanly social
functions. Medical specialisms such as neurology, gynecology, and surgery,

struggling with related disciplines to carve out their theoretical and clinical territory, appropriated the uterine theory if and when it supported their professional and professionalizing claims. Hall and Storer were gynecologists; Laycock, a surgeon; Freud, a neurologist.[13] The practice of psychotherapy, moreover, was already under way in Geneva and Germany when Freud and Breuer began treating patients cathartically. While the uterine theory added little to the foundational concepts of a functionalizing psychotherapy, the sexual theory, on the contrary, added much. But the psyche-soma debate, contested within and shaped by the shifting medical models of the body, by the production of pathological anatomy and neurophysiology as scientific discourses, made it historically possible at the end of the nineteenth century for psychoanalysis to constitute itself and, in the twentieth, for it to mobilize its concepts and transmit them along scientific networks.

At this historically opportune moment, Freud found around him the concepts he rewrote as what I have called a "rhetoric of hysteria." His representation theories may be interpreted, then, as having emerged from and revised already lively medical debates about psycho-physical correlation and causation. His early work rethought anatomy by asking what loci on the body received, and in the brain transmitted, sensations and messages of function or dysfunction. Arguing against his teacher Theodor Meynert, into whose laboratory he had first been welcomed, and from which he had then been excluded, Freud maintained that the body's periphery as pictured in the brain was not a "topographically exact image" but a representation of certain individual elements. When, as I argue in Chapter 1, Freud moved hysteria from the discourse of neuroanatomy to that of psychology, it was his training in neuropathology that enabled that move. For the young Freud could localize a lesion with the best of neurologists. His aphasia research of 1891, moreover, appropriated John Hughlings Jackson's doctrines to disprove Paul Broca's 1861 and Carl Wernicke's 1874 cerebral-localization theories; he protested that brain-localization researchers had confounded physiological with psychological data and asserted, instead, the importance of cerebral functioning. The "Project" of 1895, as I argue in Chapter 1, articulated a "theory of psychical functioning" with a "quantitative" "economics of nervous force."[14] Yet when he differentiated organic from hysterical paralyses, as I have already suggested, Freud found himself on the most fragile, albeit flexible, of plausible bridges, the representational, in which images that "stood for" or implied the body's periphery traversed the mind-body gap. Freud represented the nervous system in organic paralyses as interrupting transmission of images in brain and spinal cord and so producing lesions; in hysterical paralysis, whatever constituted "lesions" ignored "localization or extent" and behaved, as I have said, "*as though anatomy did not exist or as though it had no knowledge of it*" (*SE*, 1: 168–69).

To resolve the problem of hysteria, whose symptoms mimicked organic illness, however, Freud needed the theoretical concepts of neuropathology. Indeed, I maintain in the second section of this chapter that Charcot's science enabled Freud to situate organic against hysterical paralysis and so constitute physiological as opposed to representation paralyses. For Charcot's neuropathological practices of observation, inductive reasoning, nosography and nosology, and clinical picturing produced cutting-edge scientific theories; despite his misapplication of some research practices and principles, Charcot's laboratory work foregrounded psycho-physical reflex concepts. His two-dimensional maps and sketches, moreover, mobilized these neuropathological concepts, making them available for, and indeed visible to, a wide medical and nonmedical audience, and made it possible to transport them to other research settings. At the Salpêtrière, Freud had witnessed science in the making, as Henri Babinski dubbed the practices of Charcot's Tuesday lessons. He had watched a master neuropathologist at work in a variety of institutional spaces, including laboratory, amphitheater, consulting office, outpatient clinic, and on grand rounds. Translating these scientific hypotheses from Paris to Vienna, Freud began to reason about and sketch the clinical picture of hysterical as opposed to organic paralysis.

II

Charcot's excellence as neuropathologist positioned him perfectly to confront the differences between neurological injury and hysterical imitation of organic disorder. In his research on nervous diseases, Charcot articulated clinical observation with basic scientific work in anatomy, pathology, and, later, physiology; he used the institutional resources of hospital, laboratory, amphitheater, and cabinet to produce the findings that witnessed to the facts of tissular structure, symptom morphology, and disease entity. Charcot's lectures on localization, moreover, deployed new scientific theories about brain and spinal physiology. Microscopic experiments, he explained, enabled him to deduce morbid alterations from the normal state of tissues; macroscopic anatomy charted the alterations possible in the nervous system. In his lectures on spinal cord topography, Charcot claimed that his research on pathological anatomy had joined with experimentation to advance neurological knowledge beyond what his confrères knew (Charcot 1877, 2: 159–62, 226–27). He used Paul Flechsig's research on spinal cord development and Gustav Hitzig and Eduard Fritsch's on electrical stimulation of localized animal cortical centers to illustrate his points. Indeed, experiments in brain stimulation and extirpation of cortical matter performed by other researchers during surgical operations on living subjects, Freud asserted, had confirmed Charcot's views about localized brain centers that controlled specific motor functions (SE, 3: 15). Charcot's institutional setting, however, soon made it possible for his research to expand. When an 1870 organizational rearrangement at the Salpêtrière mandated that hysterical and epileptic patients be housed separately instead of together, Charcot found himself forced to distinguish between epileptic fits and hysterical attacks.[15] Faced with a hospital ward full of convulsive women in need of reallocation, he set out to observe the temporal succession of symptoms during epileptic fit, localized related irritations of the cerebral cortex, and, drawing on "anatomo-patholog[y]," "pathological physiology," and postmortem results, used the tools of neurophysiology, pathological anatomy, and large-scale observation to make hysteria a verifiable disease entity (Charcot 1877, 1: 301, 296). Indeed, Charcot made hysteria modern by submitting it to the mediation of the laboratory, the workshop in which the binarism of nature/culture was being both constituted and deployed to produce the facts that scientists said witnessed to their truths.

In coordinating neuropathological findings with clinical observations, Charcot put in place a sophisticated anatomo-clinical method at his Paris hospital. According to Mark S. Micale, he formalized the French tradition of bedside clinical instruction as the "leçons du mardi" and used both leçons and Friday lectures to win allies for his research from a wide medical audience (Micale 1985, 709–10). He had dissected, microscopically examined, and diagrammed cortical lesions in aphasia patients, he taught, and so could correlate postmortem outcomes with clinical observation of symptoms in living and ill patient bodies (Charcot 1889, 3: 142–50). He was particularly pleased, in the lesson of December 4, 1888, to present fresh autopsy results from a male patient he had demonstrated the week before; carefully prefacing his remarks with declarations of sorrow about patient mortality, Charcot provided "extracts from protocol" to justify his diagnosis that grave epilepsy and chorea had occurred together in the patient—whom physicians had earlier and regularly misdiagnosed as syphilitic (Charcot 1975 [1887–89], 2: 128–29). Autopsy of Charcot's maidservant, Freud reported after having attended the lessons (implying that Charcot had hired her to gain access to her corpse!), proved his diagnosis of paralysis as the clinical expression of sclerosis (SE, 3: 14).

As a neuropathologist, Charcot in fact practiced the ideology of professional charisma. Indeed, his observational strategies often seemed enigmatic, as Georges Guillain reports in his biography. Each morning, Charcot consulted with patients in his cabinet. The patient under scrutiny undressed; the intern read a clinical case summary; Charcot listened silently; he "looked, [and] kept looking at the patient," requesting him to move, inducing him to speak, examining his reflexes and sensory responses. A second patient would follow, and then a third. Charcot silently compared the symptoms he had observed. After the morning's consultation, one of his students claimed, he would rise from his chair, instruct his interns, and, followed by his staff, return to his carriage, nod to his entourage, and—"without a word"—leave. "I cannot tell you, but I know it is this disease, I can sense it," Pierre Marie reported that Charcot sometimes said impatiently after a consultation. These anecdotes about Charcot's "mysterious silence" are clearly apocryphal; his awestruck students mythologized medical observation as "meticulous clinical scrutiny."[16] Indeed, his silence about diagnostic procedures and outcomes reserved him sole authority for prognostic forecasting and singular responsibility for clinical certitude. It protected him from dangerous questions about the clinic's distribution of credit and distinction and constituted its mission as focused on his influential leadership and expert professional identity.[17] Deploying the technologies of physician authority, which granted him a set of prophetic powers, Charcot performed an inspirational call to students and doctors alike to declare allegiance and devotion to his scientific mission.

Charcot's neuropathological clinic produced impressive research results, at least in part because he "practis[ed] nosography," as Freud dubbed his observational style and descriptive technique (SE, 3: 12). Charcot systematically described disease characteristics and so identified disease entities, creating coherence within a disease category while accounting for its difference from and similarity to others. His work on hysteria declared it a verifiable disease entity even as it differentiated the disease from other related syndromes. Neurasthenia and hysteria, he said, which resembled one another, often coexisted in the same subject and so presented a descriptive or "nosographic problem" (Charcot 1975 [1887–89], 2: 132). Because both diseases presented with multiform, incomplete, or protean symptomatologies and inconstant symptomatic succession, the clinician had to observe and describe only the "*essential* and *constant*" ones, as Lester S. King calls them, in order to classify the two as separate disease entities (King 1982, 119–23). Here, Charcot deployed the structures of charismatic professional authority to support his practice of nosography, or disease description, itself dependent on the technologies of observation. Charcot constantly defended, Freud said, the "purely clinical work . . . in seeing": "look[ing] again and again at things he did not understand" and "deepen[ing] his impression of them day by day," comprehension would suddenly "dawn" on him and produce order out of chaos. The clinical picture had emerged (*SE*, 3: 12–13). Charcot's scientific authority, Freud said, guaranteed the "genuineness and objectivity of hysterical phenomen[a]"; it identified hysteria as a stable and certifiable disease entity that would "continue to designate a coherent group of facts or events nosographically intertwined one with the others" (*SE*, 3: 19; Charcot 1975 [1887–89], 2: 37). As Charcot deployed traditional medical strategies of observation, nosography, and nosology in researching hysteria, the disease could routinely be submitted to more rigorous kinds of experimental and laboratory technologies, as we shall see in Chapter 3.

Charcot deployed a variety of legitimate scientific strategies for creating nosological certainty about hysteria as disease entity. Most prominent, perhaps, was ideal-type substitution. From observations of epilepsy and hysteria Charcot constructed clinical pictures that were characterized by, as Freud said, "the constant combination" of repeated and related groups of symptoms into "nosological" pictures. The master then could distinguish the disease's ideal "type" with a "certain sort of schematic planning," and, using these types as a point of departure, his "eye" could see the long line of ill-defined or less significant cases, the "*formes frustes*," which diverged from the type and obliterated one or more of the clinical picture's traits (*SE*, 3: 12; *SE*, 1: 134–35). He labored, Charcot said, to "track down" the distorted or disfigured *formes frustes* so as to arrive at the "types from which they derive[d]." In a lesson on gastric tabes, he showed how he had constructed the ideal type from lists of recurring symptoms of crisis and fit; that "type" headed Charcot's hierarchy of pure-to-impure cases, with extreme and clearly recognizable tabes higher in order, status, and rank, and rare and anomalous cases lower on the list (Charcot 1975 [1887–89], 2: 329–38 [February 19, 1889]; also 2: 234, 487–88). Pierre Janet described Charcot's ideal type as "an ensemble of symptoms that depend[ed] on each other, which then [were] arranged in hierarchies, [could] be classed in well-defined groups, and which above all by their nature and combinations clearly distinguish[ed] themselves from other neighboring maladies" (quoted in Didi-Huberman 1982, 28). Arguing from effects to causes, Charcot said, from clinical observations to descriptions, and with physiology as foundation, the nosographer produced inductions rather than a priori deductions (Charcot 1877, 3: 8). This methodology identified the typical case and, therefore, all other cases as imperfect or partial examples of the ideal disease type. Indeed, ideal-type substitution managed scientific uncertainty by systematically submitting symptomatic ensembles to the dictates of two-dimensional systems and so simplifying representations of nosography. It enabled Charcot to fulfill his role as leader and spokesman, to tout his hospital's laboratory technologies, and to present his findings as authoritative. It was, as discussed in Chapter 3, a conventional representational strategy for scientific mobilization of concepts, one that Charcot appropriated and transformed to suit his charismatic role and research mission.

He had discovered ideal-type substitution's usefulness for nosography serendipitously, Charcot said, as a way to manage symptom multiformity. Surrounded absolutely with confusion when he had first inherited the hospital service, wondering why his cases did not appear in medical texts, feeling powerless and irritated that he could not diagnose his patients, he had suddenly intuited that he confronted a specific disease, hysteria major. According to the rules of ideal-type substitution, grand hysteria, then, was everywhere and in every case a "unity," "one and indivisible." If a researcher possessed the "key," he could immediately call on the type already constituted in his mind, and, after a certain time, could say: "Despite the immense apparent variety of phenomena, it's always the same disease." Here, Charcot deployed the traditional medical modes of observation and differential diagnosis. In a lesson on hystero-epilepsy, he presented a patient who hallucinated, talked to herself in terror, and suffered bodily contractions and hysterogenic zone sensitivity; he showed this multiplicity to be not a "succession of attacks" but one, single "developing attack," an ideal type of grand hysteria. Demonstrating the grand attack's ideal type, the patient presented the epileptoid phase, with its subdivisions of tonic and clownism; the phase of grand movements, the *arc de cercle*; the hallucinatory phase; and *attitudes passionelles*. (Charcot 1975 [1887–89], 2: 36; id. 1971, 116–19). Charcot's clinical picturing of hysteria as a classifiable disease entity characterized by multiform and pro-

tean but nevertheless systematic symptomatologies represented a significant advance in research on the illness that still seemed to belong, as
Charles Lasègue said, in "the wastepaper basket of medicine."[18] For most
physicians continued to treat hysteria as had the Salpêtrière earlier in the
century and as, according to Susan Leigh Star, medical professionals invariably respond to disease entities that cannot be fully classified: when
research events did not fit taxonomic categories, medical workers solved
unsolvable problems by creating "garbage categories" and shunting un-
manageable, incurable, or undiagnosable patients into other domains of
care.[19] But Charcot had made hysteria a credible diagnosis, one deploying conventional medical technologies and backed by scientific laboratory
research.

Charcot's nosography represented hysteria as a disease that could, as I
have already suggested, be clinically pictured. For using the technologies
of ideal-type substitution and medical observation, Charcot assembled the
list of symptoms that characterized hysteria and enabled diagnosis. While
Charcot did not use the term "clinical picture," as I do, as a trope for
medical representation, it served his need to mobilize research findings
through the energy of metaphor and through simplified representations
of the ill organism. Marshaling the facts of neuroanatomy and the neurological concepts of localization, organic function, and disease seat, Charcot figuratively mapped the symptomatic body. Janet reported that the
Salpêtrians repeatedly observed disturbances of sensibility as "sharply defined spots, islets of anæsthesia . . . scattered irregularly over the body
without any apparent order"; they sketched insensibilities of limbs or
parts as "*anæsthesias in geometrical segments*": "anæsthesia 'in shirt-sleeve,'"
for example, or "leg-of-mutton sleeve" (Janet 1901, 1: 8). Janet's tropes
mapped the hysterical body's as-yet-unknown geography and "clothed"
its terrain, created a topographical surface picturing of internal somatic
disorder.

Freud observed similar research phenomena. Disturbances of sensibility, he said in an 1888 encyclopedia entry, served a central diagnostic
function, for, playing a relatively small part in organic brain disease, they
helped distinguish hysterical from organic symptoms. Hysterical anesthesia of the skin—more common than that of mucous membranes, bones,
muscles, sense organs, and intestines—could produce feelings of anesthesia, hyperesthesia, or analgesia; affect sensations of temperature, pressure,
or electricity; disorder muscular sense; or impair the sense of touch—and
no other. Moreover, spots of insensibility exhibited the "greatest freedom

in their extent" and "degree of intensity"; overstepping the body's "mid-line at some point"—perhaps including the whole tongue, larynx, or genitals—hysterical hemi-anesthesia freely distributed its forms in "disseminated foci" over the body (*SE*, 1: 43–44).

This Salpêtrian "picturing" of hysteria not only statistically correlated symptoms or deciphered the symptom as sign, but subsumed both as it figured the body. The body's volume had become a representational space mapped by dispersed areas functionally distinct from one another, separated by virtue of differences from a norm and one another, and definable by particularized laws of operation. Only figures could represent this enigmatic illness, by mapping the hysterical body with lesional contiguities and simultaneities (Charcot 1889, 3: 264–65). A readable set of deformations, of anatomical anomalies, regionalized and so constituted the body through metaphorical representations of its disease localizations, seats, and sensate dysfunctions.[20] These representational strategies—clinical picturing, mapping, and troping—enabled the clinic's mobilization of its research findings, its translation of credible research results into the amphitheater and to other research centers. His experimental anatomo-clinical work, Charcot said, had produced more knowledge about the body than had either the "agency of anatomy" or "experimental physiology alone" (Charcot 1889, 3: 11). Publicizing Charcot's theories in Vienna, Freud maintained, with the master, that the "work of anatomy" was finished and organic theories of nervous disease were "complete" (*SE*, 1: 10).

Charcot's maps displayed, even as they failed to theorize, a representation theory of psycho-physical correlation. Although the disease inscribed symptoms on skin as spots, islets, and sleeves or in muscle as paralysis, catalepsy, or limp, Charcot's research maps did not address the concomitant problem of etiology. The seat or original site of attack, "hysterogenic points," as Charcot called them, seemed central. They caused fits but could also cause their cessation, could locate anesthetized areas or spots of heightened or diminished sensibility; demarcated from the remainder of the spatial body, they might through the *aura* (a sensation that rose around the body prior to attack) become complicitous with other apparently segregated places on the body.[21] Hysterogenic zones from the first, however, were characterized by a certain functional ambiguity. Like paralyses, some zones obeyed "anatomical," some, "psychic laws." They refused, moreover, to obey the laws of organic nerve injury: while a paralyzed hand should have produced anesthesia on the forearm, Janet admitted, where the muscles did not work, it nevertheless desensitized the hand and wrist instead (Janet 1901, 2: 229). Such hystericized zones, Freud said, could be situated in the skin, bones, mucous membranes, and sense organs, but had a "predilection" for (in women *and* men) an abdominal area corresponding to the ovaries, the crown of the head, a region under the breast, and (in men) the testes (*SE*, 1: 43). He would later say they represented "tactile" and "visual perceptions" of the familiarly known body—for patients did not, after all, know neuroanatomy as did the physician (*SE*, 1: 169–70). Yet this mapping of the hysterical body gradually subsumed the anatomical need for disease seat or localization. For hysterogenic zones fashioned the body as a spacio-temporal form on which deformations could be read not from lesion to disease, but symptom to semiology. Hysterogenic zones thus inscribed the symptomatic body with a set of readable figurations—spoken, as Freud would later say, in the "common language"—that defined dysfunction through the grid of a rudimentary psycho-physical representation. Charcot's metaphorical mappings suggested, even as they denied, that representation was the best plausible bridge between the hysterical psyche and its body's figurative and imitative symptoms.

Indeed, Charcot had discovered without knowing it the enabling principle of hysterical psycho-physical representation, the functional lesion. Because, he had first assumed, the nervous-system lesions that characterized hysterical disturbances of sensibility, motor activity, and perception could not be located at postmortem, such symptoms must be caused by a kind of lesion analogous to yet different from a physiological wound. Yet certain hysterical lesions, Charcot claimed, reproduced systematic hemi-anesthesias, and, therefore, he could differentiate organic from hysterical hemi-anesthesias. When presenting a paralysis induced by suggestion, he said, "If you ask me in what part of the brain the lesion is found, there you'll find the centers of the arms and hand; from the nervous point of view, however, sensation resides elsewhere." By the laws of association, then, "when you had the idea that your hand was numb, your hand was already numb; if you thought of moving your hand, your hand had already moved" (Charcot 1971, 103). Rather than localize lesions, then, Charcot's anatomy regionalized the body with a semiotic that signified dysfunction through functional metaphors. In hysterical paralysis, Freud said, appropriating Charcot, a "functional or dynamic" lesion, completely "independent . . . of the anatomy of the nervous system" and untraceable at postmortem, impaired and altered motor or sensory or sensible function (*SE*, 1: 169–70). The hysterical body had become at once a surface to be read semiologically and a spacio-temporal structure through which disease might radiate, might transmit nervous messages, images, or representations.

Charcot's notion of functional lesions, of course, could not withstand scientific debate. Unverifiable in the laboratory, observable at neither postmortem nor bedside, the functional lesion was, after all, a metaphor. Yet as metaphor, it served Charcot well to redirect research away from physiology and toward hypnosis and suggestion, toward a reflex theory of psycho-physical correlation. Charcot's two-dimensional maps, however, clearly displayed the figuratively anatomized hysterical body that disobeyed both the laws of neuroanatomy and of association. His theories, which suggested psycho-physical representation in a rudimentary way, which were fashioned in and through his simplified figural sketches, leveraged his laboratory's findings outside that research space, soliciting scientific allies for his neuropathological project. Mobilizing the concept of functional lesions, Charcot argued forcefully against the uterine theory, which, he said, his predecessor Briquet had demolished. Yet Charcot's two-dimensional maps sketched the hysterical body as anchored by other female reproductive organs, the ovaries. Localizing hysterogenic spots in female ovaries and male ovarian zones, practicing the therapeutic technologies of ovarian compression, icing, and palpation, the clinic confined hysterical representations of sex on the wards to physiologically based theories of reflex action. The female reproductive organs anchored and sustained the clinic's representational modes of topographical mapping and tropological explanation. Although he had sought to banish sex from his theoretical discourse and graphical modes, Charcot reinscribed female sexual anatomy into his research, effectively articulating sexuality with representation. He forcefully leveraged the clinic's scientific findings into other theaters of proof, putting sex on display for an audience of physicians, researchers, and Parisian medical consumers.

Appropriating the conceptual tools of Charcot's neuropathology, Freud rewrote his mentor's technologies of clinical picturing and graphic representation. He did so by rewriting sex. Nosographically describing anxiety neurosis, for example, he sketched its clinical picture: symptomatic general irritability, anxious expectation, a *"quantum of anxiety in a freely floating state"* (Freud's emphasis), anxiety attacks or equivalents of anxiety attacks, night frights, vertigo, phobias, gastric disorders, paresthesias (sensations like those of hysterical aura), and chronic feebleness, lassitude, and fainting. This clinical picture, like Charcot's of "grande hystérie," combined the multiform symptoms of disordered sensibility, motor convulsions, and hallucinations. Freud differentiated his new clinical entity, however, from both neurasthenia and hysteria, the two diseases whose symptoms most resembled anxiety neurosis, by revising Charcot's figurative mappings. Hysterical and anxious patients complained of aurae, hypersensitivity, and pressure-points (the equivalent of hysterogenic zones, discussed at greater length in Chapter 3); whereas the hysterical patient's organism converted excitation provoked by psychical conflict, the anxious patient's converted somatic excitation. The diseased body "accumulat[ed] excitation," a somatic, indeed sexual, excitation that had been deflected from the psychical sphere (*SE*, 3: 92–108). If the psyche could not manage exogenous or endogenous sexual stimulation, moreover, the organism also "*transpos[ed] affect.*" Here, Freud "practiced nosography," describing psycho-physically informed clinical pictures of nervous disease. Yet Freud's neuropathology had foregrounded what Charcot's had rigorously suppressed. For Freud aggregated symptoms around sex as a psycho-physical category. He correlated the details of a multiform symptomatology and sketched a complex clinical picture more coherently than had Charcot.

While Charcot has been excoriated for producing the symptoms he claimed merely to observe, his practices were entirely consonant with those of nineteenth-century science. In Chapter 3, I argue that, through its laboratory reproduction of symptoms and its technologies of presentation, the Salpêtrière made hysteria modern. Dedicated to clinically picturing hysteria by isolating its symptomatology and etiology, the clinic's researchers deployed traditional scientific procedures for producing experimental findings: Charcot's, Charles Féré's, and Alfred Binet's work with hypnotized research subjects tested the somatic effects of dysfunctional physiological states; Pierre Janet's, the psychical effects of disordered sensation, perception, and self-representation. Moreover, the Salpêtrière's research demonstrates that, as in all scientific research, the laboratory's work of purification produced the natural events it claimed to reproduce, invoking its hybridized research objects, fabricated by the work of mediation, to witness to scientific truths. Yet the practices of science—the institutional structures of laboratory experimentation, scientific demonstration and debate, and amphitheatrical presentation—were entirely social and socialized. Despite nineteenth-century scientists' claims that they reproduced nature in the laboratory, the mute facts that witnessed there to nature's truths were themselves constituted through routine work, usually by hierarchically organized collegial groups.

Making hysteria modern, however, the Salpêtrians performed the double move of conceptual purification and mediation: they constituted nature and the social as belonging in distinctly different domains, and, at the same time, fabricated hybrid figures that were translatable along scientific networks. What Latour calls "the modern critical stance" insisted on the asymmetry of natural events and socially produced knowledge, even as it elided its own creation of this conceptual opposition. In Charcot's laboratory, I argue in Chapter 3, the hypnotized hysteric was produced as a hybrid and used as a representative specimen of research findings. An "inert bod[y], incapable of will and bias but capable of showing, signing, writing, and scribbling on laboratory instruments before trustworthy witnesses," the hysteric graphically confirmed scientific truths. Endowed with "semiotic powers," the malady of representation contributed to the inscription of new texts: the documents of experimental science, the pictorial iconographies of naturalized yet hybrid figures. In addition, the hysteric could be staged in the amphitheater of proof, where dysfunctional bodies mutely spoke even as they danced, disrobed, and hallucinated (Latour 1993, 10–24). Thus the clinic's mission to document the truths it constituted through the reproduction of psychical and somatic states positioned Freud, however indirectly, to theorize modern concepts of psycho-physical representation. Freud translated the laboratory's research findings into his consulting room, itself a "laboratory" of sorts in which psychoanalysis worked to produce modern, indeed, sexual subjectivity. From my perspective of psycho-physical theoretical production, Charcot's experimental research made possible modern scientific discourse about a subjectivity anchored in, yet radically different from, the body that housed it.

CHAPTER 3

"Experiments made by nature"

The Seventh International Medical Congress of 1881, which convened in London, was a "glittering Victorian spectacle." Invitations were sent to 120,000 physicians, heads of state, and members of the "medical public"; 3,000 doctors attended 119 section meetings, which produced 2,400 pages of reports; the prince of Wales delivered opening remarks to foreign, religious, and medical dignitaries. British and French railways and steamship companies had offered special fares to encourage international attendance. Congress officials entertained their guests lavishly: a soirée at Alfred de Rothschild's, a garden party at Baroness Angela Burdett-Coutts's, a Guildhall reception featuring choral singers, a *conversazione* at the Kensington Museum complete with electric light; excursions to Hampton Court Palace, the Royal Seabathing Infirmary at Margate, and the sewage farm at Croydon. Speaking after a gala dinner at the Star and Garter Hotel, Jean-Martin Charcot denounced the British Cruelty to Animals Act of 1876 and its restrictions on animal experimentation as hypocritical, given the English aristocracy's prized and ritualized "sport" of foxhunting. Most spectacular of all, perhaps, was the final dinner, served to 1,200 people at the Crystal Palace; a post-feast fireworks display featured "fire-portraits" of the most famous physicians in attendance from England, Germany, and France: Sir James Paget and Professors Bernhard Langenbeck and Charcot.[1]

The scientific talks must hardly have seemed less spectacular. Although Charcot's demonstration on tabes stimulated wild applause, the German antilocalizationist Friedrich Goltz and the British localizationist David Ferrier took center stage in a scientific showdown. At the morning meeting, Goltz presented his experimental findings on laboratory dogs. First, he opened a suitcase he had placed on the lectern and exhibited a dog's skull, which retained only a tiny portion of brain; next, a dog from whose brain he had removed several cortical lobes. Neither the dead nor the demonstrated animal, Goltz said, had been sensorially hindered or had its motor functions impeded by tissular removal, as would have been the case had Ferrier's localization research proved true. In a heated debate, Goltz declared Ferrier's theory "completely wrong," "beyond a shadow of a doubt"; Ferrier replied that Goltz's experiments would not translate to human anatomy since in dogs such effects were transient, whereas in humans and monkeys, they were permanent. That afternoon, a group of specialized medical observers traveled to Professor Gerald Yeo's laboratory at King's College, where Ferrier had been working, and both researchers presented their animals. Goltz demonstrated his decorticated dog's mobility and responsiveness to commands and stimuli, and measured, with an aesthesiometer, signs of canine displeasure at injuries to the skin, all to verify his theory that brain functions were not localized in specific cerebral centers; Ferrier showed two monkeys whose brains he had experimentally lesioned to show that brain functions were, in fact, localized. Watching one monkey limp around the demonstration room, Charcot recognized the resemblance to one of his own brain-damaged patients and exclaimed, "Mais c'est une malade!" ("But it's a patient!")[2]

This now-famous medical congress excited serious scientific controversy. Ferrier's monkeys and Goltz's dog were killed and autopsied to verify the neurologists' claims and a medical examining committee adjudicated: whereas Ferrier and Yeo had indeed lesioned the monkeys' brains in exactly the areas they had claimed, Goltz had not destroyed as much of his dog's brain as he had believed. The victory went to Ferrier, and, although Goltz continued during the 1880s to reject the implications of brain localization research, by 1892, he had joined ranks with the physiologists. "I am not at all fundamentally opposed to the question of the localisation of cerebral functions," he declared in that year, staking out a functional rather than anatomical view of localization (Spillane 1981, 393–96). The much-talked about Ferrier-Goltz presentations, like the rhetorical and scientific mode of demonstration in general, presented a hypothesis that physicians, neurologists, and physiologists had been attempting to secure as truth. Observers learned from the debate that scientific certainty did not automatically occur, but rather was produced through experimental research and scientific competition, through the staging of complex medical commitments and acting out of strategic stands. Routinely presenting research as spectacle, scientists moved laboratory findings into the amphitheater of proof. For laboratory work demanded translation to other research sites through the work of medical representation, demonstration, and documentation.

The medical spectacle did not end with the congress's closing address. The Victoria Street Society, Britain's most prominent antivivisection group, prosecuted Ferrier under the law of 1876 for having performed "frightful and shocking experiments"—without permission from the Home Office—on the animals he had demonstrated at the congress. During the resulting trial, a series of scientific witnesses testified that Yeo had actually performed Ferrier's surgeries, and that Yeo's licensure and use of anesthesia represented both lawful conduct and lack of cruelty to animals. Ferrier was acquitted. Ferrier's arrest and trial, however, excited publicity in the medical and popular press both in England and abroad. Indeed, precisely because brain localizationists had successfully leveraged their research results into the public domain, a group like the Victoria Street Society had to deploy the laboratory's findings to argue its ethicalizing and moralizing claims. The Physiological Society, itself founded as a professional interest group in response to the 1876 law, had enjoyed a propaganda bonanza at the congress, making "sweeping and well publicized" claims about the ways in which physiological experimentation advanced scientific work. Other medical commentary accused the antivivisection society of "advertising" its anti-science positions and arousing public ire at acceptable experimental procedures; it trumpeted Ferrier's localization theories as having already issued in and as heralding great surgical breakthroughs on humans. Moreover, Ferrier's trial helped construct collegial networks and theoretical alliances between physiology experimenters and other medical specialists; it earned him the monetary and moral support of professional associations and the medical press—indeed, ensured his future financial success. Ferrier's private practice, conducted while he also consulted at the National Hospital for the Paralysed and Epileptic (popularly known as the "Fits Hospital"), prospered after the post-trial publicity; his research, which he had previously funded from his own pocket or through small private grants, could now be conducted on a larger, more lavish scale. The publicity surrounding the congress and the Goltz-Ferrier showdown popularized the vivisection debate and forged in the minds of medical men and the public alike a link among, as Susan Leigh Star reports, "issues of scientific method, vivisection, medical professionalism, and localization theory."[3]

The Goltz-Ferrier debate also raised larger questions about the purpose, goals, and social uses of experimental research in medicine and the basic sciences. These problems of method and methodology, professional credibility and authority, and of neuroanatomy's relation to the emergent science of physiology, would likewise surface in the hysteria discourse. As Charcot moved out of strictly neuropathological research and into experimentation on hysteria, he implicitly joined with the professional physiologists in demonstrating somatic dysfunctions to produce knowledge about malfunctioning bodies. Although he never fully rejected neuroanatomy, Charcot embraced physiology's conceptualization of functionalism, and the Salpêtrière, as I shall show in this chapter, provided a clinical domain in which physiology could become increasingly credible, documentable, and, indeed, leverageable as scientific theory. Although I drew primarily on Charcot's lessons and lectures in Chapter 2, in this chapter I examine hospital and iconographic texts as well as Charcot's statements about the clinic's research mission to justify and advertise the benefits of experimental research. These scientific practices, I maintain, exploited and produced the nature/social binary through the mediation of the laboratory. In the second section of this chapter, I argue that Charcot's experimental research on hysteria staged physiologically dysfunctional bodies, naturalizing even as it hybridized its research subjects, its quasi-objects, to use Bruno Latour's term. In the third section, I show that Alfred Binet's experimental psychophysiology refined Charcot's physiological discourse of functionalism, while Pierre Janet's theories of perception, cognition, and personality produced plausible bridges between motor acts and split-off mental states. An emergent psychoanalysis necessarily appropriated the findings of Charcot's laboratory. For the laboratory work of mediation, which produced research subjects—whether decorticated dogs or hypnotized hysterics—as hybrid, also invoked the work of translation, which deployed medical representations to transmit research findings along scientific networks. As Freud participated in creating cutting-edge research, he joined with the hybridizing practices and networks of nineteenth-century science in order to make hysteria modern.

I

"Mais c'est une malade," Charcot had exclaimed at the 1881 Medical Congress (Star 1989, 105). His remark was widely cited in the medical and popular press. For whether uttered in astonished scientific recognition or for the sake of self-aggrandizement, Charcot's metaphor manipulated the resemblance between animal and human subjects, between Ferrier's limping decorticated monkeys and his own paralytic patients. But such similarity—and the generalizability of research results—were not this unproblematic. Citing John Hughlings Jackson, whose phrase, "experiments made by nature," appeared widely in the scientific literature, Ferrier argued the inadequacy of data provided by the study of already diseased organisms. "Experiments on animals, under conditions selected and varied at the will of the experimenter," he said, "are alone capable of furnishing precise data for sound inductions as to the functions of the brain and its various parts; the experiments performed for us by nature, in the form of diseased conditions, being rarely limited, or free from such complications as render analysis and the discovery of cause and effect extremely difficult, and in many cases practically impossible" (Ferrier 1876, xiv; quoted in Star 1989, 103). Speaking as a neuropathologist, Charcot disagreed. Animal experimentation alone, he said, could never supply sufficient material or produce proficient enough results to advance medical research. Carefully collected clinical observations, interpreted with physiological and anatomical knowledge, could produce spontaneous experiments in the human subject (Charcot 1877, 2: 5–17). Pathology could confirm the fit between a projected lesion and a symptomatology, but "with the help of new means of anatomical study," pathology had "advance[d] beyond [what] experimental research" alone could teach the scientist. Whereas research on experimentally lesioned animal subjects could not automatically and predictably produce evidence generalizable to humans—as Ferrier himself had demonstrated in his showdown with Goltz—disease, Charcot observed, "daily produce[d] such lesions," and "topographic anatomy" enabled him to localize them with the "greatest precision" (Charcot 1877, 2: 5–17).

In 1865, Claude Bernard had advocated experimentation as the "foundation for scientific medicine" (Bernard 1949 [1927], 204–5). Bernard defined "experimental pathology" as "the application of the analytical method to the study of disease," as an inquiry into disease causes, symptoms, and courses "*by artificially creating similar disorders* in animals whose organisation closely resembles our own" (Bernard, "Lectures on Experimental Pathology," quoted in Figlio 1977, 276–77). Bernard was a student of François Magendie's, whose school had practiced unlimited and almost random vivisectional experimentation and aroused protest from Britain's anti-vivisectionists as from German and French scientists, and his experimental program foregrounded modes of knowledge and methodology rather than laboratory procedures. Between midcentury and the 1880s, however, it became clear that experimentalists ignored the clinic at their peril; clear, too, that clinical evidence could support laboratory results in the production of scientific knowledge. Correlating observations from laboratory and clinic, the researcher could more forcefully mobilize his findings and leverage them outside the laboratory. And while Bernard had argued for the artificial creation of disorders in animals, medical men continued to maintain that evidence obtained from the observation of already existent patient disorders should be included in research programs. Yet hoping that his work would disseminate "the scientific spirit" among physicians, Bernard had sought to produce a clear demarcation between clinical observation and laboratory experimentation. While observation passively noted phenomena, he had said, experimentation created, defined, or produced phenomena; experimentation controlled observed events and compared facts, producing credible observations, which, in turn, produced scientific ideas (Bernard 1949 [1927], 5–6).

Deploying these experimental principles, the Salpêtrière's laboratory reproduced, tested, and recorded evidence of dysfunctional physiological states.[4] Because researchers lacked the ability to recreate the organic states in nervous diseases, Charcot said, they sought to "artificially reproduce" pathological states; experimental conditions copied as closely as possible other, earlier, experiential conditions; researchers tried specifically to imitate a paralysis exactly as it would have been seen "in nature." This "power to reproduce a pathological state" was essential to the clinic's work, Charcot explained, for researchers could control a theory only when they possessed the means of duplicating morbid phenomena. This "mode of experimentation" possessed the advantage that certain stigmata could be made "enduring," and many deformities "reproduced exactly," ensuring the laboratory's opportunity to test and measure them. No "experimental physiologico-pathological research," Charcot claimed, had "reproduced artificially [and] with more fidelity" to nature the bodily states the Salpêtrians had observed and recorded. Charcot's conceptualization of laboratory methodology and practice, which adhered to the traditions of experimental medicine, depended in large part on the theory that reproduced events mirrored, imitated, or copied exactly those in nature. Having duplicated natural experience, scientists could endlessly and infinitely recopy it. "C'est de la perfection," Charcot said of the power to replicate natural events in the laboratory and to duplicate that reproduction on other occasions (Charcot 1971, 99–101; id. 1889, 3: 89, 307).

These assumptions—which portrayed the scientist as discovering rather than constructing nature—ignored the laboratory as mediating between a never perfectly observed nature and its never exactly framed or structured copy. They occluded, moreover, a problem to which Bernard continually referred scientists: the inevitable contamination of objective observation by active experimental interventions. Yet as knowledge in the nineteenth century became technologized and identified with unlimited intervention, Karl Figlio argues, the kinds and levels of bodily interventions multiplied and intensified, becoming increasingly justifiable, especially in research that, like Charcot's, depended heavily on reproductive modes of laboratory experimentation (Figlio 1977, 277). Indeed, the laboratory was central to what Latour calls "the practices of purification," the construction of the natural and the social as distinct from each other, and to "the work of mediation," the production by scientific practices and professional networks of the research subject as hybrid. For, whether limping decorticated dog or paralytic patient, the nineteenth-century research subject had been fabricated by the laboratory. Existing in that intermediary domain, that subject was neither purely natural nor purely social. It was at once natural and social: physical matter appropriated by the laboratory's practices but fashioned through the work of groups as part of a collectivity. Indeed, created to speak the laboratory's truths, it was at once natural, social, and discursive: materially real, like nature; medically represented, like discourse; and fashioned through laboratory work practices, like and by social groups. Witness to the experimental production of knowledge about nature, the hybrid research subject could be subjected to the work of translation, as I have suggested in Chapters 1 and 2: demonstrated to medical audiences, exhibited in a theater of proof, transported along scientific networks to new research sites, and so used to generate conceptual and theoretical production (Latour 1993, 6–24). Charcot's laboratory participated in this nineteenth-century project to hybridize even as it disarticulated the natural from the social. Indeed, Charcot has been widely misunderstood by twentieth-century theorists who misrepresent his work as unique precisely because they fail to see that science always thus functions to constitute the modern world.[5]

To reproduce natural pathological states in the laboratory, the Salpêtrière deployed hypnosis, which, Charcot said, exhibited three nosographically distinct stages. The operator induced "lethargy" by pressing on the closed eyelids or asking the subject to fix her attention on one object; sleeping, relaxed, or anesthetized, her hyperexcitable body enabled experimental testing of contractions caused by pressure and friction, stimulation, blows, or massage. Raising the eyelids or causing nervous shock with bright light or violent noise produced paralytic "catalepsy"; the entranced subject underwent testing of muscular rigidity or bodily posing. Rubbing the top of the head, closing eyelids, or demanding fixation induced "somnambulism" and so receptivity to suggestion, habitual anesthesia, or hypersensibility; because the subject could move, speak, and display a variety of psychological phenomena while somnambulous, experimenters could study hallucinations, dramatized emotions, and histrionic acts.[6] In practice, the distinction between catalepsy and somnambulism tended to break down during research, but these, nevertheless, were the clinic's favored hypnotic states.

Charcot dubbed the Salpêtrière's brand of hypnosis "grand hypnotisme" to distinguish it from the "petit hypnotisme" of his competitors. Freud, too, made this distinction when he assigned Hippolyte Bernheim only the later, inferior, hypnotic technique (*SE* 1: 77–82). And because their nerves were already deranged, Charcot theorized, only hysterics could manifest the signs of grand hypnotism; although not all hysterics exhibited grand hypnosis, then, all subjects who did were hysterics. "Le grand hypnotisme, c'est l'hypnotisme des hystériques," Charcot epigrammatized (Charcot 1971, 100). This faulty syllogism, based on the notion that hysterics possessed a special sort of somatic reproductive potential, grounded the clinic's research in what would prove to be false assumptions about hysterical physiology.

The laboratory's primary hypnotic technologies included "the touch, the gaze, and the word." The operator could submit his subject to sudden or to weak and prolonged exposure to electric, incandescent, magnesium or sunlight; ask her to fix her gaze on a brilliant object; loudly bang a tam-tam or sound brass instruments; softly play a diapason or monotone; strongly excite the senses of taste, smell, or touch, especially the hypnogenic zones; or submit the skin to soft contact, warmth, or magnetization.[7] If the operator spoke the subject to sleep, however, her "imagination" controlled the unfolding events; if she had submitted voluntarily to the experiment and had a "vivid" fancy, the magnetizer could simply stretch his hand suddenly to her head and she would fall asleep instantly, as though she had been hit by lightning, Charcot troped.[8] Binet and Féré, the clinic's experimental experts, recommended mechanical action or instrumental stimulation to induce hypnotic states; Désiré Bourneville, the Salpêtrière's iconographer, recommended that the operator mix his modes of incitement to achieve optimal hypnotic results.[9] Freud summarized the clinic's techniques: the operator influenced the subject psychically with suggestion, physiologically through fixating procedures or bodily applications (with, for example, hands or magnets); or by inducing auto-suggestion (*SE*, 1: 96). Still, Freud recommended talking the experimental subject into trance: making him comfortable, darkening the room, loosening tight clothing, maintaining silence; and then requesting him to fixate, all the while speaking softly about the observable oncoming sensations of sleep (*SE*, 1: 105–14; *SE*, 2: 108).

The Salpêtrière's experiments reproduced and examined reflex physiological functions during hypnosis, which Charcot believed altered the nervous system's physiology. The laboratory thus produced "displacements of excitability" through external bodily stimulation, testing muscle contracture, paralysis, cutaneous and subcutaneous sensibility, and other deviant physiological phenomena (*SE*, 1: 77, 97). First, the researcher strapped the lethargic subject to chair or table, then tested for and observed muscular or nerve contraction. He stimulated the skin, muscles, tendons, or nerves by "mechanical action" (shocks or blows, pressure, kneading, or massage) or "mechanical excitation" (touching, pinching, or pricking). Exploring different bodily zones, he struck, pinched, or pricked arms, legs, or trunk; he kneaded, stroked, or massaged face, head, neck, or breast. When testing the face, Paul Richer reported, the researcher could induce expressions of attention, pain, aggression, or laughter. Charcot demonstrated that "methodical electrical exploration" by faradic and galvanic current also produced muscular contraction; he struck tendons or pulled on limbs to induce involuntary gestures and movements that patients repeated for hours (Charcot 1889, 3: 116, 191). Permanent contracture could be produced by moderate shock or blow, violent shock, or repetition of several heavy shocks; in subjects with a high degree of neuromuscular hyperexcitability, simple pressure or friction on the tendons proved as efficacious as shock and produced better precision and intensity of contracture (Richer 1885, 544–53). Researchers tested muscle contracture, Richer summarized, by manipulating limbs and applying "energetic [percussive] shocks" to the body; they observed superficial cutaneous excitations by softly touching, pinching, or pricking (when violent pinches, profound prickings, or heavy pressure produced no effect); they evaluated muscular jerking by attaching the lethargized subject to a machine whose weights and belts applied force to, for example, limbs or head (Richer 1885, 539–75, 606–29). Based on neurological notions of the reflex arc as emitting, transmitting, and unifying the body's nervous messages from organ to system, the laboratory's tests produced knowledge about physiological functions and disorders.

Binet and Féré justified the clinic's experimental method of reproducing pathological states as necessary, in fact, to produce objective truths. While the "ancient magnetizers" had been content simply to observe hypnotic phenomena, modern experimental researchers "provoked" psychic phenomena by suggestion, "observed" those phenomena in the research lab, and then "described" them in print and picture. But rather than passively observing, Binet and Féré warned, the modern researcher must actively demonstrate the "reality" of suggestive phenomena, submit those observed phenomena to regulated experimentation, and produce objective signs irrefutably to demonstrate the test's truth (Binet and Féré 1887, 139–40). Here, Binet and Féré followed Bernard's recommendations for experimental modes of knowledge production; Bernard's formula of experimental creation, definition, and production of observable phenomena became, in their modern laboratory, provocation, observation, and description. To verify particularly mysterious stigmata, Pierre Janet reported, staff members used inventive observational procedures. Taking patients by surprise during the night and using precaution not to wake them, researchers pinched or pricked to test bodily sensibility and based conclusions on patient groans or somnambulous speech. Injecting morphine, applying chloroform, and forcing ingestion of alcohol tested whether insensible patients could be rendered sensible (Janet 1901, 2: 228–29, 357). The laboratory's experts knew that these active experimental interventions—especially those dependent on technologies of the touch—presented a set of serious scientific problems. For despite the clinic's sophisticated rhetorical address of research problems, the group's procedures raised a host of logical and ethical questions about, for example, the nature of active experimental intervention, the kind of suffering caused research subjects, and the replicability of results in other research domains.

Binet and Féré sought to stabilize and guarantee the laboratory's provocation of natural but dysfunctional states. Before performing somatic tests, they cautioned, operators must "indicate the somatic state of experimental subjects" and precisely determine the laboratory's operative procedures. If researchers broke either rule, they had committed an error

in method, for only pre-measured physiological, pathological, and laboratory conditions permitted comparison of similar experimental events—a
comparison to be carefully undertaken, or deplorable confusions might
well follow (Binet and Féré 1887, 138). Yet laboratory procedures introduced technical uncertainties into the clinic's physiological experimentation. For despite procedural preplanning, Binet and Féré admitted, morbid states did not present to the worker with constancy, since patient constitutions and organic functions caused disease forms to vary. Despite the
experts' extensive advice, ensuring that the procedure undertaken replicated a previous one seemed impossible at best, for the lab could not sufficiently measure or control provocation by mechanical action. The light-
ness of the operative's baton-touches to the skin, for example, or the intensity of the hammer strokes he delivered to a limb might vary widely
from experiment to experiment. Although the clinic had worked to perfect its equipment's instrumental calibration, mechanical or instrumental
excitation scarcely seemed more manageable. The same light, placed in
the same place, and illumined for the same length of time to the same
subject; or the same object, shown to the same subject; or the same faradic charge delivered to the abdomen might or might not repeatedly de-
liver the same physiological stimulation or arouse the same response. Binet warned that the experimenter must pay careful and continual attention to his modes of excitation; for somatic displacement of excitability
and the mental phenomena it provoked had to be measured in fractions
of a second (Binet and Féré 1887, 117–19; Binet 1894, 27–29). The difficulty of measuring and controlling the output of research instruments,
then, might expose laboratory findings as fabrications and jeopardize the
clinic's mission to produce reproducible research outcomes.

The relationship between researcher and experimental subject might
also expose the laboratory's reproduction of natural states as fabrications.
Recalling the "magnetic rapport" employed by the early magnetizers,
Janet acknowledged that somnambulous subjects obeyed only the operator who had induced sleep, would suffer no one else to touch them, and
sometimes failed to feel, see, or hear anyone else. This state of "electivity"
or "exclusive attention," he argued, was essential to the operations of experimental hypnotism.[10] Richer called it "a state of *fascination*" in which
the subject would violently rebuff anyone who attempted to intervene in
the mutual hypnotic gaze (Richer 1885, 180; emphasis in original); Binet,
a "*state of subjection*" in which her "leader" "led" her, demanding obedience (Binet and Féré 1887, 133; emphasis in original). This reciprocal

binding by word, gesture, and gaze, Charcot hinted, subjected the subject to a will more powerful than her own, that prepared her to be "penetrated" by the researchers' "power."[11] Attempting to delimit hypnosis's "immense" experimental "domain," Binet and Féré recommended that operators resist irresponsible or unconscious suggestion and advised that they implant suggestions with as few words or gestures as possible. For gestures, if used repeatedly and often, Binet and Féré warned, might produce "*trained* subjects" practiced at "*auto-suggestion*"; endlessly reproduced words, touches, and gazes might suggest to the subject the symptom she copied or performed (Bourneville and Regnard 1879–80, 3: 458–62; Binet and Féré 1887, 127–37). The reciprocal hypnotic rapport, then, soliciting fascination and implanting subjection in the research subject, threatened to contaminate objective observation and prevent reproducibility of research findings. Indeed, it threatened to expose laboratory reproduction and provocation as the work of mediation, as the creation of hybrid research entities, which masqueraded as discovered truths yet were, as I have already suggested, quasi-objects fabricated of nature and by discourse and collective scientific work practices.

To forestall questions about research findings, the clinic focused on technologies of laboratory inscription, on precise measurement and technical precision of obtained experimental results. "Snellen's letters" (a rudimentary eye chart) and "Flees' box" tested for reflex disturbance in the eye and discriminated hysterical from real blindness; the anesthesiometer measured not only skin but deep muscle reflexes; the dynamometer measured the force of muscle contractures; the pneumograph, placed on the chest of cataleptic subjects, measured regularity of breathing; the "perimeter" measured the width of the visual field (Janet 1901, 24, 190–91; Charcot 1889, 3: 308). The laboratory's grids of specification and modes of documentation inscribed experimentally provoked nervous, muscular, or cutaneous movement. The perimeter graphed narrowed vision or a restricted range of color perceptions; the pneumograph, labored or irregular breathing; the dynamometer, muscular contraction during the lifting of imaginary weights. These sophisticated technological instruments not only functioned to delimit the causes of observed phenomena but produced greater refinement and precision in research results. Influenced by cutting-edge laboratory technologies like Étienne-Jules Marey's odeographic notation (which measured the velocity of runners, horses, and carts), myographic measurement (for the expenditure of muscular energy), and chronophotography (for decomposing motion into time rather than simply space), the Salpêtrians' graphic method deployed various instruments of notation to read and register the body's signs of movement, force, and dynamism. It sought to inscribe in a documentary record the facts provoked and demonstrated in the laboratory, to represent those facts not as created by scientific practices but as testifying to natural truths (Latour 1993, 27–29; Rabinbach 1986, 484–89).

To control for procedural failure and research complication, the laboratory chose its experimental subjects carefully. Bourneville counseled researchers that choosing a hysteric ensured hypnotizability; the best subjects, Richer said, looked nervous or neuropathic and so displayed their predisposition to hypnosis (Bourneville and Regnard 1879–80, 3: 462; Richer 1885, 535). He had selected "sincere" and "susceptible subjects," Charcot told students, subjects whose "phenomena of the self" were "clouded" and who, "fully sensible to his suggestions," would accept his suggestions without resistance (Charcot 1975 [1887–89], 2: 10–11; id. 1971, 100–101). Indeed, reactive subjects might sabotage the clinic's results. For despite their fascinated subjection, somnambulous and cataleptic subjects could move, think, and talk and so interfere in carefully delimited laboratory operations to falsify research findings. The goal of hypnotic research, Binet and Féré said, was the "objectification of subjective troubles"; and while they no doubt meant by "subjective troubles," "known only to the research subject," precisely because objective and subjective phenomena resembled one another, simulation could never be ruled out in the laboratory (Binet and Féré 1887, 139–41). Charcot disagreed. While simulated, voluntarily exaggerated, or imaginatively created disease symptoms represented the hospital's largest clinical problem, simulation could be controlled in the laboratory by research supervision and experimental regulation (Charcot 1889, 3: 14–18; id. 1877, 1: 230). The laboratory's machinery detected subject simulation or "fraud." Charcot placed one hystero-epileptic patient on the stool of an electrical machine to check for signs of fatigue; when she experienced a "more or less *genuine* nervous storm," the experiment ended (Charcot 1889, 3: 42; my emphasis). Janet called patient deception, simulation, and fraud an "altogether crude and insufficient" explanation for the problem of procedural failure. "If the [hospital's] hystericals *did* simulate," he asked, "would they allow themselves to be caught in snares as obvious as those that are laid for them?" Had they "come here to boast of their anæsthesias?" Janet proposed that the disease's universal and historically stable symptomatology, the pain to which experimental subjects were submitted, and the neuroanatomical knowledge necessary for patient to fool doctor—himself armed with traps to "unmask fraud"—ruled out simulation as a laboratory problem (Janet 1901, 32). Yet when Bernheim criticized the Salpêtrière's research results as grounded in methodological error and operator suggestion, he rightly located simulation as having contaminated the laboratory's graphic record of procedural precision.

Justine Etch——'s is a representative case. To document her hysterical urine retention, the laboratory produced an especially complex graphic record. Although she routinely ate the same amount of food, and the staff observed her for signs of digestion, Justine alternately produced virtually no urine or a large quantity. This disorder occurred three times between May 1, 1875, and June 30, 1875, when her urination returned to normal (Bourneville and Regnard 1879–80, 3: 155). The clinical staff monitored and graphed the amount of her urine that they had collected. Justine was routinely examined, and her other symptoms were duly noted in the hospital chart, a document that tracked and noted somatic fluctuations of weight, temperature, and the like, schematically recording her condition. Bourneville's iconographic account of her case reproduced that objective record to document its procedures and to justify the hospital record as factual. Whether, however, patients' bodies actually "retained" urine could neither be clinically observed nor documented as natural or truthful. British doctors had theorized at midcentury that hysterics vomited the urine their bodies refused to void urethrally, or that—adding simulation to the mix—they drank and then vomited the urine they secretly collected; some medical workers believed hysterics blocked urine flow by inserting pebbles or gravel into their urethras, or thereby cunningly produced "stones" in the chamber pot.[12] The Salpêtrians likewise feared that such symptomatologies would be viewed as ludicrous unless they were carefully observed, controlled for, and appropriately documented. Ward nurses therefore examined Justine's bed regularly to ensure that she did not deceive researchers by voiding her urine in hidden vessels; they kept catheters out of her reach. Watched night and day, Justine was often straitjacketed in bed and liberated only at mealtimes. Fearing that other patients would imitate her symptoms, clinicians controlled her access to other inmates; Charcot placed her near two bedridden patients devoted to her well-being who, he said, would readily reveal to him "any trickery." Indeed, Charcot declared women to be the "best possible police" of one another, for, presumably from love of gossip, they invariably failed when fomenting plots together. Without the hospital's "customary surveillance," as Charcot called it, the clinic could not successfully control its patients' bodily functions, verify and regulate their symptom production, and enable the laboratory to produce value-free research findings. Only a well-policed hospital mechanism could oversee the crowded wards, Charcot said, and protect the laboratory against every possible cause of experimental error.[13]

Charcot's experimental research was neither unprecedented nor without impact on the medical field. Richard von Krafft-Ebing, like Charcot, ran hypnotic experiments at his laboratory in Graz, and, in the case of Ilma S., with whom I opened this book, he produced an evidentiary compilation of hospital charts, experimental procedures, research results, and patient and family narratives that sought to record the facts discovered by hypnotic laboratory research. Nonetheless, like the Salpêtrians, Krafft-Ebing's staff encountered the problems of simulation, imitation, sabotage, and resistance. When he won his patient's confidence, Krafft-Ebing said, he turned an "unwilling" into a cooperative experimental subject. Yet Krafft-Ebing's documentary text reproduced a clear record of Ilma's experimental interventions. She sometimes refused, for example, to accept suggestions or enter *rapport* with the physician; while under hypnosis or auto-hypnosis, she instructed the physicians as to what commands to offer her; she became "sexually forward" and resisted the posthypnotic suggestion that she "act with chastity." Angered by the suggestion–implanted branding and subsequent bandaging of her body, Ilma refused immediately to heal; enraged by her clothing's disarray and the exposure of her body (which the checking of bandages necessitated), she placed papers between her skin and underwear so that she could check, after hypnosis, whether the researchers had exposed her breasts or genitals to view (Krafft-Ebing 1896 [1889], 31, 98–99, 102–7).

The Salpêtrière's inmates likewise had only a few strategies with which to sabotage the clinic's research methods.[14] They attempted to escape from the hospital—and sometimes did so; they sexually provoked the staff; they staged erotic tableaux, as I demonstrate in Chapter 6. Nevertheless, the experimental subject's consent to repeated poking, hammering, and hitting, to laboratory hypnosis, suggestion, and documentation was institutionally conditioned and produced through the work of mediation, a set of scientific practices shared by physicians across Europe. Yet information about reactive patient intervention in research procedures, which was marginalized by most experimental documentation, surfaced primarily in records like Krafft-Ebing's, in which, as I argue in

Chapter 6, one patient's pathography framed the experimental discourses of graphological measurement and laboratory inscription. These discourses, moreover, made the work of mediation possible. The laboratory's two-dimensional representations not only transported research findings along scientific networks, but made the research subject hybrid, a being both natural and social.

Despite its cutting-edge graphic documentation, the Salpêtrière's hypnotic experimentation quickly became the subject of scientific debate. Physicians other than Krafft-Ebing questioned the credibility of Charcot's ideal-type hypothesis, his subjects' presumed malleability, and his experimental methods. The Belgian physician Joseph Delboeuf accused the clinic of educating its hysterics in imitation; the German neurologist Carl Westphal criticized Charcot's research move away from neuropathology to hysterical physiology; the British psychiatrist Charles Bucknill accused him of experimenting on patients with suspect "moral character" (Delboeuf 1886, 146–71; Ellenberger 1970, 96–97; Macmillan 1991, 51–54). S. Weir Mitchell found the "ideal type" of *grand hystérie* clinically unreproducible in the United States and hinted in *his* lectures that the "admirable" Charcot was faking it (Mitchell 1885, 30). The American neurologist George Beard came to Charcot's defense: although Charcot had made "serious mistakes of inference," he said, and although his research subjects were "waste products thrown off in the evolution of the race," Charcot's work on trance phenomena had produced "true" scientific results.[15]

The bitterest "skirmishes," as Janet called them, took place on the "battlefield" at Nancy, between "Charcot's lieutenants" and Bernheim's staff (Janet 1925, 1: 183–92). For Bernheim's experiments had failed to replicate Charcot's "lethargy" and had, he said, been unable to confirm its existence. His experimental magnetic "transfers" of sensibility, paralysis, and anesthesia had not moved symptoms from one bodily site to another, Bernheim said, unless he repeated the procedure, describing the acts he would make (as Charcot often did in the amphitheater), or unless he performed it days later on a somnambulist who had watched the first experiments. Bernheim was forced to conclude that Binet and Féré had suggested symptomatic transfer to their subjects, however inadvertently. The Salpêtrians, he said, had subjected hysterics to a "special" and "false training" that produced its own reproducible symptomatology as "*suggestive hypnotic neurosis.*" Based on false research assumptions and unreliable provocation procedures, Charcot's observation had proven "deceptive" and his physiological theories "fundamental[ly in] error." Charcot's research, Bernheim concluded, deployed the "experimental illusions" that only hysterics were hypnotizable, that hypnosis simulated neurosis, and that researchers could hypnotically reproduce hysterical symptomatologies. "It is upon experiments of this kind," Bernheim scoffed, "that M. Binet builds up psychological theories, which he speaks of as *experimental*!"[16]

Freud, too, eventually rejected Charcot's experimental enterprise. For Charcot's physiology had ignored what would soon seem almost obvious: that hypnosis involved the psyche in its physiological productions; that reflex theories of psycho-physical correlation and causation could not account for experimentally induced transfers of sensibility or disordered gaits or facial grimaces. The question of simulation and Binet and Féré's differentiation of objective from subjective experience hinted at this problem, a problem the Salpêtrière's laboratory had addressed only from a physiological perspective. Indeed, Freud acknowledged in 1888 that, if the clinic had psychically implanted hypnotic phenomena in research subjects through suggestion, its experiments had produced enormous "errors in observation." Hysterics would have exhibited, if that were the case, no medically significant hypnotic characteristics; researchers could freely have produced any symptomatology they desired in hypnotized subjects; and study of major hypnotism would not have elucidated physiological alterations in the nervous system. If Bernheim's theory that suggestion was the key to all hypnotic phenomena prevailed in the scientific community, Freud also knew, Charcot's motives would become suspect. Had the master fabricated a symptomatology and taxonomy based, not on observation, but on his own unconscious suggestions? Freud was forced to conclude, with Bernheim, that Charcot's "neglect of the psychical factor of suggestion [had] misled a great observer into the artificial and false creation of a clinical type" through the "capriciousness and easy malleability" of his research subjects. Attributing this failure to Binet and Féré, Freud maintained that Charcot's experimental methodology was scientific and his observed symptomatology correct: hypnosis created physiological as well as psychical modifications. Yet after his 1889 pilgrimage to Nancy, Freud condemned Charcot's exclusively nosographical approach, the clinic's hypnotic research solely on hysterical subjects, differentiation of major from minor hypnotism, and the hypothesis of three major hypnotic states and their characteristic physiological phenomena. All these theories would prove scientifically "worthless" if Bernheim's critique were proven right (SE, 1: 77–78).

Although Freud was indulging in hyperbole, the clinic's experimental hypnotic research did prove scientifically valueless for exactly the reasons he had stated. I do not mean, however, to impugn Charcot's motives. For the Salpêtrière did produce cutting-edge scientific knowledge by using conventional scientific practices until, producing diagnostic inflation, mixed diagnoses, and largely untestable conclusions, Charcot introduced hypnosis as a standard mode of laboratory operation. Although I argue in Chapter 2 that Charcot's theories adumbrated a rudimentary psycho-physical representation theory, his reflex physiology nevertheless failed precisely because it undervalued the organic consequences of psychic events. Indeed, Charcot's hypnotic experimentation, I argue in the next section of this chapter, theoretically suppressed the psychical aspects of the physiologically based reflex acts it everywhere displayed. Yet the Salpê-trière's modes of scientific presentation and experimental representation, to which I now turn, would assist Freud's move to theorize representation as a plausible bridge between psyche and soma. For Freud had witnessed at the Salpêtrière not only the fabrication of reflex notions of psycho-physical correlation but, as spectator of Charcot's *leçons*, the work of labo-ratory mediation masquerading as the reproduction of "natural" patholog-ical events. Staged as a physiological reflex disorder, hysteria had become part of nineteenth-century scientific medicine's debate-as-spectacle. And by "staging," as I note in my introduction, I mean the public showing of what had been rehearsed many times in the laboratory, the performance before an assembled medical public, not solely of research results, but of a charismatically imbued mission.[17] Leveraged into theaters of scientific proof, then, the laboratory work of mediation invariably created new regimes of representation and occasionally contaminated forms of docu-mentary proof.

II

As my presentation of the Ferrier-Goltz debate at the beginning of this chapter signifies, experimental research at midcentury justified its proj-ects by invoking the nature it sought to replicate and investigate. Re-searching the organism's nature, mid-century scientists constructed, as Donna Haraway suggests, a hierarchy of natures that could be read syn-ecdochically in either direction. The natural body's organic functioning meant that the social body worked homologously, despite the separation of nature from the social; nature, the new transcendental signifier, governed all proficiently. Science could therefore interpret nature, the repository of organic rules, by investigating natural objects, which, displaying themselves to the investigator, could be used to produce knowledge, not only about nature, but about the social aggregate. Bernard had represented the experimental method as both a seductive and policing interrogation of the natural object under scrutiny. The "man of science," he said, possessed an "ardent desire" for knowledge; while "the observer listens to nature," the "experimenter, stand[ing] face to face with nature," "questions and forces her to unveil herself."[18] Bernard's portrait of nature's charm and the scientist's seduction represented the research subject as naturally available for scrutiny, as penetrable by the aroused scientist. Yet the courtship of nature by science took place not in the abstract but on the material bodies of human and animal research subjects. Thus knowledge could be produced, Bernard believed, only if experimenters undertook active interventions, carefully delimited causes for observed phenomena, and, through improving technology, produced greater refinement in reproducibility of research outcomes with a large number of experimental subjects.[19] Justifying their penetration by objective observation and experimentation, scientists sought, moreover, to leverage their research results into the social domain, responding to questions that surfaced around issues such as vivisection, surgical responsibility for pain and mortality, and reliability of research subjects. As Judith Butler argues, the identification of nature as a passive surface, "outside the social and yet its necessary counterpart," was not only a product of nineteenth-century science but a justification of its own constructive and productive activities of investing meaning and significance in empirical observations (Butler 1993, 4).

At the end of the century, Charcot could thus invoke the "claims of science" to justify and validate his experimental program. When he became professor of nervous diseases in 1882, Charcot used the occasion of his inaugural address to advertise his project, begun in 1870, to make "this great emporium for human suffering" a "regularly organized teaching and research center for diseases of the nervous system." He hoped, Charcot said, to "convince even the most incredulous" populace of the Salpêtrière's research "opportunity" and its "practical significance"; he therefore strove to ensure that the clinic demonstrate its "full value" by routinely "produc[ing] evidence."[20] The Salpêtrière, a metaphorical marketplace of misery, not only represented the dysfunctional body, then, but subsumed and denied its suffering as well. Reaching a wide medical and nonmedical audience, Charcot popularized hysteria and viewed that popularization as part of his mission to produce and justify basic scientific research. Indeed, the Parisian mix of institutionalized state support, bureaucratic interest in scientific progress, physician free access to fees and payments, and a supply of cooperative outpatients seeking the most comprehensive consultations available produced a widely ranging medical field in which researchers found themselves institutionally positioned to exploit an almost free market in experimental research opportunities.[21] The clinic served the social body by translating human suffering into scientific knowledge and so performing a valuable social function inexpensively. And although Charcot did not intentionally distort scientific research in the interests of a political position, the Salpêtrière's commitment to laboratory reproduction, as Janet later admitted, managed research findings to successfully leverage the research mission's message into the cultural and social domains.

The social apparatus of hospital confinement for incurables, moreover, supplied the Salpêtrière with, as Jan Goldstein says, an inmate "clientele of lower-class hysterics."[22] These women without class status or privilege had little recourse against the uses to which they were put while incarcerated, for although upper- and middle-class hysterics might seek treatment at private *maisons de santé*, public asylums sequestered impoverished neurotics, incurables, and those identified as social deviants. The Salpêtrière was, as Mark S. Micale calls it, a "psycho-geriatric institution" in which severely diseased patients, some hospitalized since childhood, made their homes and awaited their deaths. Everyday life in the hospital's dwelling cells was lived in a miniaturized Salpêtrian city within the Paris that surrounded it (Micale 1985, 715–16). A nineteenth-century medical ethicist identified the inhabitants of urban hospitals, indeed, as individuals "constrained by an excess of misery to exchange their liberty for help which is too often niggardly; unfortunate people rejected by the families they have exhausted and who, often having chosen neither their shelter nor their doctor, have not been able to subscribe legitimately to the punishing and sometimes onerous conditions to which they nevertheless find themselves submitted" (Lens 1818, 28: 101–10; quoted in Figlio 1977, 284). Freud understood this situation only too well. Researchers waited for years to prove organic change or physiological impairment in nervous diseases that were not immediately fatal (and therefore did not quickly provide a body for autopsy), and "only in a hospital for incurables like the Salpêtrière was it possible to keep the patients under observation for such long periods of time" (*SE*, 3: 14). Indeed, Charcot asked, "Where else would one find . . . so much patient material" so "particularly adapted" to the study of nervous diseases? (Guillain 1959, 49). His "living pathological museum" served the "exigencies of scientific progress" by collecting specimens of disease states and so producing state-of-the-art findings in anatomical pathology and experimental physiology.[23] All mankind would benefit, scientists agreed, from the suffering of a poor few.

While in my analysis the hospital's pathological ascendancy intersects more forcefully with social class than with gender, lower-class women at the Salpêtrière bore a disproportionate burden of scientific experimentation. When Charcot expanded the Salpêtrière's facilities to include outpatient consultation in 1879, and, in 1882, created a small hospital section for external patients and ambulatory sufferers, he added middle-class, neurotic, and male patients to his clinical sample. Charcot's Friday lectures had presented both male and female cases to verify his work on organic nervous disorders, and as the Salpêtrière began to serve temporarily hospitalized and external patients, Charcot could also study and treat inmate men with transient nervous disorders.[24] But while male patients were submitted to somatic testing's pokes, pinches, and pricks, they were subjected neither as often nor as rigorously to the extensive experimental regimes undergone by the Salpêtrière's long-term residential female inmates. The clinic's documentary evidence of research procedures, patient management, and experimental findings, moreover, pictured primarily women patients. Georges Didi-Huberman (1982, 32) notes that the *iconographies* photographed only female invalids; Richer records no laboratory procedures undertaken on male subjects (Bourneville and Regnard 1879–80, 1: 66, 133); and Janet (1901, 91) says that the Salpêtrians experimented solely on hysterical women. Indeed, Charcot had conceptualized female hysteria by the late 1870s and applied it in the early 1880s to an ever wider range of medical populations; he produced for hysteria, as Micale says, "nosographical inflation": a continually expanding classificatory group of clinical phenomena characterized the disease, which could then be diagnosed in men and children as well as in women (Micale 1990a, 373). Still, the experimental work that grounded the clinic's research, governed its laboratory provocation, and produced its descriptive nosography had been performed primarily on residential female patients. The application of the hospital's research technologies to a small population of men, then, does not alter the fact that the clinic used female experimental subjects disproportionately to produce research findings.

While Didi-Huberman's and Janet's statements about the absence of male patients in the clinic's iconographies and experimentation clearly hyperbolize, Richer's representation of the Salpêtrians' research as though performed solely on women may have been ruled by the goal of representability. Although the *Leçons du mardi* pictured and so documented testing of male hysterical subjects, these men, who were in general not severely afflicted by the disease, did not represent the clinic's best research subjects. Nor did they represent the best models to be pictured as proof that the research was, in fact, reproductive and naturally mimetic. That hypnosis produced physiological changes in the nervous system, and that the laboratory's work reproduced naturalized disease states in hypnotized subjects, for example, had been demonstrated through presentation of hypnotized subjects in the amphitheater. The hospital collected exemplary and representative pathologies, and statistically analyzed their modes and frequency of occurrence, to demonstrate the research's evidentiary truth. The hospital's larger documentary mission, however, demanded another register of representability: the verisimilar and documentary arts. This brand of scientific realism sought to establish experimentalism's careful reproduction of nature, the scientist's stance as objective observer, an iconographic subject matter of naturalized bodies and physiognomies, a certification of statistical validity for the experimental findings, and an implicit analysis of the institution's productive deployment of its research mission. The clinic made use, then, of patient misery to measure and mimic the body, to refine reproducibility of research results, and to leverage its knowledge production outside the laboratory and amphitheater.[25]

The Salpêtrians' publications depicted the clinic's research as documenting naturally known events and objects. In the 1870s, Richer began quickly to draw patients he observed during the four phases of fit, and the clinic's research publications reproduced the "facsimile[s]" he had "sketch[ed] from nature." But while figurative delineation represented the contorted body, photography produced a more perfect copy of nature's disease. Touting this technological invention's usefulness for documenting laboratory research, the Salpêtrians invariably coupled it with the procedures of observation and the production of truth. The camera, for instance, was as "crucial to the study of hysteria as the microscope was to histology."[26] The photographic plate, Richer said, possessed the "unimpeachable character of truth"; and "as for the truth," Charcot announced, "I am absolutely only a photographer; I register what I see."[27]

Technologically reproducing an image of the naturally deranged hysterical body, the photograph superseded the sketch, and the photographic plate became, as Albert Londe, director of the photographic studio, said, the "true retina of the scientist" (quoted in Didi-Huberman 1982, 32). Yet the clinic's pictures were nevertheless posed, as Didi-Huberman suggests. These photographic portraits called attention to their artifice even as they naturalized the bodies of the women who were their models. Scantily draped, the hysteric looked at once seductive and innocent; attired in apron and cap as peasant, domestic worker, or country girl, she seemed demure and obedient. She moved around the Salpêtrian byways, between attacks, the photographs implied, attired in her daily dress, and the photographer's shutter had simply caught her unawares: she was paradoxically "real" and representable. Seized as object and image, fixed in representational space, she documented the research outcome she had been framed to represent as natural.

In representing as natural the body they portrayed, the Salpêtrians exploited the female body's "nature," a body already associated with the natural and reproductive categories of material life. This association of nature with the female material, natural, and naturally reproductive body can be traced, Butler argues, to the linguistic etymologies of *mater* and *matrix* (the womb), and so to the problematic of reproduction, and, from there, to the "classical configuration of matter as a site of *generation* or *origination*" (Butler 1993, 27–55, 31). And, as Donna Haraway argues, although the nature/culture and sex/gender discursive and research fields are not identical, they intersect, especially in the nineteenth-century sciences in which the "organism—animal, personal, and social—became the privileged natural-technical object of knowledge." The nineteenth-century body, as Haraway says, was a historically specific somatic form appropriated by and converted to the uses of sciences that represented the anatomical and physiological organism by specifying its natural functions. Nineteenth-century science thus produced, not an "unmediated natural truth of the body," but a specific "bio-political" form that anchored and supported experimental regimes of knowledge production (Haraway 1989, 287–90). Yet the hysteric's iconographic image identified her as what Latour calls a modern scientific "quasi-object": a figure more fabricated, more social, more collectively manufactured than the nature she supposedly illustrated; more real, more nonhuman, yet more objective than the photographic record projected (Latour 1993, 49–59). Acknowledging the laboratory's instrumentalized view of inmate women while obscuring their hybrid status as quasi-objects, Féré called the clinic's hysterics "the frogs of psychology" (quoted in Ellis 1930 [1894], 382).

The Salpêtrians' iconographies generalized truths about hysterics as individuals and in the aggregate. Richer's pictures collected, classified, and charted the contorted movements he had observed at the clinic. His sketches depicted representative modes of attack, and, gathered together, they inventoried hysteria and fixed one comprehensive model for all other portraits of the disease. Thus a list or line of sketches represented characteristic forms the body assumed in, for example, hystero-epilepsy or hysteria major. This table of truth generalized a disease paradigm from individual hysterical attack; it produced a body of knowledge from an individual knowledge of bodies. Published in a volume with portraits of other hysterics, the clinic's photographs technologically inventoried insanity. These mental states as they appeared on the face and figure were, the iconographies implied, both typical and representative of a characteristic somatic form of ecstatic fit, pose, or attitude in passionate imaginings.[28]

The *Iconographie photographique de la Salpêtrière*, then, as its title stated, collected icons, images, or figures that represented the real states they purported to copy, portraying as discovered or "found" the meanings it had fabricated in the laboratory. Emptying the image of its history, the iconography made of Augustine, for example, an ideal type, perfectly representing Charcot's observational technology of ideal-type substitution; her particular contingency left behind, Augustine became, not a subject with her own life story, but a signifier in Charcot's semiology. As a mute entity in the iconographic record, she signified only because, fashioned as hybrid by the laboratory's collectivity, she had been mobilized as quasi-object to demonstrate its scientific truths. Both a socialized fact and a human turned into a natural object, the hysteric served, paradoxically, to warrant the modernizing work of Charcot's iconographic record: to guarantee the separation of objects from subjects, to produce norms of physiological function guaranteed by anomalous dysfunction, to expose the laboratory's mediation even as it obscured experimental hybridity. Catalogued and inventoried in the laboratory's iconographies, when she was leveraged out of the laboratory and popularized as experimental facticity, the hysteric illustrated deviance (Latour 1993, 22–24).

Like other nineteenth-century technologies for representing individuals as typical yet statistically deviant, the Salpêtrière's iconography participated in the modern production, individualization, and classification of the subject. Cesare Lombroso's anthropological iconographies of prostitute and female criminal physiognomies and Havelock Ellis's single and aggregate picturing of the criminal deployed a set of scientific and technological principles much like those Charcot had used at the Salpêtrière. All three drew upon the nineteenth-century discourse of functionalism and dysfunction. Alphonse Bertillon's 1879 anthropometric method, Carlo Ginzburg says, which collected in personal files a set of minute bodily measurements, initiated the European effort to identify and classify the individual through the "criminal photographic archive." Francis Galton's 1888 invention of fingerprinting as a simpler means of collecting and classifying data, and J. E. Purkinje's 1823 histological analysis of cutaneous system physiology, made medicine the "art of individualizing" (Ginzburg 1989, 119–23). The uses to which these sciences were put in a modernizing society that needed efficient methods of individual identification and social control, in an increasingly industrialized economy based on mass production of marketable goods and the continued creation of new, often colonial markets, produced a discourse of the individual grounded on emergent physiological principles and the scientific, technological norms they made it possible to construe.

The anthropometric method, physiological science, and the photographic archive joined to produce a normative notion of the individual. Lombroso's criminal, a product of abnormal biological conditions and adverse social circumstances, displayed deviant physical, mental, and nervous characteristics. When female, she flouted natural (especially maternal) duties, sexual behaviors (through precocity, "virility," and cross-dressing), and moral categories (corrupting sentiment, love, and piety). A product of degenerate heredity and pathological milieus, the female offender displayed "moral and functional anomalies." Lombroso used and cited Richet's, Binet's, and Charcot's laboratory research: he tested physiological functions, measuring reflex action, narrowing of visual field, muscular strength, acuteness of touch, and sensitivity to faradic current. Measuring with dynamometer, sleigh, algometer, and electrical meter, Lombroso tabulated the sensory capability of his prostitute research group, locating, he said, prostitutes' greatest (and "natural") sensory dullness in their clitorises and their least in the palms of their hands.[29] Havelock Ellis's sexologized version of the criminal, although less thoroughly measured, tested, and graphed, also represented the same statistical urge to constitute functional and moral norms by measuring dysfunction and deviance. Bourneville's iconographies deployed a nineteenth-century research technology and documented a biologico-moral project to fix the individual who demanded to be identified and managed for the good of the social group.

Charcot's laboratory and its scientific representational projects, then, linked the hysteria debate to modernizing social-scientific practices. Indeed, Charcot had constituted his reputation by cannily turning traditional scientific strategies into spectacle. Conjoining a medical mode of presentation with the nineteenth-century Parisian theatricalizing of private as though it were public life, Charcot staged hysteria for a medical and subcultural public.[30] "Designed and arranged" to attract attention, Janet said, and to "captivate" an audience with "visual and auditory impressions," the much-discussed Salpêtrian "dramatizations" had not been confined to the lectures on hysteria (Guillain 1959, 55). The young Freud, too, confessed that "ill-disposed strangers" might think the clinic quite "theatrical" (SE, 3: 18). André Pierre Brouillet's often-reproduced painting A Clinical Lecture at the Salpêtrière showcases Charcot's position as "the most celebrated doctor of his time." While Brouillet depicts the hysteric as a medical object that solicits spectators in an institutionalized setting, not the doctor-patient couple but Charcot's empty chair occupies the picture's representational center. Sitting beside a table loaded with instruments that signify the master's technical credibility and scientific prowess, the chair represents Charcot's newly awarded official professoriate, which addressed, he said, the "wants of education" and the "exigencies of scientific progress" (Charcot 1889, 3: 7–8). Often misread as a portrayal of the master's professional charisma at work exploiting and spectacularizing woman, Brouillet's painting instead, I would argue, represents the proliferation of scientific networks, the spokesman's address of a male audience and his solicitation of professional allies.[31] Widening outside the picture's frame, the circle of spectators includes the painting's viewer, himself figuratively joining the well-instructed listeners; widening beyond the spectator, the painting represents Charcot as a man widely perceived as part of France's gloire and an "asset" to the "nation" (SE, 3: 16). Seeking allies and followers, Charcot had made himself a public figure, worthy of portraiture and fame. Brouillet brilliantly represents, then, the theatricalizing moves that modern scientists used, in the work of translation, to constitute networks and mobilize adherents.

Indeed, the "School of the Salpêtrière" was, Freud hyperbolized, "Charcot himself." That school gathered around Charcot a scientific network of young men who, participating in his research, guaranteed the future of French neuropathology. Several had themselves, Freud admitted, risen to prominence and made "brilliant name[s] for themselves" (*SE*, 3: 15). Freud was wrong, I have said in Chapter 2, about Charcot's continuing scientific reputation; he was not wrong, however, about the fame of Charcot's star pupils. I now turn to two, Alfred Binet and Pierre Janet, to argue in the next section of this chapter that Charcot's short-lived glory nevertheless produced important scientific sons. Binet and Janet revised Charcot's quickly discredited neuropathology of hysteria, initiating and constituting, respectively, the discourses of psychophysiology and cognitive psychology. Charcot's experimentally produced reflex theories of hypnotic hysterical physiology became, to use Latour's terms, a "hard" science of psychophysiology and a "soft" science of psychology (Latour 1993, 55). Binet and Janet modernized for the twentieth century Charcot's research on an enigmatic disease whose somatic symptoms had no apparent organic cause. Extending the laboratory's reach into the discourses of the quantitative and social sciences, they created new scientific networks and leveraged Charcot's work into social, cultural, and educational domains even he could not have imagined.

III

The "present conception of hysteria," Janet told an audience of Harvard medical students in 1906, depended on the research and work routines of the institution in which it had been studied. Chiefly devoted to the study of somatic accidents, paralyses, and contractures dependent on nervous system disorders—more "neurologic than psychiatric"—the Salpêtrière had "determined the direction of the studies on hysteria" (Janet 1965 [1929], xii–xiii). By 1906, however, hysteria had become a "mental disease" and Charcot's somnambulism had gone out of style, like "our grandmother's hats" (Janet 1925, 151). Indeed, Janet had begun to psychologize hysteria by 1892, describing it as "an emotional malady" that was characterized primarily by "mental accidents" rather than physical stigmata (Janet 1901, 486–87). When Janet inherited leadership of the Salpêtrière's laboratory in 1890, he deployed the experimental principles and methodologies already in place: the scientific method of observation structured his research, he said, as he applied a "clinical method" to "diseases of the mind." But Janet also distrusted an overly scrupulous reliance on experimentation, which, he believed, could confirm observation and clinical therapeutics in only a small number of cases. "Psychology," he said, "is not yet advanced enough to admit of many precise measures." To

"take a microscope and engage in rough anatomy [of the mind]" exposed
the researcher of mental disorders to charges of "not knowing what [he]
look[ed] at" (Janet 1901, xiv). As Janet suggested, the laboratories in
which scientists researched hysteria in 1906 addressed questions not about
reflex dysfunction but about cognition, perception, and personality. For
despite Binet's and Janet's differences of approach to psycho-physical correlation and causation, Charcot's star pupils studied mental rather than reflex functions. Janet's lecture, moreover, correctly located institutional research sites as central to a disease's nosographical description and nosological delimitation. Indeed, as Bruno Latour reminds us, "No science can
exit from the network of its practice" (Latour 1993, 24).

Binet exploited the Salpêtrière's experimental methods, which he had
helped to consolidate, to elaborate a hard science of psychophysiology.
While working with Féré, he had practiced experimental observation,
had mapped hysterogenic zones, tested for sensation by twisting, pricking,
and pinching, and asked research subjects to locate body parts that had
been rendered insensible or paralytic by hypnosis. He called his laboratory an experimental "workshop," a regulated work space in which the
researcher provoked, classified, and documented psychopathological states.
To perform this task, Binet coupled what he called "introspection" with
objective observation. Appropriating Charcot's observational style of looking, he silently scrutinized bodies while his own skills of analysis delimited and constructed theory; he measured individual cases against types
and construed taxonomic groups. Binet's research, moreover, like Janet's,
measured the intensity of excitations and sensations, produced dysfunctional mental states through physiological and functional alteration of excitation. Provoking sensory hallucinations, a well-known psychical symptom of somnambulism, he suggested to a hypnotized research subject that
she see serpents, and, *voila*, she saw; that she comprehend the sense of the
words "the color red," and she understood; that she see a scene at a Bona-
partist salon, and she announced the names of hallucinated attending lu-
minaries. But Binet also made explicit the problems the clinic's experimental work had encountered, but that Charcot had covered over. How
could the experimenter provoke hallucinations with his words? Did this
phenomenon occur in the lives of normal individuals? How could the
clinic control the subjective nature of experimentally provoked hallucinations and account for their personal and perhaps simulable nature? (Binet
1886, 32–36).

Binet's psychophysiology laboratory at the Sorbonne researched the higher mental functions. Presenting and justifying experimental psychology, he hoped to show, Binet said, that he could study modes of complex thinking, aptitudes for spatial and temporal perception, and the faculties of judgment, reason, and sentiment with sufficient precision for his findings to have scientific value. He parried questions about how one could experimentally study invisible phenomena, such as thought, by invoking the scientific method: the experimenter actively produced the phenomena he studied; experimentation could modify and manipulate the research subject in only two ways, with *"excitations,"* which provoked sensations, and *"acts,"* which could be interpreted as mental states. Although, he said, this definition might have seemed narrow and overly material, only in this way could he test thought processes; for only when a material object or agent produced an excitation, and only when that excitation caused a direct, nearly immediate, effect could the experimenter measure higher mental functions and laboratory inscription record them. And, Binet stressed, his laboratory studied the ways in which sensation produced thought, introspection, memory, attention, and imagination. Rather than simply sensation or movement, Binet provoked and observed complex perceptual, speech, and language acts—the "whole ensemble of reactions" of which the laboratory was the "theater" of proof (Binet 1903, 2–5). Indeed, Binet's experimental psychophysiology spawned new social sciences. Ernest Solvay, whose Belgian institute applied the physiological studies of Marey and Angelo Mosso, the 1890s inventor of the ergograph, used Binet's psycho-physical studies of intelligence and mental fatigue to sociologize fatigue in military, educational, and other modern institutions (Rabinbach 1986, 489–93).

Binet's laboratory later invented the social-scientific discourse of psychometrics. In his experimental psychophysiology, Binet refined the research strategy Charcot had called "interrogation." He recorded and documented the questions he asked a subject, for example, in an experiment on musical memory. What do you remember of the performance's harmony? Its timbre? How loudly did you hear it? Did listening to the music affect your larynx or breathing? Articulating medical history-taking with the experimental collection of sensory data, Binet invented the questionnaire as a mode of obtaining quantitative information about subjective experiences and events (Binet 1894, 48–51, 131–54, 101). Binet's psychophysiology departed from Charcot's, however; sophisticating scientific practices of experimentation and representation, Binet could more credibly record subjective mental functions and more critically classify them than could his mentor. His experimental method of provocation, observation, and description did not bear the relation of copy to original, Binet asserted, but, assembling sufficient differential statistics, repeated reality by manufacturing it in the laboratory. Stressing the modern work of purification—which constituted nature as separate from the social—Binet moved the school of Charcot away from demonstrating dysfunction toward an experimental psychophysiology that, privileging functionalism, also served the sociologizing urge to individualize and classify the subject. His laboratory produced quantitative data that became, in the hands of educators and social scientists, a vehicle for establishing norms against which qualitative differences among individuals could be assessed: Binet's psychometrics did "psychology with numbers," he said (Binet 1969, xii–xiii; id. 1894, 103–30).

Binet's experimental science, then, constituted the methodologies that, emerging from the laboratory of "hard" science and into the "soft" social sciences, investigated not just the nature the laboratory claimed to have discovered rather than produced, but the social categories that it had claimed to exclude. Making this doubly dualistic move, Binet's laboratory, like others in the early twentieth century, increasingly separated nature from the social even as it created hybrids that contaminated the purity of binary thinking (Latour 1993, 49–59).

In his laboratory, Janet rewrote the Salpêtrière's research as an experimental psychology. Janet believed, with Charcot, that hysteria disturbed somatic functions and, when paralysis disobeyed the laws of anatomy, signified a disorder in the nervous system and cerebral cortex. Yet he paid increasingly little attention to the clinic's physiological and reflex theories. While Charcot had staged contortions, paralyses, and physiological dysfunctions in their multiform guises, Janet examined patient sensation, perception, and self-representation, portraying the hysterical body as cognitively and psychologically dysfunctional. Janet's experiments sought to produce, observe, and describe psychological phenomena involving, he said, "images and movements." His improved methodology, Janet explained, placed the research subject in "simple and well-determined circumstances" and investigated acts and words. When her perceptions and sensations were experimentally deranged, the hallucinating subject heard bells when none rang or trumpets when none sounded; saw flowers, birds, snakes; smelled odors; tasted water as wine; raised imaginary weights. The experimenter evoked in the subject's consciousness "all the phenomena" that corresponded with "real impressions made on the different senses." If the operator suggested to Bertha, for example, that she was dancing at a ball, she ceased to see the room around her and believed herself to be in a ballroom with many costumed people; she would laugh to one, bow to another, dance with a third. These psychological phenomena, moreover, could be tested on the body. The researcher's suggestions to the hypnotized subject produced, in some hysterics, "marked points" or "suggesti[ve] marked-points" (Janet 1901, 231–37). Like hysterogenic zones, these points, perceived by the listening subject and inscribed on the body by the operator's words, reproduced the same hallucinated scenes, sights, and movements every time. When "*certain [of the hysteric's] representations [were] too strong, certain associations of ideas too easy,*" her corporeal stigmata and accidents, moreover, could only be characterized as psychical. Indeed, when Janet said "*hysteria is an ensemble of maladies through representation,*" he meant, not only that hysterics misrepresented their somatic experience to themselves, as I suggested in Chapter 1, but that experimental presentation and scientifically controlled management of representations could derange the hysterical body. "*Modifications of the body which [were] caused by representations,*" he said, qualified as "hysterical." Janet's experimental psychology made central to laboratory research the psycho-physical representation Charcot's theories had adumbrated but refused to embrace (Janet 1901, 488; Janet's emphases).

Janet's laboratory, moreover, studied patient self-representation and so produced a "graphics of pathological psychology" (Janet 1901, xv). Observing patient speech in an experimental setting, Janet inscribed the patient's words, writings, and narrative as the central "document" of psychological laboratory inquiry. His hysterics performed their false sensations and produced movements or images appropriate to the hallucinatory scenes they played out. Their perceptions mimicked dreams, he said, and reproduced acts, words, and "enacted" scenes. Misinterpreted by previous researchers as simulation, malingering, and imitation, the hysteric's special gift of neuromimesis, or imitation of various symptomatic states, made her move immediately from perception to action without conscious association of perception and ideation. She acted, Janet said, as though she experienced "*diminution or suppression of the synthesis which constitutes personal perception.*" She failed to process as ideas systematically unified yet different visual images, that, anchored with motor images, located her as a conscious subject in space. This, in turn, produced a diminished "*personal synthesis,*" for, automatically repeating former associated ideas to herself without having a personal perception of having perceived herself, the hysteric

mechanically repeated past suggestions and inventions without representing herself in new circumstances; she acted "without any originality" or
"recent invention" in responding to the external world. Such mechanical
reproduction of the self in space seemed an "act" because it failed to connect personality, recollection, and conscious perception during an act's
performance (Janet 1901, 232–33, 238–48; Janet's emphases). The hysteric
misrecognized and misrepresented herself to herself, dramatizing her subjectivity as purely repetitive or fragmented.

Janet's experimental psychology made it possible to imagine representational plausible bridges between psyche and soma, to constitute physiology as separate from psychology. Charcot's reflex physiology had, as I
have said, explored but failed to theorize representation theories of mind-
body correlation and psychopathological causation. His staging of dysfunctional motor acts and dislocations of individual bodies from perceptual self-location had rudimentarily articulated this research problem. But
Janet's reconceptualization of such physical self-positioning as a problem
of faulty visual and motor images moved the discussion significantly away
from reflex and toward representation theories, away from the discourse
of physiology and toward psychology. For the hysteric's unanchored motor acts and diminished ability therefore to constitute personal perception
became a question of personality as well as self-representation. Because
what Janet called "personal synthesis" constituted a bridge between unanchored motor acts and dissociated perceptions of the person as person,
it also enabled the conceptualization of acts as performing activities outside perception, cognition, and self-consciousness. Janet's experiments
demonstrated, and his work theorized, that experimentally deranging
perception could create, and the researcher provoke and observe, psychological events otherwise unavailable for investigation.

The malady through representation, as Janet called hysteria, fascinated
experimenters and the medical public alike because it challenged nineteenth-century notions of the subject's ability intentionally to choose and
undertake purposive activity. Hysterical indifference, Janet said, represented a "lack of will." Having no perseverance, the hysteric could "do
nothing seriously"; lacking forethought, she knew not how to "adapt the
present to the future." She could undertake neither continuous achievement nor willed personal initiative; neither sustain temporal sequence nor
view herself as implicated in consequential events. An automaton rather
than a person acting with a sense of voluntary activity, the hysteric was
unable to initiate new acts, to adapt herself to new circumstances, to re-

unite and synthesize psychological elements not yet systematically grouped. She could not undertake "conscious and personal acts" connected to an idea of her personality. She suffered, Janet said, from splitting of consciousness or mental dissociation. And mental health depended entirely upon the capacities for will, intention, choice, and agency. Sanity relied, Janet said, on an "equilibrium between the automatic force of the past and the conscious and voluntary effort of the present." "Our moral health," he declared in addition, "depends altogether on the limitation which these two psychological activities exercise upon each other" (Janet 1901, 249–50). Memory, then, managed the subject even as the subject managed his or her everyday life through memory's faculties.

Janet associated this willful self-representation in and through time as anchored by a coherent and unified subjectivity. The subject was subject, he said, to an "I" located within its own experience. "It is I, we say, who, before executing it, have foreseen this act; it is I who, at the moment of accomplishing it, feel that I am performing this action; it is again I who later keep the remembrance of it. I connect it in every respect with my character, with my sentiments and with my ideas; I consider it henceforth as an integral part of my personality" (Janet 1901, 249). Lacking the sense of herself as a speaking subject, an "I," the hysteric could hardly be subject to and for herself. Failing to create and sustain a unified sense of herself with her particular values, ideas, and emotions, she could neither perceive nor represent herself as coherent, as constituting herself in the present through her memories of herself and others. Although a normal subject, of course, did not always and in every circumstance interpellate herself, as Janet's imagined "I" did, she was capable of remembrances, had produced habits that reproduced past acts, and, although not completely freely, had chosen voluntarily to act in a consistent manner. Characterized by temporal disarticulation, a lack of voluntary action (however constrained, as Janet admitted), and an inability to represent herself as subject to herself—as an "I"—the hysteric as figure challenged nineteenth-century values of autonomy, will, intention, and individual agency. Failing to be a coherent subject, the hysteric troubled the purity of subject/object binarisms, oppositions aligned with those of culture and nature, even as she served to constitute their difference.

In his Clark University lectures on psychoanalysis, Freud acknowledged his debt to Janet and the School of the Salpêtrière. When he and Breuer published their "Preliminary Communication," he said, they had been "completely under the spell of Charcot's researches." Mesmerized by the master, they had equated Charcot's somatic traumas and hysterical paralyses with their patients' psychical traumas, translating physiological as psychical dysfunction. Breuer's notion of "hypnoid states," Freud said, was "itself nothing but a reflection" of Charcot's artificial reproduction of traumatic paralyses under hypnosis. Yet, because Charcot had not adopted a "psychological outlook" while Janet had attempted to conceptualize the "peculiar psychical processes present in hysteria," he and Breuer had followed Janet's example, making mental splitting and personality dissociation central to their emerging theories and clinical practices (*SE*, 11: 21–22). And although Breuer had developed his notion of hypnoid states solely on the basis of Janet's *Mental State*, indeed, on the very passages I have discussed, Freud sought early to criticize Janet's theories. Thus splitting of consciousness, Freud said, failed to view the capacity for conversion—"the psycho-physical aptitude for transposing very large sums of excitation into the somatic innervation"—as characteristic of hysteria. Janet depended too fully, too, on notions of degeneracy, mental insufficiency, and hereditary etiology then prevailing in France. Misreading Janet's notion of "psychical synthesis," Freud parodied his portrait of the hysterical personality in a "homely but clear analogy." Janet's hysteric, he said, was like "a feeble woman who has gone out shopping and is now returning home laden with a multitude of parcels and boxes. She cannot contain the whole heap of them with her two arms and ten fingers. So first of all one object slips from her grasp; and when she stoops to pick it up, another one escapes her in its place, and so on." Freud suggested here that his own representations of hysterical subjectivity solved the problems of will, cognition, and the unconscious for which Janet's theory could not account (*SE*, 3: 50, 249; *SE*, 11: 21–22). Indeed, Freud dissimulated his debt to Janet precisely because his psycho–physical representation theory depended on Janet's experimental psychology.

The School of the Salpêtrière participated in discursive moves to modernize the subject, the object, and discourse. Charcot's laboratory exploited the enigmatic illness that was partly organic, partly mental to produce the disease and its sufferer as hybrid. Partly natural as human organism, partly created by scientific collectivities, the hysteric helped Charcot to theorize the body as physiological and reflex and, at the same time, as available to suggestive, and so psychological, influence. Privileging physiological dysfunction, however, Charcot created a wide range of symptoms that counted as hysterical; enlarged clinical pictures, ideal-type substitution, the hierarchization of symptoms as *formes frustes*, all enabled the clinic's diagnostic inflation of the disease's incidence even as the laboratory adhered to conventional scientific practices. The exaggerated diagnostic situation at the Salpêtrière produced mixed or hybrid diagnoses, generating a massive patient pool from which researchers drew subjects. A product of experimentation, the hysteric became a quasi-object. She was an object of scrutiny because she suffered a fragmented subjectivity; she was real but also circulated in the hospital's social and laboratory space, linking researchers and imitative patients together in a collectivity; she was discursive and so representable, narratable, and (photo)graphable. She witnessed to the laboratory's truths, representing somatic dysfunction on her body: in the hospital's charts, records, and iconographic publications; on stage at the amphitheater of proof. Both naturalized and sociologized, the hysteric served the Salpêtrière's move to modernize a historically problematic disease.

In "experiments made by nature," then, the late nineteenth-century laboratory provoked, observed, and described physiological dysfunctions that could then be said to inhere in nature. At the same time, the laboratory dissimulated its collective function to fabricate what counted as natural. Through the mixed work of translation and purification, then, scientific researchers mobilized the hysteric to display their discovery of natural facts even as they suppressed her hybrid, indeed fabricated, status. Thus the hysteric, an enigmatic figure that had for centuries somehow muddied the distinction between the psychic and somatic, became a trope the laboratory could exploit to energize its generative scientific mission. Charcot's laboratory participated in a series of late-nineteenth-century projects that sought to imbricate—and to separate—nature and the social, object and subject. This mediatory project took place in the laboratory, where scientists produced new, indeed modern, notions of what constituted nature, the social, and discourse. Elaborated beyond its strictly medical models, the laboratory's research could be leveraged outward, into the world of social aggregates and social-scientific projects.

At century's end, the hysteric emerged as a central and representable figure in the discourses of neuropathology, psychopathology, gynecology, psychoanalysis, and cultural mimesis. As trope, she was translatable across disciplinary and professional boundaries and so could be used to engineer transitions in conceptual thinking. Indeed, her figure made it possible, as I argue in Chapter 7, to constitute newly representational texts; as lecture became spectacle, and case study became case history, the hysteric energized the production of both. Charcot had created wide-ranging interest in the hysteric as figure and so leveraged his scientific influence, his clinic's prestige and credibility, to constitute a large audience for hysteria. Following yet revising Charcot's doctrines, Binet and Janet used the hysteric to produce in their laboratories newly emergent discourses of psycho-physical correlation, which, even as they manufactured hybridity, sought to purify the distinction between nature and the social. An enigmatic psycho-physical entity, the hysteric constituted and scandalized the divide between binaries even as she facilitated the figurative and rhetorical crossover that located modern subjectivity in, even as it differentiated it from, the body. The hysteric served, too, alongside other newly fabricated hybrid or intermediary figures—such as the criminal, the pervert, and the barbarian—to measure and classify the individual, to normalize deviance, and to constitute the social aggregate. Nineteenth-century scientists had used the hysteric to construct plausible bridges between psyche and soma even as they mobilized her figure to leverage their research findings into social and political arenas—as I claim in Chapter 5—and to make the laboratory the locus for manufacturing facts about nature, subjectivity, and the discourses that linked and differentiated them. The hysteric's status as quasi-object, then, enabled the modern production of the subject as distinct from the object, the social as different from the natural, the emergence of psychologies, sociology, even the critical study of science that researches the researchers who created her.

I have said that Freud dissimulated his debt to Janet. He did so, I argue in the next chapter, to distinguish his new science from Janet's, to represent psychoanalysis as clinically efficacious, and to claim priority in scientific circles.[32] Whereas Janet had based his theories on "laboratory experiments," Freud said, he himself had theorized "with therapeutic aims in mind" (SE, 11: 22). In Chapter 4, although I do not endorse it, I follow Freud's differentiation. Doing so facilitates my analysis of the treatments available to nervous patients. The therapies from which Freud borrowed and later departed, I argue, treated the physiologically based reflex body. Isolation disciplined, while psychotherapy persuaded, and, as the rest cure, reeducated dysfunctional individuals. Freud's and Breuer's cathartic treatment, however, sought to cure patients by activating a complex array of psycho-physical affective behaviors. While Breuer's theory of catharsis relied on reflex theory, as I demonstrate in Chapter 1, Freud's application of affectively charged treatment deployed, not only neurological discharge patterns, but psycho-physical notions of self- and object-representation, subjective experiences of pleasure and pain, and cognitive appraisals. I argue, in Chapter 4, that nineteenth-century treatments for nervous disease, whether disciplinary or productive, were reeducative. Altering this concept of cure, Freud made its tutelary relation into the transference, creating an appropriate mental medication for the modern psycho-physical and self-representing subject.

CHAPTER 4

Fat and Blood, and How
to Make Them

"Anyone who wants to make a living from the treatment of nervous patients," Freud said in his autobiographical study, "must clearly be able to do something to help them." But Freud increasingly found the "only two weapons" in his "therapeutic arsenal"—electrotherapy and hypnotism—inefficacious in treating the symptoms of nervous disease. Electrotherapy "was of no help whatever," he said; and although hypnosis helped patients remember pathogenic events, his replacing of their fears with suggested maxims or didactic injunctions failed to restore them to health (*SE*, 20: 16). Moreover, he was unable to hypnotize every patient or to achieve somnambulism, or deep but active sleep, with those he did hypnotize. He implored his resistant patients to cooperate. "You are going to sleep!" he assured them. "But, doctor, I'm *not* asleep," they remonstrated. "I don't mean ordinary sleep; I mean hypnosis," Freud would insist.[1]

Could he, Freud wondered, really create a peculiar and curative psychical state merely by holding up his hand and demanding that his patient "go to sleep"?[2] Consequently, he took Hippolyte Bernheim's "astonishing and instructive experiment[s]" as a "model," he said, for an altered clinical procedure. For when Bernheim had uttered a "mild word of command" or pressed his hand to a patient's forehead, Freud realized, "lo and behold!" she had overcome posthypnotic amnesia. He could likewise induce remembrance, Freud speculated, with a touch of the hand and an authoritative order. He commanded his patient to lie down, close her eyes, concentrate, and fix her attention; he "obliged" her to communicate the reminiscences from which she unknowingly suffered. When a patient could produce no memories, Freud placed his hand on her forehead or took her head in his hands and demanded that she "think of it under the pressure of [his] hand." Surprised that the new procedure "scarcely ever left [him] in the lurch" and yielded "precise results," that it indicated the direction analysis should pursue and so enabled termination, Freud began systematically to apply his "pressure" technique. He had transformed hypnosis, he later said, into a new treatment technology based on the cardinal rules of patient discursive non-omission and physician tactile abstinence.[3]

The treatments available for nervous patients in the 1880s all sought to remake the subject by treating the reflex body. Isolation, rest cure, hypnotic suggestion, and psychotherapy operated, in theory, on the twin principles of functionalism and productivity; all refashioned sick into healthy individuals able to cope with the emotional stresses of late-nineteenth-century work and family life. During the 1870s, I argue in Section I of this chapter, physicians treated patients by regimenting somatic and affective life, calming and quieting excited nerves, and restoring the body to its proper economy. The rest cure invoked nature as justifying its largely social mission: to restore wasted women to productive positions of domestic middle management. Engineered in and transferred from the hospital, as I maintain in Section II, the rest cure's educative medical treatments remade the subject by remolding the material organism. Psychotherapies, whether hypnotic or "rational," I suggest in Section III, performed a more persuasive but no less tutelary and sociologized mission. Especially when practiced on hospitalized or outpatient working-class sufferers, suggestion-based therapies diagnosed as ill individuals incapable of working and restored them to fully functionalized labor. The rest cure, as my chapter title suggests, made fat and blood and so produced healthy, well-functioning individuals; suggestion, hypnotism, and psychotherapy regulated the mind to suppress and deter the negative ideation that caused the soma to sicken. Using concepts about the naturalized body to fashion the useful and healthy tutelary subject, these treatments read social, usually moral, functions by synecdoche from the (mal)functioning reflex body, as described in Chapter 2. Clinical production of the well-functioning individual, then, served even as it scrutinized economic modes of social organization. For the late-nineteenth-century individual worked in settings that demanded efficient interaction with others and a fully intentional sense of independent choice and capable agency. Participating in the laboratory's work of purification, described in Chapter 3, these nineteenth-century therapies helped constitute the modern separation between nature and the social even as they deployed ideas about nature to support their sociologized mission.

Freud's early clinical practice participated in the functionalizing of late-nineteenth-century individuals. In Section IV of this chapter, I treat *Studies on Hysteria* as a single text that demonstrates Freud's shift from physiologically based cures for the reflex body to psycho-physically based cures for the modern subject. For while he had prescribed the rest cure and hypnosis for Emmy von N., he had allowed Lucy and Elisabeth (whom he could not successfully hypnotize) simply to lie quietly and talk (*SE*, 2: 113, 138, 145, 153). Indeed, after Emmy, Freud increasingly challenged functionalizing rest cures and psychotherapies. Questioning their adherence to prevailing nineteenth-century notions of individual will and intention, fully conscious choice, a capacity for uninterrupted work, and the absence of unpleasure, Freud fashioned a hybrid, psychoanalytic subject characterized by counter-will, unconscious ideation, undischarged affect, and attraction to dysfunction. In Freud's and Josef Breuer's cathartic treatment, enforced performance of recovered affect healed the patient; this therapy for excitation gone awry discharged overloaded nerves and enabled the patient to create an appropriate set of self- and object representations. Indeed, catharsis depended upon a theory of affects, which, as defined by Otto Kernberg, involves psycho-physical behavior patterns that conjoin cognitive appraisals, facial communicative patterns, subjective experiences of a pleasurable or painful nature, and muscular and neurological discharge patterns. Freud's theory of affect, which Kernberg's elaborates, portrayed subject and object as reciprocally configured, for self- and other representations, created in moments of peak affect, constituted the psycho-physical subject. Misrepresenting herself in self- and other representations, the hybrid hysteric acted her affect-laden object relations, usually with family members and always in scenes or scenarios.

Here, Freud encountered a problem that all nineteenth-century tutelary psychotherapies addressed: the relation of the family to the nervous patient and to disease onset. Steeped in the theory of pathological milieus, the psychiatric, psychopathological, and neuropathological communities had identified families as neurogenic; Freud transmuted this degenerate, hereditary social unit into the arena of modern self-representation and subject formation. The tutelary relationship between patient and physician likewise transformed this relation, for psychotherapies became historically possible and widespread as treatment options when family life became available for scrutiny and interrogation. Thus the psychoanalytic patient, constituted partly as subject and partly as object, was refashioned by another collectivity, the patient-doctor dyad, in reciprocal but authoritative rhetorical and affective interaction. Since it so widely defined the matrix of subject/object and natural/social oppositions, Freud's early theory of affect seemed the first, best conception of psycho-physical theory. As this chapter suggests, then, Freud transmuted reflex theories of psychopathological causation to constitute a plausible representation bridge between psyche and soma, natural organism and social-familial relations. This theory posited a subjectivity rooted in, yet radically separate from, the body, as Freud's consulting room became a laboratory for fashioning a new kind of psychoanalytic subject.

I

In "Die Behandlung gewisser Formen von Neurasthenie und Hysterie," his 1887 review of S. Weir Mitchell's *Fat and Blood, and How to Make Them* (1879), Freud praised Mitchell's rest-cure regime of "rest in bed, isolation, feeding up, massage and electricity" as a useful treatment for nervous exhaustion when practiced in a "strictly regulated" environment (*SE*, 1: 36). Enforced restriction of voluntary motor activity seemed the cure's key, for rest reduced the patient's lived experience to just the body's involuntary processes—digestion, elimination, sleep—as prescribed and controlled by the physician. Mitchell ordered bed rest for six weeks to two months; he refused the patient the right to sit up, sew, write, or read, and even, on occasion, to turn over in bed without aid. "Sometimes I think no motion desirable," he said, since the "moral influence of absolute repose" determined recovery (Mitchell 1879, 43–44). But without motion or exercise, the quieted and calmed body might sicken in other, unaccountable ways. To preserve muscle and nerve tone, Mitchell prescribed massage and faradization: "exercise without exertion." No spot on trunk or limbs, no tender zone, remained unrubbed—although women with sensitive abdomens or ovarian tenderness needed special care. "A practiced rubber," Mitchell averred, would "by degrees intrude upon the tender regions, and will end by kneading them with all desirable force" (Mitchell 1875, 83–102; id. 1879, 57–58). Touching, kneading, or stimulating the body according to anatomical plan mapped its sensations and calmed sensitive zones. These treatments quieted the nervous body, produced and managed its limited excitations, and strictly regulated its physiological responses. Mitchell's therapy cured the nervous patient by treating her disordered and overly excited reflex body. Always on the verge of

excess motion, heat, or activity, this forcibly nonfunctioning body demanded regulation even as it threatened to elude it.

Mitchell also managed the sickened organism's consumptive economy. His dietary regime controlled the flow of fluids and solids into and
out of the inert body. First only milk, then raw beef tea, and later solid
food, infusions of iron and occasionally alcohol went into the body on a
regulated basis. Menstrual blood, urine, and stool came out. The physician exercised complete authority over all excretory activities: some patients might walk to the bathroom, some were ordered to use a bedpan.
If the bowels did not move, Mitchell recommended clysterics and diuret-
ics; should these fail, he applied an electrical battery to "move" the in-
testinal "fibres" and "act on the sphincter" (Mitchell 1885, 23–24, 259).
Indeed, Mitchell suspended massage during menstruation because, he
said, kneading might block an excitable patient's flow of blood. The resting, reflex body, then, also entered into an economy of gain and loss. Pale
and weakened, the wasted hysterical body, once plump to "excess," now
needed fattening. Although subject to fluctuation or variability, the body
needed a "standard share" of flesh verifiable by medical measurement and
treatable by medication; "each individual," Mitchell believed, "should possess a certain surplus of this readily-lost material." The "impoverish[ed]"
blood and tissue needed "nutritive prosperity," a plenitude defined by its
difference from anemic lack, a gain confirmed by its variation from loss
(Mitchell 1879, 23–24, 13). The reflex body ran, then, on an economy of
exchanges with the nurturing or depleting social world.

Treating the sickened body, then, Mitchell also inserted it into a larger
economic system. Mitchell's therapeutics strictly regulated the resting
body's entrances and exits, not only to fatten it, but to routinize its fatten-
ings, to authorize its intake and eliminations, to control its movements,
both voluntary and involuntary. For the regulatory practices of Mitchell's
cure depended not only on a stationary, bedded body but on a homeo-
static hospital surrounding the site of care. Yet the power Mitchell exercised in his hospital wards—an impressive and authoritative power, no
doubt—was not, if we look carefully, oppressive, even if apparently so, but
rather productive. The body at rest, mapped by the attendant's touch,
charted by the hospital's documents, mastered by the doctor's orders, and
readied for return to productivity, indeed grew fatter, rounder, and therefore, according to doctor and patient, abler and more vital. Making fat
and fortifying blood, Mitchell's cure for the most part restored its patients
to the health, well-being, and sense of capability they desired, to a satis-

faction many women voiced in the appreciative letters they wrote the doctor after their treatments.[4] The rest cure submitted the sickened body to a regimen of careful consumption and fleshed out the wasted body; that flesh was a visible sign of certified and verifiable cure. Drawing on the two major nineteenth-century notions of the body as a system of dynamic exchange—that every body part is related to every other, and that the system functions by structured intake and outgo—Mitchell constructed a bodily economy and situated that body within a series of economic calculations (Rosenberg 1985, 40–42). Indeed, a certain "permanent profit" accrued to all parties to the rest cure's quieting and plumping of the fatigued and wasted body. The doctor produced a restored body, a cured individual, who returned to her home no longer depleted and ready to reenter its economic systems and relations.

In his first cathartic cures, Freud, too, treated the reflex body through rest cure in a strictly regulated environment. When he met Emmy von N., a 40-year-old upper-class Russian, she lay resting, inert, on a sofa. Freud observed her tic-like facial, neck, and hand movements, heard her stammer, "clacking," and obsessive anxiety-laden verbal explosions. She must have been, he concluded, under the influence of a recurrent and horrifying hallucination. Emmy had been raised by an overly strict mother, Freud learned, had married a middle-aged, wealthy industrialist at 23, and been ill since her husband's death by stroke some 14 years earlier. Although she had tried the water and massage cures, Emmy nevertheless still complained of depression, pain, and insomnia. Freud demanded that she enter a nursing home, where he visited her twice daily; he ordered warm baths, performed massage, and implanted hypnotic suggestions. To reduce gastric pains, he "stroked" and reassured his patient; to restore sensibility, he applied the faradic brush; to alleviate pain not caused by the treatment, he "massage[d] her whole body." Fearing, like Emmy herself, that menstruation would halt her massage, Freud hypnotically reregulated the flow he had earlier set at 28 days. Unlike Mitchell, Freud did not totally isolate his patient; he allowed her to read, write letters, and visit with her daughters. Under Freud's care, Emmy lay quietly in bed, slept well, and, he said, visibly improved.[5] When she relapsed after months of relative health and so returned to therapy, Freud prescribed a "feeding . . . up" regimen. She gave her food to the house porter's children; she refused to drink water: Freud ordered improvement. "I'll do it because you ask me to," Emmy conceded. When she developed her old gastric pains, Freud hypnotized her; when, in "open rebellion," she still refused to take fluids, Freud announced that if, after 24 hours, she did not drink, he would terminate her therapy, and the next day found her "docile and submissive." Freud had not yet theorized resistance or the transference, but he sensed that Emmy's disobedience called into question the rest cure's efficacy. Indeed, Freud here stumbled on the rest cure's failure to theorize psycho-physical correlation or to treat psychopathological conditions. For treating the reflex body by economizing its exchanges and regulating its dynamic interactions with its environment produced a patient, as Freud said, both docile and submissive. When Freud visited her estate nine months later, moreover, Emmy had grown positively "stout" and seemed, he said, in "flourishing health" (*SE*, 2: 81–82; *SE*, 20: 16; *SE*, 2: 83–84).

The rest cure represented wasted women as demanding the authoritative intervention of a medical man who, invoking nature, rebirthed and reeducated her. His power infantilized the patient, who, Mitchell said, necessarily exhibited "child-like acquiescence" to her doctor's commands, who became "contented and tractable" as her body ballooned. The milk diet, troping the doctor-patient relationship as that of mother-child, made the patient a figurative baby and metaphorically reproduced the "nursing" situation.[6] Milk and milk alone, delivered on the doctor's schedule, served as first step in the rest regime; the cure's strictures mimicked, as well, developmental stages from infancy through adolescence, and, finally, to maturity. One childlike patient, "rapidly weaned," quickly increased her intake of solid food; having been put to bed, Miss B. was gradually allowed to move her legs, sit up, stand, "creep" about the room, and walk with three crutches—each less supportive than the previous one—until her body became upright and her character healthy. "You see," Mitchell concluded, "that, following nature's lessons with docile mind, we have treated the woman as nature treats an infant."[7] Miss B. had been reborn, her body retrained, and her character developed. Whereas Freud described his patient as "docile," Mitchell mistakenly imagined himself to be so.

As did so many other nineteenth-century moral treatments, the rest cure depended on a tutelary relationship. The inert patient was a receptive vessel for the doctor's moral persuasion. "If the physician has the force of character required to secure the confidence and respect of his patients," Mitchell said, "he has also much more in his power, and should have the tact to seize the proper occasions to direct the thoughts of his patients to the lapse from duties to others, and to the selfishness which a life of invalidism is apt to bring about. Such moral medication belongs to the higher sphere of the doctor's duties, and if he means to cure his patient permanently, he cannot afford to neglect them" (Mitchell 1879, 45–46). Narcissistic, self-gratifying, and failing to perform her duties to family, friends, and community, the bedridden female invalid needed moral reeducation by a pastoral yet calculating professional man. His power, then, resided not only in his regimentation of the diseased body but in his prerogative tactfully to persuade by seizing the opportunity to redirect his patient's moral attention. The cure could only truly be "permanent," then, when the physician exercised his professional power with the care of a moralizing father who, knowing woman's duties in the private domain, could reeducate her to selflessness and devotion to others. Mitchell's benevolent paternalism, the category truly attested to by the appreciative letters from his patients, suffused his professional functions with the aura of vocation: he performed spiritual work for women, work from a "higher sphere" than the solely material realm. Having cared for and regulated her physiological functions, the physician altered a patient's "moral surroundings" and, with "unbending will," paradoxically instructed his childish patient in a feminine version of this very willpower. In some cases, he taught self-control over bodily functions such as vomiting or diarrhea that were not normally volitional; because they had been caused or aided by "expectant attention" to her body or "morbid watchfulness" for symptoms, retraining could submit these involuntary functions to moral and ethical (self-)regulation. The patient's "disorder," Mitchell told his fellows, was simply bad "habit"—poorly planned and executed routine—and only "her own will," when given "moral training" by the doctor's delegates, could permanently restore moral order.[8] Like F. C. Skey's mid-century therapeutics, which taught nervous English girls "backbone," like George M. Beard's, which taught profligate American men moderate material and bodily consumption, Mitchell's cure educated wasted American women to a morally hypostatized and ethically idealized "self-support" (Mitchell 1879, 97).

Yet Mitchell's cases demonstrated that, paradoxically, social constraints and cultural practices depleted organisms that had once been well:

[Mrs. C.] undertook, at the age of sixteen, a severe course of study, and in two years completed the whole range of studies, which, at the school she went to, were usually spread over four years. An early marriage; three pregnancies, the last two of which broke in upon the year of nursing; began at last to show in loss of flesh and color. Meanwhile she met with energy the multiplied claims of a life full of sympathy for every form of trouble, and, neglecting none of the duties of society or kinship, she yet found time for study and accomplishments. By and by she began to feel tired, and at last gave way quite abruptly, ceased to menstruate five years before I saw her, grew pale and feeble, and dropped in weight in six months from one hundred and twenty-five pounds to ninety-five. Nature had at last its revenge. Everything wearied her: to eat, to drive, to read, to sew. Walking became impossible, and, tied to her couch, she grew dyspeptic and constipated. The asthenopia which is almost constantly seen in such cases added to her trials, because reading had to be abandoned, and so at last, despite unusual vigor of character, she gave way to utter despair, and became at times emotional and morbid in her views of life. After numberless forms of treatment had been used in vain, she came to this city and passed into my care. (Mitchell 1879, 84–85)

Mrs. C.'s remarkable intelligence, fortitude, and energy paradoxically put her at risk. Studying too hard, serving out too much sympathy, meeting the needs of too many family members and social relations, giving birth too many times in too short a period, Mrs. C. had performed too well the tasks demanded first of the single (but exceptional) girl, then of the married woman and mother. Yet Mitchell called Mrs. C.'s cure "complete and permanent," for, although her continuing partial blindness enfeebled her ability to accomplish intellectual work, after a month of rest she menstruated, and eighteen months later, she became pregnant (88). Representing women's "natural" propensity for bodily bloating on a regular schedule, the rest cure associated nature with the female material, natural, and naturally reproductive, body, as I suggested in Chapter 3. The configuration of matter as a site of generation or origination and the etymologies of "matter" and "matrix," as Judith Butler proposes, may account for the links among the ultimate combination of fattening, required rest, and confinement to the reproductive female body (Butler 1993, 27–55, 31).

I do not mean to suggest that social constraint caused mental illness, for disease causation is complexly constituted within a matrix of psychical, physiological, material, and social forces. Yet Mitchell quite rightly assumed that Mrs. C.'s ability fully to perform reproductive and domestic duties would identify her as recovered. Indeed, his rest-and-infantilization regime had made the wasted Mrs. C. into a "healthy and well-cured woman" able to resume her "place in the family circle and in social life" (Mitchell 1879, 97). Once more a productive family member, the domiciled woman thus again managed the regimes of production and consumption in a domestic domain. Indeed, the house's economic schedules, productivities, and sequestration seemed homologous with the hospital's, the site at which she had been reeducated by a radical reduction to an involuntary bodily economy of intake and output.[9] As wife and mother, Mrs. C. oversaw family and domestic production and circulation of products, from the material making and giving of breast milk, to the preparation and elimination of food, to the calculation of domestic purchase, waste, and expenditure. The domestic woman's healthy body also proved useful in the domain of work and social relations, for fattened with fetuses she (re)produced new managers—both male and female—for increasingly complex business and household economies. If she were ill, her productive and reproductive duties would go undone and the household would sicken. When Mrs. C. or Emmy von N. became tied to her couch, the wife's work of middle management—overseeing servants' labor, children's education, domestic relations, emotional satisfactions, social and intellectual contact with the world at large—would not get done. Wasted solely to a bodily experience of pain and fatigue by social and domestic work, made desperate and depressed by her inability to perform that work, the middle-class woman was submitted to a medically reproduced "natural" and involuntary somatic life that subsequently restored her to the same domestic social domain. In a doubly dualistic move, the hysteric had become natural object and matter that, remade as tutelary subject, encountered the same synecdochically produced biologico-moral responsibilities. Paternalistically reeducated in the cultural values of willpower and fully functional agency, fattened women such as Mrs. C. became more productive wives and household managers.[10] Submitted to a therapeutics that produced plump bodies out of wasted ones and functionalized upper-middle-class subjects, rest-cured women experienced themselves, not only as healthy, but as happy.

As productivity and the purely volitional became hypostatized in the late nineteenth century, individuals who lacked capability had become available for designation not only as sick but as dysfunctional and abnormal. For, as I suggest in Chapter 3, studies of the social aggregate had also begun, alongside the binaries natural/social and matter/subject, to constitute the opposition normal/pathological. And, according to Georges Canguilhem, while somatic disease may be described and diagnosed with more empirical precision and better standardization than can mental distress, both kinds of disease not only disable but isolate and alienate the ill individual, inasmuch as both patient and healthy people impose renunciations and limitations on the person so diagnosed. Indeed, the notion of health or normality, Canguilhem believes, indexes not reality but social values. For while individuals hold particular beliefs at particular historical moments, these beliefs are shaped by and constructed within social relations and are lived out as though they possessed relatively stable meanings. Nineteenth-century subjects had come to value "a long life, the capacity for reproduction and for physical work, strength, resistance to fatigue, the absence of pain, a state in which one notices the body as little as possible outside of the joyous sense of existence." Physicians thus measured physiological "functional constants" and "hormonal and nervous functions of regulation" according to their notions of statistical averages and norms and prescribed the appropriate medications for patients.

Indeed, as I have indicated with regard to Mitchell's "fan mail," the patient decided whether and when she had deviated from and when she returned to a normal state of health. Becoming normal, Canguilhem says, meant "taking up an interrupted activity"—even if at a reduced rate—rather than suffering impotence, helplessness, disability, and lack of capacity. Shaped by the social milieu, health, Canguilhem says, is itself a normativity that, paradoxically, limits and defines a subject's "maximum psychic capacity" without identifying a conceptual ceiling for functioning (Canguilhem 1978 [1966], 63–68). Thus the social shapes the natural, submitting matter to dictates produced by socially generated notions; conceptually separate from the natural, the social nevertheless governs it by synecdoche, working from binaristically differentiated domains (subject/object and social/natural) viewed as economically homologous. Capacity, ableness, and capability are ever-increasingly valued in an industrialized and contracturalized society as more and more complex activities are included under the rubric of the normal; for only highly volitional, well-disciplined subjects can fulfill their productive and reproductive functions in such societies.[11] Mitchell's hysterics—like Charcot's and Freud's—once wasted, but now stout, had been translated across a binary and back again, to become normative, healthy, satisfied, and fully functioning individuals. They became tutelary subjects.

When Freud prescribed the rest cure to treat Emmy von N. in 1889, he, too, hoped to normalize a haute bourgeois individual. As with Mrs. C., Emmy's domestic and marital responsibilities, intensified by the death of her husband during her second confinement, had strained her capacity, paradoxically, to perform them. Unlike Mitchell, however, Freud conceptually foregrounded the role of wife as middle manager. He observed that Emmy managed a complex set of domestic economies and public interactions as well as had her industrialist, entrepreneurial husband. Having withdrawn when ill into total isolation, for example, Emmy nevertheless helped manage her husband's large industrial business, supervise her children's educations, and correspond with "prominent people in the intellectual world." She fulfilled her obligations so capably, Freud noted, that no neighbors knew she was ill or identified the distinguished-looking visitor as her doctor. Her "moral seriousness," excellent education, love of truth, and intelligence and energy ("no less than a man's," he proclaimed), in short, her "unblemished character" and "well-governed mode of life," should have guaranteed her excellent capability and full capacity in her responsible tasks. Astonished by the "wide . . . circle" and "whole extent of her duties, occupations and intellectual interests," Freud decided, ironically, that an "*excess* of efficiency" had caused her disease (*SE*, 2: 102–4, 83; Freud's emphasis). While maintaining social networks and business relations, the upper-middle-class woman could, like Emmy, be consumed by her own conscientiousness. Emmy was not unique in Freud's and Breuer's practices, moreover, for Anna, Lucy, Katharina, Cäcilie, and Elisabeth, too, possessed intellectual gifts, exceptional talent, high moral character, and the capability to function fully—and with a perseverance as dedicated as a man's—in the middle-managerial work their class-position offered or demanded of them.

Freud had discovered, in fact, that illness was embedded in, he said, "human," "social," and "family circumstances" (*SE*, 7: 18). Yet Freud's rest cure brought to light the problem with domestic economies that Mitchell's sequestration had misread and, as I discuss in my next section, Charcot's hospital isolation ignored. Whereas Mitchell regarded Mrs. C.'s restored menstruation and eventual pregnancy as proof of the cure's and his patient's productivity, Freud wondered whether Emmy's biologico-moral responsibilities had tended toward sickening her. For maternity—the work of reproduction in the domestic domain—demanded not only physical stamina and physiological vigor but affective, emotional capability as well. And, in the realm of moral duty, Emmy judged herself as dysfunctional; she chastised herself, Freud said, for failing fully to create a sense of love, care, and nurture for her clearly troubled daughters. Emmy confessed to disliking her second child, who, she said, had never slept, learned to walk late, developed enigmatic paralyses, and suffered hallucinations, and had eventually been diagnosed as imbecilic. "I was not fond of the child," she apologized, but "one could not have guessed it from my behaviour. I did everything that was necessary. Even now I reproach myself for being fonder of the elder one" (*SE*, 2: 60–61, 54, 64). But Emmy's elder daughter's "menstrual troubles" and unsuccessful gynecological treatment had caused the mother "fits of despair," "impos[ed] fresh duties on her," and intensified her own nervous condition, the "storms in her head," as she called them. Emmy's accountability for superintending her sick daughter's medical care, both her children's educational positions, possible vocations, and hoped-for marriages had made her nervous and anxious. The cultural dictate that she enjoy motherhood and love her children equally had likewise caused her, as Freud said, to "blame herself severely for the least signs of neglect" (*SE*, 2: 59, 80, 65). Maternity's moral obligations, generated by synecdoche from material functions, put Emmy at physiological and psychological risk. And these case histories about representative women suggested that hysteria hardly attacked an unhardy few. The disease's history and nineteenth-century diagnostic statistics sustained that view.

A profoundly responsible and demanding position—by which I mean both job and social location—late-nineteenth-century bourgeois wifehood and maternity was situated at a point of historically specified stress that, in the new discourse of health and pathology, identified as ill the woman who failed to perform its functions perfectly. For the middle- or upper-middle-class female found herself constrained by contradictions and necessarily responding to conflicting cultural demands on both body and psyche. A less industrially developed society might merely have demanded that women be fat and fertile; a more aristocratic society might have removed mothering responsibilities from upper-class women, delegating the rearing of their children to nurses and tutors; and a less industrialized and business-centered society might not have needed managers, but late-nineteenth-century culture overinscribed the demands on and overrefined the definition of wife- and motherhood. Functioning to produce goods having exchange value, focused on manufacturing and on national and international marketing, late-nineteenth-century Atlantic-community societies had come to value a moralized "productivity" as defining bourgeois manhood. For a bourgeois widow like Emmy von N., who was faced with an impossibly defined task, an unreachable idealization incompatible with the demands of everyday life, motherhood imposed a set of responsibilities that might increasingly incapacitate her. Serving the social goals of productivity, the ethicizing hypostatization of "motherhood" produced an overdetermined cultural position even as its increasingly visible usefulness in an exchange economy fashioned a specifically tailored set of functions to define the creature who could fulfill its contractual demands and practice its sociologized skills.

Mitchell failed to see the relationship of the rest cure to the cultural valuation of domestic economies because, in the 1870s, the status of this belief as ideology had not yet become available for scrutiny. He represented the hysteric from within a valuation of productivity that viewed her as simply incapable of functioning and, therefore, as monstrous. Her "caprices" and "selfish despotism" made a "willing slave" of mother, sister, or whatever other devoted female relation managed the sickroom; producing care, sympathy, and self-sacrifice to excess, that nurse, in turn, could be consumed by the incapacitated girl. A "vampire who suck[ed] the blood" of healthy household members, the hysteric could, Mitchell hyperbolized, easily kill three generations of nurses (Mitchell 1879, 36, 96, 37, 32). Mitchell's hysteric, the vortex into which all female household energy was drawn, perverted social and familial relations between women. But her finely drawn figure had not yet brought to light the cultural overdetermination of domestic and somatic economies. Mitchell left untheorized the household exchanges at work in the sickroom as well as the home's homologies with larger economic systems in the local, national, and international marketplace. Neither did he analyze the hysteric as situated in a system of bodily consumption and production—and that body as constituted through social systems based on cycles of production and consumption. He replicated a widely held medical and popular notion of bodily economics even as his rest cures naturally reproduced plump and so healthy bodies. Fat and blood appeared to Mitchell naturally biological, simply material for his "making."

By 1889, Freud nevertheless understood that rest-cure technologies, however problematic, yielded patient benefits beyond the purely physiological. Indeed, Freud sensed that the rest cure produced complaisant subjectivity so well primarily because it worked at the site where soma and psyche converged. Calming while it fattened its patient, the rest cure participated in constructing, even as it drew its sustenance from, normative values about health as signifying lack of excess or anxiety. Doubting that permanent well-being accrued in rest cure or hospital therapies, however, Freud put aside his electrical apparatus and stopped prescribing baths, massage, and feeding up. In Emmy's case, Freud treated a depleted reflex body that needed restoration through material means; while he had initially prescribed systematic kneading and faradization of sensitive muscles for Elisabeth von R., he was nevertheless "preparing the ground for psychical treatment" (*SE*, 2: 138). And, although he did not understand the connection between Elisabeth's uncommon hysterical symptoms and the events of her illness, Freud knew her symptoms had seized on an organic disorder to signify a psychical meaning. Like Charcot before him, Freud had "abandoned the treatment of organic nervous diseases"—an unpromising profession, he said, in any event. Unlike Charcot, however, he had begun treating the "crowds of neurotics" who hurried, their problems unsolved, from one physician to another (*SE*, 20: 17). The treatments this crowd of neurotics consumed sought to persuade, rationalize, hypnotize, and moralize patients into health. Historically originating in hospital-based treatment technologies of "moral management," such psychical treatments, as I show in Section III of this chapter, illustrated the complex notions of health produced, by synecdoche, from soma to sociality and recirculated back to institutionalized managements of the body. In Section II of this chapter, however, I examine historically earlier, even if simultaneously occurring, hospital-based isolation therapy, a disciplinary treatment in which the charisma and authority of the physician made the disordered patient into a docile and well-disciplined subject.

II

Born out of carceral treatments for seemingly dangerous members of the underclass, European psychotherapies became respectable when redesigned to treat dysfunctional members of the middle and upper classes. When shopping for a doctor, the soon-to-be-named Wolf-Man was referred to Geneva's foremost psychotherapist, Paul Dubois, and to Vienna's new psychoanalyst, Sigmund Freud. The Russian aristocratic expatriate and his primary physician, journeying toward Switzerland, stopped first in Vienna and, after one visit, chose Freud as analyst. The prospective patient described meeting Freud as "encountering a great personality": his "penetrating" gaze, "self-assured manner," and "inner serenity" immediately inspired confidence. Compelled and attracted by the great man's personality, the Wolf-Man gave up the medicalizing treatments of sanitarium, bath, and rest cure to begin "working together" with Freud, who, he said, exercised a "purely human influence" on his patients. In addition, Freud fully explained to this patient his "new science of the human psyche," which corrected classic psychiatry's definition of nervous illness as somatic. This nevertheless tutelary figure "educat[ed]" his patient in psychoanalysis, in making unconscious material conscious. Describing this theoretical shift from soma to psyche and the changed treatment modes that accompanied it, Freud insisted that the Wolf-Man must talk his way to improved mental functioning. "Up to now," Freud told the Wolf-Man, who was obsessed by anal and sexual primal scenes, "you have been looking for the cause of your illness in your chamber pot" (Wolf-Man 1971, 135–44).

The move toward psychical therapy had begun with moral treatment. Championed by Pinel as early as the 1820s and theorized by Jean Esquirol in 1832, the moral treatment's primary therapeutic strategy, hospital sequestration or "isolation," stressed the twin themes of the physician's healing influence and the neuropathic family. Grounded in the sensationalist psychology of pathological milieus, isolation therapy removed patients from their habitual activities, submitted them—willingly or unwillingly—to activities in a domain governed by the physician and reconstructed their psychologies by banning pathological ideas. It represented the patient's family, not as blameworthy, but as incidentally involved with madness through its proximal care of an insane group member.[12] In "Hysteria" (1888), Freud reported that the disease demanded treatment with "isolation from the circle in which the outbreak occurred" and "removal of the patient from his regular conditions." Isolation enabled strict medical supervision and close physician attention to patient problems; avoidance of "all emotional excitement" soothed stimulated nerves; and application by hospital attendants of a "strengthening remedy"—massage, faradization, and bathing—encouraged health, Freud said, regardless of the disorder's severity. Freud prescribed for his upper-middle-class patients four to eight weeks of bed rest at a good sanitarium, hydrotherapy, gymnastics, and attendance by a trained nurse. A "happy combination" of traitement moral and rest cure, hospital sequestration supported the physician's moralizing influence with nutritive technologies deployed in an institutional setting. Freud called the recovery produced in this strictly regulated hospital environment "magical and permanent" (SE, 1: 54–55; French in the original).

Unlike the rest cure, moral treatments must be interpreted as originally disciplinary. Rather than infantilize, reparent, and reeducate the mentally disordered individual, the physician punished and reconstructed her. At midcentury, the British ophthalmologist Robert Brudenell Carter translated isolation directly to private practice from the asylum, institutionalizing patients in home-based or private board-and-care operations

under a regulated system that produced even as it deployed strict physician authority. Carter "train[ed]" the unstable, childish, and passionate
women who had been voluntarily placed in his care by dictating their
habitual activities and moral behaviors. They had to eat what and when
the doctor commanded and behave like ladies. If a patient violated the
boarding family's rules, she was to be shut up alone in a room, or, if in
company, shunned by the family members, who had been instructed to
remain silent in such cases. Carter's reconstruction program, as he called
it, punished bad-tempered girls, destroyed "bad habits and deceptive
practices," inculcated "good principles" and "good conduct," and so fashioned a tractable female subjectivity. Importing to England what the
French alienists called a *relation de tutelle* between authoritative doctor
and reconstructable patient, Carter sought to articulate a specialized
medical tutelage. He advised physicians carefully to select the moment
they struck the treatment's "first blow," whose "direction," "force," and
"power" determined "patient submission or resistance"—and any opposition, he warned, could render inefficient the doctor's "weapons of defence" (Carter 1883 [1853], 115–46).

This figurative war against the patient could best be waged, moreover,
in specialized hospitals for hysteria. Although Carter justified his project
(as would Charcot 40 years later) by touting its "great benefits" to "society
at large," the institution he proposed to create would incarcerate miscre-
ant working-class females. "Industrial" and financially "self-supporting,"
it would enforce occupation and labor, well spiced with gymnastic exer-
cises and, strangely enough, pugilistic training. When allied with an "em-
igrant society," the hospital would teach inmates the duties of colonial
wife- and motherhood and so, presumably, make them voluntarily or involuntarily available for transportation to the colonies. These malingering
patients, he implied, whose hysterical diseases simulated organic symptoms, deserved the treatment they endured.[13] Although it attracted little
attention in 1853, Carter's disciplinary sequestration regime appears in-
credibly prescient, and would seem historically appropriate—if severely
in need of revision—by the 1870s, the heyday of rest cures for the middle
class.

In European hospitals for the poor, however, isolation remained a
viable moral treatment. In the 1880s, Charcot advanced the implicit,
emerging critique of bourgeois marital and familial alliance that justified
sequestration regimes. The Salpêtrière's theoreticians represented the physician as an authoritative—indeed, charismatic—professional and the pa-

tient's family as neuropathic. Hysterical patients, Charcot said, demanded competent, authoritative, and experienced management—"a kind but firm hand, a calm demeanour, and much patience." After the recalcitrant parents of one hysterical, anorexic outpatient acquiesced to hospitalization at the Salpêtrière, the incarcerated girl began to eat, submitted to hydrotherapy, and recovered, confessing to Charcot that his "triumph" over papa and mamma, his "determin[ation] to be master," had convinced her of her disease's seriousness and persuaded her to stop practicing self-starvation.[14] Deploying these tactics, Charcot—like Mitchell—fattened his hysteric, constructed a no-longer-wasted daughter, and justified his isolatory regime by a charismatic performance of benevolent professional paternalism. Advocating an outpatient's removal from home and separation from parents and family, Charcot blamed a mother's séance for the epidemistic paroxysms of her three young children. Parental influence had proved in this case, Charcot said, "particularly pernicious." For although most parents fostered their children's deceits, this mother had yielded to her children's every whim, had created a deleterious environment in which epidemism, imitation, and deceit flourished, while the overly solicitous father had belligerently opposed hospitalization. Housed at the Salpêtrière, away from their pathogenic parents and separately from one another, he said, the children gradually recovered.[15]

But Charles Féré, the clinic's expert, perfected disciplinary treatment technologies to superintend the neuropathic working-class family. Féré proposed that, being hereditarily predisposed to nervous disorder, degenerate parents inevitably transmitted disease to their neurotic children. The Salpêtrière's hysterogenic parents, moreover, intensified even as they sought to soothe their offsprings' fits, and, in a perversion of generational nervous energy, could themselves contract nerves from their children. Often infected by alcoholism, syphilis, or other hereditary diseases linked with social or sexual transgression, this working-class family's disorders could be cured only in a sanitized space from which such immoral influences were expunged. For, Féré speculated, domestic disorder infected, not just the diseased body or family, but the body politic as well. Seeking to restore and maintain social homeostasis, Féré recommended juridical regulation of degenerate families and prescribed wide-scale public health and sex-education regimes for France's children.[16] And, once in place, these health-inducing programs could spread as readily as had the illness that had spawned them, when recovered individuals carried well-being back to degenerate affiliative groups. In already well-regulated families,

Féré implied, the conjugal unit completed the physician's paternalistic task, supporting the good habits learned as protection against the dangers of working-class life.

The psychotherapies that emerged contemporaneously with isolation fashioned functional individuals able to perform the work routines and sustain the social relations appropriate to their class positions. Dubois practiced psychotherapy on sequestered middle-class nervous patients; Joseph-Jules Dejerine, on working-class invalids. At the Salpêtrière, Dejerine's post–Charcot wards—called the Salle Pinel—linked an outdated disciplinary isolation with surveillance to regulate the body, and with humanistic tutelage to teach correct moral thinking. A powerful head nurse oversaw well-regimented wards, and the doctor prohibited trips home, letters, visitors, or social conversation; nightly psychotherapeutic sessions reeducated misguided minds. When they were removed from neuropathic families, these disordered individuals responded well to tutelary discipline. No longer plagued by inappropriate involuntary movements, disabling anesthetic zones, unwanted mental representations, weakened will, and morbid ideas, the working-class women hospitalized in Dejerine's service gradually returned to life outside the Salpêtrière as functionalized and normal individuals. Esquirol, who had heartily endorsed isolation as a treatment for the masses, had theorized it as monitoring deviance among a populace that endangered the social order; Dejerine added liberal benevolence to sequestration and surveillance of patient behaviors. But by century's end, disciplinary regimes seemed appropriate only for working-class patients, who, if they were lucky, might find themselves in Dejerine's strict but nurturing care.[17] The middle-class medical consumer, Dejerine knew, demanded sympathy and solicitude from the physician, and professionalized charismatic discipline had gone out of style.

By the 1890s, psychical treatment tailored for the middle classes had begun to treat the mind rather than the body. Less disciplinary but no less functionalizing than hospital sequestration, Paul Dubois's psychotherapy relaxed the rest cure's regulations, permitting hospitalized patients to read, sew, walk, and have visitors, allowing patients to board in the countryside and live, he said, just as they liked. Yet, like Mitchell, Dubois reeducated nervous, helpless women, who, under his care, learned the cardinal virtues of middle-class life, willed productivity and determined capability. After examining a hysteric who had failed to improve with rest, hydrotherapy, strychnine injections, and ovariotomy, Dubois diagnosed not organic paralysis but feelings of helplessness and powerlessness. "Your trouble is psychic, entirely psychic," he explained to his hysteric; "you have no need of material treatment." "Very well," this intelligent and tractable patient replied, "I see that I must change my whole manner of looking at my trouble. Why has nobody told me this before?" Days later, she sat up in bed, opened the curtains, wrote a letter, and wiggled her feet. "All the old helplessness of nine years' standing had disappeared under the influence of an idea," Dubois claimed.[18] Like the cops, monarchists, and enslavers Dubois troped as controlling human volition, the therapist reregulated the will to limit patient expectations and intentions, fashioning individuals who wanted less from life and so could purposefully function within their newly defined needs. Indeed, as Canguilhem suggests, the middle-class nineteenth-century individual had assimilated the sociologized notions of self-diagnosis, self-limitation, and self-renunciation; had adopted the values of long life, uninterrupted work, resistance to fatigue, and absence of pain—all lived out as though they possessed relatively stable meanings for individual experience, however elusive and ever-expanding they might seem. After having undergone Dubois's psychic treatment, one satisfied Geneva patient said, "the will drops passively into the beaten path" that "sentiment and reason have worn for it" (Dubois 1908 [1905], 54–57).

While Dubois represented the physician as exercising the tutelary skills of sympathy, patience, gentleness, and tolerance, he nevertheless saw patient recovery as dependent on his authoritative, if unobtrusive, use of power. Although he knew threats and intimidation produced medical results, Dubois deplored treatments imposed "crudely and by constraint" upon "susceptible ladies" by doctors ready themselves to exercise (and to recommend to husbands) "too severe an oversight" of patient activities. If imposed upon an invalid without her consent, Dubois maintained, psychic therapy would not work (ibid., 356). Still, Dubois sometimes quietly bullied his patients into freely choosing psychic treatment. Early in his career, he used "therapeutic feints" or a "little subterfuge" to heighten the effects of hypnotic suggestion: he prohibited a girl's return to her congenial boarding-school and recommended home recovery instead, and her cough immediately disappeared; he told a mute girl she would talk the next day and prescribed a harmless painkiller, and, minutes after swallowing the pill, she spoke (ibid., 313–18). When the "rebellious" Mlle H——— claimed that she could not suppress her convulsive attacks by "voluntary effort," Dubois threatened to submit her to surveillance by a nun she hated; the patient came to her senses, Dubois said, got into her bed, and voluntarily controlled her convulsions (ibid., 425–29, 351–55, 394). Although these negative suggestions obviated patient policing, Dubois nevertheless demanded that the patient purposefully embrace his own version of voluntarism, demonstrate confidence in his diagnosis, and evidence docility and tractability if she wanted to heal. Describing the physician as a "man of heart" able to "put himself in the place of those who suffer," Dubois troped therapeutic power as emanating, not from an "iron hand" in a "velvet glove," but from a "sensitive" hand that, extended to the patient, offered him company on the journey to health (ibid., 277, 357).

Yet psychical treatment's power ultimately derived from the doctor's ability to persuade the patient to embrace moral action. Because a "little philosophic counsel" treated nerves more effectively than "half an hour's faradization," Dubois prescribed daily patient-doctor conversations. He questioned his patients about their childhood circumstances, familial relations, and sexual lives; and he permitted patients to talk without interruption—even when "confessions" became "prolix and diffuse" (ibid., 234–43). He tolerated, indulged, and forgave his hysterics' whims and caprices, reorienting them toward positive future goals. He counseled Mme W—— to cultivate altruism for husband and family as an antidote to her helplessness, self-reproach, "diseased egoism," and "increasing incapacity." He advised Mme V—— to return to her "normal life," but not, it would seem, to rejoin the husband and daughter from whom she had lived apart while studying philosophy (ibid., 428–29, 388–91). Although he rejected Roman Catholic confessionalism, as appropriated and deployed by the psychotherapeutic movement, Dubois delivered "sermons" on stoicism and optimism; exhorting that patients choose to recover, he said, he "preached" the "conviction" of "assured cure" to chronically disabled patients.[19] Representing his vocation as pastoral, then, the psychotherapist had himself become minister to psychoneurotics burdened by the dark anxieties of incapacity, lack of will, and feelings of helplessness.

Freud and Breuer's new clinical practice met the historical requirements for designation as a psychotherapy. Yet Freud had nothing but contempt for what he called "ethical encouragement" or "moral instruction." Dubois's patients, he later sneered, left treatment with "feelings of contrition" and "the best resolutions," but any "clergyman" could have given similar advice.[20] How, Freud wondered, could persuasion produce an improved, although constrained, individual voluntarism? How could traumatically induced symptoms be preached away? As Freud struggled to differentiate hysterical from organic paralysis and so to revise current theories of psycho-physical correlation and psychopathological causation, he moved not toward psychical treatment but toward hypnosis. He wanted, after all, to treat an enigmatic ailment that involved the soma in the psyche's griefs, that inscribed in and on the body the symptoms of personal suffering. Persuasive psychotherapy left the body out of treatment; rest cure, the mind. Neurologists, he said, accounted for hysterical paralyses by assuming them to be "founded on slight functional disturbances of the same parts of the brain which, when they were severely damaged, led to the corresponding organic paralyses" (*SE*, 19: 191). Freud worked, then, to invent a psycho-physical treatment that could cure both psychical difficulties and symptomatic physiological ills. Hypnosis seemed the most promising possibility, for as Hippolyte Bernheim had said, "tout est dans la suggestion" (quoted in *SE*, 1: 101).

Yet the cures practiced at Nancy, I argue in the next section, were no less functionalizing and physiologically based than was the rest cure. For despite the insistence on suggestion as "key" to hypnosis, Bernheim's hospital treated the reflex nervous body. It returned to productive and domestic work normalized subjects able to live within the constraints of working-class marital, family, and social relations. Functionalizing the sick individual, Bernheim's cure normalized the sufferer who had fallen ill through the operations of pathological milieus: the factory laborer, the sex worker, the domestic manager, the overburdened student. Freud's attempt to follow Bernheim's therapeutic practices, when he had rejected Charcot's, made it possible to treat the bourgeois subject who intended to follow, yet failed to heed, the normalizing formulas of social, and proscriptive, regimes. Hypnotically treating his haute bourgeois female patients, as had Bernheim, Freud failed to produce conscious capacity and willful endeavor as cure. He discovered, instead, that unconscious counter-ideation sabotaged capable acts, fully embraced choices, and willful intentions. Yet Bernheim's attempt to functionalize the reflex body made it possible for Freud to treat his frustrated, dysfunctional, and unhappy patients differently.

III

"We suppress the pain, we modify function, we let the organ rest, we calm the fever, we retard the pulse, we induce sleep, we encourage secretion and excretion, and, acting thus, we permit nature the healer . . . to accomplish [her] work." Bernheim used this humble claim to justify the spectacular hypnotic cures and elaborate experimental apparatus that Freud had witnessed at Nancy. The physician applied to the body "only functional medicament," and hypnotic therapy proved to be one of his best functionalizing treatments. Bernheim's "medicine of the imagination" helped the patient transcend the disease's complaints, for rather than provoke contracture, paralysis, pain, or anesthesia as had Charcot, Bernheim's therapeutics neutralized such morbid phenomena by displacing patient attention from them (Bernheim 1886, 408–9, 207). "Pain," Bernheim said, quoting Joseph Delboeuf, "makes the patient think of his trouble; and thinking of it, he exaggerates it. Hypnotism, which distracts his attention, acts in a contrary way upon the pain; it diminishes it by making us think no more of it" (ibid., 411). Mending the mind, Bernheim believed, meant helping the patient notice the body as little as possible. Although Freud believed that Bernheim's imaginative medication traduced the boundary between voluntary bodily action and involuntary ideation, Bernheim himself treated the reflex, material body, invoking ideation only when moral-ethical questions of capability and character were at stake (*SE*, 20: 17). Indeed, the conflict between Bernheim's school at Nancy and Charcot's at the Salpêtrière had focused, at least in part, on whether hypnotism weakened healthy individual wills and character. And, as Bernheim knew, those questions necessarily involved social relations.

Bernheim updated the earlier medical concept of pathological milieus by locating his deviant patients firmly in social hierarchies and functionalized spaces. His working-class clients brought to the hospital a variety of organic and nervous complaints directly linked to their work routines and everyday lives. An accountant worried about his debilitating writer's cramp; a housepainter suffered from lead poisoning, three dressmakers from hand tremors, and a student from inability to concentrate; bricklayers, miners, railway workers, and laborers presented painful neuralgias; servant girls needed treatment for physical injuries, anorexia, and unwanted pregnancies or births—the hazards of life in the streets or work in an upper-class family (whose sons and fathers might well view the domestic worker as sexually available). Like his pregnant and battered serving-girl patient, Bernheim's other female subjects presented symptoms linked to domestic (but middle-class) life: married women had endured miscarriages, stillbirths, marital separations, divorce, and family violence; mothers who had borne and nursed many children suffered obstetrical or menstrual complications; a teenage prostitute who had left her family because of "domestic trouble" presented with neuralgia, anorexia, anesthesia, catarrh, and attacks of weeping. Whether male or female, Bernheim's patients suffered, his case studies suggested, primarily from work-related complaints. Participating in and helping promote the new "science of labor," Bernheim studied, noted, inscribed, and treated the fatigued and ill working body that had demonstrated its inability to perform industrial tasks, social functions, and technical duties. Indeed, the science of work depended on the processes and functions of industrial, as opposed to artisanal or skilled, labor, and those laborers increasingly found their way to research laboratories, outpatient clinics, or hospitals like Bernheim's and Ambroise Liébault's (see Rabinbach 1986, 489–98).

Whether they labored in factory, parlor, mine, or shop, these persons' productivity, their ability to perform routine or assigned tasks while on the job, governed their movements into and out of the hospital. If they could not work, they hospitalized themselves, often repeatedly. A miller, unable to labor for a month, entered the hospital; he left weeks later, able to resume work; remained well and worked for three weeks; fell ill; and returned to the hospital once more. If patients could not function at work, they identified themselves as sick; the clinic's staff agreed and so diagnosed them. Had these men and women continued laboring, neither they nor their doctors would have defined their conditions as demanding treatment. The student, for example, hysterical since early adolescence, sought no medical help while he "was not incapacitated for work" or "study"; when he became "powerless to work physically or intellectually," his physician referred him to Bernheim. Indeed, restored patient ability to perform tasks served Bernheim's experiments well, for hypnotized female patients sometimes worked around the hospital, sweeping wards, ironing linen, making beds, or washing windows, all while being observed. When they were able to return to work, the hospital designated patients as "cured." "Goes out as servant and does her work well," Bernheim wrote about one young female hysteric; of a baccalaureate student, he said, for "three years he has been unable to work as he has worked this evening, three consecutive hours" (Bernheim 1886, 296, 293, 315–18, 306, 375, 293).

Although he failed to theorize women's reproductive and domestic routines as "labor," Bernheim's female patients, like his male ones, reported renewed ability to demonstrate performance and capability at work as central to notions of cure. Despite residual choreic movements, a teacher instructed her class; a young factory girl "returned to work" after four weeks' absence; a young dressmaker, unable to walk after having been kicked by her drunken husband while she was pregnant, could move around the shop without pain (ibid., 311, 325–26). The hospital's cures, moreover, aimed to produce, not only effective, but happy, contented, and self-satisfied individuals. Wives once again loved husbands; mothers breast-fed their babies; "*insubordinat[e]*," "*indolen[t]*," and "disobedient" children no longer ran away from home, wet their beds at night, threatened to kill themselves, or threw "fits of passion" (ibid., 320–21, 339–40, 350–53). Bernheim's therapeutics helped the body, he said, by "provok[ing] useful reflexes" and, through "cerebral docility," transformed ideas of cure into "reality" (ibid., 133). By "reality," Bernheim clearly meant something like "useful everyday life," a life in which his patients felt well and acted fully functionally. The suggestive-hypnotic cure implanted and affirmed patients' ideas of physiological ableness and mental health, turning nervous individuals toward positive personal and social goals—goals appropriate, of course, to their position as members of the working class. These patients, whose labor enabled their survival, returned to work capable of performing their assigned tasks and fulfilling their obligations in an industrialized, contractual society. Canguilhem's notions of the concept of health, discussed earlier in this chapter, correctly identify nineteenth-century subjects as valuing the "capacity for reproduction and for physical work, strength, resistance to fatigue, [and] the absence of pain." Bernheim's functional medicine, then, produced a highly desirable mental state, in which his patients noticed the reflex body as little as possible, aside from the sense of health.[21]

The medical definition of health, as Bernheim's case studies demonstrate and Canguilhem suggests, is both economically based and historically situated. Physical and psychical wellness and the capacity to perform work signified normality in the late nineteenth century at least in part because an increasingly industrialized society demanded such labor. The articulation of well body with healthy mind, in fact, was grounded in a notion of contractual balance between parallel aspects of the person. John Hughlings Jackson's and Freud's theories of psycho-physical correlation and psychopathological causation, despite their differences, could thus appropriately become available for conceptualization, and so be produced, in a society whose economic and manufacturing sectors both supported and helped construct such notions of normality. And as Bernheim's hospital shows, not just the definition of health (as produced by the social structures with which it cooperated), or wellness's relationship to labor per se, but the motive and incentive for putting these definitions and articulations into practice on a large, institutionalized scale served to help fashion and then mythologized the able reflex body as central to healthy subjectivity. Bernheim's hospital technologized and institutionalized the production of functionally able individuals capable of sustaining their efforts to work. Invoking but transforming early-nineteenth-century medical notions about pathological milieus—the workplace, the troubled family—Bernheim participated in sustaining the circulation of value and profit in a society that contracted for wellness.

Bernheim's cure also participated in a culturally defined gendering and moralizing of work that obscured, even as it depended upon, contractual economies. Bernheim hoped that moralizing suggestion would prevent an ex-prostitute inmate from taking lovers: she had become "docile" and "reserved" and would no longer walk the city with "unmistakable companions of her profession." But this girl refused to go home to her family, took again to the streets, and became once more a *puella publica* (Bernheim 1886, 307). Rather than return her to work, the hospital aimed to rehabilitate her for the more appropriate sexual labor of eventual wife- and motherhood. Yet her continuing participation in erotic economic transactions outside the home, transactions unaccompanied by emotional exchange, meant she had not been cured; her body's location in social space outside the domestic domain, her choice to walk openly in the streets, her intention to sell sexual pleasures to men able and willing to pay, all defined her labor as work—but as unproductive. Her sexually available female body, an unreproductive male pleasure, and the public display of sexual economies normally romanticized and contained in the home vindicated the clinic's continued identification of this worker as "sick." While the capacity to labor usually constituted the definition of cure, paid sexual work by working-class women for the benefit of working- and middle-class men did not count. Medical-ethical hypostatizations of capability both justified the technologizing of health and normativity and identified some work and some workers as outside the system that valued, shaped, and sustained wellness.

Although he treated bourgeois and haute bourgeois rather than working-class patients, Freud's early hypnotic treatments also functionalized the reflex body. In 1892, Freud implanted posthypnotic suggestions that enabled a hysteric who had failed to breast-feed her first child to nurse her second infant. The young woman struggled against her symptomatic vomiting, insomnia, agitation, and depression, refusing to eat and attempting to feed her child despite her apparent lack of milk. The woman's "capability," Freud believed, her "quiet common sense" and "naturalness," made her a good candidate for cure. Like Bernheim, he used suggestion to regulate the reflex body; he therefore contradicted his somnambulous patient's anxieties and exchanged her unwelcome ideas with his own functional and normalizing moralisms. "Have no fear!" he commanded; "You will make an excellent nurse and the baby will thrive." After hypnosis, the woman ate her evening meal, slept, and successfully fed her infant the next morning. When the next meal caused relapse, however, Freud implanted the suggestion that his patient angrily accuse her family of disabling her nursing by starving her; and despite her husband's surprise at her subsequent outburst, the woman was cured—and this time it took. After her third confinement and another successful treatment, Freud's hysterical patient confessed why she had proven so difficult a patient and her family had appeared so ungrateful: she had been ashamed that hypnosis had worked to cure her when, notwithstanding all her "will-power," *she* had felt utterly "helpless" (*SE*, 1: 117–20).

Confronted with this hysteric's exasperated hopelessness, Freud felt forced to conceptualize the involuntary mental processes involved in hypnotic cure. For this young mother was determined to carry out her "intention" of breast-feeding and, although she set out to accomplish her task without hesitation, she behaved as though she had willfully chosen "not to feed the child on any account." The "psychical mechanism" of his patient's "disorder," Freud said, demonstrated that "*intentions*" or "*expectations*" could, depending on the individual's certainty or doubt of an intention's or expectation's outcome as action, produce antithetical ideas that undermined willful choices. "I shall not succeed in carrying out my intention," a patient might ruminate, "because this or that is too difficult for me and I am unfit to do it." While individuals endowed with the "powerful self-confidence of health" suppressed, inhibited, and denied antithetic ideas, the neurotic patient paid "great attention" to counterintentions. In neurasthenia, intensification of "volitional ideas" and concomitant "distrust of the subject's own capacity" produced "*weakness* of will"; in hysteria, dissociation of consciousness disconnected intention from volition and, as a consequence, the inhibited antipathetic idea "put itself into effect [*sich objektiviert*]" by "innervation of the body" producing "*perversion* of will." Aware of and astonished by her own "resolute but powerless" will, a patient would become victimized by "*counter-will*" (*SE*, 1: 120–23;

Freud's emphases). In this case of "occasional hysteria," Freud had revised hypnotic treatment beyond Bernheim's imaginative medication by foregrounding the attractions of incapacity, helplessness, and dysfunction.

Indeed, Freud here began a project to reinvent late-nineteenth-century notions of the functional subject. His lexicon of perverted will and counterwill, for example, of his patient's lack of self-assertion and failure to perform, brought to light in a new way the problem of voluntary acts. The young mother's desperate insistence on her own willpower—as with Freud's on her capability, her heroic struggles against her disorder, and her earlier and painful renunciation of nursing—illustrated the centrality of instrumental will to late-nineteenth-century individuals and their families. This woman's fury at her inability to succeed opened an ever-larger space of voluntary functioning to which she aspired but which she could not reach; it emphasized as well her family's inadequacy to cope with incapacity. For not only had this hysteric's biologico-moral functions of feeding and emotional bonding been deemed, after her first birth, a "failure," but that failure had also necessitated the hiring of a wet nurse and, after the second birth, of two family doctors (including Breuer) and a specialist in hypnosis (Freud himself). Happily for its functioning, this family could afford to hire such medical professionals, whose work for members of the upper classes was particularly labor-intensive. The doctor's psychologizing of voluntarity, moreover, covered over a moralizing imperative. When the patient's body became "innervated," its nerves overstimulated and so unable to convey messages from brain to milk glands, she could be characterized as suffering, not from disease, but from disorder or perversion (SE 1: 118–23). Yet Freud's *hystérique d'occasion* could not control her behavior. While she fell ill only in the breast-feeding situation and on those occasions when called upon to nurse her newborns, involuntary ideas paralyzed her body's voluntary actions and activities. The nursing situation identified pure volitionality and full individual capacity as powerful incentives to moral and dutiful action, as highly respected domestic virtues, and as reified desires.[22] The wasted or hysterical woman seemed herself proof that the space of the purely voluntary, the will to perfect performance, and the normativity of health, had become thoroughly problematic by century's end.

Successful treatment in Freud's case of occasional hysteria addressed the link of moral intention with bodily incapacity. Although he had represented pure will as an ideal, Freud nevertheless proposed increased capability as one definition of cure, for neurotics were "incapable of enjoyment and of efficiency" (SE, 2: 154; SE, 16: 453). Hypnosis could functionalize these patients by ridding them of painful or anxious ideas and implanting "effective counter-ideas." Physicians who opposed hypnotic suggestion by defending a supposedly imperiled "personal free-will" and psychiatrists who dosed their patients with bromide, morphine, or chloral, both failed to understand this, Freud said: patients suffered less and "perform[ed] their duties better" after they'd been hypnotized (SE, 1: 93–94). Hypnotic treatment, then, proved more successful than purely reflex physiological or persuasive psychical treatments would. Indeed, Freud judged his and Breuer's hysterics, Anna O., Emmy, Lucy, and Elisabeth, as restored to health when each, relieved of mental anguish, became "capable of successful effort" at intellectual or domestic work (SE, 2: 154). Freud had restored his occasional hysteric to a health uninterrupted by inappropriate involuntary ideas, weakened will, and morbid ideas; hypnotic suggestion had normalized her bodily reflexes, resituated them in domestic systems of labor, and returned the body to its reproductive tasks. Without having infantilized or reeducated her, Freud had returned the hysteric to household and family functioning, making her a productive wife and mother, or other worker. Yet he had also begun to formulate theories of psycho-physical causation, to complicate modes of treatment for the reflex body, and to conceptualize the counterideation that would eventually hybridize nineteenth-century notions of fully capable—or of reeducated, tutelary—subjectivity.

Freud provided numerous reasons, retrospectively, for having rejected hypnosis as his central treatment technology. First, he said, he found it unreliable. Because it did not treat hysteria's causes, it only temporarily alleviated the disease's symptoms. A "capricious" treatment with "lack of permanen[t]" effects, hypnosis worked with some patients but not with others, and the doctor never knew why; it did not prevent the adoption of new symptoms to replace the old or protect against relapse (SE, 16: 449–50). Precisely because she invariably relapsed, he had brought to Nancy a hysterical "woman of good birth" whom he hoped Bernheim could cure; but failing, too, to somnambulize her, Bernheim confessed that, whereas suggestive treatment worked in his hospital's amphitheater, it did not in his private practice, where Freud and this hysteric apparently consulted him (SE, 20: 17–18). Indeed, Freud could neither replicate in his Vienna consulting room the "suggestive atmosphere" and hypnotic *milieu* of Bernheim's hospital and Liébault's outpatient clinic nor persuade his "patients of a higher social class" to discuss their ailments "before a large crowd"; he treated patients "*tête-à-tête*" instead, which posed a new problem (*SE*, 1: 100, 107–8 [French in the original]). When an especially acquiescent patient embraced him after waking from hypnotic sleep, for example, Freud "was modest enough," he said, not to attribute it to his own "irresistible personal attraction"; after the embrace, physician and patient tacitly agreed to discontinue treatment. Grasping the mysterious erotic element that produced hypnotic rapport, Freud strengthened his decision to abandon hypnotism (*SE*, 16: 449–50; *SE*, 20: 27).

Not the patient's seduction while hypnotized, however, but hypnosis's seduction of the doctor accounts for Freud's insistent repetitions of this anecdote. Working with hypnosis was "positively seductive," Freud said, because it overcame his feelings of "helplessness" to cure nervous disorders. Indeed, when the occasional hysteric, to whom he had restored the ability to breast-feed, and her family, to whom he had returned a functional, dutiful household manager, failed to welcome him as "saviour in the hour of need" or to note his "remarkable achievement," Freud found their recalcitrance and grudging thanks more than a little annoying. For he thoroughly enjoyed the "reputation" he had achieved as a hypnotic "miracle-worker," the "credit" he had been given for "great therapeutic success" (*SE, 20*: 17; *SE*, 1: 106, 119–20; *SE*, 2: 164). Freud's sense of and desire for success, however, involved the charismatic professionalism common to tutelary cures; reimagined and retheorized, that tutelary relation, structured by grids of power and helplessness, would appear in psychoanalysis as transference and countertransference, and would invoke the affective, unconscious, and intersubjective structures of analytic work. When Freud recommended that Emmy replace warm baths with cool ones, for example, she had objected but said that she would try again, if he liked; he implanted the posthypnotic suggestion that she ask for cool baths; when the cold bath depressed her, Freud told her that she had "asked for it." She would forget earlier therapies, he suggested, and stammer when trying to name the sanitarium where she had been treated; she did. She would ask Freud for wine at lunch, although she did not drink it; she did. She would find that no doctor but Freud could successfully hypnotize her; she did. The outcome of this "struggle," as Freud called it, preserved even as it produced the hypnotist's power and authority. And although Freud acknowledged that he had "abuse[d]" hypnosis by playing "practical joke[s]" on Emmy, he had not yet transmuted the charisma he had witnessed, as spectacle, at Nancy and the Salpêtrière into transferential power (*SE*, 2: 101, 108, 80, 67–68, 84–85). Nevertheless, having inherited a "legacy" from the hypnotists, Freud summarized, psychoanalysts were the "legitimate heirs" to that power (*SE*, 19: 192; *SE*, 16: 462).

Freud's insistence that psychoanalysis originated in hypnosis, which appears often in his historicizing texts, has been widely misunderstood.[23] As my Freudian epigraph to this book demonstrates, Freud viewed psychoanalytic emergence, as do I, as a multiply determined and highly mediated event, as a palimpsestic set of discursive acts, transmissions, and recursive activities. While in some documents he doggedly insisted on his own scientific priority and on the myth of his lonely creationism, in others he carefully assessed the influence of various scientific discourses on his own theoretical production. And hypnotic research in the 1880s, he maintained in 1923, had produced a "decisive turn" in theories about the "enigmatic" disease, hysteria—"prototype" for the "whole species" of neuroses. Hypnosis addressed psychical questions that the neurologists— with their respect for "chemico-physical and pathologico-anatomical facts," for the physiological research of Gustav Hitzig and Eduard Fritsch, David Ferrier and Friedrich Goltz—had neglected. Indeed, Bernheim's work had demonstrated that "mental influences" could produce "somatic changes" and, because of posthypnotic behavior, those mental processes could be described as "unconscious"; through hypnotism, the unconscious had become "something actual, tangible and subject to experiment." Its deployment at Nancy, Freud said, had moved hypnotism into "the sphere of psychology." Looking back in 1923, however, Freud clearly inflated the psychical claims of Bernheim's hospital, for the treatments at Nancy could only retrospectively, after the institutionalization of psychoanalysis, be said to have anticipated the emergence of the unconscious as a concept. In a moment of mature but unprecedented generosity, Freud also applauded Janet's contribution to this emergence, even as he circumscribed its value for theories of psycho-physical correlation and psychopathological causation. For despite Janet's belief in constitutional incapacity and hereditary transmission (which limited his experiments' value for psychoanalysis), Janet's hypnotic research on *idées fixes*, Freud said, anticipated the emergence of the unconscious (*SE*, 16: 191–95; *SE*, 1: 75).

Not hypnosis, however, but Breuer's work with Anna O., Freud said, was the "decisive factor" in the emergence of psychoanalysis as a clinical practice. For the first time, the symptoms of a puzzling neurosis "turned out to have a meaning": they involved an "impulse to an action" that had been "suppressed"; they appeared "*in place of* actions that were not performed." The etiology of hysterical symptoms, then, led the researcher to consider "the subject's emotional life (to affectivity) and to the interplay of mental forces (to dynamics)," two concepts central to the historical production and emergence of psychoanalysis (*SE*, 19: 191–93 [Freud's emphasis]; *SE*, 1: 75). And here Freud recursively invoked a concept central to his psycho-physical endeavor. For affect, which he here rather narrowly defined as the "subject's emotional life," had been, in his early work with hysteria, more widely conceived as a psycho-physical category. In the next section of this chapter, I argue that Freud's originary mythology—that psychoanalysis emerged from hypnosis—served to obscure catharsis as "the immediate precursor of psycho-analysis" and to consign Breuer to the ranks of Charcot, Janet, Bernheim, and Mitchell—those perduring yet eclipsed precursors. Indeed, Freud later claimed to have abandoned cathartic treatment because it was merely, he said, a "new medical procedure" (*SE*, 19: 193–94). From my perspective of psychophysical representation, however, Freud's rejection of abreaction and cathartic treatment eliminated from theoretical production the most flexible and capacious psycho-physical concept in the psychoanalytic vocabulary. For the theory of affects that had early been articulated by Breuer linked psycho-physiological behavior patterns, cognitive appraisals, subjective experiences of a pleasurable or painful nature, and a muscular and neurological discharge pattern (Kernberg 1991, 5). Articulating acts, subjective experiences, cognitions, and self- and object representations, a theory of affects could fashion, represent, and clinically treat the modern psycho-physical subject.

IV

The cathartic method deployed the clinical practices of remembering, abreaction, and patient self-representation. While all hypnotic treatments mobilized the "physiological changes" produced by hypnosis to correct the "displacements of [nervous] excitability" that occurred outside consciousness, cathartic treatment retrieved forgotten pathogenic material from the unconscious.[24] A theory of affect anchored and sustained cathartic work, for the patient abreacted displaced excitation only when appropriately affect-laden speech expressed traumatic, hitherto forgotten, events; if a response to stress or trauma was suppressed, the affect associated with it would remain bound and the individual would fall ill. Despite its clinical focus on affect, Freud and Breuer's *Studies on Hysteria*, which I treat in this section as one extended clinical example and theoretical text, almost serendipitously produced the concept of the unconscious and concomitantly proposed repression as the force that constituted its contents. Soon seeking to break with Breuer, moreover, Freud foregrounded repression and sexuality as central to psychoanalysis and so occluded both the concept of affect and the clinical practice of cathartic abreaction. Yet, I maintain, Freud's marginalization of both affect and abreaction removed the innervated body from therapy, foreclosing for the moment theoretical clarification and development of the psycho-physical concepts of repetition behavior, transferential affect-laden acts, and patient self- and other representation. Although the body is everywhere implicated in psychoanalytic practice and theory, Freud fully theorized his psycho-physical notion of representation only recursively, by resurrecting a long-suppressed theory of affect.

Grounding cathartic treatment in notions of reflex action, Breuer made nervous discharge central to the new therapy. External physiological stimuli produced "incitement," he said, which aroused the urge to use "increased excitation functionally"; or it aroused "excitement," which sought discharge, sometimes violently or pathologically. Active affects leveled out increased excitation by "*motor* discharge" (shouting or jumping for joy, increased muscular tension, angry words and retaliatory acts), allowing excitation to "flow away" in movements such as "aimless pacing up and down"; mental pain, too, deployed motor discharge (difficult breathing, acts of secretion such as sobs and tears), but, by association with various ideas of pain, its motor activities released emotion. The physiological disturbances of nervous system dynamic equilibrium by "non-uniform distribution" of excitation, then, produced the "psychical side of affects" and, in mental pain, restricted ideational association. Paralyses, anxieties, or suppressed angers, however, could not discharge in motor acts. To overcome this theoretical difficulty, Breuer again invoked association. These dysfunctional motor states gradually leveled out excitation, substituted nonmotor for motor acts, or associated current ideas with recovered memories. If affects could not discharge excitation either through associative or motor activity, the quota of affect would accumulate, Breuer said, and cause unpleasure (*SE*, 2: 199–203, 223–24).

Because it involved pleasure and unpleasure, Breuer's theory adumbrated a more inclusive psycho-physical category than reflex-action theory alone could propose. While Breuer's method treated the reflex body, it also called into being a conception of the body and, concomitantly, a therapy that functioned through differing notions of psycho-physical correlation and psychopathological causation. For the neurological notion of reflex acts, which suggested the notion of unconscious ideation, Breuer said, solicited a psychic therapeutics. Abreaction treated hysteria by facilitating discharge into motor or associative acts, by unblocking blockages and circulating signifying bodily matter, by producing, for example, the flow of words or tears. Without a bodily act that signified a memory's pathogenic meaning, cathartic treatment could not achieve cure, and that symbolic or signifying act could only be thought about in terms of affect. During catharsis, the patient "gave verbal utterance with the most violent agitation to matters whose accompanying affect had hitherto only found outlet as an expression of emotion." This affect, either an emotive state or a quantity of nervous excitation, had to be discharged by "*energetic reaction*," by acts of the "voluntary or involuntary reflexes" that ranged, Freud said of his psychotherapy, "from tears to acts of revenge." The patient thus "work[ed] off" the "sum of excitation" appropriate to a past and forgotten, now remembered, situation (*SE*, 2: 101, 6–8).

Language often served as "substitute for action," moreover, for the flow of angry, vengeful words could discharge pathological and blocked feeling or excitation. Although deeds most effectively discharged blocked affect, talk alone sometimes sufficed to stand in for reflex acts: an insulted patient, for example, could reply abusively to his enemy even if he could not hit back. Indeed, in some instances of unblocking—in lamentations, tellings of secrets, or confessions, for example—words served as the only substitutes for deeds (*SE*, 2: 8; *SE*, 3: 34–39; *SE*, 2: 40). Hysterical symptoms, Freud said, disappeared when therapy had "*succeeded in bringing clearly to light the memory of the event by which it was provoked and in arousing its accompanying affect, and when the patient had described that event in the greatest possible detail and had put the affect into words*." Cathartic cure, then, produced remembered scenes in which the body was once situated, stimulated neurological and muscular discharge appropriate to those scenes, and so enabled the patient cognitively to appraise and emotionally to assess the past in light of present needs. Although Freud could not yet have articulated this complex concept of psycho-physical affects, he and Breuer had already described its constituent acts and events, psychical structures, and retrospective reconsiderations.[25] "Telling things is a relief," Breuer said, invoking reflex acts as theory; "it discharges tension even when the person to whom they are told is not a priest and even when no absolution follows" (*SE*, 2: 6, 208–211).

In the "Project for a Scientific Psychology," as I argue in Chapter 1, Freud, too, had thought discharge central to theory and clinical practice. Yet he theorized the bodily acts that made discharge meaningful specifically as repetitions and self-representative images. Because the nervous system retained a trace of their sensory qualities, repetitions of painful experiences produced affect, he proposed; when memory of such painful events could no longer arouse affect, the memories became simply mnemic images. If an idea met a conflicting and *"untamed mnemic* image," however, the sensory qualities it retained produced a feeling of unpleasure and an inclination to discharge—together, the two were a particular affect—and so interrupted ideation. Yet Freud was not satisfied with this notion, for, he asked, what "happens to *memories* capable of affect till they are *tamed?"* Repetition could not weaken, for, in theory, it strengthened, an association; memories must thus have been subjugated and bound by the ego, producing facilitations, releasing affect, and stimulating feelings of unpleasure (*SE*, 1: 380–81). Affect, then, especially when theorized neurologically, was a complex psycho-physical event that included reflex discharge, voluntary and involuntary behaviors, ideation and suppressed ideation, remembered images or self-representations, and emotive responses. Acted out during catharsis, such signifying psycho-physical events, widely conceived, could alleviate patient distress.

But why, Breuer and Freud wondered, did hysterical patients fail to discharge excitation through motor acts or abreaction as normal individuals did? The *Studies on Hysteria* everywhere illustrated Freud and Breuer's primary answer, that certain social circumstances caused patients to restrain emotive and motor reactions to stressful or traumatic events (*SE*, 2: 1; and see Laplanche and Pontalis 1973, 2). Their patients' symptoms were invariably, Breuer and Freud observed, embedded in personal histories, themselves embedded in family histories, social relations, and situational circumstances. Anna, Emmy, and Elisabeth, for example, had nursed young and old relatives out of the womb or into the grave, thus sowing in themselves the "seeds of disease." Indeed, Anna's *"absence[s],"* aphasias, hallucinations, and oral disgusts, Emmy's neck cramps and leg pains, and Elisabeth's leg pains and difficulty walking all developed while they nursed sick fathers. In Emmy's case, Freud analyzed these social circumstances precisely as necessitating suppression at an overdetermined site of nurture, sympathy, and biologico-moral responsibility. Emmy's neurotic incapacity, inhibition of will, and fear of performing certain actions originated in demands her mother had made upon her little girl.

She had naughtily refused to eat her meat, Emmy said of her young self;
two hours later, her mother had forced her to eat the cold flesh and congealed fat and had threatened to punish her if she did not. Years later,
Emmy had eaten meals with her sick (perhaps syphilitic) brother yet
feared she would mistakenly eat with his knife and fork and herself fall
ill; soon after, she had nursed her consumptive brother, who spat into an
open spittoon across her dinner plate, and she had hidden her anxious
disgust for fear of hurting him.[26]

Social and familial decorum demanded that Emmy bear the responsibility of daughters and future mothers. She politely suppressed her feelings of physical disgust, subdued the fears her sick siblings aroused, and
quelled the rage her mother's threats caused. Rather than communicate
feelings, this obsessive family economy circulated congealed or contaminated fluids, either into individual bodies or across social spaces, and fashioned a small, helpless subject, situated in an economic matrix, destined
to become speechless and hysterical. Not surprisingly, Emmy had grown
into a responsible mother, businesswoman, intellectual, and haute bourgeois domestic middle manager who suffered periodically from her inability perfectly to control the circulation of nurture, money, and words
within her family and outside her household. For the late-nineteenth-
century bourgeois family that had, as discussed earlier in this chapter,
overinscribed the demands on wives and mothers and overrefined the
definition of wife- and motherhood, made women responsible, not only
for the circulation of goods and emotions in the domestic domain, but for
family health and well-being, for the management of social, generational,
and sexual relations.

Freud and Breuer's theory did not yet conceptualize the links among
the family, abreaction, and affect. Freud saw Emmy's self-suppression as
caused by and within family networks of communication or symbolic
circulation of putrid bodily matter, and he read these family relations, by
synecdoche, from expressive reflex suppression to psychical sickness.
Nevertheless, Freud had seen that hypnotic suggestion successfully recirculated the occasional hysteric's breast milk, as I suggested in Section III,
only when she acted out her affective situation and "br[oke] out against
her family with some acrimony": "What had happened to her dinner?"
the doctor demanded that she cry; "did they mean to let her starve? how
could she feed the baby if she had nothing to eat herself?" When he suggested that the patient remonstrate against her mother in a way "quite
unlike herself," Freud caused the occasional hysteric to enact her rage and

helplessness at being unable to breast-feed, and, by implication, to act out as well her displeasure at her family's insufficient nurturance (*SE*, 1:120). This synecdochic mode of reading the soma and the homologous social-familial "body" treated only the reflex body; yet the occasional hysteric's psychomotor behavior presumably pantomimed her familial situation. Other patients' illnesses likewise dramatized family circumstances. Mathilde H. wept "floods of tears" under hypnosis and confessed that she had become depressed when her mother broke off her engagement; the morbid mood had lifted only on that day's anniversary (*SE*, 2: 163–64). When a patient suffering from disturbed gait mentioned her fiancé's death, Freud insisted that "something else had happened" to cause her paralysis, that she had not told him everything; she uttered "a single significant phrase," and her father—who, interestingly enough, attended his daughter's hypnotic sessions—"began to sob bitterly" (*SE*, 2: 100–101). Displaced from daughter to father and circulating in the cathartic situation, these tears symbolized something about a father-daughter relation. They suggested, in fact, what Freud had not yet theorized: that affect and its abreaction involved, in a fundamental way, members of a family in particular relations with the hysterical patient. I do not mean to suggest, however, that these cases adumbrate oedipal family relations. Rather, they suggest a theory of affect widely defined as a psycho-physical category of somatic mechanisms, acts, and behaviors, of cognitions and emotions, and of self- and other representations.

Freud's notion of affect began to take shape as a psycho-physical category in Lucy's and Elisabeth's cases. In Chapter 1, I suggested that this theory of affect could be used to explain several early cases of hysteria and paranoia. Only in *Studies on Hysteria*, however, did Freud publish and so mobilize this theory for dissemination to a wide medical audience. Lucy's uncommon hysterical symptom—desensitized nasal sensation with symptomatic smells of burned pudding or cigar smoke—and the three scenes she reproduced in therapy, for example, seemed to signify a highly charged affective situation. In each scene, Lucy had been subjected to sudden action (her affectionate charges had torn her mother's letter from her hands) or angry words (her employer had demanded that his chief accountant not kiss his children and had been furious at Lucy's dereliction of duty in allowing a lady visitor to kiss them). These outbursts had caused her to fall ill.[27]

But why, Freud wondered, had Lucy's body accumulated the sum of excitation linked to these scenes and so excluded them from associative modification, causing her uncommon symptoms? He was not satisfied with his explanation; although "it all sounded highly plausible," he had "missed" something, "some adequate reason why these agitations and this conflict of affects should have led to hysteria." Although he did not yet recognize it, Freud here forcefully linked affect with unconscious ideation, for Lucy's sensitivity to smells symbolized the conflict between her ideas of familial duty and her erotism. Her promise to her charges' mother, a distant relation of her own mother's, that she would "take [the children's] mother's place," signified the site Lucy wished to occupy as her employer's wife, a place she knew she must leave, a place the letter from her mother symbolized and countermanded. In Lucy's case, the social circumstance of her position as both governess and distant relation had produced the conditions for such conflict; the affect associated with her desire—her employer's angry outburst had caused "a stab at [her] heart"— had been dissociated from its unacceptable idea, which had been *"intentionally repressed from consciousness,"* and the sum of excitation attached to it had taken the "wrong path" into "somatic innervation" (*SE*, 2: 114–16; Freud's emphasis). Here, Freud had conjoined the elements of affect theory as psycho-physical representation: Lucy's sensitivity to slights and thus her perception of violent anger as trauma, her emotional response to her role-incongruous social circumstances, and her refusal to represent to herself her hoped-for pleasure, all cooperated to produce hysterical conversion of psychical conflict into physical symptoms.

In Elisabeth's case, an undischarged quota of affect also involved conflicting ideation, constraining social and familial circumstances, and misrepresentation of hoped-for pleasure. And once again, these elements all emerged in the scenes Elisabeth reproduced in the therapeutic situation. Her first symptoms, Freud said, had appeared after she had experienced "blissful feelings" with a young man she hoped to marry and returned home to find her father, whom she was sick-nursing, close to death; the conflict produced by this "situation of incompatibility" caused erotic ideas to be "repressed from association" and the "affect attach[ed] to that idea" intensified or revived her physical pain. But again, Freud was not satisfied with his explanation; he looked for other nursing scenes and discovered that Elisabeth's "tormenting sensations of cold" had emerged when, at her father's call, she had jumped from bed, her feet bare, onto a cold floor. But Elisabeth herself discovered how her situation had produced her central symptom: her father had daily rested his leg, while she changed the bandage, on the now-painful spot on *her* leg from which her hurt radiated

(*SE*, 2: 146–50). Freud confessed that he had no idea how this conversion of conflicting idea and affect into symptom came about. His theory, he said, called for closer examination.

We may ask: what *is* it that turns into physical pain here? A cautious reply would be: something that might have become, and should have become, *mental* pain. If we venture a little further and try to represent the ideational mechanism in a kind of algebraical picture, we may attribute a certain quota of affect to the ideational complex of these erotic feelings which remained unconscious, and say that this quantity (the quota of affect) is what was converted. It would follow directly from this description that the "unconscious love" would have lost so much of its intensity through a conversion of this kind that it would have been reduced to no more than a weak idea. . . . The present case, however, is not well fitted to give a clear picture of such a delicate matter. For in this case there was probably only partial conversion; in others it can be shown with likelihood that complete conversion also occurs, and that in it the incompatible idea has in fact been "repressed," as only an idea of very slight intensity can be. (*SE*, 2: 166–67)

Elisabeth "wished to forget, and therefore intentionally repressed" or "inhibited and suppressed" her erotic thoughts: not the traumatic loss of her father, her young man, and her brother-in-law, not the social circumstances that forced her to suppress her feelings, but repression caused her symptoms. In foregrounding repression as his primary psychical mechanism, however, Freud necessarily emphasized conflicting ideation rather than or apart from affect, since the theory of repression necessitated that affects were not repressed. Marginalizing his earlier theory—that the special social and familial circumstances impinging on women caused affective suppression, but not in any singular ways—Freud substituted the repressive hypothesis for a theory of affect as a structure of feelings, behaviors, and acts that represented the subject to and for herself.

Yet Elisabeth's symptoms demand interpretation from a matrix of affective forces. For her leg pained her at the site of connection with her father's body; her motor paralysis signified the upsurge of her erotic pleasure while walking with her brother-in-law; her social circumstances and familial relations demanded that she suppress her feelings about both pleasure and affect-laden object relationships. For, Freud said, in Elisabeth's case a "certain quota of affect" attached to her "ideational complex of erotic feelings" was converted into somatic pain. "[W]hat *is* it that turns into physical pain here?" Freud asked, and replied, "something that might have become, and should have become, *mental* pain" (*SE*, 2: 166). This same mechanism worked, moreover, in "healthy" people. A "quantitative factor" accounts for the pathogenic action of "affective tension"; the "strength of recollected affects" and of "fresh ones" may, when accumulated beyond a person's tolerance, cause illness. Yet "even a hysteric can retain a certain amount of affect that has not been dealt with," Freud said, confounding the connection between affect-induced hysteria and tension-ridden health. Further complicating this affective calculus, Freud invoked the example of a healthy woman whose "annual festivals of remembrance" both constituted and facilitated her health. This "highly-gifted" but nervous lady, who had nursed a number of loved ones to death, performed the "work of reproduction" by visualizing the "scenes of illness and death" on their anniversaries; her "outbursts of weeping" during these "celebrat[ions]" enabled her to remain healthy. "I must emphasize once more," Freud insisted, "this woman is not ill; her postponed abreaction was not a hysterical process, however much it resembled one" (SE 2: 162–64). This fertile problematic—the affective economy, its causative action in health or hysteria—supported Freud's early notions of hysteria, although conversion, repression, and trauma obscured its usefulness for theoretical production.

Hysteria, the representative disease of late-nineteenth-century women, constituted the field on which to theorize the convergence of psycho-pathological affects. This psycho-physical matrix included but was not limited to psychomotor symptoms; acknowledged or unacknowledged pleasure; significant perceptual images, behaviors, and acts; ideation and counterideation; and structures of feeling. Located in the affect-laden late-nineteenth-century bourgeois family, the female body proved a particularly appropriate plastic surface on which these forces converged. Nerves could map motor malfunction in muscles, transmit messages of dysfunctional sensation to skin, and misconstrue perceptual self-representation— but only if the body were theorized as located in a complex field of psycho-physical representations. Freud's haute bourgeois patients, situated in a historically produced family whose primary functions had altered from economic to affective, enabled his conceptualization of this field in which psychomotor behaviors, self- and object representations, affective discharge, and a subjective sense of pleasure or unpleasure converged. Yet his foregrounding of repressed sexuality and concomitant suppression of affects blocked Freud's ability fully to theorize this matrix, and blocked, as well, his production of other concepts associated with abreaction. Indeed, Freud and Breuer coined the neologism *abreagieren*, Laplanche and Pontalis note, and Freud appropriated for psychoanalysis the term *agieren* (which had the same etymological root but did not generally refer to action in German usage) to express the ways subjects mobilized object relations to act out unconscious fantasies, wishes, or desires (Laplanche and Pontalis 1973, 2, 4). Although it involved the same impulsive quality and economic quantity (or quota of affect), the concept of affect-driven behavior invoked, not only emotive discharge or motor action, not only abreactive acts, but a structure of object relations and subject and object representations that played themselves out in fantasied scenarios.

I have used Otto Kernberg's vocabulary of affects throughout this section because Kernberg posits affects as multiply functioning bridges between soma and psyche, subject and object, allowing him to theorize a complex psycho-physical model for psychoanalysis. For, Kernberg believes, Freud's sense that affects must be discharged rather than repressed, that decrease of psychic tension produces pleasure and increase, unpleasure, simplifies a complex intrapsychical structure. He defines affects as "psychophysiological behavior patterns that include a specific cognitive appraisal, a specific facial pattern [that represents the communicative pattern an affect invokes], a subjective experience of a pleasurable and rewarding or painful and aversive nature, and a muscular and neurovegetative discharge pattern" (Kernberg 1991, 5). From this perspective, Kernberg says, affects link biological instincts with the intrapsychic organization of drives. Affectively invested object relations energize the physiological body; erotogenic zones activate physiological functions and generalized bodily zones called into being by the interactions of child and mothering figure. Drives make functional corresponding affect states, which include a self-representation created by an object relation during a moment of peak affect. This affective situation frames the reciprocal relation of subject and object, then, and becomes part of the subject's cognitive appraisal of experience. Desires, wishes, or fantasies produced by these intersubjective relations aim to reinstate or avoid similar peak-affect experiences; unconscious fantasies thus emerge from and are connected to subject and object representations that, stored as affective memory, constitute subjectivity. Affects, then, form and are formed by intrapsychic structures and self-representations, shape and are shaped by object relations and object representations. Affects constitute, in addition, the unconscious fantasmatic that governs repeated actions produced through and by them. Kernberg calls affects the "building blocks," the representatives or "signal function for the activation" of drives (ibid., 3–20). Deploying reflex and representation theories of psycho-physical correlation, Kernberg elaborates Freud's notion of the plausible bridges between psyche and soma and, in addition, situates those connections within erotic, emotive, circumstantial, and intersubjective structures.

Kernberg's theory of affects also elaborates the ways in which perceptual, cognitive, psychomotor, and repetitive or characteristic behaviors play themselves out in the psychoanalytic situation. Kernberg's model of analytic discourse constitutes a wide range of patient affective physiological discharge patterns and/or psychomotor behaviors as communicating subjective experience to the analyst; these symptomatic actions and acts trigger transferential and countertransferential relations, reproducing and reconstituting primitive affect-laden object relations. Whereas Freud theorized abreaction by observing the circulation or expression of signifying bodily matter during catharsis, Kernberg theorizes the emotive, communicative, and physiological matrix that situates and constitutes the body as mediated by, inscribed with, and produced through the instinctual, objectival, and self-representative activities it remembers and recounts during the analytic hour. Indeed, I would like to return to Emmy von N.'s case to show that Kernberg's theory of affects appropriately accounts for the complex field of forces and significations Freud witnessed in his consulting room but could not fully interpret. Here, the theory of scenes I outlined in Chapter 1 helps me identify visualized scenarios as affect-laden representational texts. Emmy "saw" her scenic "pathognomic reminiscences" with "all the vividness of reality," in "plastic form" and "natural colour"; she narrated them in "rapid succession," as a "single sentence" or a "single episode in four acts." The cathartic work recaptured the first, traumatic scene by narrativizing it as an origin, Freud said, and an incompletely recounted story produced no therapeutic effect.[28]

Yet Emmy reproduced under hypnosis the psycho-physical behavior patterns Kernberg identifies as constituting affects. When confessing that men had hidden in, or tried to enter, her rooms at night, Emmy's facial patterns and muscular movements expressed fear and anxiety: she stammered, rubbed her hands, ground her teeth, and her body "gave a violent start." Freud watched Emmy's whole body become "unceasingly restless," her facial features grow distorted, and her hands press to her forehead during the "storms in her head." He listened to her helpless and yearning repetition of her own (and her daughter's) name: "Emmy," she moaned repeatedly, expressing her subjective experience of anguish during a past period of pain when her daughter's illness, fresh household and family responsibilities, and her own returning nervousness made her feel helpless to confront her life's chaos and confusion. The hypnotized Emmy explained this phenomenon to Freud, for her affect pattern included a (repressed and remembered) cognitive appraisal: this hypnotic bodily state, she told Freud, "was a repetition of the many fits of despair by which she had been overcome during her daughter's treatment" (*SE*, 2: 78–80). Despite her self-constraining demand that she mother perfectly, the already considerable demands placed on her by her social and familial circumstances prevented it. Indeed, Emmy's attacks forced her to confront *her* helplessness to control her daughter's health and behavior. Her fits reenacted an affective and psychomotor pattern that articulated psycho-physical behaviors and self-representations associated with helplessness, lack of or excessive discipline, and inadequate maternity.

Emmy also explained her anorexia as originating in affect-laden object relations. The story included these events, some of which are discussed earlier in this section: her mother had forced her to eat congealed fat; she had eaten meals while fearing contamination from her brothers' bodily fluids; she had contracted a catarrh (the illness's precipitating event) from bad drinking water. Connected to memories of disgust, the act of eating had attracted to itself a sum of affect, Freud said, that remained undiminished precisely because Emmy had been forced to suppress rather than express it. Indeed, her inhibitions of will and inabilities to act depended upon "the presence of affectively-toned and unresolved associations," which, incompatible with other ideas, prevented their association one with another (*SE*, 2: 82–89). But because he could not yet formulate a theory of affects as a matrix of psycho-physical behaviors, events, emotions, and representations, Freud focused on symptom formation rather than symptomatic repetition, on patient narration rather than the psycho-physical pattern of affective behaviors Emmy's acts expressed.

Emmy's case represented the affect-laden object relation of mother and daughter, moreover, as central to female subject formation. For Emmy's distorted facial patterns, disturbed motor behavior, and neurovegetative discharge patterns all expressed and repeated her subjective experience, produced in moments of peak affect, of her mother's violent disregard of her needs for symbolic and literal nurture. Her therapy not only confirmed her cognitive appraisal of her mother's disciplinary severity, but she reexperienced, in the reproduced scene with her mother, its associated affective pattern as explaining her other, seemingly unrelated, symptoms of complex affective disability as daughter and, later, as mother of daughters in a relentless repeated fantasmatic structure of psycho-physical affects and behaviors. Indeed, Emmy's, Lucy's, and Elisabeth's cases all clearly articulate the ways psychomotor behaviors, sensory dysfunctions, cognitive appraisals of family relations and social situations, subjective experiences of pain and unpleasure, and self- and object representations formed during moments of peak affect functioned psychopathologically and were later expressed in the therapeutic situation.

In *Studies on Hysteria*, Breuer and Freud had demonstrated that an affect-laden object relation, situated in the bourgeois family, produced a dysfunction that often played itself out in the realm of psycho-physical pleasure or erotism. Yet when Freud retrospectively commented on these cases, he criticized himself and Breuer for failing to view his hysterics' symptoms as originating in sexual experience. He had not expected that sexual neurosis produced hysteria, he said, when he had treated Emmy, Lucy, and Elisabeth; fresh from the school of Charcot, he had regarded "the linking of hysteria with the topic of sexuality as a sort of insult," just as his patients did. Yet the case historian had indeed viewed Emmy's case as an anxiety neurosis owing to sexual abstinence that had mixed with hysteria, Lucy's as a marginal case of "pure hysteria" with an "unmistakable sexual aetiology," and Katharina's as a "virginal anxiety" that combined anxiety neurosis and hysteria (*SE*, 2: 260). Freud's rueful declaration that he had mistaken the sexual origins of hysterical symptoms, moreover, was contemporary with his work on anxiety neurosis, itself rooted in sexual dysfunction. In the essay that distinguished neurasthenia from anxiety neurosis, which I discuss in Chapter 2, Freud clinically pictured the disorder's symptomatology and assigned to it an etiology in disturbances of the sexual life. Accumulation of sexual excitation, deflected from the psychical sphere, had produced his patients' neurotic somatic symptoms (*SE*, 3: 90–108). Whereas Freud had discovered the problem of the transposition of affect in anxiety neuroses, he had not yet begun to theorize its relation to sexuality. When returning to this problem in 1925, however, he proposed that unpleasure and anxiety could arise only by viewing anxiety as a "reproduction" or representative of "an affective state in accordance with an already existing mnemic image." Here, Freud knew he was "leaving the realm of pure psychology and entering the borderland of physiology" (*SE*, 20: 93–94).

When he criticized his therapeutic work with Emmy, Lucy, and Elisabeth as having ignored the sexual basis of neurosis, Freud had come to view sexuality as psychoanalysis's central psycho-physical category. Indeed by 1905, he had substituted a theory of sexuality for that of affect.

And sexuality seemed an appropriate field in which to theorize a hybrid psychoanalytic subject. For sex was, like affect, a matrix on which somatic events, emotive experiences, and self- and object representations converged. Sexuality constituted and was constituted by psycho-physiological behavior patterns that included specific "cognitive appraisal[s]," facial expressions that represented communicative and affective patterns, "subjective experience[s] of a pleasurable and rewarding or painful and aversive nature," and "muscular and neurovegetative discharge pattern[s]" (Kernberg 1991, 5). I have borrowed Kernberg's terminology here to illustrate how apparently easily the concepts of affect and sexuality may be co-construed. Indeed, I argue in the next chapter that, appropriating the conceptual tools of sexology and sexual pathology, Freud imagined sex in his earliest work as a neurological, sensation-saturated reflex entity constituted by zones of care. Unlike the sexologists, however, Freud represented the sexed body as always already dysfunctional, as inscribed by the traumas and disabilities of object relations and family scenarios. This physiologically inflected sex, I argue in Chapter 6, would eventually be transmuted by the very forces of psychical origination and affective relation Freud had discovered and then suppressed in his work with Emmy, Lucy, Elisabeth, and Katharina. Indeed, in Katharina's case, however sketchily, Freud would investigate the ways in which sexuality, affect-laden scenarios, self-spectatorship, and self- and object representations were structured within a fantasmatic field. But first, I argue, Freud appropriated and revised sexological notions of the body, marginalizing affect as psycho-physical concept and installing the male subject at psychoanalysis's center, where he would remain until 1920.

CHAPTER 5

The Logic of Sex

"No woman is sound, healthy, and complete unless she possesses breasts that are beautiful enough to hold the promise of being functional when the time for their exercise arrives, and nipples that can give suck," Havelock Ellis declared in *Sex in Relation to Society* (1917, 24). Female dysfunction during nursing, Ellis said, doubled the rate of infant mortality in the first year, produced unhealthy children, failed to improve the race, and nullified the mother-child bond. "The breast," Ellis continued, "with its exquisitely sensitive nipple, vibrating in harmony with the sexual organs, furnishes the normal mechanism by which maternal love is developed. No doubt the woman who never suckles her child may love it, but such love is liable to remain defective on the fundamental and instinctive side." From the breast, it seemed to Ellis, all affective life flowed— whether the individual capacity to love or the social and historical fate of nations. Yet Ellis struck chords familiar to nineteenth-century sexual scientists. Indeed, the discourse of sexology conceptualized as its productive rhetorical terms anatomical sexual difference and physiological sexual functioning, and as its logical concepts, the sex instinct and the heterosexual reproductive imperative. Freud's desire to cure his "occasional hysteric" (see pp. 146–49, above), to functionalize her breast milk and return her to managerial domestic life, then, and Mitchell's hope to reeducate women, through rest and reparenting, to full and voluntary capacity, participated in shaping this discourse through clinical practice. Yet these notions constituted, even as they were constituted by, cultural notions of the body's natural sexual activities.

The discourses of sexology and sexual pathology represented the sexed body as grounded in a neurological model. Reflex acts, cortical centers, and nervous system functions, I argue in the first section of this chapter, conceptualized this body as physiological and profoundly functionalized. Sex researchers deployed the laboratory to support the study of sex. As had the Salpêtrians, the sexologists observed, tested, and graphed the body's everyday sexual life to produce this representation of its normal and normative functions. Indeed, their research portrayal of sex was constituted by and reproduced the same binarisms that Charcot's clinic had used to anchor and support its work. Grounded in the logical opposition pathological/normal, sex research produced a hypersensate body that functioned by virtue of nervous, reflex acts and that failed to function if perception, transmission, and mental representation went astray. Still, sex researchers represented this normalized body not simply as itself either functional or dysfunctional, for sex, unlike hysterical attack, usually involved more than one subject. The question of couples and coupling, I argue in Section II, demanded that sexology describe sex as occurring, not only within one body, but with partners, and sexological research, as a result, collected patient narratives to verify its research findings, justify its physiological theories, and document its scientific credibility. Sexology's primary representational mode—with which physicians translated their research results to other scientists and the medical public—deployed patient interrogation and pathography (or patient autobiography), case study, and editorial compilation to document sex as the fundamental truth of modern subjectivity. The binarism nature/social, as a result, grounded the representation of sex more profoundly, although differently, than it had grounded experimentation on hysteria. For the oppositional thinking at work in the medicalization of sex could be leveraged to justify dominant social values, as I argue in Section III.

Indeed, whereas the Salpêtrière's portrayal of experiments made by nature elided the social basis of questions about, for example, the usefulness of incarcerated and impoverished hysterical women as research subjects, sexology's depiction of its investigations both subsumed and recirculated into the cultural and social domains questions about sexual difference, sexual practices, and gendered social relations. The discourses of cultural ethnography and criminal anthropology, moreover, appropriated sexual pathological concepts to produce as historical truths mythologies of sexual primitivism, atavism, and degeneracy. The narrativized, teleological theories of human history, civilizations, and peoples claimed scientific credibility by citing the teleological arguments embedded in sexological concepts such as the heterosexual imperative, concepts produced and reproduced by the binarisms that anchored and supported them. Observing, classifying, and documenting sex, sexual pathologists debated and circulated into the dominant culture the problematics of nature and the social (was homosexuality, for example, congenital or acquired?), normal and abnormal (when did fetishism, an often natural attachment to metonymies of a loved object, become perverse?), etiology (how did the invert, pervert, or degenerate *get that way?*), and, as a consequence, social regulation of sexualities (should the pervert be treated, forbidden to marry or reproduce, or submitted to the jurisdiction of police and the courts?). Although I do not rehearse the familiar debates about these sexological questions here, I look, in Section III, at the cultural and social consequences of sexological attempts to regulate the sexualities their discourses had helped to produce. Indeed, I represent the hybrid products of sexological science—the invert, pervert, and deviant—as highly mediated quasi-objects, created and subsumed by the modern scientific laboratory. And here the laboratory work of purification and mediation is leveraged into other social institutions and domains, as experimental researchers enter the courtroom, the school, and the brothel.

While Freud appropriated the sexual pathologists' sensation-saturated body into his early models of the sexed body, he quickly translated that model into a modern sexuality that seemed "natural," he said, only because it cooperated with cultural norms to regulate the perverse pleasures of erotogenic life. In Section IV of this chapter, I quickly sketch nineteenth-century sexual surgery's implicit and twentieth-century reproductive biology's explicit attempts to negotiate the nature/social binarism. I do so to argue that affect theory, like these other discourses of the sexed body, proposed a plausible bridge between the sexed body and unanswered psychosexual questions of pleasure and unpleasure. Because pleasure was a sexological problem and partnership a pervasive social unit for constituting and constraining pleasure, a psycho-physical sexuality involved, as had affect, self- and object representations and relatedness. Not just nervous, orgasmic discharge but the subjective experience of pleasure and unpleasure produced ongoing sexual coupling. With representation reformulated as drive theory, Freud resurrected and revised, once more, his notions of psycho-physical correlation and psychopathological causation. Yet this special sort of representation, although different from the one he had used to differentiate hysterical from organic paralyses, served to foreclose, once again, questions of subjective self-representation and affective intersubjectivity. Despite Freud's sexuality theory, the problem of pleasure and unpleasure would not go away. And the logic of sex—a phrase I appropriate from Foucault—functioned, at century's end, primarily because of the binarisms that sexology created and deployed to perform its scientific work of purification and mediation.

I

Sexology's discourse of pleasure constituted a sensation-saturated, sensualized body always already, or ready to be, stimulated. The sexologist, then, represented the body (as did Freud in his essay on organic and hysterical paralyses) as receiving sense impressions through direct stimulation of the body, as transmitting excitations to and representing them in the brain, and so producing psychosexual states. Defined by its nerve centers and peripheral boundaries, this body was a highly functionalized and functional machinery made for enticement. Sensation played over its surface from erogenous zones; it circulated nervous, chemical, or reflex stimuli. According to Richard von Krafft-Ebing's presentation of what he called, in a chapter heading, the "physiological facts," nerves in the sexological body sent sensations and impulses to the seat of sexuality in the cerebral cortex; visual, olfactory, and sensory images radiated from the periphery to the brain by reflex action; the brain returned along nervous pathways messages about, for example, innervation, ejaculation, and detumescence.[1] Using the neurological concept of disease seat, sexology functionalized the physiological body. If a man felt "voluptuous sensations" when his forehead were touched, Albert Moll wondered, did it mean the "nerves of the penis terminate[d] in the forehead"? Hardly. The seat of "voluptuous sensation," the nervous excitation that linked physiological function with pleasure, could only be in the genitals, although reflex acts by other organs could excite the sexual senses.[2] Improved technology meant that the sexologist could observe or research the physiological body's capacity for stimulation in a variety of laboratory settings, could describe arousal, satiety, and frustration as categories of sexual response and functioning. Havelock Ellis used Charles Féré's skin-sensation experiments, for example, to ground his notion that touch was the first sensory impression to prove pleasurable. Indeed, Féré's research findings on stimulation of the skin with mustard plaster, icebag, hot-water bottle, or painter's brush measured electrical stimulation with the dynamometer and muscular energy, the ergograph. Exciting the skin, which possessed special sexual sensitivity, proved tonic for sexual, as for nervous, patients (Ellis 1914, 5–9).

When sex entered the laboratory, it could be produced as scientific knowledge. Stimulated bodies bore witness to experimentally constituted truths, which were then circulated among research scientists, through the work of translation, and sociologized for a mass audience.

Sexology represented sex as instinctive and normally heterosexual. Man's "instinctive" sexual "appetite" for woman, Krafft-Ebing said, was a "mighty impulse of nature," yet woman reserved her instinctive sensual love primarily for the nurturance of offspring. But adult sexual love, which implied the presence of sexual desire, could exist only between "persons of different sex capable of sexual intercourse" (Krafft-Ebing 1946 [1886–96], 2–15). Albert Moll's paradigm for arousal as one of tumescence and detumescence necessitated that (hetero)sexual partners experience pleasure during the act of coupling. Sexual touching (which he called "concretation") produced "voluptuous sensation[s]," produced stimuli that distended the genitals, caused circulation and ejaculation of bodily fluids, genital detumescence, and emotional pleasure.[3] Clearly, Moll meant that the aroused body felt pleasure primarily because intersubjective erotic activities produced stimuli that excited physiological responses; the messages they relayed back to the body, in turn, gratified the subject's needs, both somatic and psychological. This model for intersubjective sex was both normatively heterosexual and highly functionalized: it identified as a norm for sexual functioning the characteristic action of the male sex organ; it inscribed social values within sexological statements about biological function and process; it deployed the binarism male/female to produce, through heterosexual sex, the binarism normal/pathological. Moll and Krafft-Ebing, moreover, sentimentalized the heterosexual imperative as a productive partnership in which sexual agency was assigned to the male member, affective and affiliative responsibility to the female. Yet if men engaged in sexual acts because the sex instinct drove them, and women because sentiment impelled them, men and women could hardly take the same kind of pleasure in sex. Biologically based cultural and social theories of sexual antagonism were just around the corner. Because the "laws of Nature" produced two biologically different and incommensurate sexes, Walter Heape would later claim, they disallowed sexual equality; social laws therefore rightly regulated the relations of men and women according to their biologically differentiated functions (Heape 1913, 3–35; id. 1905, 267 et passim).

Woman's pleasure served to anchor the heterosexual model on which the discourse and logic of sex functioned. Sexologists represented female sexual morphology and functions as homologous to, although different from, man's.[4] The highly excitable clitoris, "rudimentary analogue of the masculine penis," functioned solely to produce physiological "erection," Ellis said, to receive and transmit "voluptuous sensations"; the vagina, which ejaculated female sexual mucous, worked in sympathy with the womb's movements to "flash open" and "draw" in the male member; sensitive to a "look, a word, a thought, a hand on the wrist," the womb-and-vagina constituted a "living, vital, moving" organ, and made woman an active agent in coitus. Granting woman pleasure and agency in the sexual act, Ellis seemed to challenge binary structures of sexual difference that underwrote the heterosexual imperative. Yet Ellis, like Krafft-Ebing, sentimentalized woman's pleasure. Figuring the "nymphae" (a term Freud would adopt in "Dora") as valley, goddess, portal, and gate of satisfaction, as the most delicate and symbolic site of female voluptuous sensation, Ellis troped female pleasure as serving to attract the male sexually; woman's pleasure pleased not herself but her male partner, worshiper at her body's shrine. This idealized female body appeared widely in the late-nineteenth-century sexual literature, its refined and transcendentalized sexual structures represented as the liberalized potential for a more rewarding male pleasure and a more emotionally functional heterosexuality. But female physiology proved the scandal in this binaristic set of pleasures. For "voluptuous sensitivity," more widely diffused in woman than in man, meant that the whole female body could be stimulated; even in cases of clitoral amputation, a woman could take pleasure in coitus (Ellis 1906, 124–64). Ellis had dispersed erotic sensitivity over the cutaneous female body even as he sought to focus it on the genitals and erogenous zones.[5] A scandal to the binaristic system of sexual difference that underwrote the heterosexual imperative, the hypersensate female body was circumscribed by sexology's idealized heterosexual union.

Female sensation and pleasure also served and were contained by the processes of reproduction. Here, the neurologized, biological body again underwrote the production of binarisms, as birth and nurturance anchored and sustained the naturalized and normalized social functions of women. Calling the nipple a hyperesthetic zone, Krafft-Ebing noted that woman gave herself zealously to the pleasures of breast-feeding. The "voluptuous element in suckling" worked by reflex action between nipple and womb, Ellis said; the "sensation" and "sexual excitement" of breast-mouth contact "deliciously mingled" the "two supreme objects of [female] desire," child and male lover (Krafft-Ebing 1946 [1886–96], 38; Ellis 1914, 23–34). Females took pleasure in nursing, then, but that pleasure also functioned to reproduce, nurture, and nourish the human species. This aroused, excitation-loaded pleasure sustained as well the teleological theory spawned by the nature/social binarism. The "normal" male "sexual urge for women" served the "reproduction of the species" and so was "natural"; "we can hardly establish a connection between man's genital organs and his urge for women," Moll said, except from this "teleological point of view" (Moll 1931 [1891], 171–72). Woman's pleasure upheld evolutionary processes and, through the mother-child bond, the family group, and reproductive biology, the future of humankind. As Freud's occasional hysteric demonstrated, if a woman could not function productively to nurse and provide sustenance, she had failed her family and her duty as woman, her productive and functionalizing capacity in human evolutionary history.

Yet economies of excess and perversion consistently scandalized sexology's binaristic logic of the functional body. Indeed, the concept of a functionalized sex instinct inevitably suggested dysfunction.[6] If males naturally desired females, homosexual object choice became, in this binaristic thinking, unnatural. But the sensation-saturated body invited alternate gratifications, for sexology had conceptualized all the body's boundaries, its exits and entrances, its mucous membranes, as suited for sexual purposes. Secondary sexual excitations "always involve[d] the entrances and the exits of the body," Ellis said, the regions where skin merged into mucous membrane, and where, "in the course of evolution, tactile sensibility [had] become highly refined." These "frontier regions of the body," Ellis said, produced maximal sexual stimulation, for they not only produced pleasure but constituted "sexual skin centers" by reflex action (Ellis 1914, 19–21, 9). Such zones, however, undermined binaristically constituted pleasure, for they borrowed satisfaction from the genitals. Sexology's sensate body calculated pleasure, delivered under a regime of scarcity in which the ceiling on pleasure prevented excess and, if misused, deprived normal sexual aim and object choice of their energy. In males, for example, the anus might replace the penis as sole physiologically produced hyperesthetic zone, Krafft-Ebing cautioned; in hysterical women, the skin around the mammae and genitals (Krafft-Ebing 1946 [1886–96], 38–39). The body's cutaneous surfaces and boundaries, highly sensate precisely because of their biological makeup, physiologically functioning to serve individual, nation, and race, could paradoxically and perversely perform sex acts that undermined individual health, human history, and perpetuation of the species. This libidinal economy, which when normal served natural impulses and teleological human aims, was inevitably endangered by the very sensation-saturated body the sexologists had produced to constitute and sustain it.

Seeking to account for such perversion, Moll conceptualized sexual dysfunction as homologous with other physiological functional derangements. While the liver normally secreted bile, in certain disorders of the liver, the ducts failed to function and so bile reached the intestines; hunger provoked feeding, but in some pathological states, the "sensation of hunger [was] absent" although the stomach functioned normally. The "genital instinct" presented the "same morbid anomalies" as did other organic functions, for only if the instinct served reproduction was heterosexuality truly functional; "otherwise," he confessed, "one does not see why men should be urged to have connections with women since ejaculation of the sperm may be brought about in quite other ways" (Moll 1931 [1891], 171–72). Those other ways, of course, involved, among other things, entrances to and exits from the body normally reserved for gratification of other instinctual urges. Seeking to escape from the inevitable dysfunction of normal sexual aim and object choice, Moll found himself once more entrapped in the libidinal economy of excess and perversion. Always already stimulated, this body's frontier regions and zones, its excitable and structurally refined mucous membranes, seemed capable of producing a delight that threatened the natural, heterosexual, reproductive sexuality the sensation-saturated body had served to anchor and support. That sensationalized body served as the fulcrum in a series of binarisms it had paradoxically helped to produce, binarisms that, once in place, invariably seemed fragile and provisional. Constituting the dysfunction it sought to preclude, the deployment of sexuality was itself, as Michel Foucault has said, productive, for the hypersensate, polymorphously pleasured body historically and culturally enabled the intensification of sexual pleasures, the invention of sexualities, and the incitement to discourse about sex (Foucault 1978, 105–7).

The sexologists characterized their pathographers as disordered versions of unitary selves. Krafft-Ebing represented his patients as at odds with the facts of physiology and anatomy. A sexually normal individual, he said, possessed a "definite sexual personality" and desired to "perform sexual acts corresponding with that sexual personality,—acts which, consciously or unconsciously, [had] a procreative purpose." This psychosexual personality was "unchangeable" and "harmoniously" corresponded with the individual's physiological and anatomical sex. An "antipathetically" sexed person, on the contrary, displayed an abnormal psychosexual constitution, tainted sexual instinct, and neuropathic predisposition; his "feeling, thought, will," and "whole character" corresponded with the instinct "at odds" with his individual anatomical and physiological sex. Perversion articulated *"perverse feeling"* with perverse activities; normal individuals situationally engaged in such acts but did not possess a perverse personality. That identity was fundamental; it could be inherited or acquired; it served as proof of degeneration; it did not, especially if congenital, respond to treatment (Krafft-Ebing 1946 [1886–96], 282–90). Sexual identities, then, inhered in certain individuals and belonged with certain bodies but not others, and were, when normal, symmetrical with anatomical sexual morphology. Here Krafft-Ebing constituted the binarism homosexual/heterosexual, and, although he acknowledged situational perverse acts, his sexological documentary produced same-sex sexuality as, no longer a matter of "prohibited and isolated genital *acts*," as Eve Kosofsky Sedgwick says, but a "function of stable definitions of *identity*."[7] Producing his cases as representative of certain psychopathologies, accumulating their narratives as facts, Krafft-Ebing experimentally created and naturalized the pervert as surely as Charcot had the hysteric. His laboratory, however, was virtual and representational. Collected as statistics and figures to demonstrate, through their dysfunction, that functionality represented the "physiological facts," Krafft-Ebing's patients served to represent, through their difference, "normal" and everyday sexual life. Their pathological sexual practices and the pathographies that recounted them were then themselves syncopally recapped in the psychopathological case study. Producing norms and characterizing deviance, Krafft-Ebing practiced—as Binet might have said—"sexology with numbers."

In "Draft G" (1895), Freud, too, represented the physiological facts of the sexed body. His "schematic diagram" of the body's nervous pathways, bodily boundaries, and sexual objects pictured sex as a complex neurological reflex event. He explained: a psychical sexual group, stimulated by internal sexual tension, conducted "voluptuous feelings" and caused a specific (sexual) action across the ego boundary (or skin) toward an external sexual object, or its representation in the mind as image; the reaction to this act, which, with the cognitive act, crossed the body's boundary, caused sensation that, in turn, passing though the spinal center, produced reflex action; reaching the phallic or bladder-shaped terminal organ, the reflex act passed dually into the "path of conduction of voluptuous feelings" and into "sexual tension," feeding back into the psychical group responsible for arousal and so into the loop of sexual actions. Sexual anesthesia, Freud said, consisted in the omission from the specific sexual act of voluptuous feeling that, conducted into the psychical sexual group after reflex action, unloaded the sexual "end-organ"; voluptuous feeling was measured by "the amount of unloading." This neurologized body, which produced and conveyed measured quantities of nerve charge, could become anesthetic if "feelings of pleasure," linked with defense and disgust, got excluded from the psychical sexual group. The problem Freud proposed here, he said, noted the incommensurability between somatic sexual excitation and psychical response. For psychical inhibition created instinctual impoverishment and, when neurons gave up excitation, pain, a kind of "*internal haemorrhage*," a corresponding "*in-drawing*" in the psychical sphere that operated like a "*wound*" (Freud 1985, 99–104; Freud's emphases). Despite his insistence on neurological models, Freud schematized a physiological reflex sexuality that could easily malfunction. He posed the possibility, at least figuratively, of psychical interference with the logic of sexual nervous functioning.

While appropriating neurological sexological terms and concepts, Freud nevertheless systematically theorized the sexual body as traducing notions of functionalism. By 1905, he had restated and demystified sexology's binaristic discourse of normality and psychopathology. Although, he said, scientists regarded copulation as the "normal sexual aim," an act that released sexual tension and temporarily extinguished the sexual instinct, even in the "most normal sexual process" he detected "rudiments" that, if developed, would produce perverse deviations from the norm. The sexual instinct—"no simple thing"—was articulated from "components" that had "come apart" in the perversions. Translating sexology's fascination with sensationalized bodily zones and orifices, Freud proposed that perverse sexual activities either "extend[ed], in an anatomical sense, beyond the regions of the body" designed for "sexual union," or "linger[ed] over the intermediate relations to the sexual object which should normally be traversed rapidly on the path towards the final sexual aim."

Yet this identification of certain bodily regions as appropriate for sexual functioning and gratification was "often purely conventional." For although people held heterosexual kissing (which appropriated the digestive organs for gratifying a sexual aim) in high esteem, they viewed as perverse anal intercourse (which appropriated the eliminatory organs) and oral-genital sex. Nothing inhered in some bodily parts to make their use during sex natural, others unnatural, Freud said; mucous membranes produced sensations of pleasure, and only social practices policed their exclusion from sexual acts. Freud not only normalized but universalized perversion. "No healthy person," he said, existed without perversion, which "form[ed] a part of what passe[d] as the normal constitution"; the "something" that anchored perversion was "something innate in *everyone*," although its disposition and intensity might vary among individuals (*SE*, 7: 149–60, 162, 171; Freud's emphasis). Not a characterological essence, then, the perverse had a morphology. It mapped a body by regions and zones that refused to obey the laws of anatomy or of physiological function. This always already dysfunctional sexuality, with complex aim and object choice freed from anatomy and into psychoanalytic representation, suited a culture that prized functionalism but feared that dysfunction was, in fact, inevitable.

In *Three Essays on the Theory of Sexuality*, the sensation-saturated body joined a modern libidinal economy. The post-pubertal sexual aim combined component instincts and subordinated erotogenic zones to the genital zone's primacy, Freud said, yet produced the "problem of pleasure and unpleasure." The sexual aim of discharge and reproduction necessitated sexual arousal, phallic erection and vaginal lubrication; the process of sexual excitation—the nature of which, Freud confessed, was "highly complicated" and "obscure"—involved stimulation of erotogenic zones and sensory surfaces, such as skin and sense organs. How could the tension produced by sexual excitation be pleasurable? "The problem is how," Freud said, an "experience of pleasure [gave] rise to a need for greater pleasure." Freud had recourse to an earlier notion of the reflex sexual body: "fore-pleasure," an "incentive bonus" to greater pleasure, produced "end-pleasure," a pleasure "brought about entirely by discharge," a "pleasure of satisfaction" (*SE*, 7: 207–11). In this libidinal economy, fore-pleasure "endangered" the normal sexual aim, just as, in the economics of infantile sexuality, excess pleasure—refusing to obey the laws of anatomy—could produce regressive fixation, adult compulsion, or perversion. Yet that purpose was not reproduction but simply pleasure, and the infantile indulgence in body nonreproductive or goal-driven pleasure fixed the limits of, gave a direction to, and precisely calculated the quality of, purposeful adult pleasure. Although he smuggled teleological thinking back into his theory, Freud sought to free pleasure from the facts of physiology and so, as he had with hysterical psycho-physical correlation, into the realm of representation by privileging and theorizing the logical problem the sexologists kept trying to resolve, the scandal of excess and perversion.

II

Once the physiological facts of sexual function had been mobilized to produce binaristic labels and identities, the social regulation of sexuality became available for medical discussion. For the consequence of a functionalizing perspective on human sexuality and the production of pathology to prove the functional norm was the medical and social realization that pathology demanded both scrutinizing and policing. The production of a modern functional subject—one fully capable of labor and reproduction, in control of his or her intentions and choices to act, willingly acceding to his or her identity—was constituted by, even as it constituted, the sciences of the flesh, as it had been reshaped into the reflex body and functional subject. The debate about the social regulation of sexuality, linked historically and politically to psycho-physical theorizing and physiological research projects like those of Charcot, Janet, Féré and Binet, Krafft-Ebing, Emil Kräpelin, and Hugo Münsterberg, among others, took shape around questions about managing pathology and deviance. The social body, read by synecdoche from the individual sexed body, likewise demanded observation, description, and a cataloguing of ills. Several of the research scientists I have studied here, whose work crossed the boundaries between the discourses of hysteria and sexuality, wrote as well about public health. For if the conceptualization of the functioning late-nineteenth-century body worked to identify and treat pathological individuals, it could also weed out deviance from the social body. Public health thus emerged as a field of inquiry concomitantly with social anxiety about sexual perversion, child seduction, which I discuss here and in Chapter 7, and sexual crime. The production of nature/social binaristic thinking about sex, moreover, emerged as well during the historical moment when cultural anthropology began to produce primitive sexuality as antecedent to and discontinuous with modern European sexual practices. While Freud's always already dysfunctional sex hardly suited the regulatory discourse, his new science nevertheless moved forcefully into cultural speculation. As they leveraged their research findings out of the consulting office and into the social domain, sexologists began speaking within the domain of the juridical as well as the medical.

Sexologists were often consulted about legal definitions of invert sex, the specimen late-nineteenth-century pathology. Despite his psychiatric labeling of psychopathologies, use of degeneracy theory, and adoption of the congenital theory of homosexuality, Krafft-Ebing supported repeal of the section of the German criminal code that enabled legal proceedings against homosexuals. But the psychiatrist nevertheless situated his discussion of invert social lives and the nonpathological causes of homosexuality under the rubric of criminality. Classifying sex crimes in his chapter on the "pathological sexual life before the criminal court," Krafft-Ebing discriminated the medico-forensic guidelines by which criminal responsibility could be assigned—through the intervention of medical, especially psychiatric, experts—to persons accused of unnatural, immoral, or abusive sexual acts (Krafft-Ebing 1946 [1886–96], 498–614). Charles Féré, crossing from the hysteria and experimental psychological discourses into the sexological, decried the tendency toward forensic leniency in judging individuals who had acted on their anomalous sexual instincts. He called legal measures that strengthened individual motives for controlling noncommunitarian impulses "not only justifiable but needful" (Féré 1900, 343–47). On the other side of the polemic, Ellis invoked the congenital theory to anchor his liberalizing claims, arguing that neither anal sodomy nor "gross indecency," when performed in private between consenting adults, should be subject to the penal code. Ellis agreed with Moll: "An act does not become criminal because it is disgusting," he argued; "to eat excrement, as Moll remarks, is extremely disgusting, but it is not criminal."[8]

Moll's scandalous introduction of excrement into the debate about sexual criminality exposed a problem that this debate had avoided naming, and which Freud had discovered in his seduction theory. For the question of consent, when introduced into the innocence/experience binarism, profoundly troubled what had appeared simple. Whereas innocence could be defined, identified, and mythologized, consent refused to mark the opposition it had been called upon to constitute. Criminality, too, involved the category of consent or its lack, and like consent, could not easily be constructed as the binarism guilty/not guilty. Extenuating circumstances invariably arose, whether in narratives of inherited evil, predisposition to crime, or criminality acquired through exposure to other offenders or purveyors of bad habits. Disgust, as Freud would later demonstrate, could more usefully be invoked as a principle of self-regulation, although it could not be instituted at the level of social deterrent.

The sexologists solved the problem of criminality, consent, and forensic judgment of sex acts by invoking their own authority to judge. Féré invoked biology. He could find "no physiological reason" why the sexual instinct should not be controlled as were the nutritive, alimentary, and eliminatory instincts, why it should not be educated through discipline, and why it should not be subject to social regulation. Féré, like other sexologists, had implicitly aligned normal with natural sex in a hierarchical and mutually implicatory structure of the binarisms nature/social and normal/pathological; yet pathological persons were naturally so, and therefore truly sick. Perverts and inverts were not a social minority because they were "harmful and immoral," but harmful and immoral by nature and so destined to remain a minority. "Should society take away from itself the power of stopping persons because they cannot help being what they are?" he asked, invoking the congenital theory to support his position (Féré 1900, 347).

Krafft-Ebing and Féré covered over the problem underlying this discursive construction, for the assignment of the homosexual to the binaristic position of immorality and the "natural," seemed to trouble the oppositional thinking at work in the medicalization of sex. In fact, the conceptualization of the congenital/acquired binarism itself represented a kind of blockage for the theory that deployed it. For the congenital trait— whether a predisposition to hysteria or an inherent homosexuality— could occur naturally at the same moment it was defined as abnormal. Anomalous, it both deviated from the norm and served to constitute norms; those norms, in turn, could be medically or juridically deployed to constitute the identities of persons who deviated from the norms their deviance had been used to construct. Because of this circularity in the social uses of normativity, the congenital homosexual, like the hysteric, traduced categories and could be translated from one discourse to another, could function discursively to produce identifications, identities, and the very classificatory categories he or she had been used to create. But this traduction was also a problem. For, although Krafft-Ebing, Féré, and Ellis refused to recognize it as a problem, the congenital theory could no longer tolerate the nature/social opposition, and, under a different kind of critical scrutiny, the impasse it represented could be made visible. The pervert and invert, like the hysteric, were hybrids, produced by the purifying work of sexology, yet profoundly complex in their status as disordered quasi-subjects, taxonomic and representative scientific quasi-objects.

Despite Ellis's support of liberalization of statutes against inversion,

however, he, like his contemporaries, cautioned against disregarding homosexual or deviant sexual practices as a social issue. He, Féré, Moll, and
Krafft-Ebing all advised that societies protect themselves against inversion
and perversion through the purifying medicalization of sexuality. Thus,
doctors would counsel judges about the "medico-forensic" problem of
criminal responsibility in sexual cases; medicine, as Féré recommended,
would utilize periods of penal punishment to treat such degeneracy and
thus could indirectly regulate both incarceration and probation (Féré
1900, 346). Sex crimes would, as a result, become a public health problem rather than a strictly juridical matter—increasing the social power
and professional prestige of medical practitioners. Féré conceptualized the
sexual instinct, in fact, as though it inevitably needed policing; he advocated discipline of children's sexual acts through maternal sympathy, surveillance and punishment of childhood masturbation, individual and social education in the value of chastity, legislation against promiscuity, and
medical inspection of prostitutes for "contagious diseases," a measure that
had proven problematic in England.[9] Rather than discipline and punishment, Ellis preferred to consider whether treatment might protect social
groups from deviant sexual acts. Yet he recognized the difficulty of
"cure," and, in the case of homosexuality, rejected virtually all existing
therapeutic programs, including surgical castration, Krafft-Ebing's or
Schrenck-Notzing's sexual hypnotism, Moll's association therapy, and—
while recognizing its success relative to other treatments—Freud's psychoanalytic method. "I frankly confess," he said, "the remedy seems to me
worse than the disease."[10]

Unlike Féré, Ellis counseled against therapeutics that trained the invert to practice heterosexual sex. Invoking Magnus Hirschfeld, however,
he advised that the homosexual avoid marriage and reproduction. Refin-
ing and spiritualizing the invert, Ellis said, could best address both individual and social ills. Education in sexual chastity, passionate but emotional male friendship, and self-treatment in self-restraint without self-
repression would, Ellis said, produce a healthy invert rather than an
"unsexed" and "perverted" "feeble simulacrum of a normal man." Denying the usefulness to the invert of repression, Ellis nevertheless implied
that only the willful performance of self-denial could prevent homosexual activity. For Ellis had considered neither what form of self-treatment
the invert should practice nor where he should learn it. Calling for increased social tolerance rather than punishment, Ellis nevertheless helped
construct what Sedgwick calls "the epistemology of the closet." For the

invert must recognize that, if he "flout[ed] his perversion in its face," public opinion would refuse to tolerate him.[11]

Ellis advised homosexuals to "scrupulously hid[e]" their "conditions" and believed such reticence would, in turn, ameliorate their social status. Endorsing silence, apparent compliance with dominant sexual-social values, and a refusal to display homosexual object choice, cautioning against self-labeling, open speech, identificatory acts, and advocatory activities, Ellis helped consolidate the structures of closeted gay life. Until decriminalization and social liberalization of attitudes toward homosexuality, Ellis implied, invert culture should remain a subculture and homosexual acts an unspoken—because, he said, abnormal—alternative experience. Moll agreed. The closeted homosexual, he said, would "profit" general social "morale" and contribute, moreover, to the social "maintenance of morals" and "people's respect of the law" (Moll 1931 [1891], 208, 217).

Schrenck-Notzing proposed a comprehensive treatment plan for sexual pathology. Like other contemporary sexologists, Schrenck-Notzing treated deviants who had failed to observe the heterosexual, reproductive, and marital sexual-social norm. His patients, he theorized, had fallen victim to an "abnormal, dominating impulse" they must learn to control and master; the physician taught patients self-reliance, self-knowledge, and willpower. He prescribed hydrotherapeutic baths, showers, and douches; faradization; bromine preparations; hypnotic suggestion and psychotherapy; prohibited "exciting influences," "obscene reading, bad company, and pornographic pictures." For hypersexual distress, he recommended "regular sexual indulgence" rather than strategic continence, chastity, or abstinence; for impotence, a rest from intercourse; for homosexuality, sexual fantasies about women and repeated trips to brothels. He hypnotized patients, implanted posthypnotic suggestions, and often checked up on his patients' performance; specularizing the sex act encouraged patient recovery. As these prescriptions suggest, Schrenck-Notzing treated primarily male patients. Because they had more opportunity to enjoy nonmarital sexual intercourse than did females, he recognized, his hypnotic-somatic cure worked more forcefully on men than women.

Like his contemporaries, Schrenck-Notzing viewed sex as a public health problem. He proposed liberalized, professionalized, and educatory social regulation as a mode of controlling sexual deviance. "Real sexual education," he said, inculcated a sexual hygiene that, in turn, shaped sexual values. Knowing when boys became healthily sexual, a teacher could recommend an appropriately timed first sexual intercourse, could help prevent excess, infection, and procreation. Making sex visible and available for discussion, the institutionalized structures of education—teacher persuasion and observation, student imitation and admiration—could create "good habits," "consciousness of moral duty," and "discipline" rather than mechanical obedience to social rules. Cautioning that sexual conduct necessarily conformed to and was sustained by social relations, Schrenck-Notzing suggested that sexual practices be corrected by "social deterrents." To ameliorate the public problem of sexual supply and demand, for example, Schrenck-Notzing proposed easier legal access to marriage and "amelioration of conditions of life"—presumably improvements in housing, sanitation, and education for the working class. Sexual ills such as prostitution, which enabled the transfer of immorality and contagion from the public domain into the family, should be regulated, not by the police, he advised, but by medical and legal supervision (Schrenck-Notzing 1956 [1895], 38–49, 196–205).

The public health model for regulating deviant sexuality invariably invoked, as I have already suggested, cultural questions about status, class, and gender. Fears about sexual seduction, for example, had stimulated middle-class anxiety about working-class sexuality. Children might be introduced to individual or mutual masturbation, as Freud pointed out, not only by other children, but also by teachers, governesses, domestic helpers, and nurses. Servants in hotels, too, demanded greater surveillance, because they interacted with members of the middle class in a restricted but class-stratified space that mimicked the domestic by differentiating space according to the activities of eating, sleeping, and cleansing. Inmates in prisons, asylums, and general hospitals also needed watching, for, although they did not meet members of the middle class while incarcerated, once treated and cured, they circulated back into domestic and labor domains, there to insert themselves into—and possibly contaminate—families, business associations, or educational institutions. These figures appeared especially sexualizable because working-class, and therefore easily characterized by the individuals who had hired them as different from themselves and likely deviants. Institutions in which these sexual activities might be located, whether the single-sex school, the middle-class nursery, or the servants' quarters in the family domicile, suddenly invited inspection and inquiry. Calls for public hygiene, sex education, and the increased supervision of domestics and infants accompanied these pleas.[12]

Binaristic construction of deviance, then, labeled as deviants those individuals most likely to transgress the very purified, binaristic categories they had been deployed to produce. Overstepping the oppositional barrier that marked the boundary between binaristic categories, they could presumably infect individuals, especially those imagined to be innocent of sexuality, indeed outside the entire construction of such binarisms. Children, the mythologized innocents of late-nineteenth-century life, seemed endangered because their development into normal sexuality appeared so imperative—and so perilous. Deploying sex to consolidate the opposition between natural and social, the sexologists constructed as well the normal/pathological binary. These distinctions could then be used, as they were with the hysteric, to isolate and alienate pathological individuals, as both perverse patient and normal people imposed renunciations and limitations on the person so diagnosed. Sex, like health, could be viewed, therefore, as regulated by the norm of physiological functioning—and a calculus of emotional pleasure and well-being. Like health, too, sex was shaped by social milieus and cultural values.

Indeed, Freud argued that normal sexuality, like perversion and inversion, was culturally and conventionally constituted. To account for sexual unpleasure and repression, he posited as civilizing forces the normalizing mechanisms of shame, morality, and disgust, forces not operating on, he speculated, members of the lower classes, rural people, and immoralists.[13] Indeed, he represented a child's development as a process of damming up the sexual instinct through the operations of disgust, shame, and morality; these "constructions" or "dams," central to the "growth of a civilized and normal individual," were not necessarily, however, a product of education but of the body itself. The subject's developing ego interpreted the perverse impulses of erogenous zones as unpleasure; the dams of disgust and shame had been constructed specifically to oppose and resist this libido (SE, 7: 177–78, 159, 151–52). Disgust, then, served to normalize the growing body away from childhood perversity and into conventional, civilized genital sexual practices, served as well to help individuals constitute themselves as subjects and concomitantly regulate their sexual impulses.

Yet Freud represented civilized sexual morality not only as useful to the forces of ego-building and subject-making but as harshly regulatory. The nineteenth-century sexual system allowed, he said, only "legitimate reproduction"; this heterosexual, marital, reproductive sexuality produced, in turn, the frigid woman and the neurasthenic man, and produced as well the homosexual and pervert. The dominant sexual morality, moreover, exacted its demands of women but also of men, prohibiting all sexual intercourse except that practiced in monogamous marriage. Indeed, Freud argued, the premarital sexual abstinence demanded by conventional morality meant sexual intercourse in legal marriage could in "no" way "compensate" for the resulting loss of individual sensuality. Women, in particular, suffered "extensive restriction[s]" of their sexuality, while men enjoyed the benefits of a double sexual and moral standard. Quoting neurologists and psychiatrists—Erb, Binswanger, and Krafft-Ebing—Freud argued against the simplistic equation of an advancing civilization with the increased prevalence of nervous disease. Yet like these thinkers, Freud, too, imagined for an earlier historical moment and a prior civilization a more "natural" sexuality than the "civilized" late-nineteenth-century version he linked with individual impairment, sacrifice, and injury, as well as with sublimation and cultural achievement.[14] Although cultural forces produced sexuality in cooperation with the developing body, those forces so ruthlessly policed pleasure, Freud said (authorizing the repressive hypothesis), that civilized men and women no longer enjoyed it.

Freud's argument, of course, idealized the historically prior and retrospectively reinterpreted the past in light of present discontents. Moving back in historical time through structures of infinite deferral in his search for a "natural" sexuality, Freud halted at the classical antiquity he so loved and privileged its socio-sexual system and highly cultured civilization.

We must learn to speak without indignation of what we call the sexual perversions—instances in which the sexual function has extended its limits in respect either to the part of the body concerned or to the sexual object chosen. The uncertainty in regard to the boundaries of what is to be called normal sexual life, when we take different races and different epochs into account, should in itself be enough to cool the zealot's ardour. We surely ought not to forget that the perversion which is the most repellent to us, the sensual love of a man for a man, was not only tolerated by a people so far our superiors in cultivation as were the Greeks, but was actually entrusted by them with important social functions. The sexual life of each one of us extends to a slight degree—now in this direction, now in that—beyond the narrow lines imposed as the standard of normality. The perversions are neither bestial nor degenerate in the emotional sense of the word. . . . Psychoneuroses are, so to speak, the *negative* of perversions. (*SE*, 7: 50)

Invoking his reader's disgust, as had Moll and Krafft-Ebing before him, Freud did not simply represent perversion or inversion as disgusting but, going beyond his argument that culture served the embodied subject's self-regulatory activities, presented homosexuality as a cultural construct, without articulating at the level of theory the nature of homosexuality's social functions, its usefulness to the constitution of social norms and heterosexual systems. Freud's glorification of antiquity's sexual practices and social conventions suited the self-critical analysis of modern life that emerged at century's end, at least in part through such retrospective reinterpretations, and through the contestation of notions about degenerative forces at work with those of the once-dominant ideological logic of historical progress.

Yet the sexological indictment of civilization as producing increased mental and nervous disease—a purifying critique Freud considered and helped construct—neglected to theorize the structural relations and social networks that obtained between social institutions or units and individual psychologies. A more systematic analysis of culture as constructing sexuality would have to wait until the structuralist revolution of the mid–twentieth century. The structuralist theorization of sex as a cultural system of exchange would then translate Freud's modern analysis into a postmodern positing of pleasure's history. After structuralism, classical antiquity's assignment of different forms of desire to men and women can be identified as a socio-sexual system different from but no less regulatory than modern sexuality's assignment of "different sorts of sexual object-choices with different *kinds* of sexuality" (Halperin 1990, 36). The cultural restriction of female sexuality and the masculinized paradigm of sexual physiology can be identified as results of the sex/gender system's privileging of patrilineage and its distribution of gender attributes according to social norms. The heterosexual imperative that guided sexology could then also be criticized as a systematic function of social institutions of exchange (marriage) and reproduction (the family) that produce and regulate the sexuality—the bodies—they deploy. While Freud did not have access to the conceptual tools with which to produce this analysis, his representation of nineteenth-century sexuality as repressive would nevertheless support early-twentieth-century resistance, especially that of feminists and homosexuals, to the prevailing sex/gender system, which had recently become available for scrutiny. The social forms and cultural lives of homosexual and feminist groups in the United States, Britain, France, and especially in Germany, created an energetic political force and a subcultural lived experience for which experts had to account.[15]

The nature/social debate in sexology encouraged scrutiny of social conditions at home and of cultures abroad. The nineteenth-century discourses of cultural ethnography, criminal anthropology, and sexual

pathology produced a purified "nature" through discourse about "the social," thus situating what seemed pathological in a primordial past that
paradoxically predicted modern European sexuality yet had differed from
it in practice. Each discourse produced theories of natural and normative
sexuality even as each constituted the natural as somehow outside the
normative. In primitive civilizations, then, or in contemporary aboriginal
social groups, the nature/culture and pathological/normal binarisms were
aligned in an inverted ratio. If the pathological was "natural," it was so
only in uncivilized societies; contemporary civilized sex, these discourses
argued, had developed rigorous restraints—dams and moralities—against
sexual life. Paolo Mantegazza, for example, appropriated and revised sex-
pathological terminologies for an "ethnology of love." The sexual practices of indigenous, non-European people such as Africans or Australian
aborigines appeared, in Mantegazza's logic, both "natural" and atavistic in
relation to the civilizing forces that shaped European sex. He identified
masturbation, sodomy, bestiality, and lesbianism as primitive "voluptuous
sensations" (Mantegazza 1886, 102–22); he catalogued and depicted unusual erotic positions and artificial penises as sexual "artifices" (ibid.,
83–101); he represented the battling for, selection, and buying of wives as
a primitive social practice unrelated to European civilized sex (ibid.,
181–93); he presented ritual circumcision, infibulation, and clitoridectomy as savage methods of controlling female sexuality (ibid., 153–60).
While Mantegazza's cross-cultural "science" of love naturalized unnatural
sexual activities by placing them safely in the historical past, in the cultural and racial domain of the other, it endorsed as the outcome of the
civilizing process reproductive sexual relations and monogamous marriage, free partner choice, respect for wives, and affective spousal attachment. Mantegazza deployed the process of history, then, to reinforce and
sustain the binaristically produced norms of heterosexual, marital, and reproductive sexuality.

Cesare Lombroso's research performed similar cultural work in the
domain of criminal anthropology. Appropriating pseudoscientific concepts and documentary photographic techniques, Lombroso traced the
anomalous biologies, genealogies, and social conditions that produced degenerate and atavistic criminals and prostitutes. Standardizing his observations against an unspoken yet clearly assumed norm, he identified and
classified criminal individuals by picturing their abnormally shaped
skulls; prostitutes, their large thighs, short feet, small crania, and deep
wrinkles. Measuring reflex actions and testing bodily sensitivity to

pain—much as the Salpêtrians had observed and experimented on hysterics, much as Muybridge and Marey had documented the human figure in motion—Lombroso declared prostitutes' clitorises "natural[ly]" without sensation, presumably from overuse or evolutionary biological dictates. Sexual selection, he said, happily tended to weed out deformed females for reproductive tasks, for primitive men would refuse to marry and would instead "eat" them, preserving for marriage the handsome women who could contribute to racial development and historical progress. Yet because primitive females had more often been prostitutes than criminals, Lombroso said, they demonstrated the evolutionary rule of atavistic degeneracy.[16]

Grounded in and teleologized by the notion of the natural, Lombroso's and Mantegazza's theories of sexuality identified primitive, polymorphously perverse pleasures as having been modernized and become normative. Degenerate falling away from decency, then, represented a return to savagery and precivilized behaviors. By 1892, theories of degeneracy and atavism had so thoroughly entered European culture that Max Nordau could ground an aesthetic theory on its racist assumptions—and even diagnose Émile Zola as a "degenerate."[17] Deploying the natural/social binary, these theorists mythologized sex and made a functionalized, normalized sex seem modern. The savage, sexual anthropology's quasi-object, both constituted and confirmed sexual normality by violating it. Widely disseminated, coexisting among and taken up by other discourses and cultural practices, these retrospective reinterpretations of the social past appropriated quasi-experimental technologies and represented themselves as scientific.

The late-nineteenth-century production and shaping of sexuality, then, could be put to a variety of ideological and sociological uses. Sexology and cultural anthropology shared, and translated across disciplinary boundaries, rhetorical figures and logical strategies. Like Mantegazza, Ellis invoked a cross-culturally and retrospectively theorized historical past to account for modern bodily pleasures, yet he believed "uncivilized" sexual practices to be the "key" to nature's generativity; hardly atavistic, savage sex seemed to Ellis "socially constitutive" (Ellis 1952, 19). Ellis's case histories, moreover, demonstrated that modern, "normal" sexual development invariably included perverse childhood and adolescent pleasures such as masturbation, same-sex seduction, and solicitation of prostitution; that many homosexuals, moreover, considered their condition natural, even if some thought it abnormal (Ellis 1902, 233 [appendix B], 44–110).

Although Ellis's rhetoric sounds homophobic, it described the social system of compulsory heterosexuality. Allowing invert autobiographers to speak for themselves in his scientific texts, Ellis thereby justified the social deregulation of homosexuality.

Krafft-Ebing's "medico-forensic study," however, took a politically conservative stand.[18] Although he likewise endorsed the congenital theory, Krafft-Ebing idealized monogamous, affective heterosexual marriage; while such "natural instincts" often swerved toward perversity, they nevertheless grounded, he said, all ethics, aesthetics, and religions (Krafft-Ebing 1946 [1886–96], 1–24). This scientific research, portraying sensationalized and primitivized desire, thus justified a sentimentalized rhetoric of regulation of femininity, marriage, and the domestic. For Krafft-Ebing openly deployed the natural/social binary to confirm his normative views of heterosexuality. As I maintain in Chapter 6, his archivalized research on pathological sex acts and sexual character served his scientific project to normalize bodily sensation, regulate erotic pleasure, and mythologize the heterosexual imperative. In this version of sexual pathology, the pervert functioned—as did the savage in sexual pathology—to constitute normality by violating it. The discursive quasi-object, once again, confounded and created oppositional thinking.

But the sexological production of a prehistorical, naturalized, and primitive sexuality is hardly limited to the nineteenth century. All three notions appear as trace in Michel Foucault's anecdotal positing of a natural, pre-Enlightenment, rural, and childlike sexuality that, by implication, existed before the pedagogization and medicalization of sexuality, before an interrogatory machinery for "speechifying, analyzing, and investigating"; his notion of a non-Western *ars erotica* that theorizes the truth of sex as a practice of pleasure that, neither forbidden nor utilized, is valued for its quality, duration, and intensity and transmitted with "skill and severity" from master to novitiate; his adulation of a Greek moralized, yet free, sexuality that, while an ethics solely for men and masters, is based on "natural [sexual and class?] difference." Although subject to restriction, this sexuality, Foucault claims, is not organized by the "binary form of permitted and forbidden," legislated as normativity, or based on "interiorization of rules, acts, and transgressions" (Foucault 1978, 31–32, 57–58; id. 1985, 177, 116, 63). As a cliché would have it, even paranoids have real enemies; but Foucault's commitment to finding everywhere the carceral models of social regulation and knowledge/power production he looks for virtually eliminates from his work a theory of resistance to disciplinary technologies and the bureaucracies that deploy them. Nevertheless, the discourse on sexuality—even that of late-twentieth-century genealogical thinking—produces as natural a historically prior time, a socially primitive group, and an unconstrained sexuality as both antecedent to the present moment and as the repository of values not tolerated in the present. That unregulated sexuality, I would argue, functions invariably as desire in the discourse that produces it.

III

At the 1881 International Medical Congress, Robert Battey joined Charcot, Ferrier, and Goltz in discussing experimental scientific research and medical procedures. Battey had pioneered and championed an operation he called oöphorectomy, or "normal" ovariotomy (or, as James Marion Sims, the American gynecologist, called it, "Battey's operation") in which nonpathological ovaries were removed from female patients to treat symptoms such as dysmenorrhea, amenorrhea, or nervous disease. Indeed, in July and August 1872, the American, German, and British surgeons Battey, Alfred Hegar, and Lawson Tait had performed the first "normal" ovariotomies; all three doctors would become the procedure's proponents and practitioners in Europe and the United States. At the 1886 International Medical Congress, however, Battey protested that surgeons had performed his operation too frequently and for questionable indications—not only for menstrual pain or dysfunction, but for hysteria, hystero-epilepsy, epilepsy, catalepsy, and nymphomania.[19] Spencer Wells, a British ovariotomist who opposed oöphorectomy, confirmed that such surgery had been widely used to treat "general nervous symptoms."[20] By 1893, however, the medical profession had judged Battey's operation brutal and inhumane, indeed, virtually criminal. The medical societies purged from their membership the normal ovariotomists or converted them to dominant theory and practice; and the professional literature—expunging oöphorectomy from its vocabulary—represented, even mythologized, ovariotomy as the direct medical antecedent of general abdominal surgery (Longo 1979, 262).

I do not mean to ignore the real advances in surgery during this period. Ovariotomy had, in fact, saved the lives of many women with uterine and ovarian disease. Too many pregnancies and childbirths, caused by inadequate contraceptive practices; too many abdominal infections, caused by lack of antisepsis and routine surgical cleansing, had produced a plethora of vaginal and uterine disorders among both pre- and post-menopausal women. That fewer women died of ovarian tumors and cysts was a significant medical advance. Yet when surgeons deployed diseased bodies to create a scientific breakthrough, as experimental researchers had at the Salpêtrière, the female body bore a disproportionate burden of anguish and pain in the service of experimental fact-finding. The scientific work of purification and mediation used human and animal subjects that were either marginal or at risk—such as incarcerated lower-class hysterics or Goltz's decorticated dogs—to produce research findings. Once normalized or pathologized, sex could be submitted to the twentieth-century laboratory. By the 1920s, reproductive biology would, once again, have sought to modernize sex by experimenting on natural organisms in order to create facts and truths from the laboratory. Like the hysteric, the pervert, and the invert, the castrated research subject was produced as a quasi-object that both violated and confirmed binaristic thinking about sexed, sensate bodies.

As an emergent medical practice, "normal" ovariotomy and the debates that surrounded it could, however, be appropriated for a variety of ideological and sociological purposes. By analogy with male castration, oöphorectomy was indicted by its opponents as female "castration"; rhetorically, it was represented, not simply as a surgical practice, but as the "unsexing" of women. Given widespread contemporary fears about the decline of the race, labor unrest, and feminist agitation, Ornella Moscucci says, British opponents of normal ovariotomy, in particular—including feminists and anti-vivisectionists—represented this unsexing of women as a threat to marriage and the sexual division of labor, institutions that stabilized European society and reproduced social relations. During a period when, as Moscucci argues, Britain embarked on its most "ambitious programme of colonial expansion," imperialism could not succeed as a political and economic strategy without the support of productive and functional maternity. Oöphorectomy's brief popularity, Moscucci maintains, resulted not simply from medical progress in antisepsis or surgical intervention, or from medical misogyny and doctors' misuse of women, but from its intrication with the nineteenth-century social construction of femininity, women's reproductive function, and female sexuality.[21] In the professional controversy about surgical removal of healthy ovaries for the treatment of female nervous diseases, then, researchers produced scientific knowledge about the body that could be appropriated to support a gendered and sociologized functionalism.

Questionable reproductive surgery, however, hardly began with Battey's operation. In the 1860s, Isaac Baker Brown, a British surgeon who specialized in ovarian "dropsy" (or edema) and ovariotomy, introduced a surgical cure for insanity, epilepsy, and hysteria. Speculating that "peripheral excitement of the pubic nerve" (a euphemism for masturbation) was female insanity's primary exciting cause, Baker Brown's experimental surgery "freely excised" the clitoris and nymphae with scissors or knife. When Baker Brown sought to transport his research findings to other scientific centers, incensed physicians debated the merits of Baker Brown's "physiological experiment" in the medical press. Critics complained that extirpating the supposed organ of "provocation" hardly treated female nervous disease; Baker Brown, doctors said, could not demonstrate, moreover, that *surgery* had produced the stated yet unproven cure. Baker Brown performed clitoridectomy on insane inmates of the London Surgical Home, which he had founded, and, when a consulting surgeon resigned to protest surgical clitoridectomy at the Home, the Obstetrical Society of London "tried" Baker Brown for unprofessional behavior and expelled him from its membership.[22]

Baker Brown's primary accuser, Seymour Haden, based his indictment on "professional grounds," raising the specter of "quackery" and upholding the "strictest principles" of medical "honour." For as a gynecologist in a society of gynecologists, Baker Brown should have acted, Haden said, as a "custodian" of women's "honour" and therefore "constituted [himself] the true guardian" of their "interests." Paradoxically, Baker Brown claimed clitoridectomies produced more functional mid-century wives than did other treatments for female insanity and, invoking the specter of another medical battle, compared his controversial practice to specular examination of the uterus. Unmoved by appeals to medical progress, mindful of the profitability of observing women's reproductive organs, and failing to see penetrating gaze and surgical piercing as commensurate medical practices, the Society sacrificed Baker Brown to the exigencies of professionalization. In the 1880s, similar vituperation and invective would greet Robert Battey when his fellow physicians curtailed his practice in an effort to control not female auto-erotic pleasure but women's access to maternity.

The medical mavericks who pioneered oöphorectomy and clitoridectomy proposed a sexual etiology for female insanity. For Baker Brown and Battey, a woman's nervous health could be located in her functioning—or pathology in disordered—reproductive organs. The sex organs, seat of female sexuality, transmitted nervous impulses to the brain, affecting the psyche; they produced disease, by reflex action, in organs linked to uterus or vagina by the sympathetic nervous system. Neither Battey nor Baker Brown departed from then-dominant medical conceptualizations of reproductive biology, physiology, or anatomy. By the end of the century, however, reproductive biology had embarked on an ambitious program to clarify this sexual physiology. For concomitant with the historical production of the invert and pervert in sexological representations of a normative and naturalized sexual practice, sex reentered the laboratory. There, through the mediation of research collectives and networks, sex as neurological reflex would be rewritten as hormonally regulated sex—and eventually could become the immunological sex of postmodern auto-immune deficiency syndromes.[23] As the research laboratory fabricated research subjects as quasi-objects, sexual hybridity spawned modern sexed "identities," which in turn produced postmodern sexualities.

Eugen Steinach's experimental castration and hermaphroditism research, undertaken in 1894, 1910–12, and culminating around 1920, retheorized the physiological, functioning sexed body as the hormonal body. Between 1894 and 1910, Steinach's studies demonstrated that the gonads controlled the sex instinct, since castrated male rats exhibited the same unweakened "sexual excitability" as control animals. When he injected gonadal tissue into castrated male frogs, the neutered animal, demonstrating secondary frog sex characteristics, grew thumb pads and demonstrated the "clinging instinct" with females. He had proven, Steinach said, that, although the nervous system played a role in maintaining and stabilizing the sex life, the gonads and their blood-borne hormones exerted "primary causal control," for without gonadal essence, animals had "no sex life at all" (Steinach 1940, 14–36; and see also Marshall 1960 [1910], 2: 512–19; 3: 301). In 1912–13, Steinach's hermaphroditism experiments confirmed his earlier findings. Removing and implanting the gonads of infantile female guinea pigs into males, and those of males into females, Steinach established, he said, the sexual specificity of the gonads and demonstrated that the sex gland performed two endocrine functions, favoring the development of homologous and inhibiting heterologous sex characteristics. The feminized male's nipples expressed breast milk, and the animal showed a "willingness to carry out the nursing function with the same care, devotion, and patience which are natural for a normal female"; the masculinized female guinea pigs vigorously scented, pursued, and courted other females in heat, made repeated attempts at sexual contact with them, and were fought by males as though they were rivals. Such "experimental hermaphroditism," Steinach said, "had converted males into females" and females into males (Steinach 1940, 61–70; and see Marshall 1960 [1910], 3: 8–10). In 1910, Steinach removed the testicles of infantile subjects and reimplanted them in a different site in the animal's own body, proving, he said, that the glands' internal secretory function was regulated by the pituitary gland (Steinach 1940, 97). In 1917, he sterilized laboratory guinea pigs with the new x-ray technology to test whether the uterus would, nevertheless, continue to grow and develop endometrial tissue. These animals, he said, "although virginal, had been transformed by irradiation into the condition of nursing mothers" (Marshall 1960 [1910], 3: 18; Steinach 1940, 109–10).

Steinach's experiments set forth endocrine system physiology and demonstrated the functions of the pituitary gland, reproductive organs, and sexual instinct. They also inscribed cultural assumptions about social function onto the body, representing them as fact, and so as natural rather than cultural. For the scientist's observations that the male guinea pig's nursing was both "natural" and "normal" for females ignored the difference between psychological categories (such as care, devotion, and patience) and anatomical sexual structures (such as nipple and breast). When asked why castration experimentation produced scientific evidence, Steinach responded that the scientist need not refer to secondary sex characteristics (such as beard and breast) to comprehend the "thorough differentiation between man and woman," which "nature" had "carried out to the very last detail." The production of the hormonal body in the first decades of the twentieth century codified the perceived differences between male and female bodies, anatomies, and physiologies, obscuring their grounding in and circulation through cultural systems. "Everyone knows," Steinach declared, "even without books, that men are generally hardier, more energetic, and more enterprising than women, and that women show a greater inclination for tenderness, devotion, and a tendency to nestle and cling, at the same time demonstrating a practical aptitude for domestic problems" (Steinach 1940, 64, 7, 38–39). Because of the historically sustained and culturally reproduced association of woman with the body, with nature and materiality, characteristics of the female body could thus be read, metonymically, as attributes of female subjectivity and as normalized psychological femininity.[24] Steinach's research thus appropriated what he considered commonsensical perceptions of sexual difference—what Freud had called the common language of the body, transported them into the laboratory, and produced them as scientific truths.

Steinach's research sustained the production of a codified sexual difference through what Laqueur calls a "social theory of sexual incommensurability" between the sexes (Laqueur 1990, 220). His work, however, had not in fact proved his claims about sexual functioning, for the frog's "cling instinct," the rat's sexual excitability, and the guinea pig's nursing were not necessarily generalizable to humans. Whereas the frog clung to its female sexual partner because its transmitted biological characteristics and evolutionarily developed thumb pads enabled such embracing, humans had no such anatomical equipment, designed especially for clinging, that grew during and withered after the period of sexual heat. Human sexual arousal, moreover, is not periodic, as is animal heat. Human hands, infinitely more complex anatomically and equipped to perform more complicated tasks, caressed their sexual partner, as Moll's theory of concretation attempted (however rudimentarily) to demonstrate, for emotional as well as physiological reasons. Moreover, while the guinea pig's instinct, transmitted genetically from parent to offspring, necessarily included suckling her young, the human's parenting behavior could not so clearly be naturalized to hormonal flow or normalized by reference to inherited behavioral characteristics. Whereas Goltz's experiments on dogs' brains could not reliably provide the "key" to human cerebral anatomy, Steinach's experiments did, however, produce knowledge about lower mammalian endocrine systems and provide research maps for constructing human reproductive biologies. And although he did not conceptualize the ways in which his statements about social functioning read metonymically from the experimentally produced differences between male and female bodies, anatomies, and physiologies to psychical and social values, Steinach understood quite clearly that his experiments did illustrate, serve, and sustain human values about sexual behavior and interaction.

Indeed, Steinach viewed his project as settling the sexological debates about the nature/social and normal/pathological binarisms. His experimental hermaphroditism shifted masculine subjects toward feminine behavior, eroticization, and, when fully "abnormal," homosexuality. This "sexual perversion," Steinach said, which had been regarded as "an acquired variant of the normal sex instinct, and attributed to wrong upbringing, bad example, seduction, idleness, and innate immorality," could now "be based on physical causes" (Steinach 1940, 87–89). Yet Steinach knew his research results remained limited precisely because he studied animal rather than human subjects. He could not perform castration and hermaphroditism experiments on human experimental subjects, he said, "by law and common sense." He could neither "unsex boys and girls" in very early youth to create "neutral creatures," nor restore masculinity and femininity to "neutralized boys and girls." Yet the infantile castrate provided the "only really conclusive test object in sexology and in research on gonadal hormones" (ibid., 40, 43). Animal "natural hermaphrodites," while rare, did exist, however, and experimentation on them produced "additional proof" of Steinach's views. "Nature itself sometimes create[d] these bisexual creatures," Steinach said, and experimentation on such "abnormalities of nature" bore out the "deductions drawn from [his] experimental hermaphrodites." A stallion, for example, whose scrotum contained one normal and one undescended testicle, was castrated and the normal testicle removed; but only with the removal of remaining testicular tissue did the horse develop the anatomical and behavioral characteristics of geldings. "Nature," Steinach said, had thus "made an experiment which admit[ted] of the same interpretation" he had produced from laboratory castrations (ibid., 86–87, 99). Steinach could not, however, resolve his problem with generalizability. "True hermaphrodites" hardly existed among humans; while "mixed sex forms" occurred in "man," they were most often "more or less anatomically abnormal," "pseudo-hermaphrodites" mistakenly assigned the wrong sex at birth, or deviant variations from the "normal type" (such as females with large clitorises). Such human experimental subjects, Steinach knew, would hardly, if available, have produced statistically verifiable scientific results. Only during World War I did wounded soldiers provide the first human subjects for sexological and hormonal experiments made by nature.[25]

Despite his best efforts, Steinach's laboratory experiments failed to naturalize sexual behavior to an unproblematic physiology. While he had identified nature as a passive surface, outside the social and yet its necessary counterpart, Steinach knew that nature could not be so controlled. "For even in nature," he said, "the line of demarcation between the sexes" was not clear; "absolute masculinity or absolute femininity in any individual represent[ed] an imaginary ideal." Perfect specimens of a single sex seemed "theoretical ideals"; for a person could be identified as "normal" only if a certain "equilibrium" of sex hormones occurred, and, because each sex possessed both male and female hormones, such equilibrium appeared normal within wide ranges and "abnormal" only at extreme ends of a spectrum (Steinach 1940, 7, 87–89). The physiologist F. H. A. Marshall agreed. For physiology knew only that sexual characterization of individuals was not "fixed and final" but "mutable and controllable," that maleness and femaleness represented a "balance between two opposing forces" that seemed "stable and permanent" in some living organisms while "impermanent" and destabilizable in others. "No male is wholly male, no female solely female," Marshall admitted, underwriting the purifying practices of laboratory science even as he exposed the facts of experimentally produced and observed mediation (Marshall 1960 [1910], 2: 742).

The same was true of sexual object choice. While philosophers and biologists proposed, for example, that homosexuality was congenital (for it appeared at a very early age, was manifested in childhood, and occurred frequently in members of the same family), experimentation showed that experts "really knew nothing for certain" about human sexuality (Steinach 1940, 89–92). Indeed, Steinach confessed, his experiments had not "completely dispelled the darkness surrounding the mystery of sex" but had simply "lifted a corner of the veil" (ibid., 71). The ongoing scientific project to produce the truth about sexed bodies—to confirm the natural/social binary and so to consolidate the normal/pathological—nevertheless served to mobilize theory production and to construct scientific networks. Participating in the modern critique, Steinach practiced the laboratory work of mediation and purification: his experiments proliferated hybrids to separate the "natural" being from the social order, even as their existence denied that separation (Latour 1993, 27–37). By the 1920s, sexual difference and gender roles participated in this modern problematic. When Freud concluded in 1933 that "what constitutes masculinity or femininity is an unknown characteristic which anatomy cannot lay hold of," he would no doubt have sounded distinctly old-fashioned (SE, 22: 114).

I have investigated Steinach's research precisely because Freud led me to it. In the 1920 revisions of Three Essays on the Theory of Sexuality, Freud incorporated discussion of Steinach's experiments and Alexander Lipschütz's applications of them into his text but argued against their social production of functionalized sexual differences. Noting that Steinach's work illuminated the "organic determinants of homo-erotism," Freud affirmed that experimental castration and grafting of opposite sex glands into mammals affected both "somatic sexual characters" and "psychosexual attitude," both "subject and object homo-erotics." Thus when a human subject who had lost his testes through tuberculosis (and therefore behaved as though feminine, developed female secondary sex characteristics, and acted in his sexual life as a passive homosexual) had an undescended testicle from another male patient grafted into him, he again became masculine and took women as his sexual objects. But this research, Freud believed, did not necessarily prove that homosexuality was physiological and might, after additional research, validate Fliess's competing theory of bisexuality instead. Thus neither the hypothesis that inversion was innate nor the alternative, that it was acquired, could explain the "nature of inversion." Far from a "psychical hermaphroditism," psychological clinical research demonstrated that inversion and somatic hermaphroditism were instead "independent of one another." The same was true of secondary sex characteristics in relation to psychic qualities. While, then, Karl Heinrich Ulrichs explained inversion as "a feminine brain in a masculine body," Freud found "neither need nor justification for replacing the psychological problem with the anatomical one." For, he said, "we have not even any grounds for assuming that certain areas of the brain ('centres') are set aside for the functions of sex, as is the case, for instance, with those of speech." Although Steinach's discovery of pituitary tissue's role in determining the release of "chemical substances" seemed to naturalize sexuality, the "present state of our knowledge" in the biological sciences, Freud said, remained problematic. Steinach had not settled the nature/culture debates about human sexuality, had clarified neither the body's anatomical production of erogenous zones nor the nature, origin, and "basis of sexual excitation."[26] Sexuality as "normal" or "natural," then, seemed no less problematic after Steinach's laboratory experiments than it had before, just more hormonally based.

And by 1920, when Freud revised *Three Essays* in light of Steinach's research, it was no longer credible to invoke natural teleologies to support cultural theories of sexual difference. We can trace this change in Freud's reconceptualizations of reproductive sexuality in *Three Essays*. In 1905, he had assigned a teleology to a sex situated in and controlled by nature. The infantile sexual aim obtained satisfaction from stimulation of erotogenic zones that, once experienced, demanded repetition. "Nature will have made safe provisions," Freud said, that this "experience of satisfaction shall not be left to chance." In 1920, however, Freud added a footnote: in biological discussions, the scientist could scarcely avoid a "teleological way of thinking," he said, "even though one is aware that in any particular instance one is not secure against error" (*SE*, 7: 184). This rhetoric doubly removes the analyst from his investigations; as "one" replaces self-reference, error is grammatically removed from one's agency, and Freud betrays his ambivalence about declaring that infantile sexual aim and a child's instinctual gratification determine adult heterosexual object choice. In 1915, Freud qualified a teleological statement about natural sexual selection; "if such a teleological form of statement [was] permissible," he demurred, (male) libidinal excitation and sexual arousal depended on visual impressions of (female) beauty. Seeing, an activity derived from touching, thus purposefully participated—Freud maintained even as he hedged his scientific bets—in enacting, even in constituting, the heterosexual imperative (SE, 7: 156). Still, Freud deleted a similar phrase in the same edition. "It is difficult to overlook Nature's purpose," he had written, "of establishing the future primacy over sexual activity exercised by [the genital] zone by means of early infantile masturbation, which scarcely a single individual escapes" (SE, 7: 188). Having been severely criticized in 1912 at the Vienna Psycho-Analytical Society for his teleological argument that nature installed universal infantile masturbation specifically to guarantee adult genital pleasure, Freud deleted reference to nature's teleological aim as a foundation for heterosexual reproductive sexuality. Yet Freud's universalizing imperative implied that childhood masturbation was natural, and that, despite the loosening of teleological argumentation, sexuality itself possessed a force that produced heterosexuality as evolutionarily functional, even if dysfunctional perversion and inversion everywhere stalked it.

By 1920, Freud could no longer afford, nevertheless, to ignore the new reproductive biology in theorizing sex. Freud's "libido theory," as he called it in Three Essays, built upon Steinach's experiments, even as it sought to bypass their biological determinism. "It seems probable, then," he said, "that special chemical substances are produced in the interstitial portion of the sex-glands; these are then taken up in the blood stream and cause particular parts of the central nervous system to be charged with sexual tension." While still linked to the nervous system, this tension—a biological strain, or force, or stress—has altered its causal mechanism from nerve, to sexual fluid, to blood-borne hormone. But the hormonal body will not sustain Freud's metaphorical systems of psyche, somatism, and cultural circulations of value. A thoroughly modern thinker by 1920, Freud stated the incommensurability of a hormonal sexual biology and psycho-physical sexual theory. "The question of how sexual excitation arises from the stimulation of erotogenic zones, when the central apparatus has been previously charged," he said, "and the question of what interplay arises in the course of these sexual processes between the effects of purely toxic stimuli and of physiological ones—none of this can be treated, even hypothetically, in the present state of our knowledge." This "special chemistry of the sexual function," then, could tell the investigator little about psychosexual functioning. The "assumption that substances of a peculiar kind arise from the sexual metabolism" might produce new knowledge about the hormonal body but could say little about the eroto-genic body (*SE*, 7: 215–17, 219).

As the nineteenth-century neurological body gave way to the modern hormonal body, Freud departed company with biologically and phys-iologically based theories of sex. He would move, however, to redress the aporias of libido theory by invoking a special sort of representation, one different from that which he had produced by comparing the hysterically with the organically paralyzed body. Fashioning drive theory out of sex-ological concepts, Freud created what he called "representance." In this revised psycho-physical theory, the psyche functioned as representative to the organism, and organism to psyche. Yet Freud's earliest studies of sex, I suggest in this chapter's next section, constituted the binarism real/fan-tasy as allied and aligned with the sexological oppositions natural/social and normal/pathological. His work with what he called the "actual" or "anxiety" neuroses, and with hysterical patients who reported seduction, attended to the sexual practices and social values of the 1890s. While crudely physiological itself, the seduction theory gave Freud the theoreti-cal leverage to reject reductionistic accounts of biologically determined disease causation. For if nervous disease were caused by a "real" physical seduction, he reasoned, it could hardly be hereditarily transmitted or con-stitutionally degenerative. Yet Freud would abandon seduction early in his project to constitute a modern sexual theory of psycho-physical cor-relation and psychopathological causation. While the seduction theory appeared to problematize and modernize neurological theories of the re-flex body, it quickly came to seem a dead end for Freud's psychoanalytic science.

IV

Between 1895 and 1897, Freud observed the facts of seduction in a clini-cal setting as his patients, primarily female, repeatedly reported having passively submitted to sexual assault by an adult, usually their fathers. All fifteen of the hysterics he had studied before 1896, he maintained, had suffered sexual assault or repeated brutal abuse, been victims of seduction, or endured an infantile liaison. Convinced that his patients' confessions were true, Freud denied that his hysterics fabricated their memories. These recollections emerged, bit by bit, only under the "most energetic pressure" of the analytic procedure, he said, and against strong resistance; when they did become known, his patients experienced emotions "hard to counterfeit"; they had left an "indelible imprint" on the case's history and were represented in it by symptoms that could be accounted for in no other way; they were peremptorily called for by interpretation of the neurosis's structure; and therapy lagged if they were not recovered; therefore, the analyst had no choice but to reject or believe the whole (SE, 3: 153). In "The Aetiology of Hysteria"(1896), he argued that an etiological factor for neurosis could act more widely than its effect but not more narrowly (not all persons exposed to smallpox contracted the disease, but all who did must have been exposed); not simply a precocious sexual experience but a psychological precondition must have existed to precipitate neurosis, since healthy people might also recollect infantile seductions; infantile sexual scenes, which patients initially described as harmless, demonstrated great uniformity of details and caused much pain; and evidence of such scenes' reality could sometimes be procured from family members or others who had witnessed the seductions. Although he would later admit that his dependence on the real constituted a real/fantasy binarism that itself needed interrogation, Freud read these early patients' reproduced scenes as evidence of real events, the memories of which, acting as "foreign bodies," had later caused illness.

Freud's first version of seduction emphasized the child's real innocence and fragility. His rhetoric moralized even as it explicitly eschewed moralizing judgments. An "immature girl" suffered attempted "rape" and so saw "at a blow" the "brutality of sexual desire"; a child involuntarily witnessed parental sexual acts and so, observing "unsuspected ugliness," suffered "wounds" to his "childish and moral sensibilities." Freud also examined scenes of seduction with the concept of consent, a notion that had, by the 1890s, begun to figure prominently in thinking about sexual practices. Without previous seduction, Freud assumed, innocent children could not "find their way" to acts of sexual aggression, and thus neurosis could be caused only by adult violation. And such violations were everywhere enacted, Freud saw. Although pediatricians had "stigmatize[d] the frequency of sexual practices by nurses and nursery maids" (which they carried out "even on infants in arms"), children were more often exposed to sexual assaults, Freud said, "than the few precautions taken by parents" would lead him to expect. The adult responsible for a child's care—nursery maid, governess, tutor, or unhappily and all too often, a "close relative"—had violated his or her trust—for there was "no question," Freud said, of the "child's consent" in the cases he had observed. Whether "brutal" adult assault, "infantile liaison" between children (which presupposed earlier adult seduction), or "less repulsive" seductive practices, these nursery- and family-based sexual relations besmirched the innocents whose sexual development consequently went awry.[27] Freud's rendering of the ways domestic institutions, hierarchical arrangements, and dominant values put children at risk empathetically attended to, and bore the traces of identification with, victims other sexologists disregarded or sought to punish.

Yet the notion that seduction of an innocent presexual child by a tainted, perverse adult produced hysteria reinscribed even as it reimagined the old sexological arguments about whether psychopathology was congenital or acquired. Indeed, during the 1890s, the debate about the etiology of inversion had focused on seduction, on how a child with no sexual experience could have himself become a pervert or homosexual. Whereas Krafft-Ebing classed inversion as a disease constituted by sexual practices that could never excite the "normal" but only the "degenerat[e]" individual, as a characterological disorder attributable in no way to accidental or external impressions, Alfred Binet argued that accidental events caused homosexuality and that Krafft-Ebing's patients, had they been submitted to different chance childhood traumata, might have developed different psychopathologies.[28] Albert Moll acknowledged that accidental causes could precipitate sexual inversion, but he supported the congenital theory. Denying that inversion or perversion could "systematically be caused by bad habits," Moll argued, for example, that a boy who imitated dogs copulating by inserting a pencil into his anus had not acquired the habit of perverse masturbation but had inherited a predisposition to sodomy; a "normal child," Moll said, could "introduce a pencil into his rectum every day without causing sexual perversion" (Moll 1931 [1891],150–51). Albert von Schrenck-Notzing disagreed. Moll's anal masturbator set up "local irritation" sufficient, Schrenck-Notzing said, to cause "normal" sexual excitation and penile erection (Schrenck-Notzing 1956 [1895],187).

When he proposed the seduction theory, then, Freud entered a professional debate that had already generated widely different discursive positions, each buttressed by biological and cultural evidence. Situating himself within the debate, Freud tried out several notions before deciding that the binaristic logic of neurosis etiology was itself a mistake. Although Freud never stopped believing that children were physically and sexually abused by adults, he nevertheless recanted his seduction theory in a now-famous letter of September 21, 1897. He offered Fliess four explanations for his change of heart, explanations that disavowed and undid his logic in proposing seduction as theory. First, he had been unable successfully to conclude any analyses; second, he could not believe paternal perversions against children sufficiently widespread to account for the unexpected frequency of the hysteria diagnosis; third, the unconscious did not distinguish between real truth and affect-laden fiction (nor could the interpreting therapist discern the difference); fourth, unconscious memory could never fully be disclosed even in the therapeutic situation. The late-twentieth-century anger about Freud's recantation centers on his second, third, and fourth explanations. Some feminist scholars, practicing analysts, and psychoanalytic theorists argue that Freud's rejection—he "no longer believed in his *neurotica*"—favored fathers and refused to accept the reality of child sexual abuse.[29]

This objection ignores Freud's logic, however. In jettisoning seduction, Freud argued against deterministic models of disease onset and personal history, against purely physiological notions of illness causation. For only if many more children had been abused than fell ill, he reasoned, could presexual seduction be assigned as singular cause of neurosis; many other contributing factors would have to join with seduction to produce hysteria in any given individual, even after assault, and with the epidemiological frequency Freud had observed in his clinical practice. Illness could befall an adult who had been abused as a child only if other physical and psychical factors (such as constitution, psychic predisposition, and family cover-up) converged in the subject's history. Purely physiological theories of neurosis etiology, then, ignored psychical, historical, and familial circumstances.

The seduction theory helped Freud spring his thinking free from biologically based hereditary and degeneracy models of disease causation. In his early work, however, he had deployed Benedict Morel's degenerative model to argue for the hereditary hypothesis: in the first generation of a neuropathic family, one member practiced perversity; in the second, some member became hysterical, obsessive, or otherwise neurotic; in the third, the offspring might prove to be sterile. Deploying this genealogical chart,

Freud interpreted: if a hysterical patient's brother—the foot fetishist about whom I wrote in Chapter 1—had not abhorred his perversity, repressed his impulses, and replaced them with compulsive and secret sexual activities, he might not have become "abnormal" himself; "if he could be perverse," Freud said, he would be "healthy, like [his] father." Despite his sexually abusive acts (for the father had seduced his son, who, in turn, seduced his sister, into his sexual scenes), this father, Freud meant, had himself not fallen ill; but his son, who had been seduced into fetishistic activity, had become compulsive, and his daughter hysterical (Freud 1985, 213).

Yet Freud questioned the degenerative model as early as 1892. "Is heredity anything other than a multiplier?" he had asked Fliess in "Draft A." "One sometimes comes across a pair of neurotic patients who were a pair of little lovers in their earliest childhood," he later wrote; if they were "brother and sister, one might mistake for a result of nervous heredity what is in fact the consequence of precocious sexual experience" (Freud 1985, 37; *SE*, 3: 156). About one hysterical male patient who had seduced his sister and had previously been seduced by his uncle, Freud told Fliess, "you may gather from this how a neurosis escalates to a psychosis in the next generation—which is *called* degeneracy—simply because someone of a more tender age is drawn in" (Freud 1985, 222; my emphasis). What looked like hereditary transmission or even degeneracy could thus well have been caused by environmental influences and presexual sexual experiences. Thus, he reasoned, childish sexual experiences decisively influenced later sexual development because injury to an immature organ caused graver effects than damage to a mature one. Hysteria was therefore acquired through seduction rather than inherited (*SE*, 3: 202).

Collapsing metonymy into simile, Freud reconceptualized heredity as seduction. "Hysteria," he said, "results from *perversion* [Freud's emphasis] on the part of the seducer"; "heredity *is* [my emphasis] seduction by the father" (Freud 1985, 212). Freud's rhetorical construction of the theoretical binarism heredity/seduction (a version of congenital/acquired) as an identity through the copula represented a first escape from the trap of thinking with degeneracy. It allowed him to interrogate this sexological opposition, to contaminate it with everyday events, to imagine the binaristically produced empty place of third-generation sterility as occupied by an embodied victim. And Freud continued to view seduction as a problem for theory. When introducing the basic concepts of infantile sexuality—polymorphous perversity, latency, child masturbation, and component instincts—Freud presented seduction as a nursery-based activity that produced the child's body as sensate and so seducible. Although instinctual causes could arouse a child's sexual life, premature seduction could also introduce children to irregular sexual activities that nurtured their innate disposition to polymorphous perversity, present children prematurely with a sexual object for which they "show[ed] no need," and exaggerate the importance of a child's already lively scopophilia (*SE*, 7: 166–69, 187–92). "Have we not a right to assume," he asked, "that even the age of childhood is not wanting in slight sexual excitations?" (*SE*, 3: 202). These delicate sensations produced a rhetorical and theoretical instability that undermined and eventually demolished the seduction theory.

The seduced child's body enabled Freud to produce a *theory* of sexuality anchored in infantile and instinctual sexuality. Replacing the concept of hereditary prehistory with that of childhood as "something like a prehistoric epoch," Freud portrayed childhood as functioning at the level of theory only through sexuality, the diphasic introduction of which, he said, explained an otherwise inexplicable infantile amnesia (*SE*, 7: 176). The facts of infantile sexuality, moreover, could only be understood by reference to family circumstances and to bodily nursery care. For Freud represented the child's genitals, enclosed in a pouch of mucous membrane, as stimulated not only by bodily secretions, but, given their "anatomical situation," by washing and rubbing during routine toilet activities. The connection with anyone responsible for his care—but in particular with his mother—was eroticized; in Otto Kernberg's terms, affectively invested object relations energized physiological zones and functions.

At a time at which the first beginnings of sexual satisfaction are still linked with the taking of nourishment, the sexual instinct has a sexual object outside the infant's own body in the shape of his mother's breast. . . . There are thus good reasons why a child sucking at his mother's breast has become the prototype of every relation of love. The finding of an object is in fact a refinding of it. . . . All through the period of latency children learn to feel for other people who help them in their helplessness and satisfy their needs a love which is on the model of, and a continuation of, their relation as sucklings to their nursing mother. There may perhaps be an inclination to dispute the possibility of identifying a child's affection and esteem for those who look after him with sexual love. I think, however, that a closer psychological examination may make it possible to establish this identity beyond any doubt. A child's intercourse with anyone responsible for his care affords him an unending source of sexual excitation and satisfaction from his erotogenic zones. This is especially so since the person in charge of him, who, after all, is as a rule his mother, herself regards him with feelings that are derived from her own sexual life: she strokes him, kisses him, rocks him and quite clearly treats him as a substitute for a complete sexual object. A mother would probably be horrified if she were made aware that all her marks of affection were rousing her child's sexual instinct and preparing for its later intensity. (SE 7: 222–23)

This remarkable passage introduced into theory ideas that Freud knew were scandalous. Adult male love merely repeated, on a higher level, the child's sucking at the breast; nursery care initiated and produced the child's sexual sensations; his mother's apparently "pure" love inscribed his body with its erotogenic zones.

Not infantile sexuality as such, however, but its affect-laden and reciprocal fantasmatics represented the scandal of psychoanalytic theory. For cathected as sexual object by his mother's fantasy, the infant's body was marked by her touch and its sexuality constituted by her desire; his later "sexual love" for her, then, originated in hers for him. The status of the infant's fantasy—which, Freud said, "seizes upon the theme of the parents"—had first been stimulated by her having enacted on his body her substitutive sexual scenarios. For only if this was a mother's desire could the infant stand in for her sexual object. Indeed, Freud here represented object relations as initiated by parental fantasmatic sexuality: how could the child later know to take others as objects unless he himself had first been so taken? Freud here represented mothering as implanting in children the subjective experience of pleasure, as reproducing sexual subjectivity. In this version of seduction, "the shape of [the] mother's breast" became, as Freud maintained until the end of his life, the "first and strongest love object" and "the prototype of all later love-relations—for both sexes." Through her care of the child's body, through her imposition on it of her own fantasy, the mother became the child's "first seducer" (SE, 23: 222–25, 188). That seduction produced the child's sexuality as fantasmatic and as constituted by and through affect-laden object relatedness.

Yet instinct theory allowed the facts of physiology to reemerge in psychoanalytic theory. Indeed, this scene of maternal seduction produced the male subject as paradigmatic for psychoanalysis. When he had examined the "mental shapes" of children's sexual lives, Freud had, he acknowledged, taken the male child, the little boy, as subject of his investigations; he had supposed that "things must be similar" for girls, but also somehow indeterminantly different (SE, 19: 249). In fact, paternal seduction proved entirely different from maternal nursery care and affect-laden object relatedness, as I suggest in Chapter 6. In the 1920s, however, Freud transmuted the scopophilic position he had studied in hysterics, a position I sketch in Chapter 6, into the oedipalized "sexual researches of childhood." The child's instinct for knowledge, desire to know where babies came from, and the inquiry into sexual difference belonged primarily to the male subject.

The small boy undoubtedly perceives the distinction between men and women, but to begin with he has no occasion to connect it with a difference in their genitals. It is natural for him to assume that all other living beings, humans and animals, possess a genital like his own; indeed, we know that he looks for an organ analogous to his own in inanimate things as well. This part of the body, which is easily excitable, prone to changes and so rich in sensations, occupies the boy's interest to a high degree and is constantly setting new tasks to his instinct [to perform] experiments undertaken in the service of sexual research. (SE 19: 142–43)

Enjoying the sensations he produced by stimulating his genitals, the boy observed it, presumably, becoming erect and so sought to exhibit it to others and to see theirs. Surprisingly enough, however, he would eventually encounter a dissimilar one. An "accidental sight" of female genitals provided, Freud said, the "occasion for this discovery." For unusually intelligent boys would have been aroused, when observing girls urinating, to a certain "suspicion" that "there is something different here"; he would have "seen a different posture," "heard a different sound," and attempted to "repeat [his] observations so as to obtain enlightenment" (SE, 19: 143). Although, then, the boy did not set out to research the anatomical difference between the sexes, interpreting bodies as morphologically like his own, he would have found himself in the research scientist's position: looking and looking again until comparative observation of cases allowed him to produce theories; sifting and interpreting the descriptions he had fashioned to depict the difference he had seen and heard to generate a (sexual) theory.

The researching boy eventually produced a binaristic theory centered on a sensate, excitable, changeable, narcissistically cathected body part. When observation contradicted his preconception (that all humans had penises), the small scientist disavowed observation and believed he did "see a penis, all the same." Only the castration complex, which originated in the *"phase of phallic primacy,"* persuaded him to bring his inductions into line with his deductions, and to accept the fact of sexual difference. For, at this stage of infantile genital organization, "*maleness* exists, but not fe-maleness"; the operative phallic stage binary, Freud said, represented dif-ference as "having *a male genital* [or] being *castrated*"; only at puberty did the binary "*male* and *female*" obtain (*SE,* 19: 144–45; Freud's emphases). Thus the sexed male subject produced the representative schema of op-positional thinking, which was itself anchored and supported by the male/female binarism. That binarism originated with the slight but de-lightful sensations in the boy child's penis and ended by producing a the-ory that deployed binaries as its central representational and cognitive category. Not the male genital itself but its visibility privileged it within an economy of anatomical difference, made it the "natural" and uninter-rogatable foundation of oppositional thinking, made its discovery, more-over, the paradigm for childish—and perhaps all—knowledge produc-tion. And, in psychoanalytic theory, such a model for scientific investiga-tion produced, along with the Oedipus complex, the conceptualization of phallic primacy and castration that affirmed the penis as the privileged site of an unquestioned and unquestionable natural, anatomical binary.

Yet instinct theory also retheorized representation as a plausible mind-body bridge. Indeed, it more complexly rendered models of psy-cho-physical correlation and psychopathological causation than had Freud's representational theory of hysterical paralysis. First, Freud refused to *equate* instinctual with physiological stimuli, for while the latter pro-duced sensation from outside the body, the former operated as a "constant force" from within. The terminology of reflex arcs, Freud said, repre-sented "*physiolog[ically]*" the discharge of nervous energy produced by stimuli; instinct theory's "*biological* point of view," however, described the organism's management of internal excitation or needs. The nervous sys-tem as apparatus functioned, then, to reduce stimuli to the lowest possi-ble level, and its complex task to "*master*" stimuli could not be depicted by the "simple pattern" of physiological reflex arcs. For instincts made "far higher demands on the nervous system" than did external stimuli and "oblige[d] the nervous system to renounce its ideal intention of keeping off stimuli" by maintaining an "incessant and unavoidable afflux of stimulation." Yet because this system and its mental apparatus was "au-tomatically regulated by feelings belonging to the pleasure-unpleasure se-ries," a relation that fluctuated and was unstable, the plausible bridges be-tween psyche and soma needed rethinking. Instinct theory did so. The idea of instinct, Freud concluded, bridged mind and body. "[A] concept on the frontier between the mental and the somatic," the instinct was the "psychical representative of the stimuli originating from within the organism and reaching the mind," was a "measure of the demand made upon the mind for work in consequence of its connection with the body" (SE, 14: 118–22).

With drive theory, Freud had recast his concept of psycho-physical correlation by transmuting sexological thinking about the neurological sensate body. For the instinct was not simply of the body but functioned to mediate the relation of psyche and soma. Representing and serving as representative of stimuli to the mind, it measured the work that the pleasure-unpleasure relation regulated. Freud sited or situated this representation on the marker between binaries. Although he later revised this portrayal of body to mind by instinct as operating through ideational depiction of the body's delegates to mind, Freud had revised his way out of the representational dead ends sexology had produced for an emergent psychoanalysis. Freud had rejected in turn the reflex sensate body, the degeneracy theory of disease causation, and the seduction theory. Although the concept of seduction had privileged a natural childhood innocence, it had initiated Freud's researches on family circumstance. Still, he had increasingly marginalized the concept of affect, the most flexible concept with which to theorize a modern subjectivity rooted in, yet logically separable from, the body.

The suppressed concept of affect, I argue in the next chapter, constituted the psycho-physical field in which Freud articulated his earliest representation theories. Concomitant with his suppression of affect, he had nevertheless begun to conceptualize a psycho-physical sexuality at the level of theory; having witnessed the spectacle of sexual pantomime and hallucination at the Salpêtrière, Freud recalled the sexual jokes he had heard whispered at social and professional events in Paris, as I discuss in Chapter 2. In Chapter 6, I examine the hospital's charts, graphs, and iconographic texts to argue that Charcot's representational strategies depicted but suppressed a hybrid notion of sexuality. While Charcot staged the physiologically malfunctioning sexual body, Janet researched but could not yet theorize a psycho-physically sexual body. Krafft-Ebing followed the Salpêtrians, deploying hypnosis to experiment on a hysteric who had been diagnosed, in addition, with "congenital perverse sexual feeling." These laboratory networks had begun to produce a psycho-physical sex that elided, even as it sought to confirm, the opposition between the natural and the social. This hybrid sexuality, fashioned in the laboratory and leveraged into the social world, was documented and disseminated to a wide medical and nonmedical audience. Freud's cases of uncommon hysteria likewise exhibited a hybrid sexuality, but one inscribed by structures of feeling and transcribed by and within affect. I take as specimen case Katharina's girlish anxiety neurosis mixed with hysteria. For, Freud observed, Katharina's hysteria was formed and informed by affect-laden object relations, self- and other representations, sexual spectatorship, and acts of scenic self-spectatorship. This affective concept of sexuality, I argue, more complexly accounts for a modern, mediated subjectivity than could the physiological, functionalized sex Freud had appropriated from the sexologists or the spectacular hybridity he had acquired from the Salpêtrians.

CHAPTER 6

Scenes of Discovery

When Ilma S., with whom I began this book, was taken to the hospital where Richard von Krafft-Ebing practiced, the Graz police hoped to determine whether a seemingly unstable woman was psychologically able to stand trial for stealing a silver watch, two napkins, and a sheet. In the account Krafft-Ebing constructed of Ilma's past, she had fallen ill repeatedly, had previously been hospitalized and hypnotized; sent to a convent; arrested, brought to trial, and released. She had been diagnosed, variously, as epileptic, hystero-epileptic, cataleptic-hysteric, and as afflicted with "congenital perverse sexual feeling." Ilma's case did not go unremarked in the contemporary press, both popular and scholarly. Having become the subject of newspaper stories and medical articles, Ilma read, one day, about the experiments performed on her at Budapest and so fled the clinic. At Graz, she again appeared in medical narrative, however, for Krafft-Ebing published her case history, complete with the documentary record of his hypnotic experimentation. He included her as well in the *Psychopathia Sexualis*, where he happily reported that her inversion had been cured.[1]

I take Ilma's case, which appeared in the sexological and experimental psychology literatures, as one among many texts that demonstrate the intersection of the discourses about hysteria and sexual pathology, which shared and traded concepts of soma, psyche, and sickness. For in addition to sexual perversity, Ilma suffered bodily hypersensitivity, anesthesia, fainting fits, and hallucinations, all symptoms easily translatable from the research on hysteria to that on sex, or from sex to hysteria. Like the hysterical body, the body produced and documented by the sexual pathologists had, moreover, been mapped, charted, and narrativized. It, too, had been zoned by sexual stimulation and potential pleasures. Yet, unlike the neuropathologists, the sexologists had studied a primarily male patient population, as Chapter 5 of this book demonstrates. Largely absent from the case histories, documentary records, and pathographies or self-narratives, women seemed reluctant to speak about sexual pathology—or, as Havelock Ellis remarked, doctors found their stories difficult to elicit or listen to. But physicians had listened to and observed hysterics for decades, for centuries. Whether caused by "*secrets d'alcove*" or "*la chose génitale*," whether cured by "Rx Penis normalis dosim repetatur!" or sexual abstinence, hysteria had long been associated, however subtextually, with female sexuality—as Freud's reports of Breuer's, Charcot's, and Chrobak's "passing *aperçu*" or two, demonstrate (*SE*, 14: 13–15). Indeed, hysteria seemed transparently identifiable as a complaint that belonged historically and naturally to the biological woman. Deeply implicated in social assumptions about gender, the disease had been discursively produced by, even as it helped sustain, reiterated cultural binarisms and norms. While Briquet had initiated a medical move to theorize hysteria as socially situated and caused, Charcot and others had scoffed at such notions of discursive production. But that the sexed body, the family, and modern subjectivity were sociological constructs seemed to Freud everywhere implicit in sexology's logic. Rejecting his Paris master's take on hysterical sexuality, Freud transformed the conceptual apparatus for theorizing its somatic and psychical morphologies.

In this chapter, I demonstrate that sexological discourse played a crucial role in constituting modern subjectivity. The documentary modes with which physicians depicted hysterical sexuality and psychopathological causation suited a subjectivity anchored in, but conceptually separable from, the body. Those models of subjectivity, I argue, involved intersubjective acts of looking, seeing, and mirroring; these acts constituted the image of self as other, the scene as functioning through screen memories, and the scenario as a fantasmatic or unconscious structure of wished-for pleasure. In the first section of this chapter, I present a sexological model for self-representation as plastic and self-reflective. This portrayal of pleasure traduced, even as it sustained, the usual depiction of perversion or inversion. Documenting perverse desire, the sexual pathologists collected patient cases as examples; publishing patient pathographies, they anchored the binaristic concepts of disease causation discussed in Chapter 5. I argue in Section II of this chapter that, charting and recording daily somatic dysfunctions, the Salpêtrière's staff depicted a sexuality characterized by scenic hallucinatory wishes for pleasure. Documenting a pathological reflex sexuality that suggested affective disturbance and psychopathological causation, the hospital nevertheless failed to conceptualize either at the level of theory. Freud, who himself observed these hysterical performances, suppressed their significance until, as I suggest in Chapter 1, he created the concepts of scenic reproduction, representability, and, as I elaborate in Section III of this chapter, self-spectatorial subjectivity. For seeing represented images of herself in scenes of wished-for pleasure, the psychoanalytic subject doubly identified with an (impossible) image that both was and was not herself. She surveyed her self- and object representations, her scenes and scenarios, and in doing so, situated herself in her affect-laden history. That history, moreover, was invariably embedded in family and social circumstances; those object representations, usually of parental figures, invoked multiple identifications with objects and longings for pleasure. In the psychoanalytic situation, I argue, the patient became hybrid, became subject to herself in scenario, object of analytic investigation, subject of case history, and objective or goal of theoretical production. Appropriating from neuropathology and sexology a subtextual set of sexual tropes, Freud invented a complex theory of sexual subjectivity as constituted by self-dramatizing and self-reflective spectatorship. That self-portrayal linked affect-laden acts, self- and object representations, and fantasied or memorialized scenes in a highly mediated, hybrid being.

Freud's theory of subjectivity also suited the modern project to separate subjects from objects, material things, and nonhumans. Fabricated in laboratories and by scientific networks, the quasi-objects of psychopathological and sexological discourse all exhibited hybridity; pervert, invert, and hysteric were constituted by and through the intersection of natural and social categories even as they were created to shore up oppositional thinking, as I argue in Chapters 3 and 5. Fashioned by scientists whose discourses had been mobilized to create professional and theoretical alliances, these intermediatory figures were translated from discourse to discourse, laboratory to laboratory. I have dealt, in Chapter 3, with the Salpêtrière's "experiments made by nature," the laboratory production of quasi-objects that demonstrated the clinic's physiological theories about dysfunctional patients; here, I maintain that the refusal to conceptualize sexuality as central to subject formation limited the clinic's ability to interest others in its scientific project. The sexologists, I argue, effectively linked subjectivity with sex, interesting a wide audience, including Freud, in their research. Observed in the sex doctor's office and documented in scientific, often widely available and repeatedly published texts, this sexual quasi-subject shored up the moralizing binaries that constituted some individuals as normal, others as pathological, even as it titillated and stimulated members of the mass audience these volumes secured. Freud's consulting room, perhaps a more virtual laboratory than those of the sexologists, produced a complex theory of subject formation that participated in, even as it interrogated, the modern project safely to separate the experience of subjects from the world of objects.

I

Sexology shored up its fragile binarisms by claiming documentary truth as its primary research and representational goal. As sexual scientists, the sexologists sought, first, to reproduce fiducial findings about sexual dysfunctions that occurred in nature so as to confirm and verify their status as dysfunctions; and, second, to assemble and reproduce a sufficient sample of such sexualities to prove their findings credible and their research generalizable. By virtue of the binarisms sexology worked to produce, dysfunction could be measured against function, and abnormality against norms, even if those norms were known only implicitly. And, although sexologists, like neurologists, tested and physically examined their patients' bodies, the sexologist could not (usually) enter the marital bedroom or visit the brothel and so could not observe his patients' couplings. He necessarily produced his research findings, then, by listening to patient narratives about intersubjective sex acts, about autoerotic fantasies, and about partnered and singular perversions. The sexual pathology discourse recorded the voluptuous sensations and recounted the sexual activities of perverts and inverts: rapists, erotomaniacs, exhibitionists, voyeurists, and sadists. The sexologist's subjects were virtually all male, and, as a result, they represented sexual arousal—whether the pleasure in looking, the ways dreams caused "pollution," or the enjoyment of anal sex— by charting the physiological course of male erection and ejaculation as related by male patients.[2] Sexological documentation, then, reinscribed, even as it supported, sexology's binaristic representation of male sex and masculine subjects.

Krafft-Ebing documented sexual psychopathology by collecting evidence, compiling statistically significant research samples, and classifying dysfunction according to a complex set of labels. Researching sex in much the same way that Binet had studied the higher mental functions, Krafft-Ebing assembled a significantly large sample of patient narratives, nosographically described the pathologies he had observed, and nosologically classified them with sufficient precision and control for his findings to have scientific value. His research method of observation and examination, disease description, and scientific classification compiled taxonomic groups and assembled differential statistics that justified his classificatory schema and claimed credibility for his representational project. His text did not copy an original psychopathology, he implied, but illustrated and enumerated that reality by statistically counting, cataloguing, and labeling it. Yet enumerating psychopathologies that were not mimetic copies, Krafft-Ebing produced more psychopathologies. He measured the reported intensity of excitations and sensations against other such reports; he invented labels to characterize their essences and appropriated others: "voyeur," "masochism," "sadism," "fetishism" (the last of which he borrowed from Binet). He medicalized and subsumed patient stories into psychiatric case study:

R., aged thirty-three, servant, was admitted suffering with *paranoia persecutoria* and *neurasthenia sexualis*. Mother was neuropathic; father died of spinal disease. From childhood he had an intense sexual desire, of which he became conscious as early as his sixth year. From this age, masturbation; from fifteenth year, *faute de mieux*, pederasty; occasionally, sodomitic indulgences. Later *abusus coitis in matrimonio cum uxore*. Now and then even perverse impulse to commit *cunnilingus* and to administer cantharides to his wife, because her *libido* did not equal his own. His wife died after a short period of married life. Patient's circumstances became straitened, and he had no means to indulge himself sexually. Then masturbation again; employment of *lingua canis* to induce ejaculation. At times, priapism and conditions approaching satyriasis. He was then driven to masturbate in order to avoid rape. With gradually predominating sexual neurasthenia and hypochondria came beneficial diminution of *libido nimia*. (Krafft-Ebing 1946 [1886–96], 76–77)

Here, Krafft-Ebing recounted the physiological facts of a patient's sexual dysfunction. Syncopally rehearsed patient life events had point and significance, in Krafft-Ebing's case studies, only if they rationalized sexual functioning. Yet Krafft-Ebing's case studies suppressed their most interesting questions: about the reasons for sexual unpleasure, the link between neurosis and libido, the social arrangements that supported and sustained sexual dysfunction, for example—even the narratively sequenced implication that R.'s wife died as a result of perverse marital sex.

When his readers consulted him (or mailed him pathographies suitable, they hoped, for diagnosis), Krafft-Ebing absorbed their tales, too, into his representational project, adding them, in turn, to revised editions. By its twelfth edition, the *Psychopathia Sexualis* was an archival tome documenting the doctor's classificatory categories and clinical pictures more than the sexualities it purported to portray. Indeed, the pervert had acquired the status of statistic. His case no longer important, except as an instance, his self-representation serving only to illuminate an argument about an identifiable perversion, the individual pathographer became a representative case. Krafft-Ebing's sexual science thus proved the incommensurability of natural or normal with pathological sex, even as it endlessly discovered, documented, and clinically produced intermediate figures. The "third sex," as Magnus Hirschfeld called the homosexual, confirmed the truth of the two-sex theory, even as it covered over its contradictions. Compiling a collection of pathographies, labeling and objectifying their tellers, and making their cases representative of this or that highly nuanced category, Krafft-Ebing medicalized and moralized sexual (dys)function.

Albert Moll and Havelock Ellis constructed their research credibility not by compiling perverts as statistics but reproducing patient pathographies verbatim. These autobiographies recounted perverse sexual adventures; the scientific text in which they were embedded was sensationalized by their narratives. Unlike Freud, as I discuss in Chapter 7, neither Moll nor Ellis detailed the choices he had made in recording these reproductions. For Moll and Ellis, the problem that needed documenting was neither representative nor uninterpretable. While Krafft-Ebing had amassed individuals as classifiable quasi-objects, doing, as I said in Chapter 5, "sexology with numbers," Moll and Ellis sought to humanize the quasi-object by calling attention to his status as quasi-subject. Ellis did so by seeking to normalize aberration from various social-scientific perspectives. He maintained, for example, that the concept of bisexuality was historically recuperated to serve various discursive propositions; that organic bisexuality, constituted by Greek philosophers as the key to sexual inversion, had been revived by nineteenth-century philosophers both homosexual and heterosexual; that latent bisexuality had been theorized successively by Darwinian science, psychiatry, psychopathology, physiology, and reproductive biology. Whether or not his readers agreed with Ellis's genealogy, they would no doubt have agreed with his conclusion: that, by 1900, the concept of bisexuality had passed into "current thought." Ellis likened inversion, moreover, to a variety of constitutional abnormalities and anomalies such as color blindness, none of which, he argued, constituted a "diseased condition" or a morbidity. The invert, Ellis said, was, then, not only the "victim of his abnormal obsession" but of "social hostility." Nevertheless, the "emotional, enthusiastic nature of the congenital invert," Ellis argued, would make possible his acceptance of an aesthetics of the self inherited from the Greeks, with its valuing of human dignity, temperance, and chastity (Ellis 1936 [1897], 314–19, 338–39).

Moll, however, reproduced patient pathography to document deviance. In one of his representative cases, a young man tells about his seduction by the family's gardener. Moll recounted the youth's story of watching his seducer exhibit his erect penis; of embracing and kissing, mutual masturbation, and anal intercourse; of the youth's urge to look at male buttocks—not having his lover's at hand, he gazed backward at his mirrored own. Looking, moreover, set the sexual scene. "I showed him my penis," Moll quotes; "he touched it and his touch gave me a voluptuous sensation; a sensation, not entirely physical, but brought on by the idea that it was this beloved man who touched me. Then we became more and more intimate. Very soon he showed me his member, and gave in to my desire to let himself be masturbated by me." Here, Moll reported yet ignored sex as a psycho-physical category; he presented this narrative, instead, as evidence of exhibitionism, voyeurism, sexual inversion, and homosexual masturbation and penetration. Using the rhetoric of sensation-saturated bodies that I characterize in Chapter 5, Moll portrayed homosexual bodies as capable of anomalous arousal and intensification. These sensation-seeking and sensationalized bodies performed not one but many deviant sexual activities; as lovers, these two men had appropriated every bodily frontier region for pleasurable sexual activity, had used each mucous membrane and nongenital zone to enjoy stimulation, voluptuous sensation, and orgasm (Moll 1933 [1897], 85–89). Moll's sexological representation theorized this sensational body, sensationalizing, in turn, its own discursive production of the documentary pathographical record.

Allowing the youth's tales of sexual acts and fantasies to enter scientific discourse, however, Moll conceptualized a spectatorial sexual subjectivity. For even as he documented homosexual sex as dysfunctional, Moll also reported the youth's pleasure in looking, not only at bodies, but at images, representations, and his own reflection. In fact, Moll here represented the homosexual erotic act itself as a "mirroring," an inversion and imaging of the selfsame body in sex; a picturing of the object as (like) the subject, and the subject as like the object. Moll reproduced the youth's pathography, then, to represent homosexuality as a sort of projective identification, an inmix of identification *and* desire, a desire to both *be* and *have* the phallus. Yet this double move also represented the homosexual as hybrid: a perfect example and perfectly representative case of self- and other representation gone awry, the invert could be mobilized to engender sympathy with a deviance that was, as a result, more fully understood as deviance. Indeed, in this homosexual version of the lady-screws-the-gardener myth, class transgression also situated perverse acts in social relations different from the norm. This pathographical crossing of class and heterosexual boundaries contributed to the text's capacity to titillate— and the reader's self-protection against somehow seeing himself reflected in its penetrated, self-mirroring discourse. Moll represented this sexuality as perverse and, at the same time, made his reader party to this perversion, inviting complicity in constituting titillation (and perhaps readerly auto-arousal) as a perverse pleasure even as he sought to moralize his reader's response to invert sexual acts. Moll's representative case could only be read as sensational, as simultaneously shocking and thrilling.

But Moll's invert raised an unsettling question: was the homosexual different from or like other subjects? Despite their differences, these sexologists all described a sexual "third" kind of being that confirmed the existence of, even as it eluded and scandalized, the binary categories of subject and object. Appropriating patient pathographies to serve their research projects, sexologists represented the homosexual as pervert, deviant, or anomaly to document the truths about subjectivity that they claimed their science had discovered. Sexology represented those truths, then, as central to the making of modern, individual men. Sexual subjectivity was normal or pathological, both naturally occurring and socially constituted. As such, the homosexual served to illustrate what Bruno Latour calls the "modern constitution," the stated state of affairs in which the social and natural, the subject and object, are safely separated from, yet everywhere implicated in, one another. This separability guarantees that, as Latour says, "there is no common measure between the world of subjects and the world of objects," even while, at the same time, it measures human and things, objects, or animals with the same technological tools (Latour 1993, 52–62). Doubly contradictory in forming its truths, the modern science of sexology guaranteed that sexual subjectivity was normally neither perverted nor inverted by documenting a long list of sexual perversions and narrated inversions.

The scientists at the Salpêtrière followed a different course, as I argue in the next section of this chapter. They, too, observed sexual perversions in action in wards and laboratory, but safely separated sexual subjectivity from their research findings by disguising it as physiological dysfunction. Unlike Charcot's, Krafft-Ebing's clinic at Graz exploited the hysteric's perverse sexuality, translating her across disciplinary discourses and between laboratory settings to mobilize conceptual production. Freud's use of the hysteric to theorize psycho-physical sexuality, as I discuss in Section III of this chapter, interrogated, even as it sustained, the binaries of subject and objects, normal and pathological. For translating the hysteric from one research discourse to another, Freud constituted a theory of the self-spectatorial psychosexual subject. In doing so, he posed a question being asked throughout the sexological literature: was the homosexual produced by social or natural events?

II

The Salpêtrière's laboratory provoked, observed, and described hysterical symptomatology, as noted in Chapter 3, as though it were naturally occurring and graphically naturalizable. Yet Magloire-Désiré Bourneville and Pierre Regnard's *Iconographie photographique*, its summary medical histories and diaries of hospital treatments, suggested that hysterical sexuality everywhere bore the traces of social values and collective activities. In Celina Marc——'s hystero-epilepsy, for example, Bourneville and Regnard recounted a story of working-class female sexual desperation and domestic difficulty framed as though the patient's history were purely medical. A fourteen-year-old apprentice washerwoman, Celina often amused herself sexually, stayed away from home all night, gave false addresses, and played "husband and wife" with men. She became sexually involved with a man named Ernest, strolled with him in the evening or went to his rooms; they argued; she fell ill with vaginismus and ended up at the hospice of St. Vincent de Paul. After she fought with her employer, Celina's family placed her as apprentice first to a fruit seller, then to a washerwoman, and finally to a boot stitcher. She fought with her stepmother, who threatened that, if she were not obedient, Celina's father would be forced to choose between his wife and daughter. Accosted by a man in the street one night, Celina was then attacked by a dog and taken to the hospital, where she dreamed of menacing figures that looked like hybrid men/dogs. When home once more, Celina fought again with her stepmother, continued to have sex with Ernest, and fell ill with vaginismus. She began to behave strangely, to babble about men and marriage, about envying women with infants. After a dental operation, Celina experienced a nervous attack and was taken to the Salpêtrière (Bourneville and Regnard 1879–80, 1: 111–49).

Celina's medical history was firmly embedded in social circumstances. It referred to family dysfunction, sexual abuse, and class and gender oppression. Constrained by her choices of how to make a living, Celina sought to marry. She became sexually involved with a variety of men and, strolling in the city, presumably identified as a prostitute, she was a target of urban sexual violations. By putting her at risk of abuse and disease, her sexuality endangered both her health and her ability to secure her future in marriage and motherhood. Having been identified by her family as ill, Celina pronounced herself cured, interestingly enough, when, after escaping from the Salpêtrière, she had intercourse without vaginal pain. She therefore defined functional female heterosexuality, practiced with a possible future partner, as health. The hospital's medical history, however, which suggested a correlation between working-class female sexuality and hystero-epilepsy, rightly refused to identify class conditions and social relations as the cause of Celina's nervous disease. Conceptualizing a functional working-class female sexuality, I would argue, lay outside the Salpêtrians' field of inquiry and Bourneville's documentation of it. An urban hospital, outpatient clinic, and residential ward necessarily served a working-class population; a research laboratory specializing in reflex and hypnotic experimentation produced physiological findings rather than therapeutic outcomes. The hospital deployed respectable, but hardly innovative, medical and isolatory therapeutics to produce the haphazard cures that seemed secondary to the goals of research.

The Salpêtrière's iconographic record documented daily somatic treatments for symptoms diagnosed as reflex and physiological. Once in the hospital, Celina underwent treatment interventions that focused on her genitals and reproductive organs. For she had presented with "pronounced erotic tendencies," and her attacks of convulsion, *arc de cercle*, aura, ovarian pain, and delusion demonstrated reflex disorders. Charcot and other staff members stopped her attacks by compressing her left ovary on February 21 and 23, 1872; and on April 12, by doing so with her right ovary. Celina suffered not only disordered sensation and movement but erotic delusions. In the hospital record, she is represented as hy-

persensate and hypersensual, even, in a displaced localization, as symbolically orgasmic: her "physiognomy expressed lively pleasure"; raising her
pelvis and repeatedly thrusting it forward, she cried, "ça y est!" "papa,
papa!" or "Ernest, Ernest!" with "satisfaction"; her mouth foamed with
abundant saliva. On November 5, agitated, singing, and attempting to
embrace ward assistants, Celina consigned herself to the straitjacket.

The clinic ignored Celina's hallucinatory, clearly sexual and self-representing, subjectivity. Treatment reflected, instead, the diagnosis of reflex
erotism. On November 22, her cervix was cauterized with a hot iron; the
speculum entered her vagina with difficulty, occasioning pain and a return of vaginismus. In February, April, and June 1874, Celina's cervix was
again cauterized. In 1874 and 1875, she received anti-spasmodics, ether,
amyl nitrate, and chloral. The staff iced her abdominal ovarian region and
again cauterized her cervix. By summer 1875, Celina had become irritable and menacing; she broke things and sexually provoked staff members.
For contractures and hallucinations, she received morphine injections that
probably produced her new symptoms, cold sweats, twitchings, and
swellings. In 1876, Celina was photographed; in 1877, she and another
young woman patient, Geneviève, twice escaped from and were twice
returned to the Salpêtrière. After somatic and hypnotic treatments,
Celina had become less rather than more capable, was drug addicted, sexually aggressive, and physically disruptive. The summary discussion of the
medical case blamed her family's medical history and paternal alcoholism, her "deplorable education" and "vagabond existence," the "vicious
habits" she had learned in infancy (presumably masturbation), and physiological traumatism for causing and prolonging Celina's illness.[3]

Like Celina, Geneviève had been diagnosed, not only as a hysteric,
but with eroticized motor and sensory disorders. She, too, had been sexually active at 14, but, unlike Celina, she had lost her lover, Camille, at 15.
After his funeral, Geneviève had escaped from her father's house through
a window, fled to the cemetery, and thrown herself on her lover's grave in
a cataleptic trance. She had been hospitalized, douched, and bathed at
Poitiers; at 16, despite painful menarche, she was pronounced improved
and placed with a private nurse; at 17, her belly distended from menstrual
distress, she had again been hospitalized; the nuns thought her pregnant,
and, until a midwife reversed their diagnosis of pregnancy, they had "per-
secuted" Geneviève. Removed to the ward for the insane, she had been
treated with belladonna, which caused visions and hallucinations; she had
cut off the nipple of her left breast, the record states, for no apparent rea-

son. She fled the hospital with her student lover, went to Paris, and, during an attack in the street, was arrested and taken by police to the Necker Hospital; more attacks landed Geneviève, on December 6, 1864, in the Salpêtrière.

Although they were diagnosed as physiological, Genevieve's eroticized disorders were embedded in social circumstances. She reported there that she had won the nuns' confidence during her earlier hospitalizations, had been permitted to wander the hospital freely, and had roamed the streets of Toulouse and Paris in borrowed clerical costume—sleeping in trees, undressing to wash her chemise, and begging bread. In August 1867, Geneviève gave birth to a daughter at the Salpêtrière; unable to breastfeed, she assented that her child be sent out to nurse. In 1872, again hospitalized, Geneviève entered Charcot's ward, where the diary record lists treatments for repeated hospital stays through 1877. Although her medical history does not, like Celina's, record her as presenting with a symptomatic "vagabond existence," homelessness clearly contributed to Geneviève's distress. Her sexuality, like Celina's, also exposed her to the abuse, precocious pregnancy, and dysfunctional maternity the record depicts her as having experienced. Like Celina's, Geneviève's medical history portrays a woman's complex and problematic social relations as resulting in ill health and disabled subjectivity.

Although the hospital treated Geneviève's symptoms medically, theatricalized self- and object representations of erotic and religious deliria nevertheless appear central to her case. The hospital documented her characteristic scenes photographically as well as in writing: she dramatized "lubricity," for example, in disordered movements, trances, and sensations; she would drop her body on the bed, lift up her chemise, open her thighs, and, addressing an assistant, lean toward him while saying, "Embrace me, give it to me, take my . . . " Geneviève's "scenes," repeated and repeatedly documented, flaunt a carnivalesque erotism, complete with baring of body, smacking of buttocks, and thrusting of pelvis. The summarizing commentary, in fact, reports that Geneviève "fancied" herself visiting her dead lover, Camille; imaged herself as St. Theresa, and as Louise Lateau, her sister. Pantomiming an aggressive, easily available, self-offering, and frenzied female sexuality, Geneviève's scenes represented her situation as a woman who, homeless and vagrant, used her sexuality strategically both inside the hospital world and on the streets.

I do not mean to suggest that the conditions of working-class life produced Geneviève's hysteria, but that her self-representations in hallucinatory gesture and imagined scene dramatized her subjectivity as shaped, at least in part, through social and familial circumstances. A working-class woman whose vagrancy, linked in the public mind with deviant female sexuality, got her in trouble with, for example, the police, nursing nuns, and Salpêtrière staff, Geneviève's histrionic representations characterized her in situations of risk. Like Freud's hysterics' scenes, which, as discussed in Chapter 1, contained the same figures or elements rearranged in different contexts and transferred onto other figures, Geneviève's scenes restructured and depicted her experience as hallucinatory representation. Her object representations of lovers and others pantomimed her wished-for pleasures and played themselves out as eroticized, hallucinatory scenes and scenarios (Bourneville and Regnard 1879–80, 1: 70–90). Her self-representations, acted to and for the staff as audience, demonstrated that hysterical sexual dysfunction demanded to be theorized as a psycho-physical disorder.

Nor do I mean to imply that the Salpêtrians intentionally mistreated Celina and Geneviève. The staff's nosological descriptions and diagnostic judgments implemented the then-standard medical course for treating mixed hysterical and organic illness. Yet, as the record suggests, the recently medicalized nineteenth-century hospital could induce—and certainly worsen—disorders. It proved difficult to cure a long-term residential patient population that, geriatric or severely dysfunctional, had little hope of living the productive life viewed outside the hospital as normal and normative. The laboratory's experimental findings, moreover, mapped deranged somatic sensation and demonstrated disordered physiological function. The clinic's representation of Geneviève's sexual scenes thus failed to become meaningful as other than renderings of an amorous or lubricious female, and so were suppressed; eroticism entered the documentary record only in photographic subtitles. Indeed, the hospital's record depicts the Salpêtrians' refusal to conceptualize sex as a strategy for medicalizing an otherwise illogical disease. The Salpêtrians' representation of hysterical sexuality, finally, suggests the fascination and disgust that this transgressive female figure excited. Her sexualized psychomotor behaviors, theatricalized self-enactments, and hallucinated scenarios flouted civilizing forces and staged a grotesque, denuded, outrageous sexuality that, although it could be observed, demonstrated, and even documented, could not yet be conceptualized at the level of theory. Indeed, as I suggest in Chapter 4, the relatively stable meanings nineteenth-century subjects attributed to health—a long life, the capacity for reproduction and for physical work, strength, resistance to fatigue, and absence of pain—meant that normalcy specifically precluded the suffering, impotence, helplessness, disability, and lack of capacity suffered by incarcerated hysterics at the Salpêtrière and elsewhere (Canguilhem 1978 [1966], 63–68).

Indeed, the Salpêtrians' hypnotic experiments and therapeutics were not unique to Paris, or even to France, the hotbed of hysteria. Using technologies that resembled Charcot's, Krafft-Ebing experimented on Ilma S.'s mixed hysteria at his clinic for nervous diseases in Graz and demonstrated it in the medical amphitheater at Steiermark. Krafft-Ebing's *An Experimental Study in the Domain of Hypnotism* (1896 [1889]) seemed guaranteed, however, to prove the hysteric a sexual pervert. At the beginning of the book, Krafft-Ebing reproduced the autobiographical story that Ilma had written at his request, a story detailing not only her medical history but the events of her sexual life, the family and social relations that constrained and conditioned her experience. She recounted, as essential to her story, a series of suicides as familial medical history, and said she feared a similar sad fate for herself. According to her autobiographical account, she had fallen in love with her cousin "as only a woman can love a man" and, according to her brother's account, "surrender[ed] herself . . . sexually" to an unnamed engineer and been rushed back to the convent by her angry father; she had also, while at the clinic in Budapest, fallen in love with a sister of charity. "The passion was sensual," Krafft-Ebing said, and greatly "disturbed the patient." Indeed, Ilma had proved a problem, too, at the Rochus Hospital, where she had not only suffered frequent hystero-epileptic seizures but had demonstrated symptoms of "perverse sexual feeling" that, when expressed, proved "troublesome in the ward." Moreover, as we have seen, Ilma had dressed as a man and been hired to tutor two children, whose mother had sexually approached the "quiet teacher with the girlish face." In addition, she had worked for a railway company, and, so as not to "betray her sex," had "carouse[d]" with her fellows, cursed, and visited prostitutes. Having an insider's view of masculinity, Ilma said, she had taken an "unconquerable dislike" to men and their motives and found herself powerfully, indeed passionately, drawn to sympathetic, intelligent women and girls (Krafft-Ebing 1896 [1889], 1–20). Identified as hysteric, transvestite, invert and pervert, Ilma had escaped to Graz, only to find herself in 1887 once more arrested, hospitalized, and subjected to hypnotic experiments.

Indeed, Ilma S.'s case illustrates the ways in which scientists translated the hysteric into the discourse on sex, and the pervert to hysteria. For Krafft-Ebing reported her case in his research not only on hypnotic experimentation but on sexual psychopathology. And although his experimental research had recounted but suppressed sex, Krafft-Ebing's *Psychopathia* foregrounded sex as a diagnostic category. A conventional medical case study, Krafft-Ebing's sexological representation opened with Ilma's family medical history of "bad nervous taint," paternal alcoholism, maternal apoplectic paralysis, sibling hysteria, and multiple family suicides; it continued with her medical history of irregular menses after age 18 and adolescent catalepsy and hysteria. It documented her psychopathology in syncopal detail. Ilma had indulged in a passionate love affair, sensual enjoyment, and, after her lover abandoned her, frequent masturbation. She had cross-dressed as a tutor and been courted by her mistress. She had worked as railway employee, visiting brothels with, and listening to vulgar stories told by, her male companions. Reassuming female clothing and failing to earn a living, she was subsequently arrested for theft, diagnosed with severe hystero-epilepsy, and sent to the hospital, where doctors discovered her sexual inversion (Krafft-Ebing 1896 [1889], 294–95).

Here, her case illustrated a different diagnosis, and the case study's shaping of her narrative deployed a teleology that, as differential diagnosis demonstrates, produced a different plot of the same story events. For the diagnosis *is* the anagnorisis and the askesis in this narrative; all events serve to produce it, despite the doctor's having retrospectively rearranged and so manufactured it. While the hysteria diagnosis was consonant with but not dependent upon Ilma's gender, the diagnosis of sexual inversion, which was usually attached to men, labeled her as not only ill but deviant. Her "romantic life," simply transgressive when acted out as a hysteric with a male partner, became symptomatic of psychopathology when with a female. Ilma had violated several cultural assumptions about femininity, for she admitted that she had responded to her male lover's passion, had enjoyed cross-dressing, and had, in addition, acted or spoken sexually to nurses and female patients. So abnormal was Ilma's love for a sister of charity (a detail, interestingly enough, expunged from the sexological case study, where Krafft-Ebing stopped short of implicating a religious functionary), that she had been diagnosed, variously, as hystero-epileptic, cataleptic-hysteric, and psychopathological ("congenital perverse sexual feeling"). In diagnosing deviance, the sexological case foregrounded Ilma's subversion of sexual and social functions, her crossings of cultural boundaries, her enjoyment of pleasures, costumings, or practices identified as perverse.

But such translations and rewritings raised questions about research reliability. The documentary report of Ilma's case in Krafft-Ebing's *Hypnotism*, with which this book and this chapter open, included the daily notebook of experimental laboratory and clinical treatments, narratives that recount two demonstrations (one at the clinic, the other before the medical society), the patient's and doctor's stories—including family letters and the subject's autobiographical life history—as well as professional comment, discussion, and debate. Because medical men who had attended his demonstration had questioned the patient's reliability, Krafft-Ebing stated in the pamphlet's preface, the record also included independent testimony by authorities and individuals that attested to her story's truth—aside from the "romantic auto-suggestive embellishments, delusions of memory, and gaps in her life history" attributable to hysterical grandiosity and amnesia. Indeed, Krafft-Ebing said in a long footnote, he gave sufficient weight to other versions of Ilma's case to shake his confidence in his patient's story. Although she had told the same tale twice to family members, although her confessor had inscribed it in an intercepted letter and so borne witness to another and similar retelling—one with, a reader might expect, significant credibility as a private but institutionally authorized "confession"—her family judged Ilma's story "romantic." The doctor discounted the priest's knowledgeability, credited the convent abbess's denial of Ilma's story's truth, and judged his patient's story hallucinatory. Still, invoking the factual findings of physiology, psychology, nervous pathology, moral therapeutics, and legal medicine, Krafft-Ebing characterized his work with Ilma as an investigation into the psycho-physical phenomena of hysteria. His experiments at Graz, he said, charted the "physiology of the human mind," the relationship between "the psychical and the corporeal world" (Krafft-Ebing 1896 [1889], v–viii).

In this case, however, Krafft-Ebing foregrounded the problem of medical representation and judgment. Indeed, he modeled and thematized the process of medical documentation in his text about Ilma S.'s sexual subjectivity. This documentary record of experimentation and its concomitant winnowing of narratives sought to produce a factual version of the events surrounding Ilma's illness and mental distress. Questions of medical legitimacy and physician authority, of patient narratorial and memorial reliability, of the interpretive status of gapped and fragmented narrative, all surrounded the medical inscription of symptoms as signs, of clinical pictures as genuinely descriptive, of the laboratory's ability to guarantee its research credibility. Only documentary representation, then, served to guarantee truth, and Krafft-Ebing portrayed that documentation as consisting primarily of narrative interpretation, sifting, and judging. Diagnosis depended on, treatment issued from, and recovery was created by the doctor's correct winnowing of patient, medical, historical, autobiographical, and testimonial narratives. The evidence assembled here, Krafft-Ebing's record attests, acquired its credibility from the very fact of the doctor's ability correctly to read the evidentiary texts and to produce, after tallying observation and physical examination with the narrative documents, a theory about Ilma's perverse subjectivity.

Here, Krafft-Ebing leveraged his skill and his laboratory's research into the social domain more effectively than Charcot had leveraged his, for Krafft-Ebing's psychopathological research could be used to alter social structures and values. Ilma had presented to the clinic with conventional hysterical amnesia, declaring herself innocent of the theft for which she had been arrested by the Graz police; she was, as noted, judged able to stand trial, but was treated for mental illness rather than convicted of a crime. The subtitle of Krafft-Ebing's *Psychopathia, A Medico-Forensic Study*, indicates that scientific translation of sexual subjectivity from one research setting to another also enabled its outreach beyond the laboratory. For, as suggested in Chapter 5, the discourse and practice of medical forensics gave sexologists access to domains other than the amphitheater, experimental laboratory, consulting office, or hospital ward. As observers, witnesses, and virtual judges, their expertise earned them opportunities to enlarge their sphere of interest; and their professional observations of sex enabled them to interest often-fearful others in deviance and pathology. The research on sex, then, addressed itself to social ills, declaring that its practitioners could judge and enforce the normative values on trial in Europe's courts and bedrooms.

Krafft-Ebing's documentary record nevertheless demonstrated its status as a physician construction. Indeed, it is not central here whether Krafft-Ebing believed his patient, according her story the status of fact and granting it the authority of self-representation. I do not mean to suggest either, however, that Ilma's story was true because it was experientially authoritative. Nor do I mean that Krafft-Ebing abused his position as doctor. Rather, I mean to position Krafft-Ebing's documentary report as representing a set of problems inherent in diagnostic technologies. For

Krafft-Ebing's record of experimental research does not only demonstrate the separation of laboratory observation from the social and sociological categories constituting the disease it scrutinizes and its uses when circulated back into the social domain. It foregrounds, in addition, the problem of medical interpretation itself: the ways in which the patient's narrative shaped her experience, itself shaped by the constraints of work, class, gender, and family; the ways in which medical observation constructed cases through the presentation of patients, interpretation of symptoms, and reproduction of patient histories; the ways in which medical discourse tallied different narratives to bracket certain events, foreground others, and so legitimate a constructed version of medical truth. Krafft-Ebing's experimental record shows how research produced medical knowledge of patients based on experimentation, case presentation, disease nosology and nosography, narrative winnowing, and evidentiary representation. His text demonstrates, as Bourneville and Regnard's does not, that scientific knowledge and the quasi-objects it investigated were products of scientific networks and practices. It demonstrates, too, that perverse objects could produce research truths primarily because of their translatability. Itself a narrative reproduction of assembled narratives, observation descriptions, examination results, and documentations of experiments and treatments, Krafft-Ebing's case study proved that medical credibility was produced on the site of multiple and conflicting claims to truth. And Ilma's case seemed perfectly suited to demonstrate the hysteric's or pervert's translatability, for Ilma, a vagabond, like Celina and Geneviève, performed her translatability between laboratory sites.

The treatments documented by the Salpêtrière's photographic iconographies and medical charts occurred decades before Freud visited that famous clinic; those undertaken by Krafft-Ebing in the same decade. But when Pierre Janet succeeded Charcot as director of the Salpêtrière's research laboratory in 1890, he introduced psychology into hypnotic experimentation. Janet's research recorded, not only physiological "accidents" (or transient somatic symptoms), but the disorders of memory and emotion discussed in Chapters 1 and 4. According to Janet, the patient's bodily attitude and movement during a hysterical attack recalled the emotion that she had experienced during the event that caused her disease. Several of his patients recollected sexual events. Lucy, for example, suffered vague sensations, genital aura, and erotic ideas when the physician touched or stimulated bodily "erotogenic" spots; during somnambulism, she hallucinated men behind her curtains, which, Janet concluded, reproduced a real, earlier happening, which she remembered only under hypnosis. She also recalled the "sufferings" she had experienced during her first "conjugal act"; for on her wedding night, her husband had infected her with a sexual discharge—perhaps, although Janet does not say so, syphilis. Unlike Lucy, seventeen-year-old Rah had endured an attempted rape, which she reported while hypnotized. Her employer, a self-styled mesmerist, had hypnotized and sought sexually to violate the somnambulous servant, but he had instead provoked convulsive attacks. Rah remembered nothing of the rape attempt, but a few days later, fell ill with absent-mindedness, anesthesia, amnesia, and aphasia. Unable to work, she returned home, where she experienced somnambulistic attacks and delusions: she jumped from beds, swept floors, and filled a wheelbarrow with sand. In Janet's laboratory, Rah reproduced these hallucinatory activities and performed these pantomimic acts under hypnotic suggestion. Although Janet identified her hauling of gravel as "associated with the fixed idea of the rape," he neither reported the source of his knowledge nor conceptualized the nature of this associative activity.[4]

Yet Janet's research clearly described the details of a psycho-physical sexuality and self-representational subjectivity. Thus body and emotion, traumatic event and forgetting, hypnotic visualizing and storytelling, sexual brutality and psychic panic, all appear here, unarticulated by a conceptual structure. Shaped by his training and research at Charcot's clinic, Janet viewed sex as a biological and medical entity and, like Charcot, he believed that to conceptualize sex as etiological would necessitate admitting his patients' lubricity.[5] But that kind of judgment—which had, in fact, already been made about the Salpêtrière's research subjects—would not only discredit the clinic's research results but morally impugn its patients. The Salpêtrians had therefore diagnosed psycho-physical symptomatology as reflex ovarian hysteria. The researchers refused, as well, to situate the sexed body in the stories their patients told. Janet recounted Rah's tale, much as Charcot had told Justine Etch's, as originating in a rape attempt, but he failed to view the event as a cause of Rah's illness. Although he portrayed Rah's hallucinatory acts as dramatizing a subjective experience of pain, a self-representation fashioned during a peak-affect state, even an enactment significant to a possible fantasmatic scenario, he did not theorize this self-representation as a pantomime of psychosexual material. For Janet could not conceptualize sexuality beyond the limits imposed by his research setting. Despite his observations of sexual trauma, his semiotics of deranged sensation and perception, his "psychological point of view," Janet's representation of the malady through representation did not portray sex as linked to the conditions of representability.

Freud would seize upon and theoretically exploit Janet's terminology, producing for the hysteria discourse a psycho-physical sexuality and self-representational subjectivity. In his letters to Fliess of December 1896 and January 1897, Freud hit upon the conceptualization Janet had missed, the psychical mechanism or "architecture" of hysteria. A hysterical attack did not, he said, "discharge" energy but presented an "*action*" that served as a "means to the reproduction of pleasure." While Freud here used the terms of affect-laden object relations enacted as pantomimic and self-dramatizing scenario, he adhered to Janet's perspective on psycho-physical causation. While perversion functioned by the "operation of erotogenic *sensations*," he said, hysteria did so by means of "*erotogenic zones*" that, in childhood, had secreted sexual substances from many locations on the body, but that, differentiated and limited by individual development and moral and cultural progress, had been abandoned. These "groups of sensations," Freud said, had "much to do with psychological stratification" and obeyed a "direct connection with the mechanism of hysterical anaesthesia" (Freud 1985, 207–13, 223). Although Freud seemed unsure of the causal mechanism at work here—how sensations produced psychical stratification, what kind of link joined erogenous sensation and hysterical lack of it—he had discovered that structures joining the sensate, pleasure body with psychic events would serve his research goals.

Indeed, Freud said, his "discovery" of a new source of "unconscious production" solved his hysteria enigma. Scenes and fantasies served as key to the "structure of hysteria," as argued in Chapter 1. "Everything goes back," Freud assured Fliess,

to the reproduction of scenes. Some can be obtained directly, others always by way of fantasies set up in front of them. The fantasies stem from things that have been *heard* but understood *subsequently*, and all their material is of course genuine. They are protective structures, sublimations of the facts, embellishments of them, and at the same time serve for self-relief. . . . [T]he psychic structures which, in hysteria, are affected by repression are not in reality memories . . . but *impulses* that derive from primal scenes. I realize now that all three neuroses (hysteria, obsessional neurosis, and paranoia) exhibit the same elements (along with the same etiology)—namely, memory fragments, *impulses* (derived from the memory) and *protective fictions*. . . . In hysteria, it is the memories; in obsessional neurosis, the perverse impulses; in paranoia, the protective fictions (fantasies), which penetrate into normal life amid distortions because of compromise.[6]

Although Freud here set forth a theory of the major nineteenth-century neuroses, their structural identity covered over the psycho-physical theory Freud was proposing. For not their coincidence down to the last detail, but their linking of memory, fiction, and fantasy made this proposal formative. The hysteric's scenes reproduced, visually and aurally, childhood memories through intermediary fictions or fantasies. These scenes, then, were representations rather than reports of real events, but that fact did not alter their importance. Indeed, these representations—memories, perversions, or projected fictions, depending upon the patient's choice of neurosis—served structurally to mediate between the registers of the real and psychical. These mechanisms constituted a series of binarisms that Freud sought to unriddle: soma and psyche, past (or childhood) and present symptom, real and fantasy, pleasure and unpleasure. And although Freud had not yet learned to read these structures or mechanisms other than symbolically—patients who had "had something sexual done to them in *sleep*" thus experienced, he said, cataleptic "attacks of sleep"—he had discovered the status and function of hysterical fantasmatics. For, since no patient produced memories without a motive, these representations recollected a repressed and, we might say, primal pleasure: attacks of giddiness or fits of weeping, Freud said, were "aimed at *another person*," the "prehistoric, unforgettable other person who [was] never equalled by anyone later," the mother (Freud 1985, 212–23; Freud's emphases). Although he would conceptualize and then suppress this affective matrix, Freud had here made it possible to theorize affect-laden object relations as central to patient self-representation and subject formation.

In Katharina's case of hysteria mixed with anxiety attacks, I argue in the next section, Freud would theorize a self-reflective and self-representative subjectivity. This subjectivity was not singular, like that of the sexologists, but constituted through and in a field of affective, sexual, and representational forces. For Katharina's hysteria presented through her disordered self- and object representations, themselves formed, at least in part, by her social and familial situation. Indeed, her father, whom Freud disguised as her uncle, had sexually approached her and was sexually involved with—would impregnate and marry—her cousin. Becoming spectator of this perverse adult sexuality, Katharina had fallen ill. Failing to recognize her "scene of discovery" as linked to her own experience, her object relations with her father, and her self- and object representations, Katharina suffered hallucinations that Freud would interpret as sexual, as displaced representations of her father's enraged face and engorged penis—the sensations of which Katharina had felt on and against her body. Katharina's reproduced scenes, Freud realized, positioned her as image in visualizable scenes, as herself yet other than herself, as subject yet object of investigation. Theorizing memory as the trace that joined psyche and soma, childhood past and needs of the present, Freud made of memory a protective screen, fiction, or fantasy that fabricated yet mediated the real through recounting. Freud's insistence on the intrication of spectatorship, representation, and the real meant that his theory violated, indeed scandalized, even as it participated in, the modern project to keep the realm of subjects safely separate from the world of objects. Indeed, psychoanalysis invented a hybrid, highly mediated subject that, articulating affect, cognition, identification, and self- and object representation, served a modernizing scientific project.

III

I take Katharina's case as "specimen" here because it links representability, self- and object representations, and the reproduction of sexual scenes that solicited and produced spectatorship. Hoping to "forget" the neuroses while on vacation in the Alps, Freud was hailed on a mountaintop by the innkeeper's daughter. This girl of 18 presented a "complex of sensations" that stood for anxiety attacks; an "awful face" stared at and so haunted her. Freud responded: "You must have seen or heard something that very much embarrassed you, and that you'd much rather not have seen." "Heavens, yes!" Katharina responded, and began her story with what Freud called "the scene of discovery." Finding both her uncle and Franziska absent from the inn one day, Katharina and her cousin Alois had "looked everywhere" for them (*SE*, 2: 125–30):

> "Why, Franziska must be in Father's room!" [her cousin had exclaimed]. And we both laughed; but we weren't thinking anything bad. Then we went to my uncle's room but found it locked. That seemed strange to me. Then Alois said: "There's a window in the passage where you can look into the room." We went into the passage; but Alois wouldn't go to the window and said he was afraid. So I said: "You silly boy! I'll go. I'm not a bit afraid." And I had nothing bad in my mind. I looked in. The room was rather dark, but I saw my uncle and Franziska; he was lying on her. (*SE*, 2: 127–28)

This "scene of discovery" thematized the apparatus and material of scenic representation, the looking subject, and sexual relations; it embedded a *mise en scène* within a self-representation of seeing. It reproduced, moreover, the spectator position, the images in and of the scene as "seen," the constitution of desire, and the status of psychoanalytically produced subjectivity. It provided for Freud, in addition, the tools he needed to conceptualize hysterical sexuality as plastic and representational.[7]

Although Freud refused to say so, Katharina's scene made her witness to her father's perverse sexuality. Looking into the darkened bedroom, through the window that framed her look and identified what she saw as "scene," Katharina observed a bedded but clothed couple in the act, presumably, of coupling. What Katharina saw and how she came to see it cannot be disarticulated in Freud's representation. In her well-known discussion of cinematic spectatorship, Laura Mulvey—following Freud—identifies two possible spectatorial relations to a viewed image. Scopophilia implies "a separation of the erotic identity of the subject from the object on the screen"; narcissism demands "identification of the ego with the object on the screen through the spectator's fascination with and recognition of his like" (Mulvey 1992, 26). Although Mulvey theorizes the filmic spectator position as necessarily male, Katharina's scene positions the girl as spectator (the boy fears and refuses spectatorship) and constitutes her subjectivity as a dialectic of multiple identification and desire. Recognizing her like in her cousin, Katharina identifies with a daughter and her seduction and feels fascination; separated from the coupling by the look's distance, she fears and feels breathless, hears buzzing in her head, and hallucinates a dreadful face—the face, perhaps, of a sexually aroused man. This sight, a complex articulation of primal scene and scene of seduction, symbolizes the sensation and upsurge of female sexuality. Katharina's cousin, figure for herself, lies under her father's body; her father, coupling with that sexually passive yet clearly compliant cousin, implicitly betrays a mother, the usual female participant in primal scene images. Katharina sees the adult world of coupling, a self-constitutive yet horrible sight for the girl, who wonders about her body's sensations and, coincidentally, stumbles on the adult "world of sexuality."

Katharina's scene of discovery produced a series of "disagreeable scenes" between her "aunt" and "uncle." Freud represented these scenes, like the traumatic scene of discovery, as involving spectatorship, distance between participant and observer, and scenic representation. During these real scenes, Freud said, the children "came to hear" things that "opened their eyes," disputes that it "would have been better for them not to have heard." In the final real scene, which Katharina told at her dialogue's end, her father broke out in "senseless rage" against her, threatening violence; afterward, if he caught sight of her from a distance, his face, she said, "would get distorted with rage and he would make for me with his hand raised"; terrified that he would catch her, she had run away (*SE*, 2: 129–32). This second visualized scene, temporally the most recent of Katharina's scenes, like the hysterics' scenes discussed in Chapter 1, contained the same elements as did the first, but those elements had been arranged in a different context and transferred onto another—here unrecognizable—figure. The second scene positioned its participant and witness in different subject positions, constituting Katharina as the observed and her father as bearer of the look; she, fleeing, produced the distance required by spectatorship in this scenario. Here, her father, looking at her, desired to punish her, a punishment Freud would later interpret in "A Child Is Being Beaten" as fantasmatically signifying the humiliations and despairs of perverse female oedipal love. Moreover, as I suggest in Chapter 1, the position of spectatorship invariably structures a scenic and fantasmatic representation, one that articulates, not only desire and punishment, but the possibility of multiple identification, of hetero- and homoerotic desire. Although Freud did not invoke that structure here, he would do so when working with Dora and his own daughter, as I argue at the end of this chapter. Still, Katharina's symptom, the face that looked at her, linked the paternal stare with the dreadful face she had seen in the scene of discovery. And that hallucination reproduced Katharina's representation of her affect-laden object relation with her father, her witnessing of his sex during a peak moment of affect, her identificatory sensations of pleasure, and, in the retelling, her cognitive assessment of the remembered events.

The scene of discovery produced, in addition, two temporally prior memories of paternal sexual abuse. When the family (or father and daughter) were visiting other inns, Katharina said, her drunken father had twice awoken her at night; she had "fe[lt] his body" in the bed. She had twice awakened when her father and Franziska came to bed late; once she had found a figure by the door, and it was her father, "looking for something." But Katharina was not sure whether she had been frightened then, just as she did not understand the scene of discovery or her disgust. Freud interpreted: "She had carried about with her two sets of experiences which she remembered but did not understand," he said, "and from which she drew no inferences. When she caught sight of the couple in intercourse, she at once established a connection between the new impression and these two sets of recollections, she began to understand them and at the same time to fend them off." Katharina, that is to say, remembered her father's sexual advances, remembered that she had "noticed something between her father and Franziska" that she did not understand (*SE* 2: 130–32). Memory, then, as suggested in Chapter 1, structured a psycho-physical sexuality, or memory, banished, dissociated it from the subject who felt it. For the structure of affects that produced memory could well, as in Katharina's case, make the subject spectator of her own desire. Thus Katharina had remembered but not understood real events; her self- and object representations, disarticulated from a subjective experience of pleasure or pain, from a cognitive appraisal of those events' meaning, and a neurological discharge pattern, produced a hallucination—her father's enraged face—that joined all these affective states and structures of feeling once memory had mediated the distance between observer and seen figure, self- and object representations, and affect-laden experience.

Freud would later complicate this temporal model by theorizing the links among seeing, remembering, and retelling. In "Screen Memories" (1899), he conceptualized childhood memory as a series of "scenes" that did not become sequential until later childhood; especially intense childhood scenes, he said, served as figurative "screens"—partitions, sieves, or light-reflecting image-bearing surfaces—that associated early material with later and wishful constructions. In this complex relation between seeing and remembering, the "scene" seen through/on the screen was fashioned of elements that were "genuine" even though they were, in addition, constructed or fantasied. Freud took a patient's memory-scene as example. A boy and his cousins play in Alpine meadows full of bright yellow flowers; they tear dandelions from their girl cousin's hands; and, after she is given bread by a peasant woman, who cuts the loaf with a long knife, the boys, too, eat the delicious bread. The analyst interprets. This memory was constructed after the fact when the patient articulated two fantasies. The first: although his father's business had failed and the family had moved to the city, the patient had visited a well-to-do rural family and fallen desperately (but secretly) in love with their daughter; he had wished he had stayed home, grown up in the country, followed his father's profession, and married this girl. The second: after a later trip to the Alps, the patient had visited his uncle and cousins and realized that his father had hoped that he would marry his cousin to recoup the lost family fortune; yet he had remained dedicated to university studies and subsequently endured professional difficulty. The subject who remembered, Freud interpreted, had amalgamated two sets of fantasies of a comfortable life, projected them onto one another, and made a childhood memory of them. Thus the screen memory's intensely yellow dandelions, torn from the girl's hands, represented the adolescent's wish to "deflower" and marry her; the extravagantly delicious bread, the student's wish to succeed in a "bread-and-butter" occupation. The detail of the Alpine flowers, Freud said, stamped the "date of manufacture" on the memory, a time when the patient struggled for his daily bread and first discovered mountaineering. This memory, then, the analysand responded to Freud, recollected something that had "never happened at all" that he had "unjustifiably smuggled" into his childhood memories (SE, 3: 302–18).

But Freud defended this memory's "genuineness." A memory-trace, he said—the yellow Alpine flowers—offered the fantasy a "point of contact" with childhood experience. The memory had been produced precisely because its "raw material was utilizable." Anomalous details also bespoke the "genuineness" of the memory, despite its status as invented, falsified, and tendentious: as representation. Freud's articulation of seeing and remembering, then, made memory, much like dreams, a text that had been constructed and retrospectively projected onto a "screen" whose point of contact linked or mediated lived experience and fiction. Memory did not recall facts but produced and placed in the past representations useful for coping with present needs; the mind fabricated memories around representable recollected details. "It may indeed be questioned," Freud said, "whether we have any memories at all *from* our childhood: memories *relating to* our childhood may be all that we possess." Childhood memories, he said, "show us our earliest years not as they were but as they appeared at the later periods when the memories were aroused." Screen memories, indeed all memories, then, were sited between real events and fantasied scenarios. Like sexuality, like the structure of affects, memory constituted a scandal to scientific binarisms even as it helped construct them. Childhood memories did not "*emerge,*" Freud concluded, but were "*formed,*" and there was "no guarantee" that their "data" were literal (SE, 3: 318–322, 315; Freud's emphasis).

This remarkable formulation, like the scenic memories discussed in Chapter 1, but more complexly than they, articulated memory, invention, and hysteria through the concept of representability. In "Draft N," for example, Freud called the "mechanism of fiction" the "same as that of hysterical fantasies." "Remembering," he said, was "never a motive" in itself but only a "method," and because libido motivated symptom formation, symptoms, like dreams, depicted the *"fulfillment of a wish"* (Freud 1985, 251). Hysterical symptoms, dreams, and memories, then, were representations produced through and motivated by present needs or demands, which existed in intermediate positions between conscious ideation and unconscious wishes for pleasure, and that demanded interpretation. Indeed, the "exaggerated" details of Freud's screen memory—its "overemphasis" on floral yellowness, its almost hallucinatory "niceness" of bread—resembled nothing so much as the exaggerated sensitivities and responses of hysterics. Screen memory texts, like hysterical symptomatics, had been constructed—although without the knowledge that they *were* constructed—and, put to use by the memorializer or hysteric, they represented "genuine" yet "invented" material that the subject could not bring himself or herself to acknowledge (*SE*, 3: 317–18, 311–12, 315).

Yet Freud's analysand complained that there was "something not quite right about this scene" of flowers and bread. "I cannot help being reminded of some pictures that I once saw in a burlesque exhibition," he said. "Certain portions of these pictures, and of course the most inappropriate ones, instead of being painted, were built up in three dimensions—for instance, the ladies' bustles" (*SE*, 3: 312). This analogy, which called attention to its own vulgarity, unintentionally revealed the unconscious at work on the question of representability. For memories were textual: they demanded interpretation, were tendentious, deployed utilizable material, and represented the subject as subject through fantasmatic invention; they utilized exaggerated rhetorical details, articulated real event and unconscious desire, and represented memories as visualizable scenes. Remembrance, then, constituted visualizable "events" with unconscious needs precisely because the former met the needs of the latter for fantasmatic appropriation.

And, finally, Freud's essay presented memories as incorporating all the complex subject and object positions of spectatorship, positions that produced and constituted psychoanalytic self-representation. We imagine, Freud said, that childhood memory images arise "simultaneously with an experience as an immediate consequence of the impression it makes and that thereafter they recur from time to time in accordance with the familiar laws of reproduction." Closer observation, however, disproved this notion. In fact, childhood memory, Freud said, positioned the subject as spectator of his own childhood material. For in significant and "unimpeachable"—that is, truthful—childhood scenes, the subject "sees himself in the recollection as a child, with the knowledge that this child is himself; he sees this child, however, as an observer from outside the scene would see him. . . . [S]uch a picture cannot be an exact repetition of the impression that was originally received. For the subject was then in the middle of the situation and was attending not to himself but to the external world." Indeed, this doubled position is, as Elizabeth Grosz has suggested, an impossible subject location, which is, nevertheless, productive for psychoanalytic self-representation.[8] For memory constitutes representation as a psycho-physical category; linking subject and object representations, whether "real" or imaginary, memory also constitutes the scenario in which these visual representations are situated (whether they were serially assembled or are imaged as mirroring) and the affective sensations that structure them as scenes (in which the subject mirrors yet differs from him or herself). Whenever the remembering subject appears "as an object among other objects," Freud said, the contrast between the "acting" and the "recollecting" ego provides evidence that "the original impression has been worked over." A memory-trace from childhood was at a later date, the "date of the memory's arousal," "translated back into a plastic and visual form," but no "reproduction" of the "original impression" entered the subject's consciousness (*SE*, 3: 321). Whether memories or fantasies, psychoanalytic self-representations articulate a complex set of visualizations, sensations, perceptions, cognitive reworkings, and self-locations.

By situating the subject in the scene of spectatorship, memory makes him or her hybrid, both subject and object. All affect-laden memories, moreover, represent the subject rather than exactly recall lived events; recollection does not simply re-present childhood material but reproduces and fabricates that material, representing not its original impression but an artifact shaped, retrospectively, by present need, by past and present hoped-for pleasure. Not just screen memories, then, but all memories are worked over by the subject's unconscious. All memories, moreover, exist in the screen memory's position: as mediations between past and present, they constitute the subject as hybrid, as a kind of quasi-subject. In the psychoanalytic situation, the patient's visualized, remembered self becomes a quasi-object—fabricated by patient and analyst discourse, invented and worked over by a reciprocal and investigative collective inquiry, and then naturalized as childhood experience.

Freud's frequent tropes of painting or book publication sought to capture this hybrid quality of visual memory texts. Thus Dora's transference presented "new editions" or "facsimiles" of the impulses and fantasies aroused and made conscious during her analysis (*SE*, 7: 116). These fantasmatic new editions, moreover, located the subject, who observed herself as a child, who observed herself observing herself, within a complex spectatorial situation that represented affect-laden object relations to the subject at the moment of memory formation or arousal. She watched herself acting as she fantasmatically imagined she had acted, utilizing the distance or separation between spectatorship and seen scene to reenact past affects in the transference. This reenactment shaped and was shaped, moreover, by object relations that, formed at moments of peak affective arousal, articulated psycho-physical capabilities, psychomotor behavioral enactments, and cognitive assessments of experience to structure a subjectivity both located in and logically separable from the body. Watching herself watch herself in the psychoanalytic situation, the subject could begin cognitively to appraise her behavior patterns, her psycho-sensory symptoms, her remembered and so formed subjective experiences of pleasure and pain. Her affect-laden object relations, experienced as real and witnessed as spectator, constituted and had been constituted through a fantasmatic sense of self. That "*hysterics suffer from reminiscences*," meant, I would argue, not only that memories precipitated disease, but that the *act* of recollecting and the patient's *account* of such remembered experience, when performed by her during analysis, deployed a doubly positioned spectatorship to investigate, through representability, the subject's fantasmatic status as subject (*SE*, 2: 7).

I take Katharina's case as exemplary and paradigmatic for the emergence of psychoanalysis precisely because it sketches this mediating work of memory within a matrix of psycho-physical forces. In telling her stories to Freud, Katharina constituted her memory scenes, observed herself observing the scene of discovery, and, identifying with her like, observed herself participating in the scenario. She reproduced recent childhood memories—Freud never doubted their genuineness—replete with exaggerated details; like the screen memory's yellow flowers and delicious bread, like the ladies' bustles, the hallucinated head meant that this hysterical memory text had fastened on utilizable material to reproduce a memory. Katharina's metaphorical hybridity, her position as both subject and object, her literal and later recovered location as spectator, made her suffer from reminiscence, as did Freud's other hysterical patients. Her recollection represented in memory impressions and thoughts related to the scene of seduction—the sensations she had experienced during the time of the memory's "arousal"—and its content represented the affective structure that linked her bodily sensations, psychomotor behaviors, parental object relations, and self- and other representations. Functioning as a screen memory, the "picture" she had seen of her father having intercourse with another daughter could not "venture out into the light of day," as Freud put it, precisely because she had witnessed it before puberty; it remained unconscious and "slip[ped] away into a childhood memory" (*SE* 3: 316).

This genuine memory had nevertheless undergone a series of transformations. One forced the scenario's consequential clause into visualizable representation: the scenes of discovery, dispute, and paternal rage. Another expressed the fantasmatic sexual material figuratively, as a dialectic of identification with her cousin, betrayal by her father (of her mother, of herself), and desire to be the child her father loved. Like Freud's hysterics' scenes, which contained the same figures or elements rearranged in different contexts and transferred onto other figures, these scenes constituted a scenario. The scene of paternal rage likewise represented a scene governed by a fantasmatic, a girl's humiliation by the father who raged at and threatened her, who loved another girl like herself, who fathered a child with that girl. Katharina's hysterical vomiting signified this consequential representation. As witness to scenes, then, Katharina was both object of and subject to the effects of seduction. Her memory texts, both visual and narrative, presented genuine material and worked over her lived experience in light of her needs in the narrating present: to account for psycho-physical sexual sensations, psychomotor behaviors, and affectively constituted and subsequently represented object relations. This narrativized set of scenes and stories constructs what I have been calling a scenario, following Mary Ann Doane, who follows Freud: a constellation of objects or persons charged with significance in which the images are displayed to evoke desire in a spectator who now knows or learns to recognize the meanings embedded in them. And "as though *her* knowledge, too, had been extended by our conversation," Freud reported, Katharina promptly replied that the face was her father's; she "recognize[d] it now—but not from *that* time" (*SE*, 2: 131–32).

The scene of discovery itself identifies the psychoanalytic situation as spectatorial and specular. Katharina's case history represents Freud as analyst seeing Katharina's seeing the scene; witnessing this scene of seeing, Freud as case historian positions the narrating analysand as object and the listening analyst as spectator. Freud's spectatorship situates the work of scenic reproduction within a psychoanalytic scene; that scene, like the scene of discovery, constitutes desire through a play of identifications and looks. Indeed, the scene of discovery, its replication in the storytelling situation, and the analyst's look at the patient as she relays her scenic story of seduction, all identify the psychoanalytic situation as itself constituting a scenario, a scene of seduction and multiple identifications. Although psychoanalysis did not produce recovery through the spectacular mesmerizing of symptomatic bodies, as had Bernheim's experiments (to which Freud had played "spectator"), it reinscribed the spectatorial conditions for cure within a privatized space and clinical practice that invoked self-spectatorship. Requiring the patient to lie on a couch while, he said, he "sat behind him, seeing him, but not seen [him]self," Freud constituted the clinical setting as structuring looking, seeing, and scenic reproduction to produce the position of the remembering spectator. Both spectator of himself and image or object in scenes, the analysand is also object of the analyst's gaze and subject of countertransferential musings. Using the play of transference and countertransference, the psychoanalytic situation invokes psycho-physical sensation, self-representation, and psychomotor behavior and acts; the analyst interprets these "symptomatic actions" as inscribed by affect-laden object relations, fantasmatic rehearsals of subjective experiences of pleasure or pain (*SE*, 20: 28, 46). Freud's representation of Katharina's scenario identifies it as a "scene of discovery"—an originary scenario—for psychoanalytic theory and practice.

Indeed, Freud's suppressed and disguised self-representations cover over, even as they expose, the psychoanalytic work as work of mediation. Positioned between publication of *Studies on Hysteria* and *Dora*, for example, "Screen Memories" misrepresents its patient's identity, for the "patient," although he does not say so, was Freud himself. A university-educated man who had taken an interest in psychological questions, this patient had been cured when "Freud" had analyzed his railway phobia; the childhood scene's cousins were Freud's niece and nephew (the children of his older half-brother) and the country family the Flusses, with whose daughter, Gisela, Freud fell in love.[9] In relating this patient's childhood scene, then, Freud is both spectator and actor, subject and object; analyst and analysand. In the analytic dialogue, Freud portrays his patient as able "collaborator," as always ready to hear an interpretation, as never frustrated or angry with and always deferential toward his analyst. When Freud tells this patient, "You are going too far," the patient does not resist but becomes more cooperative; he accepts interpretations about childhood masturbation, aggressive sexual fantasies, and rampant ambition without the slightest hesitation. One conversation, free of transferential tension, rights all problems, sufficing for interpretation to produce insight, self-recognition, and recovery. Like Katharina's case, this disguised case history thematizes the apparatus and material of scenic representation, the looking subject, and fantasmatic sexual and object relations—a self-representation of seeing. Freud as patient sees the scene that Freud as analyst interprets; Freud as analyst observes and makes the patient object; the case historian represents the analyst representing the patient's self-representation. The psychoanalytic subject is hybrid, manufactured by the mediating work of psychoanalytic recollection, and made part subject, part object by the representational work of case history.

In "A Child Is Being Beaten" (1919), Freud complicated his model of self-spectatorial and self-representative subject formation. Inventing narratives around perverse acts, this fantasy represented subject, object, and action in three transformative "phases." At first, the patient knew "nothing" except "a child is being beaten," or "a child is being beaten on its naked bottom." Freud questioned his patients: who was the child? the one producing the fantasy or another? was it always the same child? who beat him or her? Eventually, the patient identified the punisher as an adult, and indeed as "the (girl's) *father*." Freud represented the beating fantasy's first phase, then, as the phrase, "*My father is beating the child*" and the second phase as "*I am being beaten by my father*." In the third phase, the subject fantasized (boy) children being beaten by a "representative of the father" as the subject probably looked on. The three phases of this fantasy, Freud said, represented three historically located versions of the girl's identifications with others or misrecognition of self, and her erotic feelings for her father. In the first phase, the subject hated the child who was beaten and interpreted it as taking the father's affection away from herself; this phase signified, "My father does not love this other child, *he loves only me*." In the second phase—which, unlike the first, was never recollected but constructed in analysis—the beating signified a fantasied substitute for sexual desire of father by daughter as well as punishment for that desire; this phase signified the girl's masochistic "humiliation" and "deprivation of love," and was repressed because it represented identifiable figures of father and daughter. In the third phase, the subject looked on while a figure from the "class of fathers" beat a boy; because punishment was displaced onto a child of the opposite sex, Freud said, the subject protected herself from the humiliations and deprivations of paternal love by removing herself as subject and her father as punisher from this fantasied situation (*SE*, 17: 183–87). As Jean Laplanche and J.-B. Pontalis have argued, the grammatical subject of this transformative but structurally consistent story could be the father, the child ("I"), or even the verb "seduces"; could be love-object, subject, or punishment itself (Laplanche and Pontalis 1986, 22–23).

But why, Freud wondered, did the conscious beating fantasy represent the act of seeing? For whether placing herself outside the scene as spectator or imagining herself the child being beaten, the subject represented herself as punished and desiring, as different from or resembling the fantasy's subject. Structuring her desire as doubly sexual, then, the subject identified with the positions of masculinity and femininity through the possibility of spectatorship: "I am probably looking on." This looking on performed cross-sexual identifications, or sexual transitivity, the ability of the subject to pass from one sex to another through the activity of self-spectatorship. Because identification could take multiple objects—like and unlike—as its models, it functioned as a mutable, almost infinitely variable, mechanism for subject formation. By adopting the position of spectator, moreover, Freud's female patients could make themselves objects, remove themselves from their beating fantasies, and disavow them as self-representations. The daughter thus looked on a scene of paternal punishment and it produced perverse pleasure; or she escaped from the "demands of the erotic side of her life altogether" and, turning herself "in phantasy into a man" without herself becoming "active in a masculine way," became "no longer anything but a spectator of the event which [took] the place of a sexual act" (SE, 17: 186, 190, 199). Here, then, the position of self-spectatorship joined with sexual transitivity—adding the binary male/female to the oppositions it mediated—to produce a modern notion of subjectivity rooted in, yet theoretically separable from, the body.

Freud's tropes for seeing, which articulated identificatory mechanisms and spectatorship as embedded in familial self- and object relations, served to make his models oedipal. For the beating fantasy took shape within the Oedipus complex's sphere, out of whose identifications, desires, and misrecognitions the child inevitably developed a normal or abnormal adult (hetero)sexuality; beating fantasies were thus "precipitates" or "scars" of the Oedipus complex (SE, 17: 193). Imagining the figure for herself as male other, female self, or children of indeterminate sex, the sexually transitive fantasizer invented her relation to her father as both heteroerotic and homoerotic. Indeed, both female and male unconscious fantasies, Freud reported, originated in and represented "*incestuous attach-*

ment to the father" (*SE*, 17: 198). Like the identificatory mechanisms that constituted and anchored it, oedipal attachment was thus doubly desirous and its object choices were reversible. Freud could only depict this transitive relationship as "perverse" because its constructed representation in the fantasy's second phase portrayed oedipal love as precisely a double and unstable desire outside the social norm. Freud invoked the infinitely multiple mechanism of regression to justify calling this desire "perverse." For the beating fantasy represented "*not only the punishment for the forbidden genital relation, but also the regressive substitute for that relation*"; its "libidinal excitation" led inevitably to masturbatory acts and produced the "essence of masochism" (*SE*, 17: 189–204). Like the structure of regressive identification in which the subject desired to *be* and to *have* the loved parent all at the same moment, the structure of this female oedipalized fantasmatic depicted the truly scandalous fact of family love: that it had inevitably to be repressed to prevent reversibility of object choice, that the mechanism by which men and women became "normal" was, in its "essence," perverse, and that oedipalized subjectivity bred a hybrid and highly mediated sexual transitivity.

Freud's essay on beating fantasies mobilized its own oedipal fantasmatic, for one of the beating fantasies Freud described belonged to *his* daughter, Anna. Anna Freud wrote about her own beating fantasies, moreover, as representative of female fantasmatics in general. Describing the masochistic daughter who turned her masturbatory fantasies into nonorgasmic daydreams (or "nice stories") as "renouncing her private pleasure" to make "an impression on others" (she might well have said "fathers"), Anna Freud argued that the fantasizer imagined a significant "developmental step" away from aloneness and alienation as a subject and toward social activity (Anna Freud 1973, 172). This daughter, who failed or refused to marry, who became one of Freud's successors and member of his scientific networks, presented her essay "Beating Fantasies and Daydreams" to the Vienna Society of Physicians. Toward the end of Freud's life, moreover, she presented her father's work to medical and nonmedical audiences alike. In September 1925, Freud entrusted Anna with the presentation of "Some Psychical Consequences of the Anatomical Distinction Between the Sexes" to the Homburg Congress.[10] At the 1927 Innsbruck Congress, Anna averted a potential crisis over the "vexed question" of lay analysis when, as the Europeans sought to force the underrepresented American contingent to accept a vote favoring lay analysis, her "girlish" voice rang out, "Gentlemen, I think we are committing an injustice" (Jones 1957, 3: 295–96). Here, Anna helped perform the work of translation undertaken by her father and his successors. For this subterranean conflict between American and European conferees eventually led to institutionalization of an International Training Commission and, later, to a struggle over the commission's right to impose standards for choosing and methods of training candidates for entry to psychoanalytic practice. Standing in for her father, Anna helped mobilize psychoanalytic theory, widen its conceptual domain, leverage it into other institutional settings (the school and nursery), and apply it to other psychoanalytic subjects (the child). Indeed, raising questions about her own sexual object choices, Anna deployed sexual transitivity to make these moves, playing the spinster adherent and "daughter" to Freud as psychoanalytic father and founder.

Freud represented psychoanalytic subjectivity, then, as hybrid, and the work of mediation as forming the modern quasi-subject. Psychoanalytic self-representation, moreover, took place in a matrix or field that constituted a wide range of mediations and transitivities. These transitivities, crossing the boundaries between the binaries of subjects and objects, social or familial groups and natural organisms, male and female, made the modern subject mobile and mobilizable by scientific collectivities. Constituted by nature, culture, and discourse, the psychoanalytic subject was inscribed through, reproduced in, and characterized by a representation that could never be described as singular, as "autorepresentation" (Borch-Jacobsen 1988, 117–19). The modern subject as self-spectator watched him or herself as scenic object and image, constituted him or herself through affect-laden self- and object representations, fabricated and formed memories and scenarios, and narrated him or herself as same- and other-sex. This hybrid, transitive quasi-subject eclipsed the hysteric, a figure that had been central to psychoanalysis's emergence. Fabricated through the work of mediation, the psychoanalytic quasi-object entered the two-dimensional realm of scientific representation; translated along scientific networks, this quasi-object entered the cultural domain, reached and acquired a mass audience of medical men and "medical public" alike. In the late twentieth century, as a result, psychotherapies are consumed by a wide-ranging group of middle-class clients, as "therapeutic culture" makes analytic rhetoric increasingly available—and desirable—for patient self-representation.

Yet representing this hybrid and transitive psychoanalytic quasi-subject to other scientists, Freud found, was a complex task. In Chapter 7, I argue that, in his early case histories, Freud confronted the problem of how to portray psychoanalytic subjectivity; this problem was central to the new scientific genre Freud created to mobilize an emergent psychoanalysis. For, having appropriated medical concepts about natural bodies and social subjects to produce a new theory and clinical practice, Freud sought to translate exemplary and representative cases out of his consulting room, as did other researchers, and into various theaters of proof. Transmuting psychiatric, neuropathic, and sexological case study into psychoanalytic case history, Freud invented a new mode of representation for transmitting knowledge about theory and practice to other research sites. In doing so, however, he discovered a problem central to psychoanalytic representation: the experimental dilemma of observation and interpretation. How must he portray the analytic subject who was also an object of investigation? How articulate individual and familial depictions of disease causation? How correlate patient psyche and symptomatic soma? How join and disarticulate doctor's and patient's narratives? In the case of Dora, Freud foregrounded these problems of psychoanalytic representation. For "Dora" serves to index both the ascendancy and the eclipse of the hysteric in psychoanalytic theory. Demonstrating the hysterical reflex sensation that had made a theory of sexuality possible, Dora also illustrated psycho-physical subjectivity, subject-object hybridity, and sexual transitivity. As scientific trope, she enabled Freud to see, yet momentarily suppress, the invert as figure capable of carrying an emergent science of modern subjectivity beyond the nineteenth-century diagnosis of hysteria. Indeed, joining forces with the sexologists, I argue at the end of Chapter 7, Freud made the homosexual the exemplary figure for psychoanalytic case history, the genre that represented and transmitted to new research domains Freud's science of hybrid subjectivity. Indeed, Dora's case of bisexual hysteria paradoxically enabled Freud to leverage psychoanalysis into the social and cultural realms, for none of his other case histories has entered the discursive domain as frequently, forcefully, or disputaciously as has hers. As exemplary figure, moreover, she enabled—indeed, invited—theoretical recursivity. Rewriting her case from later in his career, Freud could deploy Dora to assist his project to stabilize the work of translation: to delimit his new science's concepts, legitimate its claims about subjectivity, and distribute scientific credit and distinction among his psychoanalytic successors.

CHAPTER 7

Stories of Suffering

In his discussion of Elisabeth von R.'s hysteria, Freud differentiated his analytical case histories from psychiatric case studies and his clinical treatment from neuropathological practices by invoking the forms and strategies of fiction.

I have not always been a psychotherapist. Like other neuropathologists, I was trained to employ local diagnoses and electro-prognosis, and it still strikes me myself as strange that the case histories I write should read like short stories and that, as one might say, they lack the serious stamp of science. I must console myself with the reflection that the nature of the subject is evidently responsible for this, rather than any preference of my own. The fact is that local diagnosis and electrical reactions lead nowhere in the study of hysteria, whereas a detailed description of mental processes such as we are accustomed to find in the works of imaginative writers enables me, with the use of a few psychological formulas, to obtain at least some kind of insight into the course of that affection. Case histories of this kind are intended to be judged like psychiatric ones; they have, however, one advantage over the latter, namely an intimate connection between the story of the patient's sufferings and the symptoms of his illness—a connection for which we still search in vain in the biographies of other psychoses. (*SE*, 2: 160–61)

Here, Freud set his theory and practice apart from neuropathology, from diagnostics that localized and treatments that electrified pain, and his mode of case presentation from psychiatry's. Unlike the psychiatric case study, however, the Freudian case history correlated the patient's "story of suffering" with analytic interpretation of recounted somatic symptoms to produce an illness narrative that both analyst and patient found credible.[1] Although many critics have worried about the question of fictionality, or conversely, historicity, that my quotation raises, I argue in this chapter that in the 1890s, Freud created a new scientific genre that suitably represented the psychoanalytic subject and the research project that produced it.

The problem of Freud's "science" exists in a postmodern critical imaginary. For Freud's case histories were neither novelistic nor fictional. Rather, they presented a medical audience with the scientific evidence of hypothesis and theorizing; they represented translatable research findings in two dimensions.[2] Indeed, Freud practiced conventional medical technologies of direct and indirect somatic observation—palpation, poking and pricking, testing reflexes, and auscultation. He listened to patient narrative, as did the physician; he constructed a "doctor's story," as Kathryn Montgomery Hunter calls it; he wrote up cases to present to other physicians as research publications or demonstrations at medical societies. Moreover, Freud and Breuer performed "cathartic experiments." Although these "experiments" took place in the nerve doctor's consulting rooms, this space was itself, I argue, a laboratory of sorts for investigating, researching, and fabricating modern subjectivity. Indeed, Freud practiced the scientific method of observation and experimentation: he deployed the research technologies of interrogation, somatic and psychical correlation, and repeated observation of cases; he practiced nosography, disease classification, and production of taxonomies. He collected data, reproduced observable events, took a wide sample of cases, and tested generalizability against repeated observations of cases. As researcher, he clinically pictured patients' symptomatologies and portrayed patient characters; as case writer, he represented experimental results in a modernized version of case writing.

Freud worked indefatigably to create scientific networks along which his scientific practices could be distributed. Indeed, as discussed in the Introduction, Freud crafted the myth of himself as lonely creator to establish his scientific authorship: to found and institute his research credibility by sharing the details of experimental conditions; to generate arguments based on local evidence that could itself produce generalizable, indeed systematic, evidence; to justify his choice of research subjects; to identify himself as initiator of a new discourse. His successful effort at scientific self-fashioning made him a theoretical spokesman; he acquired enthusiastic allies; he helped establish new research sites over which he, as "founder," had control. These sites, quickly spreading throughout Europe and to the United States, disseminated and delimited the new sci-

ence's concepts, instituting networks of sociability, legitimating claims
about clinically produced theories of subjectivity, and distributing scientific credit and distinction among psychoanalytic adherents.[3]

But first, Freud fashioned a medical representation capable of convey-
ing the concepts, principles, and practices of his new science. Although it
adhered to the principles of scientific method, however, Freud's science of
subjectivity was not a natural science. Yet Freud's was not a "soft" or social science, either, but a natural/social science that investigated subjectivity, itself a hybrid entity constituted by and through social and familial relations, in a matrix of historical and psycho-physical self-representational
activities. Freud's first research project, moreover, uncovered the problems
of observation and experiment that "hard" or natural scientists understood but occluded. Hysteria, an enigmatic and imitative disease, called
into question the research methodologies of late-nineteenth-century science; Binet and Féré's defense of their laboratory's procedures addressed
and dismissed this methodological difficulty. Hysteria challenged, in addition, the generic conventions and formal strategies available for writing
up case study. As a result, Freud encountered difficulties in representing
his uncommon cases of hysteria: how to report a treatment of long duration, how to portray the patient's character, and what stance to take as interpreter. Reporting on cathartic experiments, the hybridized genre of
Freudian case history necessarily correlated organism, event, and memory; reconstituted individual, family, and medical histories; and reconceptualized patient's and doctor's stories. Narrative form, rhetorical persuasion, and the status of interpretation emerged as problems in Freud's new
case-historical record. Still, the incommensurability between psychoanalytic experience and its two-dimensional and therefore translatable representation was the problem that informed all the others. Unlike the natural
scientist, however, the natural/social scientist wrote into his reports the
problems of practicing science, the difficulties of interpretation and representation. Inscribing these problems into case-historical discourse,
moreover, Freud created the historical conditions for psychoanalytic recursivity. Representing a disease that had never yet been represented,
Freud often returned to his most difficult cases, revising the descriptions
of patient ailments, diagnosing his own shortcomings as interpreter, and
outlining more accessibly the concepts he had used. This recursivity mobilized Freud's research for transportation to other medical and research
sites; it served to delimit the domains in which psychoanalytic concepts
could be used and elaborated; it leveraged theory and practice into the

cultural domain. As I argue in my conclusion, Freud fashioned himself into psychoanalytic founder, authoritative reviser, and first and most legitimate historian.

I

The case study, Jan Goldstein reports, achieved currency as medical discourse because it so appropriately documented the moral treatment. Although at the beginning of the nineteenth century, Philippe Pinel believed that he had fully specified the treatment's methodology in his *Traité médico-philosophique sur l'aliénation mentale ou la manie*, Pierre Cabanis thought his predecessor's medical treatise insufficiently demonstrated the procedure's deployment. Calling Pinel's conceptualization the "fruit of observation and genius," Jean Esquirol nevertheless maintained that examination of specific cases most appropriately presented a medical observation's accuracy and the treatment's efficacy. "Little stories" (*histoirettes*)—the "true results of observation"—therefore became, as Goldstein says, "serious scientific business." Yet, Goldstein argues, case studies allowed researchers, not just to share scientific findings, but to exchange "examples of successful practice." The "little story" thus taught physicians how to implement the moral treatment's principles of gentleness (doctor-patient rapport secured the patient's confidence in the treatment), repression (the application of salutary but often coercive physician authority if gentleness should fail), destruction of pathological ideas (by turning the patient's attention away from his suffering or by startling his imagination), and management of pathological passions or affective emotional states. Pinel also cautioned the physician against overtly indicating the "intention to observe" patients or to "penetrate their secret thoughts with questions," Goldstein reports; a simple and "affectionate manner," even detective work carried on through, for example, the servants, more correctly brought a patient to obedient and tranquil cooperation with his doctor.[4] The study of these cases served not primarily to document a patient's progress toward recovery or to disseminate the rules of a scientific medicine, then, but to teach other physicians the technologies of successful clinical practice.

Despite the eclipse of moral treatment and the rise of somaticism in the second half of the nineteenth century, psychotherapeutic discourse appropriated and redeployed Pinel's concept of the "little story." The moral treatment's technologies reappeared in the 1880s as Binet and

Féré's hypnotic rapport, Charcot's masterful authority, Bernheim's suppression of imaginative attention to pain, and Freud's suggestive "wiping out" of pathological ideas. Like their predecessors, these practitioners identified case study as the appropriate form for reporting observation and examination of cases, presenting physician commentary and explanation, sharing research findings, and teaching clinical practice. All adhered to the generic conventions of medical case study. But the nature of Freud's subject, rather than his preference, forced him to rewrite case study as case history. For to cure hysteria, the malady through representation, necessitated that Freud invent not only a new treatment technique but a new form of textual verification and representation. The patient whose case witnessed to the therapy's trustworthiness—now the psychoanalytic rather than psychiatric, neurasthenic, or neuropathological patient—could no longer be portrayed by the conventions of case study. The psychoanalytic case history presented not the reflex but the representational body, accounting for the psychical inscriptions registered in the organism through the mechanisms of sensation, perception, affect, and memory; it depicted recovery as created through historical recounting and analytic interpretation. The new case history appropriately reported the clinical activities of self-spectatorship; it articulated the patient's visualizeable and fantasied scenarios with the talk that animated them, joining scene with story in psychoanalytic representation. And, finally, it mobilized the concepts and testimonies of patients to produce a theoretical and practical text that could, when translated to other medical and research sites, win allies for Freud's new science of the psycho-physical hybrid subject.

The studies Freud wrote about his first hysterical patients, however, resembled those of other neuropathologists. Here are summaries of five little stories by Bernheim, Charcot, and Freud, in each of which I have maintained as fully as possible the case's language and plot:

Case 1: Charcot. Julie M., 13 years old, daughter of a healthy military father and neurotically disposed mother (herself born to a hysterical mother and an invalid father), suffered delicate health because born prematurely and brought up by hand [i.e., was bottle- rather than breast-fed], experienced violent pain with her first menstrual periods, was exceedingly nervous, acted disobediently and moodily at the convent where she boarded, away from the military prison where her officer father served. While home for the summer holiday, Julie joined the wives' séances; while serving as "medium" she fell into a fit characterized by clownism, suffered 20 to 30 attacks a day for several months, and, along with her two similarly afflicted younger brothers, was taken to consult Charcot. While hospitalized at the Salpêtrière, Julie experienced attacks characterized by aura, movements of *arc de cercle*, and clownism, which could be stopped or provoked by pressure on hysterogenic zones located on or near breasts, flanks, calves, and elbows, but not ovaries. She displayed a narrowed visual field but no anesthesia. Charcot prescribed isolation and separation of the children from one another. After fifteen days of moral treatment, Julie was relatively well; after one month, Charcot presented her to a lecture audience; he hoped her improvement would become permanent. (Charcot 1889, 3: 198–219)

Case 2: Bernheim. Born to healthy parents, the 26-year-old Mme M. had a good constitution and had had no previous illnesses, but had a nervous temperament. She had had regular menstrual periods for twelve years, had been married at 17, had become a mother at 18, and had nursed her child herself. At 21, she had had a second child, which she had nursed for ten months; she had experienced weakness, menstrual difficulties, and, after accidents involving her children, extremely strong emotions. A few months later, she experienced two attacks of pain, choking, and anxiety while walking. Her left arm became numb, and she felt pain along the mammary line, which, if it were touched, made her cry out. Bernheim located no organic lesion, diagnosed hysteria, and treated Mme M. with suggestion, which, because she lacked faith in it, failed. She became pregnant again six months later, fell ill again and, after her confinement, could not nurse. Hydrotherapy treatments, too, failed, and, during increasingly violent fits, fevers and chills, and insomnia and anorexia, the patient became addicted to the morphine and cocaine used to treat her. She again consulted Bernheim, was admitted to his hospital, and, after a course of suggestive treatments, cured. (Bernheim 1980 [1891], 246–51)

Case 3: Bernheim. Lucie L., the previously healthy but temperamentally impressionable 11-year-old daughter of a nervous father, had become sad and agitated after a house servant was wrongfully accused of espionage by the local papers, dismissed by her father, and committed suicide by hanging himself. Lucie had been attached to this man, who had taken her to school daily. She lost her appetite, experienced nightmares about the hanging, and thought obsessively about the servant. A month later, a nervous seven-year-old friend also hanged himself, apparently as a result of autosuggestion. Three months later, Lucie had been seized by a sudden and violent crisis after dinner: she experienced aura (intense abdominal pains that rose toward her throat), suffocation, a flushed face, major convulsive movements, screams, and extreme agitation; she had called out, "Louis, Louis [the servant's name]! I'm going to rejoin you!" and had attempted to kill herself. That three-hour crisis was followed by fifteen months of attacks, nightmares, pain in the abdomen (which, when touched, caused cries), hallucinations of her father as a murderer. Earlier treatment by bromides and hydrotherapy were superseded by suggestion at Bernheim's hospital; the patient returned to her family, cured, after nearly two months. (Bernheim 1980 [1891], 244–46)

Case 4: Freud. This capable, commonsensical, natural, otherwise healthy and unneurotic young woman in her mid twenties was born into a family whose hereditary disposition to neurosis remained an open question: her mother and younger sister were healthy, but her brother suffered from a career-ruining neurasthenia in early manhood. Despite her favorable body build, this woman failed to breast-feed her first child; she produced a poor flow of milk, felt pains when the baby was put to the breast, and experienced loss of appetite, vomiting, and sleeplessness. She recovered when a wet nurse was hired to feed the child; but after the birth of a second child, the symptoms returned. Freud found her entire digestive tract sensitive and symptomatic. He treated the syndrome with hypnotic suggestion, and, despite her family's lack of cooperation, the patient was cured. She remained cured after the birth of a third child. (*SE,* 1: 117–20)

Case 5: Freud. The family circle of 18-year-old Dora included her active and talented yet tubercular, once delusional, and syphilitic father, a manufacturer in comfortable circumstances; her foolish mother, estranged from the social world by her husband's illnesses and suffering from "housewife's psychosis"; her ambitious, ex-bed-wetting brother, allied with his mother; and Dora herself, critical of and withdrawn from her mother, modeling herself on her brother, and tenderly attached to her dominating father. Freud cautioned that, despite the fact that Dora's "family circumstances" signified convergent and tainted heredity and her father's family predisposed her to illness, her constitutional predisposition (acquired through her father's tabes) more clearly put her at risk. Dora's father had brought her to treatment because she objected to his relationship with his friend Frau K., and to Herr K.'s attachment to her. She disliked her father's meetings with, presents to, and preference for Frau K.; she herself adored Frau K. She had been disgusted by Herr K.'s kissing her in his office and embracing her by a lake during a group holiday. Although Freud treated her analytically for three months, she left treatment prematurely, uncured. (*SE,* 7: 18–21, et passim)

The case study as a medical genre was constituted by, even as it helped shape and sustain, neuropathological principles of heredity and medical history. Charcot, Bernheim, and Freud open these case presentations or studies conventionally, with the patient's medical history and hereditary situation. Julie's mother's predisposition to neurosis and own hereditary taint, for example, put the girl at risk of illness. Lucie's father's nerves made his daughter vulnerable. Dora's father's syphilis and mother's "psychosis" predisposed her to disease. The heredity of Freud's "occasional hysteric" (see pp. 146–49, above) was clouded by her brother's neurasthenia. The medical history of family members helped determine the patient's disease: each patient's parents could have transmitted degenerate or nervous characteristics to their offspring and each family created the circumstances that made children ill. Although several patients in this sample had experienced no previous illnesses and had no family medical histories, their constitutions (their organic and physiological tendency to respond to particular stresses) predisposed and determined, at least in part, their dysfunctions. The patient's medical history, then, situated and accounted for her symptoms in this representational mode, symptoms that had been determined by organic predisposition and inheritance from parents. In the genre of case study, family and organism were biologically determinative categories.

The physician met the representational requirements for reporting medical history by taking family and patient histories before presenting or writing up the case. Such clinical practices inevitably and invariably supported the medical concepts that produced and shaped them. Bernheim, Breuer, Freud, and Charcot did not reproduce in their case studies or formal lectures their interrogations of patients and family members, yet clearly all took detailed family histories and considered such information crucial to diagnosis and treatment. Freud supplemented his questioning about symptoms with hypnosis; the details his patient could describe only while asleep satisfied the therapist's curiosity, Freud confessed, filled in her narrative's gaps, and helped him "wipe out" (or expunge from memory) tics, stammering, and paralyses (*SE*, 20: 19). The transcriptions of Charcot's Tuesday lessons, on the contrary, reproduced his interrogation of patients and family members. Here, for example, he questioned a patient's mother about her own, her parents', and her siblings' health:

[CHARCOT]: And your health?
MOTHER: I have never been sick.
CHARCOT: No rheumatism?
MOTHER: None.
CHARCOT: And your family?
MOTHER: One 45-year-old brother who has never been ill.
CHARCOT: And your father?
MOTHER: I never knew him—he died when I was two.
CHARCOT: And do you know how he died?
MOTHER: No.
CHARCOT: Your mother?
MOTHER: She is alive with frequent headaches.

CHARCOT: All we have, then, in this family is one member with an arthritic condition and nothing solid in the nervous system tree. (Charcot 1987 [1887–89], 75–76)

Although he could not directly observe or physically examine heredity, could not submit it to laboratory experimentation, Charcot assembled the proofs of patient heredity by taking extensive patient and family medical histories. For Charcot's theory that heredity determined nervous disease shaped his clinical interrogation even as the questions served to prove his point. His interview questions traced health back through a genealogy of wellness or illness, positioning pain, dysfunction, or nervousness in a historical family system. Deploying this representation of the family nervous system as a figuratively "branched" tree, Charcot produced the patient's hereditary situation by reading backward through his patients' and their parents' medical histories, including those of siblings when necessary, and identifying heredity as historically teleological and temporally consequential for disease etiology. Through this diagrammatic conceptualization of the neuropathological family, Charcot rigorously controlled disease causality, even when anomalous onset or symptomatology called such predication into question.

As discussed in Chapter 5, Freud questioned Charcot's notion of neuropathic family heredity and the clinical practices it supported soon after he had studied at the Salpêtrière. In his 1893 obituary of Charcot, Freud declared the master's doctrine of the neurogenic family simplistic and in need of "sifting and emendation." Charcot's overestimation of heredity as causative agent, he said, "left no room for the acquisition of nervous illness."[5] Thus the Salpêtrière's neuropathologists had mistaken heredity for the "sole true and indispensable cause" of neurosis, viewing other causative factors only as *"agents provocateurs."* Because "no such thing as chance" governed nervous pathogenesis, however, and because members of families clearly fell ill with many and different nervous diseases, Freud maintained that neurosis could surely be acquired. Thus Charcot's "retrospective diagnosis" of ancestors or absent family members, was, Freud argued, an untrustworthy clinical instrument built on unexamined assumptions about hereditary patterns of nervous disease causation.[6] If a capable woman fell ill, Freud thought, and her personal, family, and medical histories could not account for her malady, she must accidentally have undergone some unknown stress or wounding. He therefore posited trauma to be a disease etiology that was neither hereditarily nor historically determinative. As a general rule, however, he replaced Charcot's "neuropathic heredity" with prepubertal sexual seduction as etiologically determinative, identifying all postpubertal causes as provoking agents. Freud had clearly taken Dora's and her family's medical histories, and in "The Clinical Picture" of her case (from which I have taken my summary), he had adhered to the representational principle of reporting heredity, but even my quick sketch of the case indicates that Freud had, by 1900, reimagined the status of the neurogenic family. For "Dora," unlike "A Case of Successful Treatment by Hypnotism," met the representational requirements for case history rather than case study, an argument to which I return later in this chapter.

As a genre, the case study depended on a conventional notion of narrative form. The disease was viewed as originating in a recoverable cause that could be located, comprehended, and recounted, not only as disease, but as to historical origin. Case study thus deployed the representational strategies of traditional narrative beginnings, historical reconstruction, and predication of therapeutic alteration as narrative closure. The case studies I have sketched begin with the facts of birth, quantifiable measurements of age, family status, life crises, sickness or wellness. Thus Mme M. had been married at a reasonable age but given birth too early and often, and so had suffered somatic and emotional distress during postpartum nursing; the "occasional hysteric" had failed to breast-feed her first infant, developed symptoms of anxiety, and failed to feed a second baby as well. While scrupulously maintaining the representational requirements for conventional narrative structure, the case study silently collapsed two narrative temporalities. For the case study necessarily elided some stories, while privileging others. It produced narrative ends by retrospectively shaping the history of the illness (a narrative interpretation of the patient's story of suffering); it presented the doctor's story as subsuming the patient's, a point to which I shall return later. For although the doctor began to construct his story in earnest immediately after the patient presented for treatment, he wrote up the case after having sifted all the stories he had heard during the clinical work. He collated, for example, the patient's and her family's medical histories, the history of the illness, and selected details of the patient's life story, if appropriate.[7] He larded into these stories the history of the treatment as well, and, deploying the story he had constructed as shaping principle, he replotted the patient's story of suffering so as to foreground clinical practices and predict therapeutic alteration. Thus Bernheim's report on Mme M.'s cure by suggestion was shaped by and, in turn, narratively shaped her history of reproductive and menstrual difficulty. Freud's study of hysterical breast-milk blockage prophesied cure even as it recorded recovered physiological function. At the moment of telling, the doctor recounted events that had occurred at the time of patient presentation and during clinical treatment, itself a time during which he had observed and interpreted, preparing as eventual outcome the metanarrative he now used to transmit his findings to a wide medical audience. Through this complex but largely unannounced narrative procedure, the case study represented the physician's interpretive process as though it necessarily produced generalizable, stable, documentable treatment facts. The little story of clinical practice produced, most of all, functionalized patients and successful outcomes.

Medical clinical picturing sketched the patient as presenting with a specific case that could be differentially diagnosed by reasoned physician consideration (Hunter 1991, 55). The doctor assembled symptomatic events, ruled out or accepted the possibility of certain applicable disease entities, reasoned about the likelihood of several diagnoses, and then diagnosed the patient as victim of a particular illness. The concepts of medical history and heredity framed the clinical picture. Thus, despite her healthy parents, good constitution, and spotless medical history, Mme M.'s "nervous temperament" had put her at risk of illness. So, too, had Julie's exceeding nervousness. Once attributed to these patients, this constitutional or organic predisposition shaped the doctor's interpretive narrative and so his representation of symptoms, disease course, and possible recovery. Julie's nerves, moreover, when correlated with her poor health and degenerate maternal heredity, constituted a clinical picture that could be differentially diagnosed only as hysteria. These medical representations of cases could, in turn, generalize diagnostics and clinical pictures to other cases and so, at a higher level of generalization, generate theoretical abstractions. Thus Charcot's use of clinical picturing and differential diagnostics, for example, could produce the ideal types that then "typed" other sick individuals who presented at the clinic. Those types, in turn, became templates for the medical representation of disease characteristics and symptomatologies and eventually found their way into theory. Local evidence thus produced systemwide evidentiary explanations.

The case study, then, represented the patient not as an individual but as a case. The written-up case presented the patient as sufferer from a particular disease; her case was nevertheless exemplary and so appropriate for medical representation. None of the cases I have summarized, moreover, challenged medical assumptions about how to portray patients. For according to ascertainable illness categories, a case possessed a certain character, and by implication, a patient possessed a determinable personality whose traits had, perhaps, helped produce—and been produced by—the illness. The patient's character could, like her disease, be assessed and judged, as I suggest in Chapter 5; could be interpreted as participating in illness onset and possible recovery. That Julie was moody and disobeyed the sisters at her convent school seemed the appropriate attribute of a person with her particular neurogenic and representative heredity. Because she had been bottle- rather than breast-fed, Julie's delicate health joined with her heredity to produce her enigmatic but exemplary case. The patient as diagnosable and representative case, moreover, demanded that the observing and reasoning physician assume an authoritative narratorial stance. Charcot's stance as Julie's doctor produced a judging and generalizing interpretive narrative; as case writer, Charcot concomitantly eliminated interpretive anomalies to fashion Julie's case as exemplary. In accord with his function as medical observer and scientific experimenter, he portrayed her dysfunction as objectifiable and his own role as objective. His diagnosis, as a result, could be viewed within scientific and collegial networks as credible and verifiable.

Yet the clinical pictures sketched by these physicians often reported details for which heredity, medical history, or the neuropathic family could not account. These diagnoses could be made, in part, because the physician had ascertained and so could report on the patient's work habits, family experience, and social patterns up to the narrative and clinical present, as I describe them in Chapter 4 (Hunter 1991, 54–55). Bernheim, for example, portrayed familial and occupational situations as fatiguing, injuring, or disabling the women and men he treated; participating in the medicalizing of the late nineteenth-century working body, he contextualized his patients' disease stories as implicated in a larger social narrative. These patients' psychical sufferings, moreover, appeared alongside the reflex disturbances the doctors represented as characteristic of particular clinical pictures, and so cases. Bernheim's staff observed Lucie L.'s symptomatic bodily pains, hysterical attacks, hallucinations of her murderer father, and screams to Louis; these symptoms, which suggested psychic distress, entered the medical record but were not submitted to interpretation. Bernheim's imaginative medicine could generate neither the clinical practices with which to treat nor the medical concepts with which to analyze Lucie's self-representing stories and scenes. Given the material conditions of work at the Nancy hospital, Bernheim could not characterize his patient as other than a presentation-worthy example of a successful clinical intervention. Yet it seemed clear to Freud in his work with the "occasional hysteric" that clinical picturing did not always or invariably tally with characterological traits or provide a secure narratorial position from which to interpret. Despite her capability, common sense, and unneurotic health, this woman could not breast-feed her newborn infants. She was hardly a hysterical "type." Having described this discrepancy between a clinical picture and a particular patient's personality or capacity for functioning, Freud identified his patient as only occasionally, and on specific occasions, a hysteric. The discontinuity between the patient's character and the doctor's ability to construct and judge that character would make possible, in part, Freud's later rewriting of case study as case-historical genre.

Freud would exploit medical concepts implicit in the case studies I have summarized, however, to produce his new scientific genre. For while the enigmatic disease of hysteria produced exemplary and representative cases, it also challenged the representational modes of case study. In "Dora," Freud questioned, for example, the case study's tendency to type the patient. Supplementing "somatic data" with information about Dora's "purely human and social circumstances," Freud sketched "The Clinical Picture" as including, at least in part, Dora's "family circumstances." Indeed, the details that entered "The Clinical Picture" demonstrated that Freud had begun to think of such simplified tables of correlative symptoms as metaphorical representations. A trope suitable for mobilization in the dissemination of representative yet uncommon cases, the Freudian clinical picture was a field or a matrix in which multiple causations, symptomatic acts, and personal histories played themselves out. What appeared as Dora's "convergent" heredity, moreover—her father's "taint" plus her mother's neurotic predisposition and "housewife's psychosis"—could be understood as a symptomatology developed in common by co-resident family members. No longer a vehicle for hereditary transmission of illness, the family in Freudian case history constituted a "circle" and created a set of "circumstance[s]." Indeed, Freud represented this enlarged family system, not as a neuropathic unit with disabled and sick members, but as a series of erotic exchanges that stimulated fantasied self-representations and family scenarios (*SE*, 7: 18–20). Freud's revision of family circumstance paradoxically enabled him to characterize this patient as an ill individual who, however resistant to treatment, could not be represented as a type.

Dora's disease, then, was not reducible to a single and singular cause. Rather, Freud's case history suggested, it had originated in a complex set of object relations, many of them damaging to the patient, whose father had handed her over for treatment. Indeed, Freud observed here the social situation many late-nineteenth-century Viennese families experienced as necessity: the arranging of marriages, the difficulty of divorce, the performance of illicit libidinal activities, and family secrecies all demonstrated the problems and constraints of lifelong coupling in an age of increasing life expectancies. Dora's character, then, could not be predicted solely by her degenerate heredity or predicated solely on the traumatic embrace that had precipitated her illness. Freud had recast individual etiological and historical theories, individualizing the patient and situating illness within social networks and family circumstances.

Medical attention to the categories of psychic causation and social networks pressured the case study's conventional assumptions about generic representation. The case history of Elisabeth von R., which presented Freud's "first full-length analysis of a hysteria," demonstrates his revision of the case study's medical concepts and representational modes. He did not neglect to consult earlier notions of patient and family medical history, heredity, and accidental trauma, although he relegated such information to his closing discussion. But he revised the case study's technologies of patient portrayal and clinical picturing. He identified Elisabeth's father's death and her sick-nursing during his final illness as traumatic, and the daughters' social isolation as part of the medical history. But there was "no appreciable hereditary taint" on either side of her family, and despite her mother's "neurotic depression," Elisabeth's father's family and her mother's close relatives were all "well-balanced people free from nervous trouble." He portrayed his patient sympathetically, as ambitious, intellectually gifted, morally sensible, and possessing considerable independence of spirit; as proud and longing for love; as embittered by her family's failures; in short, as a woman "unreconciled to her fate." He reported the results of physical examination; he took patient histories, sketched clinical pictures, and, despite great difficulty, produced a differential diagnosis of hysteria. For, like the others in *Studies on Hysteria*, Elisabeth's case was uncommon. Unlike a sufferer from organic pain or neurasthenia, Elisabeth did not report her pain definitely or exhaustively; she did so, rather, with the "*belle indifférence*" of the hysteric. If Freud pressed or pinched her hypersensitive skin and leg muscles, her face expressed "pleasure rather than pain," and this "noticeable" but enigmatic expression could, Freud said, only be reconciled with a diagnosis of hysteria, with an unusually localized hysterogenic zone. Her presenting story, moreover, provided little to explain why she had fallen ill with this particular hysteria, why her symptoms took the uncommon form of a painful abasia. Greatly disappointed, Freud set out to ask questions physicians were not in the habit of asking. And while doctors were usually content with diagnosing the patient as "constitutionally a hysteric," Freud sought to discover whether Elisabeth was "using her physical feelings as a symbol of her mental ones" (SE, 2: 161, 136–44).

Seeking to explain Elisabeth's uncommon hysteria, Freud crafted a plausible bridge between psyche and soma that revised the concept of patient medical history as representation and self-representation. As the treatment entered its second stage, he attended fully to "the story of her illness" and its articulation with her bodily symptoms, as described in Chapter 4. Elisabeth reproduced visualizable scenes in which she had spent a blissful evening with her first love and returned home to find her father sicker; in which she had jumped out of bed, her feet bare on a cold night, to respond to her father's call. Her story reported and stimulated somatic and perceptual sensations, recounted recollected and fantasied pictures of herself, and evoked and enacted affective emotional experiences. Arousing and aroused by organic excitations, Elisabeth's scenes joined soma and psyche in her "life of memories." Yet an enigmatic pain in her leg blocked her treatment. At this point, Elisabeth herself interpreted her unusually localized hysterogenic zone as situated where her father had daily rested his leg while she rebandaged it. Her hysterogenic zone had somatically represented a psychical self- and other representation, a hoped-for pleasure and anxious fear that were formed in a moment of peak affect and, because fearful, were subsequently suppressed. It was embedded, moreover, in a network of social and familial circumstances, themselves constituting and constituted by affect-laden object relations, here with a loved but dying father. Like Frau P.'s overly sensitive genitals, Elisabeth's painful legs had "joined in the conversation"; using her pain as a "compass" to guide him, Freud had encouraged Elisabeth to continue producing the stories that recounted her psycho-physical scenes until the pain had vanished. Elisabeth improved and was now "capable of successful effort"; because her pains occasionally returned, however, Freud judged the cathartic treatment incomplete.

A serendipitous event opened the treatment's third stage. One day, Elisabeth's brother-in-law dropped by Freud's consulting rooms and, when she heard his voice and footsteps, Elisabeth's severe pains returned. She reproduced several new scenes and recollections, which culminated in her sudden thought that, when her sister died, her brother-in-law would be "free again" and she could "be his wife." The family network of object relations was now complete. The death of a father and illness of a sister had enabled Elisabeth to represent herself as beloved of her brother-in-law, an affective and pleasurable situation she could now cognitively assess and judge as inappropriate. Although his patient was "shattered" by the interpretation Freud had offered, although she attempted to reject his explanation, both physician and patient soon felt they had "come to a finish." Elisabeth's recounted scenes—psycho-physical representations of herself—had released the "quota of affect" attached to her "erotic feelings" and made clear the family scenario that had disabled her (*SE*, 2: 138–67).

No longer a "little story" of successful clinical practice, the psychoanalytic case history exposed the textual problems of interpretation, narrative temporality, and narratorial contact and stance. As he presented the procedures through which he had constructed his interpretation, Freud foregrounded the treatment history rather than the disease's deterministic origins and its therapeutic end. The treatment history, which case study had elided, raised questions, moreover, about the doctor's authority as interpreter. "The task on which I now embarked turned out," Freud said at the history's beginning, "to be one of the hardest that I had ever undertaken, and the difficulty of giving a report upon it is comparable, moreover, with the difficulties that I had then to overcome. For a long time, too, I was unable to grasp the connection between the events in [Elisabeth's] illness and her actual symptom, which must nevertheless have been caused and determined by that set of experiences." The connection between Freud's representational difficulties and his struggle to interpret Elisabeth's illness meant that the doctor's clinical procedures, hunches and guesses, questions and comments, all had to enter the discourse of case-historical report. His first interview, he acknowledged, hardly enabled him to make much "progress in understanding the case"; he did not "find it easy to arrive at a diagnosis"; he suffered "discomfiture" when his patient slyly confessed that her pains were "as bad as ever" (*SE*, 2: 138–45). Indeed, Freud looked for significance in Elisabeth's scene of first love, but patient and doctor failed to find there the psychical cause of her symptoms; he observed that her relation with her father produced pain in her right leg, but that with her young lover, in her left; he asked about the origin of her pain in walking, standing, and lying down, and so began the process of uncovering the ways her somatic symptoms represented her psychical pain. When Elisabeth confessed that the thought, "Now he is free again and I can be his wife," had shot into her head like a "flash of lightning in the dark" at her sister's death, Freud had already interpreted: "Everything was now clear." Case-historical discourse, then, foregrounded the interpretive process of producing the illness's history, which articulated the patient's story of suffering with the doctor's investigation of her somatic symptoms. It highlighted the physician's analytic work and his narratorial situation, interweaving his interpretive "explanations" with the "description of the course of [the patient's] recovery" (SE, 2: 156–61). It represented, too, the double temporality that the case study had elided. For psychoanalytic temporality retrospectively reinterpreted beginnings in light of ends, and so reconstructed the presenting story's originary teleology in light of the patient's present interpretive needs.[8]

Freud's early case histories thus represented hysteria differently than had psychiatric or neuropathological case studies. Freud had revised the etiological explanations of heredity, degeneracy, and accidental trauma and reimagined the formal strategies for beginning and ending, as for representing narrative temporality. He had reconceptualized medical history as an individual story of psycho-physical self-representation and as a series of scenes open to analytic interpretation. He had transmuted notions of the neuropathic family into a paradigmatic erotic structure capable of figural substitution and displacement, and so viewed hysteria as always already embedded in social situations and family circumstances. No longer simply an example of successful clinical practice (indeed, Dora had walked out), Freud's case history documented and disseminated the new practice's principles as well as its procedures.

Yet Freud's case history of Dora, as I demonstrate in the second section of this chapter, displayed at the level of representation the problems he had been forced to confront as he reinvented the genre. Indeed, Freud exploited the case history's double temporality, its foregrounding of narratorial stance and contact, to depict a case-historical discourse incommensurable with psychoanalytic experience. Although Freud attempted to overcome this problem through analytic appropriation and replotting of patient narrative, this incommensurability emerged as generically constitutive. Only such an inadequate standard of measure could represent the psychoanalytic patient's multiple and shifting location in self-spectatorship, her hybrid and highly mediated subjectivity. Presenting the patient as a witness to the truths of psychoanalytic practice, Freud's case histories sought to define and delimit the possibilities of meaning production in the consulting room, even as they registered this project's impossibility. As such, Freudian case history is a quintessential modern text, one that participates in the modern constitution of subjects as different from yet constructed within familial object relations and social networks. Although "Dora" has been carefully and thoroughly scrutinized by contemporary, especially feminist, critics, I briefly examine her celebrated case in the next section of this chapter, where I maintain that the problem of interpretation identifies Freudian case history as a modern and modernizing scientific genre.

II

Freud's representational difficulties were not unique to Elisabeth's or to Dora's case. In each of his case histories, Freud addressed the formal problems he encountered in representing psychoanalytic procedures and experience. Indeed, not all analyses produced material that met the generic needs of his revised case history. Dora's, Anna's, Katharina's, and Lucy's analyses were either fragmentary or otherwise incomplete, and their case histories somewhat compromised. He chose to relate neither the history of the Wolf-Man's illness nor the history of his treatment, Freud said, for fear of betraying the patient's secrets and revealing his identity; he combined instead the "two methods of interpretation." Freud had never treated Schreber, whose memoirs he analyzed, or Little Hans, whose analyst father wrote the treatment history Freud himself reproduced; both cases, however, so fully illustrated psychoanalytic principles that Freud produced for each a case history. Indeed, Freud never overcame the technical difficulties, he said, of "how to record for publication the history of a treatment of long duration." "Exhaustive verbatim reports" of the psychoanalytic proceedings would obscure rather than clarify the new method's principles; Freud conducted six or eight treatments each day and, since he refused to take notes during sessions for fear of shaking the patient's confidence and distorting his own observations, he could not simply reproduce the analytic dialogue. He reproduced his nightly notes in Emmy's case history and transcribed his single conversation—dialect and all—in Katharina's; he recorded Dora's dreams immediately after her sessions but wrote the case history after she had left treatment. Although his record could never be "phonographi-cally" exact, it possessed, Freud claimed, "a high degree of trustworthi-ness."[9] Indeed, Freud's representational strategies sought to portray the psychoanalytic situation even as they acknowledged its problematic sta-tus in case-historical discourse.

Freud's truth claims have recently come under attack by both post-modern and psychoanalytic critics. Roy Schafer argues that case-histori-cal representation obscures and elides the history of the treatment, for-mally falsifying the architectural "temporal circle" that would correctly represent the dialogic exchange between interpreting analyst and story-telling analysand. Normative life historical projects like case history, Schafer argues, are not "fact-finding expeditions" but problematic struc-tures predetermined by preparation for what will be found: "maps," "compasses," and probable "destinations" generate treatment narrative's coherent plot and produce representation as a "simplified form of tradi-tional biography" (Schafer 1980, 48–49). Donald P. Spence criticizes Freud's use of clinical narrative in explanatory case-historical discourse. Aiming through narrative unpacking to give the reader with normative competence the same evidentiary familiarity as the analyst with privi-leged competence, Freud emphasized "narrative fit" as his primary prin-ciple of plotting, Spence argues, and deployed "narrative smoothing" as his chief representational strategy. Interpretations that did not produce in-sight or were rejected by the patient, examples that disrupted the flow of narrative and so undermined the case-historical enterprise, went unre-ported. Spence calls "Dora," for example, "a narrative account which at-tempts to tell a coherent story by selecting certain facts (and ignoring others), which allows interpretation to masquerade as explanation, and which effectively prevents the reader from making contact with the com-plete account and thereby prevents him (if he so chooses) from coming up with an alternative explanation" (Spence 1987, 123, 133–34). While Schafer and Spence identify the case-historical project's problematics of biographicalism, narrative form, and reader persuasion, their accounts of psychoanalytic life history and narration naively misrepresent the generic conventions and formal requirements that constitute case history as case history.

For Freud understood clearly that these problems underwrote his representational choices. Each, moreover, addressed a formal incommen-surability between psychoanalytic experience and its case-historical re-port. The problem of persuasion, for example, governed Freud's narratorial stance toward and contact with his readers. In his case-historical introductions, he wrote out his worries about the readers his histories would (or would not) reach and sought to identify, by inscribing multiple narratees, an appropriate medical audience. These narratorial strategies to control his readers' responses and identities aimed to mediate, even as it produced, the incommensurability between the psychoanalytic experience as represented in the history of the treatment, and its report, as inscribed at the level of case-historical discourse. For the difficulties of presentation, as Freud said, forced him to make tactical choices about what to recount, comment on, and suppress. His strategy to exclude explanation of the analytic technique in "Dora," he admitted, disadvantaged the reader, who, as a result, could not "test" the "correctness of [his] procedure." But presenting simultaneously the technique of analysis and the "internal structure of a case of hysteria" would have proved impossible and would, in addition, have made the case history "almost unreadable." To have presented the technique of Dora's analysis would have required separate exposition and discussion of numerous observational outcomes and individual cases; to present the psychical structures of Dora's hysteria, on the contrary, required careful reading of her story of suffering and interpretation of her dreams, which Freud wove into the history of the treatment. The two formal requirements seemed incompatible. In addition, if he had characterized Dora as would a "man of letters," he would have simplified and abstracted her psychology and expunged from his text her love for Frau K. As a "medical man," though, he tried to "dissect" mental states and "depict" a "world of reality" replete with complicated motives and mental activities, and so, although it would "obscure and efface the outlines of her fine poetic conflict," he had to report Dora's homosexuality (SE, 7: 112, 59–60). Indeed, this very repletion made the psychoanalytic situation incommensurable with its case-historical recounting. And because the treatment history reported the analytic work—the analyst's interpretations, the patient's resistance, the transference and countertransference—its problematic status in case history was inseparable from, and in fact characterized, the case-historical project (Cohn 1992, 34–45).

The status of narrative in case-historical discourse, moreover, is problematic, not because Freud deployed narrative smoothing or sought narrative fit, but because clinical narratives themselves announce their own incommensurabilities. In medical representation, Kathryn Montgomery Hunter argues, the doctor's and patient's stories have different authors, different narrative modes, and different thematics. In the case history, too, the incommensurability between analyst's and analysand's stories constitutes a central difficulty for psychoanalytic work and, by necessity, for the case-historical genre's complex representational task. Because patient narrative's representation of the psycho-physical subject is the primary object of psychoanalytic investigation, the doctor must fashion a story that accounts for observed details; the patient must, moreover, acquire a sense of conviction that the story is credible. The differences between analyst's and analysand's stories—between storytellers, plots, audiences, and purposes—shape the representational project. While the two stories may both relate events connected with the invalid's illness, the patient's story, the analyst's story, and the case-historical narrative account tell their tales for a different purpose: the patient's to make sense of an illness that alters a life story, the analyst's to diagnose and make psychoanalytic sense of it, and the case history's to mobilize it for representation to other analysts.

As a result, the two primary tellers—analyst and analysand—select, emphasize, and organize narrative events differently, choosing different plots to sequence meaning in different ways and with different outcomes. The physician's story begins with the clinical present and interprets events historically; the patient's, with the onset of symptoms and their retrospective rereading in light of, as Hunter says, "circumstantial etiology" and "leaps to meaning." The two tellers, moreover, differ in their involvement with the events they relate. The patient speaks of her own subjective experience, guided by a sense of herself, interrupted, and hoping to recover; the physician, submitting the patient's story to observation and investigation, deploys objective medical principles of inclusion and exclusion with the goal of diagnosing, treating, and curing disease. While the patient is the subject of her own story, she is the object of the physician's; she becomes, as I argue later in this section, quasi-object of the case history's. The case-historical narrative includes, not just details of the patient's illness account, but, as Hunter says of medical case study, those of the "physician-patient encounter," rendering it "observable and intersubjective" and "open to critique." The patient's story is framed and appropriated by the case-historical narrative that represents it to a medical world. "The physician-listener turns from the patient-narrator to become a medical narrator," Hunter says, "altering the story in order to tell it to a medical audience in a medical way" (Hunter 1991, 62–63).

Although these problems and the choices they entailed emerged in all Freud's case histories, Freud foregrounded them in Dora's case. Indeed, the history of the treatment recounted a series of often contradictory stories: the patient's presenting story, the father's presenting tale, the history of the illness and its symptoms, and the analyst's narrative.[10] Although each contained as narrative kernel the same common complaint—Herr K.'s attempt at seduction—each recounted and plotted it differently, differently interpreting events and imagining outcomes. Each was told, moreover, for different authorial purposes. Dora's presenting story about Herr K.'s proposal concluded with her slapping his face. Representing her action as signifying outraged honor in the face of masculine impropriety, she sought to persuade Freud that her story of improper seduction was credible. Dora's father's presenting story, however, denied his daughter's decency. She had read Mantegazza's *Physiology of Love*, Herr K. had told him, at his house by the lake, and, being overexcited, had "fancied" Herr K.'s "immoral suggestions" and the whole scene she had described. Dora's father hoped not only to cast doubt on his daughter's story but to represent his own actions, by suppressed analogy to Herr K.'s, as honorable. Freud reconstructed both stories differently. Dora must have wanted to marry, he believed, as did other nineteenth-century women; she had therefore misread Herr K.'s "proposal" in light of her desire. Dora's father had justified his own plans and evaded confronting a dilemma by falsely posing one of his two alternatives, to seduce or to respect marital fidelity (*SE*, 7: 24–27). The clash of presenting stories, then, exposed not only the problem Freud encountered in narrating the psychoanalytic situation, but his choices about how to judge and characterize each player in the "seduction quadrille," as Jacques Lacan calls it, and how, as a result, to represent his patient and her interests (Lacan 1985, 92–104). His story appropriated his patient's and her family's presenting narratives and hoped, in subsuming both, to intervene in Dora's storytelling practices to produce therapeutic alteration.

"Dora" posed as a problem, then, the ways in which the doctor constructed and structured his interpretive narrative, its relation to the patient's story, and its status as story within case history. As the psychiatrist Philip R. Slavney claims, while the doctor uses the patient's information as "starting point," he holds in reserve, ignores, supplements, and contextualizes the hysteric's fragmentary story; although the doctor "must think critically about the narrative as he creates it," without his clinical experience, theoretical sophistication, and knowledge of cultural themes, "there would be no story" (Slavney 1990, 165–66). Medical and psychiatric tradition, then, demanded that physician narrative appropriate, interpret, and replot the patient's story of suffering. The doctor did not repeat the patient's (or parent's) presenting story, but, regarding it skeptically, constructed his own by submitting the patient's story to medical observation; he diagnostically replotted it, producing cure as outcome and end. Yet Freud's famous case history problematizes this naive assumption of psychiatric authority. Indeed, Freud began the process of constructing his story by suspending his judgment about Dora's father's tale until he'd heard Dora's. Freud's retelling of these stories repeated Dora's father's story in direct discourse and then, as the patient cognitively assessed her father's actions, summarized hers; the doctor's story followed. Here are summaries of each:

Dora's father's: He had an "intimate friendship" with the K.s, but, because Frau K. had nursed him during his illness, he claimed a special gratitude to, friendship for, and sympathy with her. Herr K. had given Dora presents to which no one objected. Could the doctor please "bring her to reason" about the scene by the lake?

Dora's: Herr K. had attempted seduction not only by the lake but four years earlier.

Freud's: Dora had felt his erect penis during their embrace in Herr K.'s office, and, displacing her sensation upward, had produced as symptoms catarrh and oral disgust.

But Dora resisted Freud's story and sought to appropriate his interpretive position. She detailed without memory gaps Frau K.'s and her father's sexual subterfuges, and, at her story's end, neither Freud nor his now persuaded reader could dispute Dora's characterization of her father's infidelity. Her reproaches against him were justified; she had indeed been "handed over" to Herr K. as the "price" of his tolerating the affair; and, although the men had made no "formal agreement," each man had clearly refused to acknowledge the other's behavior as improper so as to continue his seduction. Having concluded, as had Dora, that her father and Frau K. were enjoying a "common love-affair," the doctor found himself without room to move. Doubly bound to tell Dora's gapped story more coherently than had she, Freud seemed constrained by conventional medical forms and professional assumptions to discredit, or at least discount, Dora's "sharp-sighted" interpretations. Still, while Freud agreed that Dora had been made an object of barter, he refused to plot his story like hers. Instead, he accused her of complicity, of dismissing the affair's "true character" and, until the scene by the lake, of assisting her father's relations with Frau K. "This is all perfectly correct and true, isn't it?" he had imagined

Dora saying to challenge his interpretation; "what do you want to change in [it] now that I've told . . . you?" When Dora accepted Freud's interpretations, without her usual contradiction, and bade him good-bye warmly at year's end, Freud assumed his story's plot had prevailed. Instead, however, Dora "came no more."[11] It was neither the therapeutic termination nor the narrative conclusion that Freud had had in mind.

Freud's choices of narratorial stance and narrative form sought to remedy this clash of stories by rewriting Dora's story as concluding in marriage. For in the session before which Dora "came no more," Freud had presented a normative and prescriptive interpretation of female jealousy and marital bliss. "May you not have thought that he wanted to get divorced from his wife so as to marry you?" Freud asked her of Herr K. Moreover, Freud hinted, had Dora *been* seduced by the lake and—another implication—had she gotten pregnant, she would have been forced by social convention to marry Herr K., and so he to divorce his wife, leaving her free, perhaps, to marry Dora's father. "Indeed, if your temptation at L—— had a different upshot, this would have been the only possible solution for all the parties concerned." Perhaps, he implied, Herr K. had meant not to seduce her but propose marriage by the lake. Perhaps, had Dora listened to Herr K.'s whole story to the very end, she would have been engaged to marry him rather than scandalized. Perhaps she had intended this to happen and was "waiting for" Herr K. until she reached marriageable age, as her mother had before her her father. Divorce, exchange of partners, remarriage, and childbirth would have been the least "impracticable" outcome for all members of the seduction quadrille. This desire, Freud said, accounted for Dora's hysterical pregnancy and fantasy of childbirth "nine months later." And so, Freud thought, Dora must have felt bitter disillusionment when her charges against Herr K. evoked his denials and slanders rather than renewed proposals. "You will agree," Freud told her, "that nothing makes you so angry as having it thought that you merely fancied the scene by the lake. I know now—and this is what you do not want to be reminded of—that you *did* fancy that Herr K.'s proposals were serious, and that he would not leave off until you had married him" (SE, 7: 103, 107–08). Dora's analyst had attempted to rewrite her story of seduction as a courtship tale; for at their stories' ends, females conventionally were wed (or "terminated"). The female destiny to marry was a "crucial determinant" in the narrative's "readability," and Freud's interpretive narrative sought to fulfill precisely these requirements for readability's sake.[12]

This effort to constrain and appropriate narrative, however, produced a proliferation of texts in Freud's case-historical text. These texts, moreover, represented the problem of interpretation as central to psychoanalytic subject formation. Dora's transference, as suggested in Chapter 6, replicated her relationship to her father or Herr K. It re-presented "new editions" or "facsimiles" of childhood impulses and fantasies; during analysis, it aroused new "impressions" and inscribed in the transferential text the traces of old psycho-physical excitations. Indeed, the patient's loves, Freud later said, were a "reprinting afresh" of an old "stereotype plate"; the transference was "prototype," attaching itself in a "series" of representations with the patient's love objects and the doctor's "imago" (*SE*, 7: 116; *SE*, 12: 99–100). Dora's dreams, moreover, pictured her self- and object representations much as Elisabeth's scenes did. A spatial map of gazing, wandering, direction-seeking, letter- and encyclopedia-reading, the second dream depicted a "phantasy of defloration," at once a masculine and feminine unconscious sexual fantasy mobilized by cross-sexual identification, desiring transitivity, and hoped-for pleasure. Indeed, Dora's self-representations reproduced the position of self-spectatorship that I posit in Chapter 6 as central to psychoanalytic subjectivity. Freud recollected, for example, that Dora had said, "*she saw herself particularly distinctly going up the stairs*," when she supplemented the second dream's text.[13] Freud connected this self-spectatorship with the scene of encyclopedia-reading in Dora's first addendum to the dream-text. This visualized scene, in which Dora read a big book calmly, also positioned her as watching a picture of herself reading—without the affect Freud thought she would have felt when experiencing the scene of reading. Both scenes of self-spectatorship signified a visualized or fantasmatically realized sexual situation: the encyclopedia taught Dora about female genital parts, Freud hypothesized; the limp on the stairs represented a symbolic pregnancy and childbirth (by its symptomatic link with Dora's appendicitis). This repeated pattern of reflective self-figuration situated Dora in the double position of acting subject in, and observing spectator of, her reproduced scenes and family scenarios, an impossible position necessary for psychoanalytic mediation. Like the mechanisms Freud had assigned to screen memories, those of the visualized dream-text fabricated events around representable recollections and fantasmatic pleasures. Self-representations, like memories, did not emerge, then, but were formed and were everywhere inscribed within the retrospective and problematic interpretations of psychoanalysis.

Despite and, indeed, because of Freud's struggle to constrain and represent interpretation in "Dora," the case demanded rewriting. In 1919, Freud further problematized his earlier notion of psychoanalytic subject formation. Here is his 1905 version of the identificatory mechanisms through which Dora constituted her subjectivity. She identified with her mother by adopting a leucorrhoea; sympathetically imitated her father through her catarrh (and its upward displacement of libido); identified with Frau K. by falling ill and so expressing her unconscious love of Herr K. and her father; identified with the K.s' governess (who, like Dora, had been seduced by Herr K.'s words, "You know I get nothing out of my wife") in giving Freud (who stood in for Herr K.) two weeks' notice. Surpassing appropriate filial concern, Dora felt and acted like "a jealous wife"; her ultimatum to her father, her scenes, her suicide letter, all put "herself in her mother's place." Yet the "imaginary sexual situation" that sustained her symptomatic cough put "herself in Frau K.'s place," and, seeking in fantasy to earn her father's love, Dora identified herself "both with the woman her father had once loved and with the woman he loved now" (SE, 7: 75, 82, 107, 56–57). But Freud was not completely satisfied with this explanation. In his footnotes, the case historian asked: "If Dora loved Herr K., what was the reason for her refusing him in the scene by the lake? Or at any rate, why did her refusal take such a brutal form, as though she were embittered against him? And how could a girl who was in love feel insulted by a proposal which was made in a manner neither tactless nor offensive?" (SE, 7: 38).

Freud had failed to answer these questions in 1905, however, and, reconsidering the case in a lecture on group psychology, he acknowledged at the level of theory that Dora's symptoms represented herself as performing, and her dreams as portraying, her multiple and doubly sexed identifications. Her cough thus signified her hostile desire to take her mother's place and expressed her object-love for her father. The symptom meant, Freud said, "You wanted to be your mother, and now you are— anyhow so far as your sufferings are concerned." Yet hysterical symptom formation could also deploy the mechanism of object-choice, he said, but only if "identification has appeared instead of object-choice, and that object-choice has regressed to identification." This identification with a parent signified the wish to be, and object-choice the desire to have him or her. Dora's complex set of identifications—the desire to be and have that, when confounded, constituted her profoundly homosexual love—were represented in her symptomatic acts, her self-representational dream-texts, and her transferential text. When Dora imitated her father's symptomatic cough, her ego copied a love-object's characteristics—but a symptom could as easily have imitated a hated rival's, as in Dora's identification with (and love for) Frau K. Thus identification produced the "original . . . emotional tie" with objects, which served to constitute the ego even as the ego differentiated itself from objects.[14]

In his remarkable set of calculations, however, Freud had hardly resolved the problems that underwrote his theory of subject formation. For, as contemporary feminist critics have argued, Dora's homosexuality seems the central fact of her subjectivity, a fact Freud everywhere ignored and suppressed. Indeed, this truth emerged several times in the case history, always at moments when the analyst's attempts to interpret seemed most problematic. For in his "supplementary interpretations" of the case, Freud quietly acknowledged that Dora's multiple identifications, and consequently her homosexuality, constituted and structured her self-representations. At the end of "The Clinical Picture," Freud stranded a fragmentary and somewhat befuddled discussion of Dora's homosexuality: reported his patient's attachment to and anger at her governess and girlish cousin; her intimacy with, sleeping beside, and stories about Frau K.'s "adorable white body." Indeed, Freud normalized homosexuality, confessing that no single psychoanalysis, whether of man or woman, had failed to uncover "a very considerable current of homosexuality" (SE, 7: 60–61). In a footnote to the "Postscript," Freud again acknowledged that he had failed to discover and to inform Dora that "her homosexual (gynaecophilic) love for Frau K. was the strongest unconscious current in her mental life." Here, the "discomfiture" he had experienced with Elisabeth became "perplexity"; before he had learned the importance of homosexuality in psychoneurotics, he admitted, he had often been brought "to a standstill" during treatment (SE, 7: 120). Although these confessions interrogated, and indeed undercut, Freud's careful interpretation of Dora's heterosexual rivalries, jealousies, and motives for revenge, the case history as genre and discourse enabled such problematization. For the incommensurability of doctor's and patient's stories, which necessitated interpretation, also made the former problematic. While the incommensurability of doctor's and patient's stories, then, represented the doubled, indeed hybrid, position of psychoanalytic subjectivity in self-spectatorship, it served, most importantly, as index to the problems of analytic interpretation.

That difficulty made re-presentation of uncommon yet representative cases for other medical practitioners both imperative and problematic. For

Freud's consulting room, a laboratory of sorts for the examination and manufacture of modern subjectivity, produced a series of problematic examples of clinical practice rather than easily translatable test cases. These practices, moreover, had often failed to produce cure for the patients that undertook them; indeed, Freud eventually problematized the entire concept of "cure," calling for the cessation, not of psycho-physical symptoms, but of the "common unhappiness" of the clients and consumers of psychotherapy. Thus the patients who had been called upon as witnesses to the truths of psychoanalysis testified not to its conceptual stability nor to its successful clinical outcomes but to the problematic status of one and the impossibility of the other. Freud's new scientific genre, which claimed both its novelty and epistemic rupture with earlier structures of knowledge, thus called attention to its fragility as a form of knowledge. Indeed, the late-twentieth-century disputes about the scientific credibility of Freud's cases, his theories' replicability in different research sites, and the case histories' contamination with fictionality all arise from this representational instability and incommensurability. Rather than witness to the truth of a subjectivity located in the sexual body, psychoanalytic research subjects testified to the impossibility of producing an unproblematic subjectivity in the modern period.

The psychoanalytic subject, as I have called it, is neither singular nor univocal. The position of self-spectatorship, the intermediary location of psychoanalytic self-representations (whether memory-, dream-, or fantasmatic texts) means, as I have already said, that the psychoanalytic subject is neither wholly subject nor wholly object. I have identified Charcot's research subjects, in Chapter 3, as what Bruno Latour calls "quasi-objects" (Latour 1993, 51–55); I argue here that Freud's first research subjects—largely hysterical haute bourgeois late-nineteenth-century Viennese women—were constituted by case-historical discourse as a different kind of quasi-object. Situated on the divide between the binaries that separated subjects from social circumstances and family structures, the hysterical women who consulted Freud were both alienated from their own memories and experiences and able to reflect on them only because they were so distanced. Thus the position of self-spectatorship identified the need for self-representation and the impossibility of an unproblematic, merely mirroring self-reflection. The incommensurability of psychoanalytic experience and its case-historical report constituted the patient as the analyst's quasi-object, as a being created by the interpenetration of discourse, subjectivity, and scientific culture. Indeed, a more perfect hybrid than Charcot's staged or photographed hysteric, than Bernheim's spectacularized dysfunctional worker, Freud's re-presented self-spectator occupied the unenviable position of the subject who was both object and subject for herself, object of the analyst's investigation, and quasi-object of case-historical discourse. Created by scientific practices, translated from one research site to another, trope of logical and conceptual writing, she was a hybrid psycho-physical entity. As such, she was the quintessential modern subject, whose sense of herself was rooted in, yet seemed conceptually separable from, the body that housed her.

In the final section of this chapter, I argue that Freud's new scientific genre itself underwent constant revision. As such, it produced a new quasi-object and modern research subject: the homosexual. The infinitely fashionable hysteria diagnosis began to wane after Charcot's death, and, as I note in Chapters 1 and 3, research on the disease focused increasingly on either psychophysiology or cognitive psychology. Freud's research quickly rejected hysteria as the primary diagnostic category based on which clinical pictures could be sketched and a new discourse initiated. Indeed, while the hysteric had functioned as trope to initiate, the homosexual served to stabilize, psychoanalytic discourse. For, as Freud said, in every analysis he undertook, homosexuality emerged as a problem. The homosexual became the perfect psychoanalytic patient or case-historical quasi-object, everywhere appearing, everywhere confirming psychoanalytic concepts, networks, and social relations. Whereas the hysteric had facilitated psychoanalytic theoretical emergence, the homosexual limited terminological fluctuation and so enabled conceptual revision. Replacing the hysteric with the homosexual in case history, Freud accomplished the final task in his project to found a new science: to create networks sufficiently capacious, flexible, and extensive to transport its representative figures from one research site to others.

III

Seeking to author a new science and the genre appropriate to transport its concepts, Freud understood where and how to position himself as spokesman and "founder." He knew, too, that the hysteria diagnosis had reached the limits of its historical usefulness. "Anxious not to be restricted to treating hysteriform conditions," Freud sought other conceptual frameworks for classifying the neuroses, novel clinical practices with which to cure the uncommon diseases his taxonomies had constituted.

Finding "grave abuses of the sexual function" habitually present in his patients—whether a current sexual conflict or the traces of earlier sexual
experiences and excitations—Freud's "cathartic experiments" produced
the "apparently original discovery" that hysteria "deriv[ed from] sexuality." As Freud understood and as I argue elsewhere in this book, sexuality
was not "something purely mental" but had "a somatic side as well" (*SE*,
20: 23–27). An inclusive psycho-physical concept with which to theorize
modern subjectivity, sexuality would serve Freud's project to initiate a
new science, to fashion a new genre, to mobilize and transport his research, to win allies for psychoanalysis, and to produce new scientific
networks. That conceptualization of sexuality, I argue here, emerged first
in textually marginal sites, where the case historian could acknowledge
the problems of interpretation and theoretical representation he had encountered when revising case study as case history. There, a theory of
sexuality emerged around the figures Freud had everywhere tried to suppress: the pervert, the invert. Appropriating the central figure in sexological science, Freud replaced the hysteric with the homosexual as translatable and mobilizable scientific trope. But unlike the sexological invert,
this homosexual was a modern girl.

How else can we account for the eruption in Dora's case history of
perversion and homosexuality? Although Freud apologized, acknowledging his medical readers' skepticism, astonishment, and horror, he nevertheless confessed in "The Clinical Picture" that he talked with young
girls about topics such as fellatio. I shall not myself interpret the details of
this remarkable aside, for most have been carefully reread by feminist
psychoanalytic critics. I argue, instead, that this digression on perversion
portrays Freud's shift from hysteria to homosexuality as central to his discourse on hybrid, often dysfunctional, subjectivity. Indeed, this passage itself looks like a revision. Using the terminologies of *Three Essays on the
Theory of Sexuality*, it presents all sexuality as necessarily perverse. For instances in which the sexual function had "extended its limits in respect
either to the part of the body concerned or to the sexual object chosen"
were common and "widely diffused among the whole population," even
across different racial groups and historical epochs. Normal sexual life
was thus an "uncertainty," its acts and object choices often straying beyond "the narrow lines imposed as the standard of normality." Sublimated
perversions provided the energy for innumerable cultural achievements,
and all individuals had once—in childhood—been perverts. Thus Dora's
knowledge and fantasy of fellatio, Freud argued, derived from her per-

verse childhood thumb sucking.[15] Moreover, Freud averred in 1925, the "most important" perversion, homosexuality, "scarcely deserves the name." Traceable back to bisexuality and phallic primacy, "homosexual object choice" was once evident "in everyone" (*SE*, 20: 38). I have argued that Freud appropriated concepts and clinical practices from a variety of contemporary medical discourses to create a flexible and capacious psychophysical notion of modern subjectivity. Ending this book, I argue that the specimen pervert—the homosexual—replaced the hysteric as the quintessential psychoanalytic quasi-object and case-historical trope.

Because Dora's case exposed the instability of interpretation, moreover, it created the conditions of possibility for theoretical revision. Psychoanalytic recursivity—an activity increasingly central to theoretical production—involved reconsideration of clinical pictures, accumulation of additional observations, reinterpretation of already-presented cases, documentation of new cases and quasi-objects, and stabilization of new theoretical concepts. Psychoanalytic recursivity, moreover, functioned to marginalize hysteria, making the homosexual the perfect analytic quasi-object. Yet, I argue, figures for Dora appear throughout psychoanalysis's minor, often buried, case histories. "The Psychogenesis of a Case of Homosexuality in a Woman," viewed from this perspective, is a rewriting of "A Fragment of a Case of Hysteria" and so serves as a final specimen case for my argument that psychoanalysis modernized subjectivity. The hysterical woman disappeared from case history for twenty years, James Strachey informs us. She reemerged later, I argue, as the homosexual who had no hysterical symptoms, who resisted the interpretive and case-historical discourse with which Freud sought to constrain her. Replacing the hysteric as research subject and representational quasi-object, the homosexual became the last exemplary and representative figure of psychoanalytic case history.[16]

Both clinical picture and patient portrayal in "A Case of Homosexuality in a Woman" resemble those in "Dora." Freud began the case history with his characteristic apologies to and invocation of his readers; this "presentation," he averred, furnished only "the general outlines" of the case, while "suppressing all the characteristic details on which the interpretation is founded." Here is a sketch of Freud's clinical picture: a beautiful and clever 18-year-old girl, whose family enjoyed "good standing," was brought to treatment by her parents; they disapproved of their daughter's devoted attachment to a "questionable lady," herself "nothing but a *cocotte*" who lived and enjoyed intimate relations with a married woman friend, as well as promiscuous affairs with a number of men; they asked Freud to return their daughter to a "normal state of mind." The girl's father, Freud said, had treated his children sternly and so become estranged from them; when he had learned of his daughter's homosexual tendencies, he "flew into a rage and tried to suppress them by threats"; he had been determined to combat her homosexuality "with all the means in his power." The girl's mother, who herself suffered from "neurotic troubles," had indulged the girl's brothers but been harsh to the girl herself. The patient, reserved in her comments about her mother, provided little information about her character.

The homosexual girl's family circle, then, resembled Dora's in a number of details, including the presence of a hostile father, a withdrawn but neurotic mother, and brother(s) allied with the mother. Like Dora's, the girl's family was bourgeois and financially comfortable. The family circle might also be said to include erotic figures outside itself, as had Dora's; here, a transgressive woman who enjoyed a domestic sexual relation with a woman and extra-domestic affairs with many men. This girl, like Dora, had been handed over for treatment by her father, who, like Dora's, asked Freud to normalize her sexual desires. Like Dora, this girl had considered killing herself, but instead of writing a suicide letter, like Dora, she had thrown herself onto a railway track, winning her resistant lover's attention and her parents' lenience. And finally, the homosexual girl, resistant to psychoanalysis, left treatment early and so caused, through her self-representative fantasy, its "premature conclusion." Like Dora, this homosexual girl possessed "acuteness of comprehension" and the capability for "lucid objectivity"; she, too, had been a "spirited" and rebellious girl, and was dissatisfied with her lot as a woman. Like Ida Bauer, she would become or could be called—in a new terminology—a "feminist" (SE, 18: 147–54, 169).

Here we have another "seduction quadrille." Yet Freud attributed to this girl both the agency and the homosexual desire he had denied Dora. The girl, for example, was the seductress in this quadrille. She expressed erotic devotion to her beloved, as Herr K. had to Dora, and Dora's father had to Frau K.: she seized every opportunity to enjoy her beloved's presence; waited for her at tram stops; sent her flowers; and neglected to protect "her own reputation." When the girl inadvertently met her father on the street, he was not accompanying his beloved (and hers!); she accompanied her adored lady. While he had sought to suppress Dora's homosexual tendencies, then, confining them to footnotes and the position of afterthoughts, Freud made this girl's homosexuality the research subject of his case history. Indeed, he confessed, this girl "was not in any way ill," nor did she complain of her homosexual condition. Indeed, "the girl had never been neurotic," Freud acknowledged, "and came to the analysis without even one hysterical symptom." His difficulty in summarizing her sexual history, then, originated in her mental and physical health. The analyst found himself blocked, moreover, by his patient's lack of resistance: although she felt no urgent need to renounce her homosexuality, she hoped, for her parents' sake, to cooperate with the therapy. Freud understood his analytic task, then, not as "resolving a neurotic conflict" but as "converting" a homosexual woman to heterosexuality. By 1920, Freud understood the difficulty—indeed, the impossibility—of this task. For this kind of treatment, in most instances, merely facilitated heterosexual alongside homosexual object choice, thus restoring, he said, the patient's "full bisexual functions." "Normal sexuality too depends upon a restriction in the choice of object," Freud said; "to undertake to convert a fully developed homosexual into a heterosexual does not offer much more prospect of success than the reverse, except that for good practical reasons the latter is never attempted" (SE, 18: 148–55). As Havelock Ellis had frankly confessed, the remedy seemed worse than the disease.

Freud's theory of family circumstance had altered, too, since 1905, and so this seduction quadrille served to illustrate and confirm oedipal theory. Freud attended, in particular, to the substitutions of place in family scenarios, and to the ways in which the oedipal family formed children into subjects. Thus, Freud maintained, the homosexual girl experienced, at puberty, the feminine wish to have a male child, indeed, her father's child and an "image of him"; not she, however, but her mother, her "unconsciously hated rival," had borne the child, her youngest brother, when the girl was 16. She thereupon turned away from her father and men in general and took women as her love objects. Here, the mechanisms of identification and object choice served to form subjectivity, as discussed in Chapter 1. Yet by 1920, these mechanisms no longer operated within psycho-physical scenes to inscribe erotic family scenarios onto and within the perceptual and sensory child; they were no longer, moreover, significant problems for psychoanalytic theory. Homosexuality in the oedipal family had become problematic. For Freud had already theorized identification with a same-sex "love-object" as a kind of regression to narcissism (SE, 18: 154–58). Indeed, the adorable lady, whose slender figure and severe beauty resembled the girl's brother's, reproduced her

feminine and masculine ideal, satisfying at once homosexual and heterosexual tendencies. By positing the plasticity of identification—its difference from yet identity with object choice—Freud removed a problem
from psychoanalytic theory. At the same time, he anchored his oedipal
theory of modern subject formation. For if homosexuality were not
merely a perverse swerve away from, but a normal aspect of, heterosexuality, the normalized subject seemed everywhere perverse. The double
oedipal relation—identification with and desire for the same-sex parent—caused or expressed the unconscious changing of one's own sex; the
same-sex identification facilitated same-sex object choice. Sexual transitivity, which Jill L. Matus defines as "a continuum of sexed being rather
than a great divide between incommensurable opposites," had replaced
hysterical translatability as the mechanism that produced, controlled, and
delimited psychoanalytic theoretical production (Matus 1995, 10).

In "The Psychogenesis of a Case of Homosexuality in a Woman,"
Freud confirmed the theory that homosexuality originated in fixation on
the same-sex parent. Like Dora, the homosexual girl was ambivalent
about her mother. The girl's mother saw her daughter as an "inconvenient
competitor"; she favored her sons at the girl's expense, limited her independence, and kept a "strict watch" on the girl's intimacy with her father.
Yet the girl's homosexual object choice also expressed her seduction fantasies even as it took "revenge" on her father: she "show[ed] herself
openly" with her beloved in the streets near his workplace, daring him to
rage at her; her suicide attempt depicted her "f[a]ll" through his sexual
fault, performing and fulfilling her wish to have his child even as it punished her for it. All these facts, nevertheless, betrayed the girl's attachment
to her mother. For Freud's analysis proved "beyond all shadow of doubt"
that the "lady-love was a substitute for—her mother." Thus the girl had,
in fantasy, changed into a man and taken "her mother in place of her father as the object of her love." Her homosexual object choice imitated the
mother-fixated object choice of men, and so the girl idealized her
"adored one." This lady-love, like Frau K., both indulged the girl's passion
and betrayed it: the cocotte by spurning, Frau K. by calumniating the
impassioned girl. The homosexual girl's transference to Freud, despite its
apparent equanimity and even indifference, thus signified her desire to
wound, deceive, and take revenge on him as on her father. Freud therefore "broke off the treatment," he said, advising the girl's parents to consult a woman doctor, who could stand in for the mother as object choice
and transferential imago.[17]

The homosexual as trope thus resolved some conceptual problems for psychoanalysis, even as she facilitated its clinical productivity. Indeed, the notion of mother-fixation fixed Freud's oedipal version of family circumstance, enabling all analytic interpretation to find its origin in attachment to the same-sex parent, a seemingly universal fact in the bourgeois nuclear family. In the homosexual girl's case, mother-identification helped Freud undo a particularly knotty problem with dream interpretation. For the girl's dreams represented her longing for a man's love and for children, yet these dreams contradicted Freud's interpretation of the oedipal family scenario, which identified homosexuality as caused by regressive object choice of the same-sex parent. The dreams' status as lies, moreover, seemed to subvert psychoanalysis's theory of the unconscious. For Freud imagined some readers as asking (with "helpless indignation"), how the unconscious, which dreams represented, could lie. Yet Freud demonstrated that these dreams, with which the patient consciously sought to mislead her analyst, resolved contradictory impulses; thus the desire to please and to betray the father—or father-substitute, the analyst—existed in the same (mother-)complex. Serving as always available conceptual anchor, this female oedipal complex stabilized any ideational fluctuation in psychoanalytic theory.

Freud deployed the same logic in another case of female homosexuality to illustrate, legitimate, and stabilize psychoanalytic concepts. In "A Case of Paranoia Running Counter to the Psychoanalytic Theory of the Disease" (1915), Freud presented this clinical picture: an attractive, "distinctly feminine," and "handsome girl" of 30, who had a "responsible post" on the staff of "a big business concern," reported having heard a clicking noise while in the arms of her lover; later, seeing two men on the stairs carrying a small box, she imagined the box to be a camera, the click to have been that of a shutter, and herself to have been photographed during a compromising "scene." Although Freud did not identify this woman as "feminist," she was nevertheless a professional woman. Indeed, her elderly female supervisor played a central part in her fantasies. When her lover had entered the supervisor's office, the girl imagined he had betrayed the secret of their love affair, and, moreover, that he and the supervisor themselves enjoyed a love affair. But this case of paranoia challenged an important psychoanalytic concept, that paranoia originated in homosexual panic. "In these circumstances," Freud admitted, "the simplest thing would have been to abandon the theory that the delusion of persecution invariably depends on homosexuality, and at the same time to abandon everything that followed from that theory. Either the theory must be given up or else, in view of this departure from our expectations, we must side with the lawyer and assume that this was no paranoiac combination but an actual experience which had been correctly interpreted."[18] Did Freud have another "sharp-sighted" girl in his consulting room? The hysteric and the paranoiac, as noted earlier in this book, resembled one another in Freud's earliest musings: Frau P.'s hypersensitive genitals, like Elisabeth's painful legs, "joined in" the consulting room's conversations; Frau P.'s self-punishing and erotic scenarios, moreover, resembled those of another hysterical girl, who, from her vantage point under the bed, had been kicked while watching her father seduce a servant.

But in this paranoiac's, as in the homosexual girl's, case, Freud resolved the problem paranoia posed. For it was "easy to see" that the elderly superior, whom the girl had described as having "white hair like my mother," was a "substitute for her mother," that she had put her lover "in the place of her father," and that the "strength of her mother-complex" had driven the girl to imagine her lover and supervisor engaged in an affair. Thus the girl's "*original* persecutor" was not a man but a woman; this erotic scenario represented the girl's inability to emancipate herself from her mother's disapproval of her daughter's sexual pleasure. This girl's case was highly truncated and fragmentary. She was not Freud's patient, but had been brought twice to see Freud during her lawyer's consultation with him. While Freud's presentation of this paranoid girl does not meet the generic requirements for psychoanalytic case history, it nevertheless served a clear function for psychoanalytic theory. Although the "present case emphatically contradicted" Freud's own "observations and analyses" and those of his "friends," it in fact confirmed "the relation between paranoia and homosexuality without any difficulty" (*SE*, 14: 265–68). By betraying her mother-complex through the detail of white hair, the homosexual woman served to clarify rather than problematize interpretation. She functioned, as well, to derail anti-oedipal challenges to Freudian theory and its by now well-constituted scientific networks.

Freud's final recursive consideration of hysterical symptomatology focused, ironically, on a man, and so would seem to contradict my own interpretation. Yet "Dostoevsky and Parricide" (1928 [1927]) supports my notion that, while the hysteric initiated, the homosexual stabilized psychoanalytic discourse. Tentatively diagnosing Dostoevsky as not epileptic but hystero-epileptic, Freud sketched the novelist's clinical picture: a "severe hysteria" characterized by convulsive attacks, characterological irritability and aggressiveness, *absence*, fits of vertigo, and mimetic attacks. Dostoevsky's imitative attacks of deathlike states symbolized his identification with someone (the subject wished) dead; for the boy, this figure was the father; Dostoevsky's fits were thus a "self-punishment for a death-wish against a hated father." Yet the double oedipal relation of son to father—masculine identification with and feminine desire for him—required that castration intervene to enable the son's maturation. The novelist's deathlike attacks, then, fixed his father-identification, his aggression against and submission to the same-sex parent: "You wanted to kill your father in order to be your father yourself. Now you *are* your father, but a dead father [and] now your father is killing *you*" (*SE*, 21: 179–85). Dostoevsky's sexual history, moreover, included homoeroticism, masochism, and an extraordinary sense of guilt, all of which stemmed from his especially strong feminine component. Indeed, the masochistic self-punishment of Dostoevsky's oedipal scenario represented his disposition to femininity, which, in tandem with his innate bisexuality, made him the perfect homosexual hysteric. Imitating the father he resembled, but from whom he desired to differ, Dostoevsky could perform himself both male and female, satisfying in fantasy a masculine wish and a masochistic feminine satisfaction. Presenting with hysterical multiple and cross-sexual identifications, homosexually fixated on the same-sex parent, Dostoevsky served as exemplary and representative case for use in psychoanalytic recursivity.

Freud had undertaken and succeeded at a mammoth scientific and institutionalizing project. The Conclusion to this book assesses Freud's constitution of scientific networks, his deployment of sociabilities to create solidarity within this community, and his efforts to control the distribution of credit and distinction within these social groups. For his hands-on work practices, his control over clinical training and technologies, and his ability to galvanize followers and adherents facilitated his endeavor to institutionalize psychoanalysis as a new science. In his consulting room at Berggasse 19—amidst his antiquities, the rug-covered couch, and the stuffed bookcases—Freud had combined scientific concepts he had appropriated from a variety of medical discourses to produce a theory of psycho-physical and self-representative subjectivity. From the patients who frequented that consulting room, he heard stories of suffering that he used to transmute the scientific genre of psychiatric case study into psychoanalytic case history and then, recursively, to control and delimit the theories that anchored and supported it as a record of practice. Despite their problematic accounting for psychoanalytic experience, their incommensurable narratives, their problematic scenes of interpretation, those case histories appropriately represented their patients as hybrid subjects, their discursive function as quasi-objects. These case histories served to disseminate psychoanalytic concepts and practices, served recursively to delimit the domain and stabilize the shifts of conceptual production. As exemplary research subjects and laboratory quasi-objects, these hysterics' and homosexuals' stories of suffering, their maladies of representation, helped Freud transport psychoanalysis to other research sites along the scientific networks he himself had authorized and instituted.

Making all modern subjectivity perverse and psychosexual, moreover, Freud had fundamentally altered what we think of as "normal." For the *Three Essays on the Theory of Sexuality*, Freud said, "quite remarkably increased the number of people who might be regarded as perverts." Nearly a century later, hysteria is everywhere visible in the discourses of psychiatric and psychotherapeutic theory, cultural criticism, feminist historiography, and internecine psychoanalytic debate. As Jean Laplanche has said, psychoanalysis has invaded the social domain, becoming a cultural movement and, indeed, the dominant theory of human subjectivity in the modern period (Laplanche 1990, 124). Although he was speaking hyperbolically, Freud may well have been right when he claimed in 1905, "we are all to some extent hysterics" (*SE*, 7: 171).

Conclusion

Psychoanalysis Proper

In 1910, Freud was consulted by a "well preserved" middle-aged woman who had suffered anxiety-states since her recent divorce. A young suburban physician had advised her that, because sexual continence had caused her disease, she must return to having intercourse with her husband, take a lover, or masturbatorily satisfy herself to recover her health. Moral and religious scruples made the latter two recommendations repugnant to her, and she refused to return to her role as wife. She had become convinced that she was incurable. Her "older" and, as Freud described her, "dried-up" female companion urged Freud to prescribe a treatment other than sexual gratification; continence could not make women ill, she said, for she herself had long been a "respectable" and anxiety-free widow. Rather than discuss the young physician's handling of this case and creation of this "awkward predicament"—for he had identified Freud as the sex-treatment's author, himself as Freud's follower, and referred the patient to him—Freud in his essay questioned the young doctor's scientific knowledge and described his technical errors. He had mistaken the "sexual life" for coitus and orgasmic release and failed, moreover, to work through the patient's resistances. If the patient, Freud said, had had no hesitation about masturbating or entering into a sexual liaison, she would already have done so. The young physician, thinking his patient's anxiety an "actual" neurosis with a contemporary cause, had prescribed somatic therapy; but, Freud said, this "convenient misapprehension" prevented the doctor from distinguishing anxiety neurosis from other pathological structures and states. Freud himself believed that this newly divorced woman, who was "not yet finished with her womanhood," suffered from "anxiety *hysteria*," which indicated—given this nosographical distinction—a different clinical picture, different etiology, and different therapeutic intervention. The "three therapeutic alternatives" this "so-called psycho-analyst" offered, Freud exclaimed, left "no room for—psycho-analysis!" (*SE*, 11: 221–25).

In "'Wild' Psychoanalysis," Freud cautioned medical men about diagnosing nervous disorders without psychoanalytic knowledge or training. Although this young physician had endangered his patient's health, "wild" psychoanalysis harmed "the cause of psycho-analysis" more than it hurt "individual patients." And because internal and external threats to the emergent yet still fragile science had surfaced by 1910, Freud set out to define its "technical rules." Knowing a few psychoanalytic findings, Freud said, insufficiently prepared a physician to treat nervous patients; he needed, instead, to familiarize himself with psychoanalytic technique. But that procedure could not yet be learned from books or discovered independently without "great sacrifices of time, labour and success," and only a few physicians "already proficient" in psychoanalysis could teach it. And, Freud hinted, because *he* did not know the young physician who had prescribed sexual activity to the hysterical divorcée, the suburban doctor could not qualify to practice psychoanalysis. Although he and his co-workers hesitated to claim a "monopoly" on such psychic techniques, they had "no other choice." In March 1910, therefore, they had founded the International Psycho-Analytical Association, whose members declared their adherence to psychoanalytic principles and repudiated "wild" treatments that called themselves psychoanalysis but did not, Freud said, "belong to us" (*SE*, 11: 226–27).

Other critics have already recounted the stories of the IPA's inauguration, conflict, and struggles for priority, and I shall not do so here.[1] Yet in "'Wild' Psychoanalysis," Freud implied that, because he had successfully inaugurated a new discursive practice, he needed to declare its principles of dispersion and control its concepts' redistribution. Psychoanalytic theory had entered medical practice; new analytic ideas, Freud knew, could breed and would multiply. By 1910, he had set out to identify the doctors who could name themselves his adherents and to delimit the domains in which his practices could be deployed. Although Freud represented his institutionalizing moves as necessary to protect psychoanalysis from popularization and charlatanism—from "wild" practitioners—he was savvy enough to understand that the new science would prosper only if he organized an apparatus to secure its professional reputation, to control dispersion and transmission of its statements through periodical and book publication, to regulate its enunciatory modes and subjects by authorizing a new generation of analysts, and to legitimize its therapeutic techniques through training analyses. Promulgating a set of rules that governed the modes of psychoanalytic enunciation, the distribution of its subject positions, and the system that defined and prescribed them, Freud hoped to govern the status of psychoanalytic concepts and to regulate the ways in which they circulated. For the doctor who prescribed a satisfying sexual life as cure for the hysterical divorcée met none of Freud's rules for psychoanalytic professionalism.

Fashioning himself a psychoanalytic "Robinson Crusoe," Freud had nevertheless, by 1910, created around himself a scientific network. First in the casual Wednesday Society meetings, then at the International Congresses, and finally through the IPA, the Freud circle had created an international organization, encouraged the institution and growth of local professional societies, and spawned publication organs to govern the status and regulate the reception, use, and reuse of its theoretical statements. The newly organized group did not neglect economic and institutional considerations. Welcoming Carl Jung and Eugen Bleuler into the psychoanalytic fold, the movement gained from Zurich, Freud said, a "compact little group of adherents," a "public clinic" at the Burghölzli mental hospital that could be "placed at the service of psycho-analytic researches," and a teacher who made psychoanalytic theory an "integral part of his psychiatric course" (*SE*, 14: 27–29). In addition, Freud encouraged institutional growth of this network in other countries. He supported Karl Abraham's decision to leave the Burghölzli and establish a German branch in Berlin, encouraged organization of psychoanalytic societies in New York and Boston, and endorsed formation of the American Psychoanalytic Association. The American adherents, moreover, had professorships, and thus access to print, patients, graduate students, and research facilities.[2] In a few short years, then, psychoanalysis had begun to establish itself as not only a professional specialism but a new science, complete with collegial networks, research sites, and modes for distributing credit and distinction.

The Freud circle's members achieved group coherence by troping their network as a "band of brothers." Situated as father figure, however, Freud often stimulated rather than controlled his metaphorical sons' aggressive and rivalrous competition for his favor. Seeking to settle a squabble between Jung and Abraham over scientific priority, for example, Freud fueled the dispute. When Jung sought to "liberat[e]" himself from

Freud's paternal authority, Freud wrote him into a family romance. When Alfred Adler refused to "stand in [Freud's] shadow," Freud felt forced to "bring about" his resignation from editorship of the *Zentralblatt*, his exit from the Vienna Society, and his expulsion from all connection with psychoanalysis.[3] When Sandor Ferenczi "struggle[d] for independence," Freud berated his "rebellion and submission"; while Jung was, early in their relationship, his "favorite child," he soon became a usurper.[4] Against the figurative sons whose masculine ambition made them dispute the psychoanalytic Father, that Father "took up arms," aggrandizing himself even as he rebuked them. He declared Adler and Jung "retrograde" and their theoretical innovations illegitimate. In the epigrammatic and oracular words of Goethe's God, they would not be worth a "fart" on Judgment Day.[5] The Freud circle was thus constituted by, even as it anchored and sustained, the oedipalizing of psychoanalytic theory.

The Freud circle used this oedipal paradigm as a model for conceptual transmission along its scientific networks. Although Freud initiated this family myth, Jones—chosen son, heir, and head of the movement by 1930—popularized and disseminated it. Unresolved "infantile complexes," he said, produced rivalry and jealousy among the brothers; while the obedient sons had "come to terms with their childhood complexes" and could work harmoniously, the dissidents squabbled childishly with the papa and each other. The "backbiting" and "quarrels over priority" increased when Freud preferred Jung to the Viennese sons; banding together, Adler and Stekel rebelled against the "great Father," Jones said. Freud relished this oedipalizing game, moreover, diagnosing in his letters and conversations Ferenczi's "brother complex," Abraham's "personal complexes," and his own father and brother complexes (Jones 1955, 2: 128–29, 71, 47, 146). Edith Kurzweil notes that it was "de rigueur" among the sons to "expose all conflicts, in the name of science, as manifestations of unconscious processes"; this "reductive" semiotic habit, she says, inevitably caused "organizational headaches" that obscured the early psychoanalytic movement's structural and institutional problems. Indeed, Freud's desire for an international association imposed impractical and counterproductive rules on national associations, ignored local customs and laws, and caused frictions that were exacerbated when psychoanalysts could not separate institutional, intellectual, and emotional concerns (Kurzweil 1989, 37–42). Although this interpretive habit of reducing all organizational conflict to family tropes created even as it sought to resolve competition among Freud's heirs, the clamor to be Freud's "favorite child"

had, Jones confessed, a "material motive" (Jones 1955, 2: 128). For although dissident sons could be disinherited, those who remained—and
who thus headed up their own research units, published theoretical
polemics blessed by Freud himself, trained students and appointed their
own followers—reaped large professional benefits.

Freud may well have appropriated this clannish model for group organization, coherence, and loyalty from Judaism. A patriarchally organized religion practiced by a marginalized social group anxious about its
racial inheritance and intellectual transmission, Judaism sustained the
brotherhood's identifications with one another as members of a minority
subject to racial discrimination. I do not mean to imply that Freud and
his followers miscalculated the effects of anti-Semitism on their professional lives; they did not. But the fact of their Jewishness served their
group solidarity. "Kindred Jewish traits," Freud said, united the seven
members of the "*strictly secret*" executive counsel that surrounded and
served him; its members assured and comforted him with their adherence, swore loyalty to psychoanalysis's fundamental tenets, and replied to
criticism in his place (ibid., 152–53, 164). Judaism, moreover, provided
the conventions of sociability necessary to secure for the group a sense of
scientific community. The only "Gentile in the circle," Jones—whom Peter Gay calls a "kind of honorary Jew"—identified with Judaism and
shared his colleagues' intimacies, anecdotes, wisdom, and jokes so fully
that, he hinted, he could almost "pass" among other analysts.[6] Gentile
converts, moreover, protected psychoanalysis from appearing too Jewish,
and the first disciples' identities mattered greatly in the dissemination of
"the cause [*die Sache*]." Indeed, Freud courted Jung precisely because, he
told Abraham, only his membership in the group saved psychoanalysis
from seeming "a Jewish national affair," a "Jewish science."[7] He cultivated
the Zurich group, he told Ferenczi, "to amalgamate Jews and goyim in
the service of [psychoanalysis]." For although he felt "solidarity" with his
Jewish ancestry and the Jewish people, Freud sought to protect his new
science from contamination by close association with a marginalized minority. Moreover, he had "put up" with his fate, he said, refusing to feel
"inferior and an alien" because he "was a Jew."[8] Mimicking a minyan, the
Committee closed ranks against the gentile world, even as it sought to
camouflage its cultural and social appropriation of Judaism's characteristic
senses of loyalty, zeal, sociability, and intellectual fervor.

I have relied, in these concluding statements, on Freud's historical, autobiographical, and expository documentations of psychoanalytic emer-

gence and theorization. For in these texts, Freud sought to fix psychoanalytic concepts and, looking back, recursively to restate them, even "dogmatically," in the most "concise of forms" and "unequivocal of terms" (*SE*, 23: 144). He sought to secure, for example, the theories of resistance and repression, the unconscious, the etiological significance of sexual life, and infantile sexuality, all of which, Freud said, formed the "principle constituents" of psychoanalysis's theoretical structure (*SE*, 20: 40). He hoped, in addition, to govern the clinical practices of free association, analytic interpretation, transference, and dream analysis, which represented psychoanalysis's primary appropriable technologies. Instantiating his central concepts, Freud thus attempted to govern what Michel Foucault calls discursive additivity—to ensure that psychoanalytic theory would obey the same laws of composition at century's end that it did in 1938. But even as he sought to regulate the succession of psychoanalytic statements, he invoked the principles of discursive recurrence, reconstituting psychoanalysis's past, defining its filiations (its precedents and antecedents), redefining the terms of its possibility and necessity, and excluding discourses incompatible with it. Freud's historical project retrospectively reconstituted psychoanalysis's past even as he himself, its creator, recursively fixed its laws of composition.

I take my accounts of Freud's oedipalized relations with his figurative sons from *On the History of the Psycho-Analytic Movement*. A curious mixture of conceptual restatement and personal grievance, this history demonstrates all the petulance and rage of the betrayed papa, angered by his sons' usurpations, his own energy fueled by revenge. In this problematic history, Freud closes ranks with the submissive sons and takes a hard line on psychoanalytic concepts. As he did in "'Wild' Psycho-Analysis," Freud warns any follower who refuses to declare fidelity to psychoanalytic "facts" that he will not "escape a charge of misappropriation of property by attempting impersonation, if he persists in calling himself a psychoanalyst." His rhetorical rage defines psychoanalytic solidarity and justifies himself by oedipalizing that social relation. Here, Freud invoked nomination to identify psychoanalysis proper. For Jung, who dared modify Freud's original tenets, forged—and falsified—the true steel of the figurative psychoanalytic knife: he changed the hilt and put on a new blade, but, despite his engraving on it of the "same name," Freud said, no one would "regard the instrument as the original one" (*SE*, 14: 16, 66). Portraying a scientific network as though it were constituted by an oedipalized set of subject positions, rules for enunciation, conceptual pu-

rities, and professional authorizations, Freud played out the countertransference through which he had taken revenge on his predecessors, early
co-workers, and probable successors. Ironically enough, Freud had displayed to Fliess this mix of rhetoric, nomination, and transferential rage.
"Binswanger has just published a thick handbook of neurasthenia in
which the sexual theory—that is, my name—is not even mentioned!" he
wrote his mentor in 1896; "I shall take my cold revenge on him."[9]

Freud's "history" of his new science, moreover, stands midway in its
originator's career, an unusual position from which to historicize. Yet this
history undertakes a central historiographic project for Freud at mid career: to disguise that hysteria was psychoanalysis's clinical and conceptual
source and to foreground, instead, a theory of sexuality as its origin. He
defines as incompatible with psychoanalysis discourses not focused
squarely on sexuality. Finding the "underworld of psycho-analysis" too
"uncomfortable," Freud said, men like Jung resisted the new science's
concepts and entered a transferential struggle with him, its creator (SE,
14: 66). Although this project of discursive exclusion hardly succeeded, its
logical shift of the conditions for initiation to psychoanalytic networks
identify it as a kind of occlusion. In "'Wild' Psycho-Analysis," Freud had
berated a physician who dared call himself a psychoanalyst for having
misdiagnosed his patient as suffering a real sexual neurosis when she truly
suffered from hysteria; in the History, he berates his predecessors and early
adherents for failing to understand sexuality's centrality for theory and
thus for misdiagnosing hysteria's true etiology, sexual trauma. Logically
and grammatologically, Freud performed a chiasmus here, moving hysteria from a logically prior and grounding location to a secondary one, and
sexuality to a privileged position of origin. The diagnosis of hysteria,
once basic to psychoanalytic practice, had become contingent on the theory of sexuality. Retrospectively installing sexuality as psychoanalysis's
fundamental truth, Freud invoked a metaleptic and reminiscent temporality. For his historical representation of psychoanalysis's past put an effect of theory production in place of its cause: "we may reverse the dic-
tum 'cessante causa cessat effectus' [when the cause ceases the effect ceases],"
Freud had said in explaining hysterical trauma as a "foreign body" whose
agency, long after its entry into the body, was still at work. Thus the effect recalled and, in a way, produced its cause, just as, Freud said, "a psychical pain that is remembered in waking consciousness still provokes a
lachrymal secretion long after the event" (SE, 2: 6–7).

This historical reproduction of theory as about sexuality, however, also functioned through screen memory. For while the material in this reminiscence of psychoanalysis's first cause was "genuine," its status was also invented, falsified, and tendentious. Freud's recollection of psychoanalytic theory's origin in sexuality was "formed," and, as my reading has tried to demonstrate, its data were not literal (*SE*, 3: 319–22). For Freud's early "sexual theory," like the seduction theory, hardly resembled the theory of sexuality he posited in 1905. Whereas his first musings about the sexual etiology of neuroses considered material irritants (such as masturbation, abstinence, and coitus interruptus) or hereditary determinants as causing illness, and the seduction theory posited pre-sexual sexual trauma, *Three Essays on the Theory of Sexuality* conceptualized normal as inflected by perverse sexuality, and heterosexuality as constituted by a detour through oedipal homosexual wishes. Deploying a metaleptic logic, then, Freud replaced hysteria as psychoanalytic origin with the theory of sexuality, a theory he thus located as central to all other psychoanalytic structures and positioned as ground to all other statements and concepts.

As part of the project to stabilize, delimit, and disseminate psychoanalysis, Freud's representation of its history repeatedly sought to justify the new science's grounding in experimental method. In *An Autobiographical Study*, Freud said that he had applauded the early cooperation between Vienna's psychoanalysis and Zurich's experimental psychology because the Burghölzli—and its "friends of psycho-analysis"—produced research that experimentally confirmed psychoanalytic observations and demonstrated Freudian concepts directly to students. While Jung's "word association" tests lent credibility to psychoanalytic theory, Jung's and Bleuler's schizophrenia research offered new treatment opportunities and demonstrated in psychiatric patients mental processes akin to those of dreams and neuroses. This research confirmed Freud's findings as only experimentation could, he said, making it impossible "for psychiatrists to ignore psycho-analysis any longer." When "the Burghölzli was lost to analysis," an institutional base from which to propose theoretical statements, perform investigative research, and refine clinical practice—a place to "learn" and "practice" the "new art"—would no longer support the new science (*SE*, 20: 51; *SE*, 14: 27–28). Experimentation and the opportunity for mass observations, Freud knew, would have facilitated theory production, enabled the legitimation and translation to other research settings of psychoanalytic concepts, and created opportunities to distribute credit and distinction among psychoanalysis's supporters. But, he said in the autobiographical study, because he had stayed "in the closest touch" with analytic material, had never ceased to detail points of clinical and technical importance, psychoanalysis remained grounded in patient observation despite its poverty of experimental data.

Indeed, Freud deployed the concept of observation in his historical and autobiographical texts to define the scientific networks he and his colleagues were constructing. He judged predecessors, displaced discredited mentors, and excluded inappropriate followers. Breuer, he said, had failed as co-worker primarily because he had neglected sexuality. No previous observation had explained hysterical symptoms as had Breuer's case history of Anna O., and Breuer's cathartic treatment had stimulated Freud's "cathartic experiments," yet cathartic theory had merely "described" observations and, although it illuminated etiology, had failed to establish the disease's nature. In the "transition from catharsis to psychoanalysis proper," Freud had gone "beyond the domain of hysteria" to investigate the sexual life, he said, and, on closer observation, had produced classifiable clinical pictures of various distinctly describable neuroses, each based on a different abnormality in the sexual life, and each superseding Breuer's theoretical foregrounding of hysteria. Followers practiced scientific observation as poorly as had early comrades. Adler's investigations had "furnished not a single new observation" and Jung had turned entirely away from "observation" and "scientific logic." Both theorists, Freud accused, sought to eliminate sexuality, the Oedipus complex, and the family-complexes from theoretical consideration by backgrounding the investigation of individuals and foregrounding evidentiary conclusions based on anthropological research (SE, 14: 21–24). The Zurich school, then, had revised psychoanalysis "not on the ground of fresh observations" but on the basis of "fresh interpretations" that "made the things they see look different." Freud's articulation of observation, experimentation, and investigation justified his choices about psychoanalytic transmission and translation, justified his expulsion from its social networks of those not loyal to its concepts. Ironically, Freud invoked Charcot, a long-discredited predecessor, to warrant his own superior observations, for, like his master, he said, he "look[ed] at the same things again and again until they themselves begin to speak" (SE, 20: 52–62). Indeed, he said, psychoanalysis's teachings were "based on an incalculable number of observations and experiences, and only someone who has repeated those observations on himself and on others is in a position to arrive at a judgement of his own upon it" (SE, 23: 144). In short, only Freud and those he designated as his sons.

In *An Outline of Psychoanalysis* and *Some Elementary Lessons in Psycho-Analysis*, Freud set out the boundaries of his new science, inscribing again the conceptual split between questions of representation and functionalism. Drawing a line around the limits of psychoanalytic concepts, he both summarized and constituted the main points of his theory, describing its development and its culminating concepts. Returning again to the mind-body problem, Freud repudiated anatomical localization's conceptual usefulness for psychoanalysis. He sketched the psychical apparatus' structure, the forces active in it, and traced the ways those energies organized themselves into physiological functions. Psychoanalysis knew, he said, only two facts about mental life: the psyche's bodily organ and scene of action (the brain or nervous system) and its acts of consciousness ("immediate data" unexplainable by "any sort of description"). Attempting to "picture" the mind's apparatus as a number of interrelated "*functional systems*," Freud mapped them without reference to the "actual anatomy of the brain" (*SE*, 23: 144–53). From physiology, he turned to consciousness, a "highly fugitive state." Here, Freud criticized earlier theories of psychophysical correlation. Proposing that consciousness accounted for all mental states divorced psychical processes from external events and somatic processes. Pre-psychoanalytic attempts to move research beyond this "*impasse*" had assumed the existence of "organic processes parallel to the conscious psychical ones," which "acted as intermediaries in the reciprocal relations between 'body and mind', and which served to re-insert the psychical into the texture of life." Psychoanalysis, Freud maintained, had escaped the difficulties of psycho-physical parallelism as explanation by "energetically denying the equation between what is psychical and what is conscious" (*SE*, 23: 159, 283).

Here again, Freud sought retrospectively to discredit the origins of psychoanalysis in the hysteria discourse, eliding the complex problems he had worked through in proposing representation as plausible bridge between psyche and soma and positing, instead, the centrality of instinct theory and the sexual function. He sidestepped conceptual difficulties and defined history as, in part, personal and historiography as a recounting of the work of translation along scientific networks. In the 1935 postscript to *An Autobiographical Study*, Freud said that, since he had hypothesized as foundational "two kinds of instinct" (Eros and the death instinct) and since he had sketched the second topography (ego, superego, and id), he had "made no further decisive contributions to psychoanalysis." Indeed, he represented his work in "the natural sciences, medicine and psychotherapy" as "a lifelong *détour*" away from his earliest love, the study of culture. Freud concluded his postscript with some words on "the history of psychoanalysis during the last decade." That history listed organizational achievements in the struggle to construct scientific networks held together by sociability, the distribution of credit and distinction, and an oedipalized sense of filiation: local and international societies formed, training institutes founded, uniform instruction in place, outpatient clinics established, biannual congresses meeting, and lay analysis debated. These institutions, Freud said, performed "serious scientific work" at "a high level" of competence and credibility. Yet the history of psychoanalysis was also, he granted, entwined with "the story of [his] life." Indeed, he had, Freud admitted, more openly and frankly represented himself in his essays and case histories—however disguisedly—than did most autobiographers. "I have had small thanks for it," he averred, "and from my experience I cannot recommend anyone to follow my example" (*SE*, 20: 71–74). Nothing could, of course, have been more disingenuous.

REFERENCE MATTER

Notes

Introduction

1. I take the term "backstage," which means behind-the-scenes insider group talk, from Goffman 1959.

2. See Rabinbach 1986 for discussion of the laboratory work produced to measure the fatigue, capability, and endurance of the working body (484, 494–96, 500–512); like Charcot's, this experimental work deployed images of the body, primarily photographic ones, to document its research findings. For extended discussion of film motion study in the late nineteenth century and of Claude Bernard's, Étienne-Jules Marey's, and Eadweard Muybridge's laboratory practices and scientific methodologies, see Dagognet 1992; Cartwright 1995, chs. 2 and 3; and Williams 1986; both Cartwright and Williams bring film theories of the cinematic gaze to the study of medical research on, in particular, the female body.

3. I have appropriated this paradigm from Susan Leigh Star, whose anthropological study of the laboratory practices of the nineteenth-century brain localization researchers at the National Hospital for the Paralysed and Epileptic at Queen Square has influenced my methodology here. Like Latour, Star maintains that no science can be understood apart from the laboratory and work practices its adherents use to produce scientific knowledge (Star 1989, 166–68). Judith H. Hughes (1994) is also interested in the mind/body problem in psychoanalysis; her study, however, brings a clinical and philosophical, rather than a scientific, perspective to the study of Freud's theoretical production and work practices.

4. Madelon Sprengnether argues persuasively that Freud's identification with and concomitant fear of Emma Eckstein's bleeding body served to distance him from his female hysterics and to temper the sympathy he had so clearly displayed in writing about Emmy, Lucy, Katharina, and Elisabeth (Sprengnether 1990, 22–39); as feminist critics have repeatedly maintained, Freud has little sympathy for Dora. I take this shift in sympathetic attention (which Freud would later call

"transference") as sign and consequence of Freud's move from a somatic to a psychical intimacy with his patients. Monique David-Ménard argues, perhaps more radically than does Sprengnether, that by the time Freud worked with Dora, his hysteric "had no body" but the "body informed by the signifying elaboration of desire" (David-Ménard 1989, 64, 68; 64–82).

5. Foucault 1972, 161, 172–75, 114–15; see also Kuhn 1970.

6. Frederick Crews, for example, vilifies psychoanalysis as an "intellectual narcotic" and "pseudo science" (1986, xii–xiii; 1995, 288 et passim); Donald P. Spence proclaims psychoanalysis a fiction-constructing machine; Catherine Clément attacks the contemporary French analytic establishment for obediently following the psychoanalytic Father and for themselves producing the structures of oedipal professionalism. Peter Rudnytsky, idealizer rather than basher, expresses transferential filiopiety toward Freud's body of work. I view both the hagiographic and hostile perspectives on Freud as ideological. For critiques of oedipalized psychoanalytic adherence, see Samuel Weber and François Roustang. For a deconstructive reading of the history of madness, see Derrida 1978, 31–63, and 1997; in both essays, Derrida argues that Michel Foucault's *Madness and Civilization* paradoxically situates Freud with negativity ("as Foucault intends it . . . the historical current he is studying, the concept of madness, overlaps everything that can be put under the rubric of *negativity*" [Derrida 1978, 41]); in "Justice to Freud," he maintains that Foucault places Freud paradoxically with Nietzsche and with Pinel—yet always on the side of "Evil Genius"—and portrays psychoanalysis as discursively "whole" and self-identical, as occupying a historical origin and establishing a teleological causality.

7. Davidson 1987, 43; and see also 43–45, 61–63. I have been strongly influenced by Davidson's methodology, since he is also engaged in a Foucauldian reading of psychoanalytic emergence; he positions his argument, however, primarily from the perspective of Freud's theorizing of sexuality rather than from the ways in which the debate on hysterical physiology and psychology conditioned the emergence of psychoanalysis as a science.

8. Ricoeur 1970, 422; and see also 419–55. Borch-Jacobsen states forcefully of positions such as Ricoeur's that "these vocal declarations of rupture with philosophy appear to me as rather elaborate forms of denial" (Borch-Jacobsen 1997, 211).

9. Borch-Jacobsen 1992c, 100–108; id. 1992d, 142–47; Henry 1993, 281–316. Borch-Jacobsen supports—with reservations—the *Genealogy's* critique of Western philosophy's reliance on "the subject (of representation)"; he applauds Henry's "radical [theoretical] *positivity*" that privileges affect, the body, sensation, immanence, and "life"—in short, Borch-Jacobsen says, "all the non-representational aspects of human experience that the philosophy of the subject has so consistently avoided, neglected, or rejected" (Borch-Jacobsen 1997, 223). Harvie Ferguson views Freud's "contributions to the theory of *representations*"—of the body, body-

image, city, dreams, aesthetics, sociology, and culture—as central to his influence on the construction of modernity (Ferguson 1996, ix).

10. On hysteria as an aesthetic or poetic category, see Kahane 1995, vii–xv; Cixous and Clément 1975, 6–10. For social-constructivist accounts of the nine-teenth- and twentieth-century hysteric, see Hunter 1985, 89–115; Smith-Rosenberg 1985, 197–216; Krohn 1978, 40–47; and—for critical versions—Evans 1991; Fuss 1989, 107–12. For the hysteric as proto-feminist, see Showalter 1985, 17–18 et passim; as sorceress, Cixous and Clément 1975, 3–39. For Grosz's account of psycho-physical subjectivity, see Grosz 1994, vii–xv, 27–85.

11. See Fuss 1995, 57–82, and de Lauretis 1994, 38–54, both of whom make this point to recuperate psychoanalysis for a lesbian theory of sexuality and desire.

12. See Dagognet 1992, 65–128; Rabinbach 1986, 475–513; id., 1982, 42–62; and Cartwright 1995 for discussion of this experimental research and its laboratory practices.

13. Latour 1983, 151. On "staging" hysteria, see also Stallybrass and White 1986, 171–90, and White 1993, which uses the phrase "staging hysteria" too. The theory that the nineteenth century portrays carnivalesque transgression through the hysteric's hallucinations goes largely unsupported, however; neither archival historical evidence nor cultural theoretical argument sufficiently deepens or frames the argument (Stallybrass and White 1986, 176–90).

14. I argue here against Daphne de Marneffe (1991), who represents Freud's epistemology and clinical practices of narrativity as a break from the spectatorial and observational ones of Charcot. As I seek to show, Freud's clinical practices owe a particular debt to Charcot's, as does his deployment and revision of the Salpêtrière's representational strategies for documenting research findings on the hysterical body and subject.

15. My thinking has been influenced by Jean-Joseph Goux (1990), whose strategies for reading social and discursive interactions through the concept of homologies, elaborates on earlier Marxist structuralist modes of such reading.

16. In nineteenth-century France, Goldstein 1991 maintains, the hysteric enjoyed a "career" in the discourses of both medicine and literature. Micale 1995, 182–200, describes this cultural-medical discourse as fertile and productive. This convergence, as I argue in this book, demonstrates a larger discursive interpenetration that emerged during the 1880s and 1890s. Indeed, this intertextual play confirms Latour's theory that the "work of translation" moves research findings along scientific networks and leverages them into culture.

Chapter 1

1. Janet 1901, 2: 486–502; Janet's emphasis. Although Janet used the term "moral" in its by then old-fashioned sense of "mental" (as in "moral treatment"),

his prose nevertheless betrays a certain disdain for the weaknesses, both moral and social, of his patients. Freud and Breuer, very alive to this distinction, mention it in their *Studies on Hysteria*. For a sympathetic exposition of Janet's work, which is generally ignored, and his discursive position in the medicalization of hysteria, see Trillat 1986; for an argument that medical modernism decentered the fit as pathognomic sign of hysteria, see Micale 1990b, 80–84.

2. *SE*, 1: 161–63. Begun in 1888, this essay appeared in print five years later; yet the final section, in which Freud quotes his own paper the "Psychical Mechanism" (1893), most likely was written later than the first three. The delay of publication may account, at least in part, for Freud's discursive shift from neurological to psychological modes of explanation.

3. *SE*, 1: 163–72; Freud's emphases. As discussed in Chapter 2, Freud appropriated from Charcot the terms "dynamic" and "functional" for nonobservable lesions. Always extremely hypothetical and never theoretically stable, these concepts served Freud well in his move from organic to representation hysteria. Malcolm Macmillan persuasively argues that Freud lifted this notion of "popular language" from John Hughlings Jackson and Pierre Janet; such indebtedness nevertheless fails to cancel out this concept's usefulness for psychoanalytic theoretical production (Macmillan 1991, 71, 97–110).

4. Star 1989, 161–67. Here, Star quotes John Hughlings Jackson's 1884 paper "Evolution and Dissolution of the Nervous System" (Jackson 1932, 2: 45–75). Star's chapter on "The Mind/Body Problem" argues that researchers used the "doctrine of concomitance" and others to support their organizational segregation of research activities (Star 1989, 155–77). I have relied heavily on this argument from *Regions of the Mind* throughout this paragraph. On the mind/body problem in early psychoanalytic discourse, with the argument that Freud reconceptualized the body, which endowed the ego with meaning, producing a "bodily ego," see Hughes 1994, 21–63.

5. *SE*, 1: 169–72; Freud's emphases. The term "ego," which I use as a synonym for "self" in this paragraph, was widely used in the nineteenth century. Although twentieth-century thinkers tend to believe that Freud coined this term as part of his second topography (in which he distinguished the status, functions, and locations of the id, ego, and superego), he did not. Thomas Laycock, for example, wrote a mammoth two-volume work on the concept of ego and its relation to body; see *Mind and Brain*.

6. Although I frame this notion with Star's and Latour's conceptualizations of scientific theoretical production, I have also been influenced here by Laplanche and Pontalis; their notion that Freud's rhetorical and tropological strategies mobilized his early physiological and psychological theories has proved productive for my own thinking (Laplanche and Pontalis 1973, 449–53).

7. Latour 1986, 25. Latour is, of course, herself guilty here of invoking an energistic metaphor, as am I. For a rhetorical version of Freud's tropes, especially

of archeology, colonial conquest, and global exploration, see Bowie 1987, 14–44; for his architectural tropology as facilitating production of Freud's position in the hysteria debate, see McGrath 1986, 152–96; for a critique of the conversion theory as biological rather than erotogenic and historical, see David-Ménard 1989, 17–63.

8. By "case history," Freud means here not the published report on the treatment and its outcome but the medical history as constructed by interpolating patient's and doctor's stories of disease history and symptomatology; see my Chapter 7.

9. Yet Freud's search for the innocent and natural moment was already doomed by 1899, when he sent this note to Fliess. For the sexual theory, to which I return in Chapter 5, had produced not a real and natural sexual moment in which a child was seduced but an awareness that "the rest" could not be explained simply by supposing that a real seduction had necessarily taken place—although it might well have.

10. SE, 1: 353–59. See also Laplanche and Pontalis 1973, 111–12. For a philosophical and literary discussion of the primal scene as the fundamental (psychoanalytic) concept and as a mechanism of deferred action, see Lukacher 1987, 45–67.

11. SE, 5: 340–44; SE, 9: 159–62. For this paragraph, I have consulted Freud 1963, 146–47, because it so carefully translates the original.

12. Freud 1985, 230. Freud meant that these genealogical patterns, in which fathers seduced their offspring, protected paternal health while endangering children's, and ultimately caused degeneracy and sterility. I discuss this aspect of Freud's sexual theory (usually called the seduction theory) in Chapter 5.

13. "Multiplicity of Psychic Personalities," Freud headed a fragment in "Draft L" (1897): "the fact of identification perhaps allows us to take the phrase literally" (Freud 1985, 241).

14. Freud 1985, 213. Freud reported a similarly structured case in "Further Remarks on the Neuro-Psychoses of Defence" (SE, 3: 165–66).

15. Freud 1963, 151; SE, 9: 165–66.

16. SE, 19: 191.

Chapter 2

1. SE, 14: 13–15. Hertz 1985, 221–42, first read this anecdote as a fable of medical knowledge transmission.

2. King 1993, 3–35. In assessing hysteria's medical and scientific genealogy, Micale 1990b, 230–33, praises King's work for having corrected this pervasive misreading .

3. My paragraph, and this chapter, are influenced by Foucault's argument (1975, 126–28, 9–12) that anatomy cannot be separated from its representation.

4. Soranus 1956, 16, 26–32, 128–33; 149–54. For discussion of historically based diagnoses, see Micale 1989, 232.

5. In his preface to the 1815 American translation of the *Works of Thomas Sydenham*, Benjamin Rush identified this belief of Sydenham's—that observation should supersede theory—as one of his medical mistakes (iv).

6. Sydenham 1848–50, 2: 85–105. Rousseau 1993, 138–145, argues that, breaking with the uterine theory, Sydenham conceptualized hysteria as an imitative and psychological malady. See also Vieth 1965, 132–46, and Micale 1989, 237, which both also make some of these points.

7. The questions and quotation from Laënnec are from Foucault 1975, 175–76.

8. Hall 1827; id. 1850, 660. For a historical overview, see Shorter 1992, 40–44.

9. Laycock 1840, 6–9, 116–17; id. 1976 [1860], 1: 186–93; Beard 1879. Beard 1882 extended this argument about physiology and representation as a way to acclaim the discursive position and support the waning reputation of Charcot, to justify the cultural movement in the United States that he believed to have a scientific origin in physiology and mesmerism.

10. Briquet 1859, vii–38, 116, 190–92, 151–52, 164–66, 172–75, 187–89. Briquet conducted research over a ten-year period on 430 cases. He singled out in particular for condemnation Schutzemberger, Piorry, and Négrier, whom Charcot would later praise. Briquet presented evidence from specular examination of his own cases to show that Schutzemberger's theories were without scientific merit.

11. Briquet 1859, 40, 104–5, 116–17; 118–41; 40–41, 50–52. Briquet observed that men were twenty times less likely to contract hysteria than were women (ibid., 51).

12. Carter 1883 [1853], 2–6, 18–20, 25. Carter's work on hysteria, which in retrospect clearly looks groundbreaking, was virtually ignored in his own time, perhaps because he was trained as an ophthalmologist, not a neurologist.

13. It was an "old surgeon," hopelessly out of date in an age when knowledge had begun to grow exponentially, who objected to Freud's 1886 presentation of a male hysteric; because "*hysteron* means the uterus," witnesses reported the gynecologist to have said, a man could not be hysterical. For accounts of the meeting, see Ellenberger 1970, 437–42, and Sulloway 1979, 35–42.

14. *SE*, 1: 283–84. For discussion of this debate, see Forrester 1980, 14–39; Gay 1988, 62–63.

15. This reorganization of the Salpêtrière buildings is generally reported as fact; according to Forrester 1980 (216), the Salpêtrière records fail to verify or deny the statement by Charcot on which this belief is based.

16. Guillain 1959, 52–53. Guillain's hagiographic representation of the master and his work with students is, at present, the sole modern Charcot biography.

17. I have been influenced here by the argument of Rothfield 1992, which Athena Vrettos summarizes as follows: "nineteenth-century clinical medicine provided a central model for the development and expression of realism in the French and British novels, and . . . the attraction of clinical medicine for novelists arose out of a desire to legitimize literary authorship according to the model of medical professionalism" (Vrettos 1995, 191). My discussion of Charcot and his work with students and patients is especially indebted to Rothfield's concept of the emergent ideology of professional charisma (Rothfield 1992, 69–78).

18. *SE*, 3: 12; Lasègue quoted in Goldstein 1987, 324. In 1930, the Freudian A. A. Brill similarly called George Beard's neurasthenia diagnosis the "newest garbage can of medicine" (Sicherman 1977, 35).

19. Star 1989, 173. Throughout this book, and in particular in this chapter and the next, I have been influenced by Star's excellent account of nineteenth-century brain-localization research methodologies and by her argument that scientific knowledge production cannot be separated from the institutional forms, settings, and work practices that are constituted by the medical profession.

20. I have adapted this neurological and representational terminology from Foucault 1975, 181–91, and Trillat 1986, 20–26.

21. In "On Hysteria in Boys," Charcot lectured: "What are these *hysterogenic zones*? They are more or less circumscribed regions of the body, pressure on which, or simply rubbing of, produces the symptoms of an aura, which may be followed, if you persist, by an hysterical attack. These points, or rather patches, are, moreover, possessed of a permanant hyper-sensitivity, and before an attack are the seat of a spontaneous painful sensation which consequently forms part of the *aura*. Sometimes this latter consists of palpitations, sometimes of a burning sensation. An attack, once started, may often be arrested by energetic pressure on these same points. . . . These points are not met with on the limbs, but they are to be found on the anterior surface of the trunk in the middle line" (Charcot 1889, 3: 74–75).

Chapter 3

1. I have taken the details of this narrative from Spillane 1981, 393, deriving from Spillane's reading of nineteenth-century popular periodical and newspaper stories, journal reviews, and medical articles.

2. I take this part of the story from Star 1989, 104–5, 199–214.

3. Star 1989, 56. I have taken these details about the Goltz-Ferrier debate from a variety of sources on medical and scientific historiography. French 1970 reports on the political and cultural tactics employed by the Victoria Street Society (194–205, 310–14); Spillane 1981 discusses the neurological issues and professional problems that met in the debate (396–97); Star 1989 links the research institutions, discourses, and practices that motivate medical, social, and political

strategists (54–58, esp. 56); Reiser 1978 discusses the medical and research advances at stake in the debate (126–32).

4. Levin 1978, 43–93, argues that Charcot demonstrated physiological dysfunction in his *leçons* and lectures; the stagings of hobbled gaits, paralyzed limbs, unstable heads, and wiggling feathers have all been misunderstood as self-dramatizing parades, Levin maintains, rather than having been viewed as the display of physiological dysfunction in a scientific setting. Given my perspective on scientific networks and work practices, I agree wholeheartedly with this analysis.

5. For an example of this misrepresentation, see Georges Didi-Huberman (1982, 23–68 et passim), who judges the Salpêtrière's clinical observations as necessarily contaminated by its technologies of laboratory provocation.

6. I have aggregated details in this description of the Salpêtrians' methodology from a variety of sources: see J.-M. Charcot, "Essai d'une distinction nosographique des divers états nerveux compris sous le nom d'hypnotisme," quoted in Binet and Féré 1887, 113–17; Bernheim 1886, 87–88; Janet 1925, 1: 167–69.

7. Binet and Féré 1887, 66. Charcot dubbed operators who misapplied hypnosis "novice" magnetizers; they were, he averred, charlatans who induced mass hypnotic "mania." His practice, of course, was scientific, and his hyperbolic and ad hominem rhetorical strategies served not only to announce the fact but to make it illogical to raise another option. See Charcot 1975 [1887–89], 2: 254–55 (January 22, 1889). For more information about the clinic's campaign against the practitioners of mass hypnosis, their support for state regulation of medical practice and physician monopoly of hypnotic procedures, see Harris 1985, 223–30.

8. Bourneville and Regnard 1879–80, 3: 158–62, 150–56, 458–62, 169. Charcot attributed these methodologies to the magnetizers Deleuze and Faria, but in order to make these judgments, he must also have consulted others. Because he was so widely known and read and so well traveled himself, moreover, he would have known the scientific literature and the practitioners of magnetism and mesmerism.

9. In a search for scientific forebears and so structures of legitimation and credibility, Bourneville identified James Braid, the first "scientific" magnetizer, as the clinic's experimental father. For extended discussion of mesmerism's history, see Macmillan 1991, 32–44.

10. Janet 1898, 1: 424. Moll 1931 [1891], 165–67, uses the same terms to describe sexual attraction or "magnetism."

11. I have quoted this material from a lecture Richer recorded (Richer 1885, 162, 160–61).

12. For the nineteenth-century sources that discuss hysterical patient simulation of urine retention, see Anon. 1856; Anon. 1857; and Laycock 1840, 234.

13. Charcot 1877, 1: 234–38. Micale 1985, 710, details the hospital's structures of surveillance, its efficient deployment of ward nurses and guards, and its timetables for managing patient histrionics.

14. In *The Story of San Michele* (1930 [1929], 302–13), Axel Munthe states that attempted escapes, although punished, were not unusual at the hospital for incurables, but Munthe's testimony about Charcot's hospital and research must be judged largely untrustworthy, primarily because it so self-servingly represents Munthe as doctor-hero and rescuer of female patients. That Munthe performed hypnotic experiments on Geneviève—including this posthypnotic suggestion that she escape—seems, however, credible.

15. Beard 1882, 37. Charcot's subjects, Beard said, both in moral-scientific outrage and tongue in cheek, "would scarcely be acceptable candidates for teachers in Sunday-school." Yet Beard also identified with the medical researcher under siege, since he himself had traveled with mind- and muscle-reading demonstrations and been soundly criticized for unscientific showmanship. Some of Beard's motivation, then, must have been self-justification and staging of what he imagined as professional charisma.

16. Bernheim 1886, 90–95. Only one young patient had exhibited the Salpêtrière's three hypnotic stages at Nancy, and researchers concluded that she had learned to imitate other inmates' symptoms. Bernheim also judged the Salpêtrière's research procedures scientifically inadequate. Charcot had hypothesized, he said, from a statistically skewed sample: at Nancy, 6,000 hypnotized patients over 25 years had produced a single "*grand hypnose*"; at the Salpêtrière, too, only a few dozen examples of major hypnosis had presented during ten years. The clinic's theory of hypnotic provocation likewise seemed flawed, for rubbing the head or touching the eyes did not cause hypnosis, Nancy researchers argued; speech did (Bernheim 1886, 90–91).

17. I use the term "staged" the way Latour and Star do in their very different, yet discursively allied, ethnographic projects; see, e.g., Latour 1983, esp. 151. It is currently widely used in literary and feminist theory.

18. Bernard 1949 [1927], 5–6, 221–24. Bernard says that he is quoting Cuvier (6), but he provides no scholarly apparatus.

19. My argument in this paragraph is influenced by Figlio 1977, who argues persuasively that the link between medical technology and ethics served to objectify the patient by removing moral considerations from medical judgment (273–77).

20. Charcot 1877, 1: 1–10. Guillain 1959's translator, Pearce Bailey, renders parts of this passage differently (e.g., calling the Salpêtrière a "great asylum for human misery" rather than a "great emporium for human suffering"); see Guillain 1959, 50–54, esp. 49. This lecture is not included in Charcot's *Oeuvres complètes*.

21. My thinking here has been influenced by a variety of institutional perspectives on the nineteenth-century asylum. Goldstein 1987, 14–49, argues that the asylum cannot be understood apart from the professionalizing strategies of nineteenth-century physicians: their boundary skirmishes with priests, for exam-

ple, or their creation of patronage circles. Goldstein notes, too, that the term "police" meant, in its Old Regime usage, civilized and therefore not barbaric; it began to accrue its sinister connotations, however, during postrevolutionary centralization and bureaucratization (21, 281–82, 295–96). Robert Castel stages a Foucauldian argument: that the state in France used incarceration to control "dangerous" subjects and their strategies for resistance (Castel 1988, 151–56). Yannick Ripa deploys a Foucauldian perspective in the service of feminism: thus women, always already associated with madness, were more routinely incarcerated than were men; Ripa documents the iatrogenic nature of the asylum and seeks to recover the madwomen's voices; see esp. Ripa 1990, 12–13. For Foucault's perspective, see Foucault 1988, 180–89.

22. Goldstein 1987, 331–35. For information about prerevolutionary modes of confinement and medical and judicial sharing of the power of detainment before 1830, see Castel 1988, 16–17, 137–42. On Esquirol's "boundary dispute" with the judiciary and his introduction of "isolation" as a tactical solution to the then-ambiguous judicial process of interdiction, and on the law of 1838, which mandated asylums throughout France and sought to remove the judiciary from the incarcerative process by recreating it as wholly administrative, see Goldstein 1987, 276–321.

23. Charcot 1889, 3: 3–9. This scientific professionalizing strategy worked for and was deployed by a number of new medical specialisms. For examples, see Bernard 1949 [1927], 196–226, on the discourse of experimental medicine; Krafft-Ebing 1896 [1889], v–viii, on that of experimental psychology; Storer 1972 [1871], 207, 120–22, 213–18, 231–36, on that of asylum administration; and Spitzka 1878, 202–19, on the psychiatric side. Both Storer and Spitzka lamented the lack of experimental and autopsy-confirmed research in American asylums; such research could produce a "thorough clinical and pathological demonstration of insanity," Spitzka said, and the asylums' failure to produce "valuable and suggestive" postmortem data was an "unpardonable waste" of "rich [research] material" (Spitzka 1878, 206–16).

24. Goldstein 1987, 336–38; Micale 1990a, 372. The Tuesday lessons dated from the 1880s and presented external patients Charcot had never previously seen or treated.

25. Sander Gilman uses the term "realism," as does Lawrence Rothfield (Gilman 1993, 354–59, 379–84; Rothfield 1992, 5–14). In this book, and especially in Chapter 7, I prefer the term "documentary," which designates not a literary genre but a wider array of documents and representations (most of them two-dimensional and so easily translatable from research site to research site), all of which claim a truth-value.

26. From a review of vol. 1 of the *Iconographie* in *Progrès médical* 7 (1879): 331, quoted in Goldstein 1987, 327.

27. Richer 1885, 575, quoted in Didi-Huberman 1982, 35. Daphne de

Marneffe (1991, 79), who also notes these statements, reminds us that when technologized, photography immediately entered medical discourse and seemed especially appropriate to the documentation of mental illness. For historical and technological accounts, see Dagognet 1992, 65–128; Williams 1986; and Cartwright 1995, 107–43.

28. Goldstein believes Charcot's hysteria concept contained a "constant undercurrent of sexuality," which is photographed and subtitled but "never canalized into theory" (Goldstein 1987, 376); see Showalter 1985, 150. This analysis of the Salpêtrière's research program overstates the case to advance a feminist program. I argue in Chapter 6 that the photographic captions, on which this reading is often largely based, served to facilitate the clinic's production of physiological theories of disease symptomatology and causation.

29. Lombroso and Ferrero 1901, xiv–xvi, 99–103, 153–70, 145, 222, 128–40. Havelock Ellis undertook a similar classificatory project on the male offender in *The Criminal* (1895).

30. Munthe 1930 [1929], 293, 276; Didi-Huberman 1982, 27, 22. My analysis of celebrities has been influenced by Dyer 1986, 6–37. On spectacle, see Richards 1990, 54–56; on culture as commodity, see Lears 1983, 3–38, esp. 6–7.

31. I disagree here with readings by, for example, Showalter 1985, 147–54.

32. Macmillan argues this point more forcefully than I do, maintaining that Freud purposefully obscured Janet's priority on several research questions and, in particular, Freud's conceptualization of the hysteric's sense of her body's limbs as a "popular" or "common" notion; see "A Note on Priority" (Macmillan 1991, 120–21).

Chapter 4

1. *SE*, 20: 27–28; *SE*, 2: 108. Freud also found a smaller percentage of patients subject to somnambulism than had Bernheim; for a criticism of Nancy's experimental results as overestimating the number of hypnotizable subjects, see Thornton 1976, 176–83.

2. See *SE*, 2: 61, 77, 101. For evidence about the possibility that Freud misremembered the dates during which he treated this patient, Emmy von N., see appendix A (*SE*, 2: 307–9). It is likely that Freud first treated Emmy before his pilgrimage to Nancy, but whether the work began in May 1889 or 1888 is unclear from Freud's contradictory dating of the case. If, however, his doubts about hypnosis emerged from his treatment of her, as he says, it must have begun, James Strachey suggests, in 1888 (*SE*, 2: 307).

3. *SE*, 2: 108–11. Thus the patient reported everything that came to mind, without censoring even seemingly irrelevant details, and the doctor refrained from touching the patient's body. For a discussion of Freud's alteration of his clinical technologies from mesmerism to touch, see Didier Anzieu. I have appro-

priated the apt and succinct description of Freud's cardinal rules as "discursive non-omission" and "physician tactile abstinence" from Anzieu 1989, 138.

4. Of course, when he published these encomiums, Mitchell only repeated their praise. We may assume that some patients complained, although that enraged lamentation did not enter the cultural register until the turn of the century, when professional women writers such as Charlotte Perkins Gilman, Jane Addams, and Alice James took up their pens to indict the rest cure's practitioners, conceptualizations, and therapeutics.

5. *SE*, 2: 54–57, 72, 76, 67, 48–51. Freud's allowing Emmy to read, write, and have visitors differs from Mitchell's prohibitions, as Freud realized when he acknowledged that he did not "forbid" her such activities.

6. Suzanne Poirier mentions, but does not analyze, the rest cure's infantilization. The patient, Poirier says, "was encouraged to act like a baby, and even more important, everything in her environment assured her that it was *safe and acceptable* to do so" (Poirier 1983, 32).

7. Mitchell 1879, 75; id. 1885, 46–47. I would argue that this emphasis on the intermediate stage of patient "creeping" accounts for some curious—and generally uninterpreted—details from Charlotte Perkins Gilman's *The Yellow Wallpaper* (1899): the "creeping" figures on the sanitarium wallpaper and the female protagonist's "creeping" around the room; Gilman had, of course, undergone Mitchell's rest cure and been enraged by its enforced incapacitation of the patient.

8. Mitchell 1885, 54, 60, 256. On the fan letters and the fact that the treatment worked, see Poirier 1983, 20–22. On French doctors' supplanting clergy, see McLaren 1974–75, 39–54, and Goldstein 1987, 197–230.

9. For theorization of the concept of homology between apparently disparate bodily and social economies, see Goux 1990, 1–63.

10. See Langland 1995, 24–61, for more extended discussion of the nineteenth-century wife as a domestic manager.

11. On the mystifications and subjections of contract theory, see Pateman 1988.

12. For analysis of British asylum routines as versions of domestication, see Showalter 1985, 23–51; for discussion of French alienists' pioneering of isolation, see Goldstein 1987, 64–147, 276–307.

13. Carter 1883 [1853], 158–61. On moral treatment as a form of medical tutelage, see Rothfield 1992, 65–69.

14. Charcot 1889, 3: 210–14. Charcot did footnote Mitchell and other likeminded, but, he implied, other, less original, practitioners. For discussion of the case as a psychological but not yet discursive cure, see Forrester 1980, 8–14.

15. Charcot 1889, 3: 198–219. On the pioneering of isolation in the nineteenth-century asylum, see Goldstein 1987, 122–46, 287–92; on "Neuromimesis and the Medical Gaze," see Vrettos 1995, 81–98.

16. Féré, 1898, 1–33, 45–60, 97–100, 133–39. See also Rothfield 1992, 67–78.

17. Camus and Pagniez 1904, 206–38, 100–107. In private practice after the turn of the century, Dejerine's therapeutics resembled Freud's; he believed the first goal of a psychotherapist was to "reconstruct" or "redirect . . . the personality," and worked to "sweep away" the "emotional causes" of neurosis by exercising a "liberating action" on the mind (Dejerine and Gauckler 1913, 299; and see also ibid. 263–300). For a slightly different therapeutic regime, see Renterghem 1907, 35–49, and Nayrac 1906, 179–200. On Esquirol's treatment as classinflected, see Goldstein 1987, 285–92. In *From Paralysis to Fatigue*, Edward Shorter claims that the physicians who developed and disseminated what they called psychotherapy "manipulated" the doctor-patient relationship, that although the physician directed treatment toward the mind, the patient thought he or she received strictly medical treatment (Shorter 1992, 245, 248). I have, however, found no evidence of this in their theoretical statements.

18. Dubois 1908 [1905], 234–40, 389–92. With regard to what he and his contemporaries called "material" treatment, Dubois asked, "I wonder of what use it is . . . to poison psychopaths?" (ibid., 389). But of course Dubois's reports of his patients' gratitude and therapeutic understanding, like those of the other doctors I study in this book, are invariably self-serving and clearly seem deployed at least in part to enhance his professional reputation.

19. Ibid., 242, 240. Dubois had refused, he said, to put patients on the sofa, "yoke" them with induced sleep, fix their arms cataleptically, or impress them with the spectacle of other magically hypnotized subjects; although psychotherapy was not, hypnotism was quackery and "charlatanism" (ibid., 313–18).

20. *SE*, 14: 63–64. Here, Freud quotes one of Jung's patients and feels constrained to offer apologies and self-justifications in a footnote; the informant was trustworthy, capable of judgment, and delivered the information spontaneously. Unlike the clergyman, Freud concluded, the psychoanalyst had no "right to claim the protection of medical discretion" (*SE*, 14: 64).

21. I have used Canguillhem's concepts as a frame of reference here, and my quotations are from Canguillhem 1978 [1966], 68.

22. My discussion in this and following paragraphs has been influenced by Sedgwick 1990, 167–81.

23. See, for example, Borch-Jacobsen 1988 and id. 1994.

24. I have simplified the *Standard Edition*'s language for purposes of clarity; the full quotation reads: "The mechanism of some at least of the manifestations of hypnotism is based upon physiological changes—that is, upon displacements of excitability in the nervous system, occurring without the participation of those parts of it which operate with consciousness" (*SE*, 1: 77).

25. The "therapy" chapter of Freud's projected book on hysteria would bear the epigraph, he told Fliess, "Flavit et dissipati sunt" (He blew and they were dis-

persed); the quotation multiply referred to the Hebrew God's liberation of the Jews from Pharoh's tyranny, contemporary political oppression, and the words of the cathartic cure, which dispersed undischarged excitations (Freud 1985, 205; *SE*, 14: 42). For extended discussion of Freud's anti-Catholicism, see McGrath 1986, 152–59, 172–73, 195.

26. *SE*, 2: 24–42 [French in original]; *SE*, 1: 218–19; *SE*, 2: 88–89, 82, 58.

27. For a Lacanian reading of "scenes" in the *Studies on Hysteria*, see David-Ménard 1989, which is critical of Freud's first theory of conversion, arguing that it mystified the status of the body, and that scenarios locating the moving body in space identified the body as erotogenic. David-Ménard's reading (ibid., 22–63), I would argue, paradoxically essentializes and marginalizes the body.

28. *SE*, 2: 53, 56–57; Freud 1985, 239, 269.

Chapter 5

1. Krafft-Ebing 1946 [1886–96], 25–28. The chapter title is "Physiological Facts."

2. Moll 1931 [1891], 153, 165. Even Krafft-Ebing, whose research into aberrant sex acts hardly mentions pleasure, cited his fetishists' "voluptuous feelings." Frank Sulloway argues convincingly that Freud was influenced by Albert Moll's theories of sex; Moll (and Ellis), he says, published work characteristic of the "clinical findings and ideas" emerging from the sexology movement; Moll (and Ellis), however, were "more progressive, more biologically sophisticated, and more clinically informed" than their contemporaries, and so, in their writings, a "new perspective on human sexual development first began to crystallize into a systematic, compelling, and historically consequential form" (Sulloway 1979, 309–10).

3. Moll 1931 [1891], 101–8, 127–28, 146–55; id. 1933 [1897], 39–48, 59–68.

4. The most useful work on the nineteenth century's construction of the "two-sex theory" is, of course, Thomas Laqueur's *Making Sex* (1990), which argues that until the eighteenth and nineteenth centuries, the female reproductive organs were viewed as a variant of the male gonads; the scientific discoveries of the nineteenth century consolidated and institutionalized the two-sex theory, which then entered—or was leveraged—into culture and the social domain.

5. For discussion of Ellis's idealization of such heterosexuality in his marriage and of his extramarital relationships, see Grosskurth 1980, 135–253.

6. Davidson 1987 makes some of these same points.

7. Sedgwick means, she says, that "one's personality structure might mark one as *a homosexual*, even, perhaps, in the absence of any genital activity at all" (Sedgwick 1990, 83); see also Halperin 1990, 15–40. This labeling of individuals from a hierarchical position of social and professional authority functioned to blind the expert to his research subject's experience, Hacking 1986, 233, warns.

8. Ellis 1936 [1897], 347–55. Ellis does not follow Moll, however, who concluded that if we thought about heterosexual sex, we would find it disgusting too; we do not, he speculated, only because we routinely practice it.

9. Féré 1900, 301–32. On the contagious diseases act, see Walkowitz 1980.

10. Ellis 1902, 193–216, esp. 215, 195. Other references to Ellis in this section likewise appear in these pages. For discussion of Ellis's complex attitudes toward Freud, the sex specialist who superseded the psychologist of sex, see Grosskurth 1980, 233–35, 291–94, 387–93, 419–22.

11. Ellis 1936 [1897], 338–47, 355; id. 1902, 202. In fact, Ellis and his wife carefully controlled public knowledge and discussion of her lesbianism; as Grosskurth argues, Ellis seemed naively unaware when he married Edith that their companionate, nearly nonsexual relationship was related to her passion for women friends, a passion that Edith most likely acted out rather than simply sublimated (Grosskurth 1980, 135–64).

12. See, e.g., Ellis 1936 [1897], 125–35, 153–79, 193–95; Schrenck-Notzing 1956 [1895], 41–44, 196–206, et passim; Krafft-Ebing's case 80 (Krafft-Ebing 1946 [1886–96], 187–90); Féré 1900, 300–329.

13. Freud 1985, 163–64. Freud rightly feared his explanation would "not stand up to deeper testing."

14. SE, 9: 181–204, esp. 189, 196. "There is no question of its being able to compensate for the privation which precedes it," Freud says of compensation. Still, Freud recommended that given the difference between the sexes, men's lapses from monogamy be treated with less severity than women's (SE, 9: 196, 182).

15. On the historical construction of homosexuality from the 1870s to the 1920s, see Greenberg 1988, 400–433; for a history of heterosexuality, see Katz 1995, 19–55. For an example of the Progressive Era deployment of Freud's repressive hypothesis to criticize Victorianism, see Virginia Woolf's Orlando (1929) on female chastity as a social construction and founding myth.

16. Lombroso and Ferrero 1901, 28–32, 103–39, 220–47. See also Ellis 1930 [1894], 144–85, on sexual differences in bodily sensitivity.

17. Nordau 1895 [1892], 473–506. This hyperbolic aesthetic argument, grounded in a fictional ethnographic anthropology and a spurious biological evolutionism, quickly came to seem excessive and ad hominem in its logic.

18. A Medico-Forensic Study is the subtitle of Psychopathia Sexualis.

19. Longo 1979; Battey 1886, 483–90; Sims 1880, 622. For an account of the historical incidence of ovariotomy, see Shorter 1992, 73–86.

20. Wells 1886, 461. The first ovariotomy was performed by Ephraim McDowell, a rural surgeon in the southern United States. The first in Britain was done by John Lizars in 1824, and the operation was performed there again in 1825 and 1833 by Augustus Granville, and by William Jeaffreson in 1838. For extended discussion of the operation's history in Britain, see Moscucci 1990, 134–64.

21. Moscucci 1990, 152–60, 134–35. See also Shepherd 1980.

22. See "The Obstetrical Society's Charges and Mr. Baker Brown's Replies," *Lancet* 1 (April 6, 1867): 427–41, and a review of *On the Curability of Certain Forms of Insanity, Epilepsy, Catalepsy, and Hysteria in Females* by Isaac Baker Brown, *British Medical Journal* 1 (April 28, 1886): 438–40. The debate is summarized in Fleming 1960. See Baker Brown 1854 and 1862 on his earlier, less problematic work.

23. For the argument that the postmodern body has been theorized as the immunological body and its functions and dysfunctions, particularly in light of the AIDS epidemic, see Martin 1994.

24. Judith Butler argues that this association can be traced to the linguistic etymologies of *mater* and *matrix* (the womb), and so to the problematic of reproduction and, from there, to the "classical configuration of matter as a site of *generation* or *origination*"; see Butler 1993, 27–55, esp. 31.

25. Steinach 1940, 74, 86–89. For discussion of World War I and modern psychiatry's diagnoses of male hysteria, see Showalter 1985, 167–94.

26. *SE,* 7: 147, 139–43, 212–16. I take the final phrase from Freud's 1905 and 1915 version of *Three Essays*. As his editor James Strachey says, Freud did minor revision of this passage in 1920, primarily because he had earlier proposed sex substances as present in the body. Despite its appearing ridiculous in 1905, by 1920, Freud's notion of sexual substances seemed, with the "discovery" of sex hormones, a research-proven certainty.

27. *SE,* 3: 200, 207–8, 152–53; Freud 1963, 146.

28. Krafft-Ebing 1946 [1886–96], 82; Binet 1887. For an extended discussion of the debate, see Sulloway 1979, 277–319.

29. Freud 1985, 264–65. The debate about Freud's rejection of the seduction theory includes a variety of positions and perspectives. Masson 1983 argues that Freud abandoned the seduction theory to cover up the bungling of Emma Eckstein's nasal operation by his mentor, Wilhelm Fleiss, and because he could not accept the facts he had discovered about paternal sexual abuse of children, primarily daughters. Balmary 1982 and Krüll 1986 argue that Freud rejected the seduction theory because of his unresolved oedipal problems with his father. Herman 1981 documents the twentieth-century case for what Freud presented as (and we call) the seduction theory as widespread sexual abuse of daughters by fathers and denial by mothers. Robinson 1993 criticizes Masson's argument as an unnuanced failure to understand the continuity of seduction as theory in Freud's work, and as a misreading of the fantasy/reality binarism.

Chapter 6

1. Krafft-Ebing 1896 [1889], 1–20; id. 1946 [1886–96], 294–96.
2. Moll 1931 [1891], 93, 101, 127–28, 146, 150–53, 165.

3. Bourneville and Regnard 1879–80, 1: 114–46. The details of Geneviève's illness, which follow this narrative, likewise appear in these pages.

4. Janet 1901, 376, 403, 416–17, 440.

5. Freud, too, later said that he had first sided with Charcot in this debate and had only arrived at his singling out of the sexual factor in the etiology of hysteria, despite his own "personal disinclination," after "laborious and detailed investigations" (*SE*, 3: 199).

6. Freud 1985, 239; Freud's emphasis. The polemical value of this letter is played out in the letters' editorial commentary on it. While Masson foot-notes "primal scenes" as referring to "sexual seduction by the father" as the "source of neurosis," Strachey footnotes the same term as the "beginning of the 'dynamic' theory" of neurosis etiology and sends the reader, as well, to his earlier footnote defining "sexual scene" as the "forerunner" of "primal scene" (see *SE*, 1: 247–48).

7. In this chapter, I argue against Daphne de Marneffe's notion that Freud's clinical work superseded Charcot's because, rejecting the doctor's gaze at his pa-tients, he instituted a clinical practice of storytelling (de Marneffe 1991). In fact, as this book argues, Freud's project was much more historically continuous and scientifically accordant with Charcot's project than de Marneffe allows, primar-ily because of the focus in both theories of spectatorship, however differently lo-cated and theorized.

8. Grosz 1994, 42–46. Grosz states: "Human subjects are able to see or feel only parts of their bodies. While the extremities are most readily visible, clearly there are many parts of the body to which the subject has no direct visual or tactile access, mainly the back. And although the subject can feel many parts of its body which are not normally visible, it can at best gain a serial notion of its own bodily parts, unless it has access to a unified and unifying image of the body as a whole" (ibid., 42). While Grosz is clearly correct about the physiologi-cal, sensual, and perceptual capabilities of the body, Freud's theory accounts for that self-representation's complex impossibility.

9. Lisa Appignanesi and John Forrester also draw this parallel, although they see primarily the resemblance of settings; for the biographical details of Katha-rina's story, see Appignanesi and Forrester 1992, 103–8. The name of the girl with whom the young patient fell in love, Gisela Fluss, uncannily replicates that of an-other patient who once consulted Freud, a name that links this self-representing psychoanalytic situation with the emergence of it as discourse. When in 1903, Aurelia Kronich (Katharina) was left by her husband, her daughter, Gisela Öhm, fell ill with fever and stomach pains and Freud, who happened to be visiting nearby, attended her; Katharina's daughter, as had Emmy's, acted out the displaced desire and rage that belonged, in marital scenes, to the mother. These two Gise-las—the country girl he had loved and Katharina's daughter—identify Freud's "screen memory" as the scene of spectatorship and affective self-portrayal central

to psychoanalytic mediation, to the hybrid subjectivity formed through its visualized memories, fantasies, and scenarios.

10. Jones 1957, 3: 112–23. Freud's "mark of attention" to his daughter and Anna's performance pleased the audience, Jones said. In fact, Anna presented several of Freud's papers and addresses during the next fourteen years. In addition to "Psychical Consequences," Anna presented "Humor" (to the Tenth International Psycho-Analytical Congress in 1927), the "Letter to Dr. Alfons Paquet" on the occasion of his winning the Goethe Prize (1930), the "Letter to the Burgomaster of Pribor" on the occasion of Freiberg's installing a bronze tablet to celebrate the place of his birth (1931), and section C of Part II of the third essay in "Moses and Monotheism: Three Essays" (1939).

Chapter 7

1. In this paragraph and throughout this chapter, I have been influenced by Hunter 1991, esp. chs. 3 and 7; I alter Hunter's model, however, to refer to the structures of psychoanalytic, rather than solely medical, knowledge.

2. Many critics have written about Freud's appropriation of narrative strategies. Although often brilliant interventions into the discourse about psychoanalysis, much of this poststructuralist criticism applies a postmodern narratology to Freud's case histories and so ignores both the medical contexts in which Freud wrote and the historical locations of case history as a genre. Kofman 1991, for example, identifies Freud as a novelist and his case histories as occupying the genre of "analytic novel." Certeau 1986 locates psychoanalysis within the terrain of the historical novel. Brooks 1984, 90–112, 264–85, reads *Beyond the Pleasure Principle* and the Wolf-Man's case history as models for narrative repetition and for a hermeneutic of plot. Marcus 1985 claims the case histories represent a new form of modernist literature. Hertz 1985 compares Dora to Henry James's Maisie to explore Freud's hidden identification with Dora. Cohn 1992, 37, 29, argues emphatically against case-historical discourse's being so "gravely misunderstood" and for the notion that Freud adhered to the "narrative code of historical biography" in differentiating his scientific writing from fiction.

3. For discussion of such networks in a different historical and cultural setting, see Biagioli 1996.

4. Goldstein 1987, 80–81, 85–88. Goldstein quotes the passages from Cabanis 1815, 1: iii–xxxii, and Pinel 1806, 228–31, 222–24.

5. *SE*, 3: 23. See also *SE*, 3: 147.

6. *SE*, 3: 143–56. Here, Freud distinguished between indispensable and "universal" "*conditions*" for the production of specific diseases; "*concurrent*" and not indispensable causes; "*specific*" indispensable causes for particular diseases; and "every-day factors" that functioned as "precipitating causes" (*SE*, 3: 147–48).

7. For discussion of the double signification of case presentation and patient self-presentation, see Hunter 1991, ch. 3.

8. Because of its status as Freud's first analytic case history, Elisabeth's case has received much critical attention. Some of the points I have made about it have also been made in David-Ménard 1989, some in Kiceluk 1992.

9. *SE*, 17: 8, 13; *SE*, 2: 48, 125; *SE*, 7: 9–10, 112–13.

10. Of course, Peter Brooks (1984, 264–85) was the first critic to explore and elaborate the multiple dimensions of narrative in Freudian case history.

11. *SE*, 7: 25–30, 32–34, 47, 35–37, 59. I have emended the Standard Edition for sense in the penultimate quotation: "what do you want to change in now that I've told it you?" (*SE*, 7: 35).

12. For the articulation of figural female destiny with narrative readability, see Miller 1980, ch. 1.

13. *SE*, 7: 103, 75–77, 102, 96–100, 63, 111, 101. Gearhart 1985, 105–27, has made the point that Dora's identifications are bisexual.

14. *SE*, 18: 105–7. Quotations in my next paragraph are from these same pages. I use the terms "cross-sexual" or "sexual transitivity" rather than "bisexual" to prevent anatomy from reentering my text; for when Freud used the term "bisexual," he invariably meant something strictly biological, as had Fliess, from whom Freud had appropriated both term and concept.

15. *SE*, 7: 50–52. Gallop 1982, 132–50, argues that Freud got Dora's fantasy wrong, that rather than fellatio, she fantasized cunnilingus, the sexual act an impotent man could undertake to satisfy a woman's desire.

16. Fuss 1995, 57–82, notices this resemblance, too, but does not interpret the latter case as a rewriting of the former. De Lauretis 1994, 38–54, also treats these two case histories together, as addressing female homosexuality.

17. *SE*, 18: 156–64. Strachey explains in a footnote that Freud is punning here on the verb *niederkommen*, which means both "to fall" and "to be delivered of a child"; the pun exists in English, too, he notes (ibid., 162).

18. *SE*, 14: 263–66. Freud uses the term "girl" and emphasizes that she "looked much younger than her age" and "was of a distinctly feminine type" (263). I repeat his word in order to draw attention to her resemblance to the other homosexual girls I discuss here.

Conclusion

1. See, e.g., Kurzweil 1989, 35–81; Jones 1957, 2: 67–106, 126–51; Sulloway 1979, 419–502; Weber 1982, xv–7; Roudinesco 1986; Cremerius 1981; Ellenberger 1970; Gay 1988, 213–43.

2. See Hale 1971, 313–31. Freud mentions that professors and medical superintendents led the way to psychoanalysis in the United States (*SE*, 14: 32).

3. *SE*, 14: 48–59. Adler had said of Freud's paternity, "Do you think it gives me such great pleasure to stand in your shadow my whole life long?" (*SE*, 14: 51).

4. Quoted in Jones 1955 2: 71, 47, 156, 166; see also Gay 1988, 187–89, 201.

5. *SE*, 14: 48–62, 42–43. The Goethe text is "Mach es kurz! / Am Jüngsten Tag ist's nur ein Furz! [Cut it short! On Judgment Day it's no more than a fart!]." The words represent God's reply to Satan's charges against Napoleon. I imagine, as well, that the pun on "Jung" in "Jüngsten Tag" seemed significant to Freud the Father.

6. Gay 1988, 185. Jones 1955, 2: 48, 153–63, 44, discusses each member of the committee's relation with Judaism, judging each in terms of his Semitic characteristics.

7. Freud, letter to Karl Abraham, quoted in Jones 1955, 2: 47–48; Gay 1988, 204. Although I deploy religious terminology here, I would not analyze its organization as functioning from a position of religious or cultlike militancy, as does Sulloway 1979, 480–84. That the early movement did, however, depend on a certain religious zeal, seems clear from Jones's confession that the charge of Freud's founding a "secular religion," although a "pretty obvious caricature," also possessed a "minute element of truth" that was made to stand in place of reality (*Free Associations: Memories of a Psycho-Analyst*, quoted in Gay 1988, 175). In characterizing the Wednesday Society members, Kurzweil 1989, 37, describes Rank as "pleasant but somewhat arrogant"; Wittels as "righteous and obnoxious"; Federn as "acquiescent"; and Stekel as "disruptive and disagreeable." See also Gay 1988, 178.

8. *SE*, 20: 9. Freud said something similar—quoting the same Ibsen text— in his address to B'nai B'rith, delivered as a letter because his health prevented his attending the society's celebration of his 70th birthday (*SE*, 20: 273–74). "We Jews," he had earlier written Abraham, counseling resigned patience in the face of prejudice, "if we want to cooperate with other people, have to develop a little masochism and be prepared to endure a certain amount of injustice" (Jones 1955, 2: 49).

9. Freud 1985, 218.

Bibliography

Anon. 1856. "Hysterical Pain in the Abdomen." *Lancet* 26.1: 372.

Anon. 1857. [On hysterical monomania.] *Lancet* 24.1: 642.

Anzieu, Didier. 1989. *The Skin Ego*. Translated by Chris Turner. New Haven: Yale University Press.

Appignanesi, Lisa, and John Forrester. 1992. *Freud's Women*. New York: Basic Books.

Baker Brown, Isaac. 1854. *On Some Diseases of Women Admitting of Surgical Treatment*. London: John Churchill.

———. 1862. *On Ovarian Dropsy: Its Nature, Diagnosis, & Treatment*. London: Davies.

———. 1886. "On the Curability of Certain Forms of Insanity, Epilepsy, Catalepsy, and Hysteria in Females." *British Medical Journal* 1 (April 28): 438–40.

Balmary, Marie. 1982. *Psychoanalyzing Psychoanalysis: Freud and the Hidden Fault of the Father*. Translated by Ned Lukacher. Baltimore: Johns Hopkins University Press.

Battey, Robert. 1886. "Castration in Mental and Nervous Diseases." *American Journal of the Medical Sciences*, n.s., 92: 483–90.

Beard, George. 1879. "The Nature and Diagnosis of Neurasthenia." *Medical Record* 15: 184.

———. 1882. *The Study of Trance, Muscle-Reading and Allied Nervous Phenomena in Europe and America with a Letter on the Moral Character of Trance Subjects, and a Defence of Dr. Charcot*. New York: n.p.

Bernard, Claude. 1949 [1927]. *An Introduction to the Study of Experimental Medicine*. Translated by Henry Copley Greene, with an introduction by Lawrence J. Henderson. N.p.: Henry Schuman.

Bernheim, Hippolyte. 1964 [1886]. *Hypnosis and Suggestion in Psychotherapy: A Treatise on the Nature and Uses of Hypnotism*. Translated by Christian A. Herter. 2d rev. ed. New York: University Books.

———. 1980 [1891]. *Bernheim's New Studies in Hypnotism*. Translated by Richard S. Sandor. New York: International Universities Press.

Bernheimer, Charles, and Claire Kahane, eds. 1985. *In Dora's Case: Freud—Hysteria—Feminism*. New York: Columbia University Press.

Biagioli, Mario. 1996. "Etiquette, Interdependence, and Sociability in Seventeenth-Century Science." *Critical Inquiry* 22.2 (Winter): 193–238.

Binet, Alfred. 1886. *La Psychologie du raisonnement: Recherches expérimentales par l'hypnotisme*. Paris: Félix Alcan.

———. 1887. "Le Fetichism dans l'amour." *Revue Philosophique de la France et de l'étranger* 24 (July–Dec.): 143–67, 252–74.

———. 1894. *Introduction à la psychologie expérimentale*. Paris: Félix Alcan.

———. 1903. *L'Étude expérimentale de l'intelligence*. Paris: Schleicher.

———. 1969. *The Experimental Psychology of Alfred Binet: Selected Papers*. Edited by Robert H. Pollack and Margaret W. Brenner. New York: Springer.

Binet, Alfred, and Charles Féré. 1887. *Le Magnétisme animal*. Paris: Félix Alcan.

Borch-Jacobsen, Mikkel. 1988. *The Freudian Subject*. Translated by Catherine Porter. Stanford: Stanford University Press.

———. 1992a. *The Emotional Tie: Psychoanalysis, Mimesis, and Affect*. Translated by Douglas Brick et al. Stanford: Stanford University Press.

———. 1992b. "The Freudian Subject: From Politics to Ethics." In Borch-Jacobsen 1992a, 15–35.

———. 1992c. "Mimetic Efficacity." In Borch-Jacobsen 1992a, 98–121.

———. 1992d. "The Unconscious, Nonetheless." In Borch-Jacobsen 1992a, 123–55.

———. 1994. "The Oedipus Problem in Freud and Lacan." Translated by Douglas Brick. *Critical Inquiry* 20.2 (Winter): 267–82.

———. 1997. "Basta Così! Mikkel Borch-Jacobsen on Psychoanalysis and Philosophy." Interview by Chris Oakley. In Dufresne 1997, 209–27.

Bourneville, Magloire-Désiré, and P. Regnard. 1879–80. *Iconographie photographique de la Salpêtrière (service de M. Charcot)*. 3 vols. Paris: Progrès médical.

Bowie, Malcolm. 1987. *Freud, Proust, and Lacan: Theory as Fiction*. Cambridge, Eng.: Cambridge University Press.

Breuer, Josef, and Sigmund Freud. 1957. *Studies on Hysteria*. Translated from the German and edited by James Strachey, in collaboration with Anna Freud, assisted by Alix Strachey and Alan Tyson. New York: Basic Books. Reprint of vol. 2 of *SE*.

Briquet, Pierre. 1859. *Traité clinique et thérapeutique de l'hystérie*. Paris: J.-B. Baillière et fils, Librairies de L'Académie impériale de médecine.

Brooks, Peter. 1984. *Reading for the Plot: Design and Intention in Narrative*. New York: Random House.

Burgin, Victor, James Donald, and Cora Kaplan, eds. 1986. *Formations of Fantasy*. London: Methuen.

Butler, Judith. 1993. *Bodies That Matter: On the Discursive Limits of "Sex."* New York: Routledge.

Bynum, W. F. 1985. "The Nervous Patient in Eighteenth- and Nineteenth-Century Britain: The Psychiatric Origins of British Neurology." In Bynum et al. 1985, 1: 89–102.

Bynum, W. F., Roy Porter, and Michael Shepherd, eds. 1985. *The Anatomy of Madness: Essays in the History of Psychiatry.* 2 vols. London: Tavistock.

Cabanis, Pierre Jean Georges. 1815. *Rapports du Physique et du moral de l'homme* (3d ed.). 2 vols. Paris: Caille & Ravier.

Camus, Jean, and Philippe Pagniez. 1904. *Isolement et psychothérapie: Traitement de l'hystérie et de la neurasthénie pratique de la rééducation morale et physique.* Preface by J. Dejerine. Paris: Félix Alcan.

Canguilhem, Georges. 1978 [1966]. *On the Normal and the Pathological.* Translated by Carolyn R. Fawcett, with the editorial collaboration of Robert S. Cohen. Introduction by Michel Foucault. Reprint. Dordrecht, Holland: D. Reidel, 1978.

Carter, Robert Brudenell. 1883 [1853]. *On the Pathology and Treatment of Hysteria.* London: John Churchill.

Cartwright, Lisa. 1995. *Screening the Body: Tracing Medicine's Visual Culture.* Minneapolis: University of Minnesota Press.

Castel, Robert. 1988. *The Regulation of Madness: The Origins of Incarceration in France.* Translated by W. D. Halls. Berkeley and Los Angeles: University of California Press.

Certeau, Michel. 1986. "The Freudian Novel." In *Heterologies: Discourse on the Other*, trans. Brian Massumi, 1–30. Minneapolis: University of Minnesota Press.

Charcot, Jean-Martin. 1877. *Lectures on the Diseases of the Nervous System Delivered at la Salpêtrière.* Translated by George Sigerson. 3 vols. London: New Sydenham Society.

———. 1887. "Essai d'une distinction nosographique des divers états nerveux compris sous le nom d'hypnotisme." In Binet and Féré 1887.

———. 1889. *Clinical Lectures on Diseases of the Nervous System Delivered at the Infirmary of la Salpêtrière.* Translated by Thomas Savill. 3 vols. London: New Sydenham Society.

———. 1971. *L'Hysterie: Textes choisis.* Edited by Etienne Trillat. Toulouse: Privat.

———. 1975. [1887–89]. *Leçons du mardi à la Salpêtrière: Notes de cours de MM. Blin, Charcot, Henri Colin, élèves du service.* 2 vols. Reprint. Paris: Hachette.

———. 1987 [1887–89]. *Charcot, the Clinician: The Tuesday Lessons: Excerpts from Nine Case Presentations on General Neurology Delivered at the Salpêtrière Hospital in 1887–88 by Jean-Martin Charcot.* Translated and with commentary by Christopher G. Goetz. New York: Raven Press.

Cixous, Hélène, and Catherine Clément. 1986. *The Newly Born Woman*. Translated by Betsy Wing. Minneapolis: University of Minnesota Press.

Clément, Catherine. 1987. *The Weary Sons of Freud*. Translated by Nicole Ball, with an introduction by Ann Rosalind Jones. London: Verso.

Cohn, Dorrit. 1992. "Freud's Case Histories and the Question of Fictionality." In *Telling Facts: History and Narration in Psychoanalysis*, ed. Joseph H. Smith and Humphrey Morris, 21–47. Psychiatry and the Humanities, vol. 13. Baltimore: Johns Hopkins University Press.

Cremerius, J. 1981. *Die Rezeption der Psychoanalyse in der Soziologie, Psychologie und Theologie im deutschsprachigen Raum bis 1940*. Frankfurt a/M: Suhrkamp.

Crews, Frederick C. 1986. *Skeptical Engagements*. New York: Oxford University Press, 1986.

———. 1995. *The Memory Wars: Freud's Legacy in Dispute*. New York: New York Review of Books.

Dagognet, François. 1992. *Étienne-Jules Marey: A Passion for the Trace*. Translated by Robert Galeta with Hanine Herman. Cambridge, Mass.: MIT Press, Zone Books.

David-Ménard, Monique. 1989. *Hysteria from Freud to Lacan: Body and Language in Psychoanalysis*. Translated by Catherine Porter, with a foreword by Ned Lukacher. Ithaca, N.Y.: Cornell University Press.

Davidson, Arnold I. 1987. "How to Do the History of Psychoanalysis: A Reading of Freud's *Three Essays on the Theory of Sexuality*." In *The Trial(s) of Psychoanalysis*, ed. Françoise Meltzer, 39–64. Chicago: University of Chicago Press.

de Lauretis, Teresa. 1994. *The Practice of Love: Lesbian Sexuality and Perverse Desire*. Bloomington: Indiana University Press.

de Marneffe, Daphne. 1991. "Looking and Listening: The Construction of Clinical Knowledge in Charcot and Freud." *Signs: Journal of Women in Culture and Society* 17.1: 71–111.

Dejerine, Joseph-Jules, and E. Gauckler. 1915. *The Psychoneuroses and Their Treatment by Psychotherapy*. Translated by Smith Ely Jelliffe. 2d ed. Philadelphia: J. B. Lippincott. Reprint. New York: Arno Press, 1976.

Delboeuf, Joseph. 1886. "De l'influence de l'éducation et de l'imitation dans le somnambulisme provoqué." *Revue Philosophique* 22: 146–71.

Derrida, Jacques. 1978. "Cogito and the History of Madness." In *Writing and Difference*, translated by Alan Bass, 31–63. Chicago: University of Chicago Press.

———. 1997. "'To Do Justice to Freud': The History of Madness in the Age of Psychoanalysis." In *Returns of the "French Freud,"* ed. Dufresne, 133–68.

Didi-Huberman, Georges. 1982. *Invention de l'hysterie: Charcot et l'iconographie photographique de la Salpêtrière*. Paris: Éditions Macula.

Doane, Mary Ann. 1987. *The Desire to Desire: The Woman's Film of the 1940s*. Bloomington: Indiana University Press.

Dubois, Paul. 1908 [1905]. *The Psychic Treatment of Nervous Disorders [The Psy-*

choneuroses and Their Moral Treatment]. Translated and edited by Smith Ely Jelliffe and William A. White. 4th ed. New York: Funk & Wagnalls.

Dufresne, Todd, ed. 1997. *Returns of the "French Freud": Freud, Lacan, and Beyond.* New York: Routledge.

Dyer, Richard. 1979. *Stars.* London: British Film Institute.

Eagleton, Terry. 1983. *Literary Theory: An Introduction.* Minneapolis: University of Minnesota Press.

Ellenberger, Henri F. 1970. *The Discovery of the Unconscious: The History and Evolution of Dynamic Psychiatry.* New York: Basic Books.

Ellis, Havelock. 1895. *The Criminal.* 2d ed. New York: Charles Scribner's Sons.

――――. 1902. *Studies in the Psychology of Sex,* vol. 2: *Sexual Inversion.* Philadelphia: F. A. Davis.

――――. 1906. *Studies in the Psychology of Sex,* vol. 5: *Erotic Symbolism, the Mechanism of Detumescence, the Psychic State in Pregnancy.* Philadelphia: F. A. Davis.

――――. 1908. *Studies in the Psychology of Sex,* vol. 3: *Analysis of the Sexual Impulses, Love and Pain, the Sexual Impulse in Women.* Philadelphia: F. A. Davis.

――――. 1914. *Studies in the Psychology of Sex,* vol. 4: *Sexual Selection in Man.* Philadelphia: F. A. Davis.

――――. 1921. *Studies in the Psychology of Sex,* vol. 6: *Sex in Relation to Society.* Philadelphia: F. A. Davis.

――――. 1930 [1894]. *Man and Woman: A Study of Human Secondary Sexual Characters.* 6th ed. London: A. & C. Black.

――――. 1936 [1897]. *Studies in the Psychology of Sex,* vol. 1. New York: Random House.

――――. 1952. *Sex and Marriage: Eros in Contemporary Life.* Edited by John Gawsworth. New York: Random House.

Evans, Martha Noel. 1991. *Fits and Starts: A Genealogy of Hysteria in Modern France.* Ithaca, N.Y.: Cornell University Press.

Féré, Charles. 1898. *La Famille névropathique: Theorie tératologique de l'hérédité et de la prédisposition morbides et de la dégénérescence.* Paris: Félix Alcan.

――――. 1900. *The Sexual Instinct: Its Evolution and Dissolution.* Translated by Henry Blanchamp. London: University Press.

Ferguson, Harvie. 1996. *The Lure of Dreams: Sigmund Freud and the Construction of Modernity.* London: Routledge.

Ferrier, David. 1876. *The Functions of the Brain.* London: Smith, Elder.

Figlio, Karl. 1977. "The Historiography of Scientific Medicine: An Invitation to the Human Sciences." *Comparative Studies in Society and History* 19: 262–86.

Fleming, J. B. 1960. "Clitoridectomy—the Disastrous Downfall of Isaac Baker Brown, F.R.C.S. (1867)." *Journal of Obstetrics and Gynaecology of the British Empire,* n.s., 67.6 (December): 1017–34.

Forrester, John. 1980. *Language and the Origins of Psychoanalysis.* London: Macmillan.

————. 1990. *The Seductions of Psychoanalysis*. Cambridge, Eng.: Cambridge University Press.

Foucault, Michel. 1972. *The Archaeology of Knowledge and the Discourse on Language*. Translated by A. M. Sheridan Smith. New York: Pantheon Books.

————. 1975. *The Birth of the Clinic: An Archaeology of Medical Perception*. Translated by A. M. Sheridan Smith. New York: Vintage Books.

————. 1977. "Nietzsche, Genealogy, History." In *Language, Counter-Memory, Practice: Selected Essays and Interviews*, ed. and trans. Donald F. Bouchard and Sherry Simon, 145–68. Ithaca, N.Y.: Cornell University Press.

————. 1978. *The History of Sexuality, Volume I: An Introduction*. Translated by Robert Hurley. New York: Pantheon Books.

————. 1985. *The History of Sexuality, Volume II: The Use of Pleasure*. Translated by Robert Hurley. New York: Random House.

————. 1988. "Confinement, Psychiatry, Prison." In *Politics/Philosophy/Culture: Interviews and Other Writings, 1977–1984*, ed. Lawrence D. Kritzman, trans. Alan Sheridan et al., 180–89. New York: Routledge.

Fox, Richard Wightman, and T. J. Jackson Lears, eds. 1983. *The Culture of Consumption: Critical Essays in American History, 1880–1980*. New York: Pantheon Books.

French, Richard D. 1975. *Antivivisection and Medical Science in Victorian Society*. Princeton: Princeton University Press.

Freud, Anna. 1973. "Beating Fantasies and Daydreams." In *Writings*, vol. 2: *Introduction to Psychoanalysis: Lectures for Child Analysts and Teachers, 1922–35*, 137–58. New York: International Universities Press.

Freud, Sigmund. 1955–74. *The Standard Edition of the Complete Psychological Works of Sigmund Freud*. Translated and edited by James Strachey et al. 24 vols. London: Hogarth Press.

————. 1963. *Early Psychoanalytic Writings*. Edited with an introduction by Philip Rieff. New York: Collier Books.

————. 1985. *The Complete Letters of Sigmund Freud to Wilhelm Fliess, 1887–1904*. Translated and edited by Jeffrey Moussaieff Masson. Cambridge, Mass.: Harvard University Press.

Fuss, Diana. 1989. *Essentially Speaking: Feminism, Nature and Difference*. New York: Routledge.

————. 1995. *Identification Papers*. New York: Routledge.

Gallop, Jane. 1982. *The Daughter's Seduction: Feminism and Psychoanalysis*. Ithaca, N.Y.: Cornell University Press.

Garner, Shirley Nelson, Claire Kahane, and Madelon Sprengnether, eds. 1985. *The (M)other Tongue: Essays in Feminist Psychoanalytic Interpretation*. Ithaca, N.Y.: Cornell University Press.

Gay, Peter. 1988. *Freud: A Life for Our Time*. New York: W. W. Norton.

Gearhart, Suzanne. 1985. "The Scene of Psychoanalysis: The Unanswered Questions of Dora." In Bernheimer and Kahane 1985, 105–27.

Gilman, Charlotte Perkins. 1973 [1899]. *The Yellow Wallpaper.* Reprint. New York: Feminist Press.

Gilman, Sander L. 1993. "The Image of the Hysteric." In Gilman et al. 1993, 345–452.

Gilman, Sander L., Helen King, Roy Porter, G. S. Rousseau, and Elaine Showalter, eds. 1993. *Hysteria Beyond Freud.* Berkeley and Los Angeles: University of California Press.

Ginzburg, Carlo. 1989. *Clues, Myths, and the Historical Method.* Translated by John and Anne C. Tedeschi. Baltimore: Johns Hopkins University Press.

Goffman, Erving. 1959. *The Preservation of Self in Everyday Life.* Garden City, N.Y.: Doubleday.

Goldstein, Jan. 1987. *Console and Classify: The French Psychiatric Profession in the Nineteenth Century.* Cambridge, Eng.: Cambridge University Press.

———. 1991. "The Uses of Male Hysteria: Medical and Literary Discourse in Nineteenth-Century France." *Representations* 34 (Spring): 134–65.

Goux, Jean-Joseph. 1990. *Symbolic Economies: After Marx and Freud.* Translated by Jennifer Curtiss Gage. Ithaca, N.Y.: Cornell University Press.

Greenberg, David F. 1988. *The Construction of Homosexuality.* Chicago: University of Chicago Press.

Grosskurth, Phyllis. 1980. *Havelock Ellis: A Biography.* New York: Knopf.

Grosz, Elizabeth. 1994. *Volatile Bodies: Toward a Corporeal Feminism.* Bloomington: Indiana University Press.

Grünbaum, Adolf. 1984. *The Foundations of Psychoanalysis: A Philosophical Critique.* Berkeley and Los Angeles: University of California Press.

Guillain, Georges. 1959. *J.-M. Charcot, 1825–1893: His Life—His Work.* Translated and edited by Pearce Bailey. New York: Paul B. Hoeber.

Hacking, Ian. 1986. "Making Up People." In *Reconstructing Individualism: Autonomy, Individuality, and the Self in Western Thought,* ed. Thomas C. Heller, Morton Sosna, and David E. Wellbery, 222–36. Stanford: Stanford University Press.

Hale, Nathan G., Jr. 1971. *Freud and the Americans: The Beginnings of Psychoanalysis in the United States, 1876–1917.* New York: Oxford University Press.

Hall, Marshall. 1827. *Commentaries on Some of the More Important Diseases of Females.* London: Longman, Rees, Orme, Brown and Green.

———. 1850. "On a New and Lamentable Form of Hysteria." *Lancet* 1: 660.

Halperin, David M. 1990. *One Hundred Years of Homosexuality and Other Essays on Greek Love.* New York: Routledge.

Haraway, Donna. 1989. *Primate Visions: Gender, Race, and Nature in the World of Modern Science.* New York: Routledge.

Harris, Ruth. 1985. "Murder Under Hypnosis in the Case of Gabrielle Bompard: Psychiatry in the Courtroom in Belle Époque Paris." In Bynum, Porter, and Shepherd 1985, 2: 197–241.

Heape, Walter. 1905. "Ovulation and Degeneration of Ova in the Rabbit." *Proceedings of the Royal Society of London* 76: 260–68.

————. 1913. *Sexual Antagonism*. London: Constable.

Heath, Stephen. 1984. *The Sexual Fix*. New York: Schocken Books.

Henry, Michel. 1993. *The Genealogy of Psychoanalysis*. Translated by Douglas Brick. Stanford: Stanford University Press.

Herman, Judith Lewis. 1981. With Lisa Hirshman. *Father-Daughter Incest*. Cambridge, Mass.: Harvard University Press.

Hertz, Neil. 1985. "Dora's Secrets, Freud's Techniques." In Bernheimer and Kahane 1985, 221–42.

Hughes, Judith M. 1994. *From Freud's Consulting Room: The Unconscious in a Scientific Age*. Cambridge, Mass.: Harvard University Press.

Hunter, Dianne. 1985. "Hysteria, Psychoanalysis, and Feminism: The Case of Anna O." In Garner, Kahane, and Sprengnether 1985, 89–115.

Hunter, Kathryn Montgomery. 1991. *Doctors' Stories: The Narrative Structure of Medical Knowledge*. Princeton: Princeton University Press.

Jackson, John Hughlings. 1932. *Selected Writings*. Edited by J. Taylor. 2 vols. London: Hodder & Stoughton.

Janet, Pierre. 1898. *Névroses et idées fixes*. 2 vols. Paris: Félix Alcan.

————. 1901. *The Mental State of Hystericals: A Study of Mental Stigmata and Mental Accidents*. Translated by Caroline Rollin Corson. New York: G. P. Putnam's Sons.

————. 1925. *Psychological Healing: A Historical and Clinical Study*. Translated by Eden and Cedar Paul. 2 vols. London: George Allen & Unwin. Lectures, 1904–7.

————. 1965 [1907]. *The Major Symptoms of Hysteria: Fifteen Lectures Given in the Medical School of Harvard University*. New York: Hafner. Facsimile of 1929 edition.

Jones, Ernest. 1953–57. *The Life and Work of Sigmund Freud*. 3 vols. New York: Basic Books.

Jorden, Edward. 1971 [1603]. *A Disease Called the Suffocation of the Mother*. Reprint. Amsterdam: De Capo Press.

Kahane, Claire. 1995. *Passions of the Voice: Hysteria, Narrative, and the Figure of the Speaking Woman, 1850–1915*. Baltimore: Johns Hopkins University Press.

Katz, Jonathan Ned. 1995. *The Invention of Heterosexuality*. New York: Dutton.

Kernberg, Otto F. 1992. *Aggression in Personality Disorders and Perversions*. New Haven: Yale University Press.

Kiceluk, Stephanie. 1992. "The Patient as Sign and Story: Disease Pictures, Life Histories, and the First Psychoanalytic Case History." *Journal of Clinical Psychoanalysis* 1.3: 333–68.

King, Helen. 1993. "Once upon a Text: Hysteria from Hippocrates." In Gilman et al. 1993, 3–90.

King, Lester S. 1982. *Medical Thinking: A Historical Preface*. Princeton: Princeton University Press.

Knorr-Cetina, Karin D., and Michael Mulkay, eds. 1983. *Science Observed: Perspectives on the Social Study of Science*. London: Sage Publications.

Kofman, Sarah. 1991. *Freud and Fiction*. Translated by Sarah Wykes. Boston: Northeastern University Press.

Krafft-Ebing, Richard von. 1896 [1889]. *An Experimental Study in the Domain of Hypnotism*. Translated by Charles G. Chaddock. New York: G. P. Putnam's Sons.

————. 1946 [1886–96]. *Psychopathia Sexualis: A Medico-Forensic Study*. Introduction by Victor Robinson. 12th ed. New York: Pioneer Publications.

Krohn, Alan. 1978. *Hysteria: The Elusive Neurosis*. New York: International Universities Press.

Krüll, Marianne. 1986. *Freud and His Father*. Translated by Arnold J. Pomerans. New York: W. W. Norton.

Kuhn, Thomas. 1970. *The Structure of Scientific Revolutions*. 2d ed. Chicago: University of Chicago Press.

Kurzweil, Edith. 1989. *The Freudians: A Comparative Perspective*. New Haven: Yale University Press.

Lacan, Jacques. 1985. "Intervention on Transference." In Bernheimer and Kahane 1985, 92–104.

Langland, Elizabeth. 1995. *Nobody's Angels: Middle-Class Women and Domestic Ideology in Victorian Culture*. Ithaca, N.Y.: Cornell University Press.

Laplanche, Jean. 1976. *Life and Death in Psychoanalysis*. Translated by Jeffrey Mehlmann. Baltimore: Johns Hopkins University Press.

————. 1989. *New Foundations for Psychoanalysis*. Translated by David Macey. Oxford: Basil Blackwell.

Laplanche, Jean, and J.-B. Pontalis. 1973. *The Language of Psycho-Analysis*. Translated by Donald Nicholson-Smith. New York: W. W. Norton.

————. 1986. "Fantasy and the Origins of Sexuality." In Burgin et al. 1986, 5–34.

Laqueur, Thomas. 1990. *Making Sex: Body and Gender from the Greeks to Freud*. Cambridge, Mass.: Harvard University Press.

Latour, Bruno. 1983. "Give Me a Laboratory and I Will Raise the World." In Knorr-Cetina and Mulkay 1983, 141–70.

————. 1986. "Visualization and Cognition: Thinking with Eyes and Hands." *Knowledge and Society: Studies in the Sociology of Culture Past and Present* 6: 1–40.

————. 1990a. "Drawing Things Together." In Lynch and Woolgar 1990, 19–68.

————. 1990b. "The Force and Reason of Experiment." In LeGrand 1990, 49–80.

————. 1993. *We Have Never Been Modern*. Translation of *Nous n'avons jamais été modernes: Essai d'anthropologie symétrique* (1991) by Catherine Porter. Cambridge, Mass.: Harvard University Press.

Laycock, Thomas. 1840. *A Treatise on the Nervous Diseases of Women, Comprising an Inquiry into the Nature, Causes, and Treatment of the Spinal and Hysterical Disorders.* London: Longman, Orme, Brown, Green, & Longmans.

————. 1976 [1860]. *Mind and Brain, or, the Correlations of Consciousness and Organisation; with Their Applications to Philosophy, Zoology, . . . and the Practice of Medicine.* 2 vols. Reprint. New York: Arno Press.

Lears, T. J. Jackson. 1983. "From Salvation to Self-Realization: Advertising and the Therapeutic Roots of the Consumer Culture, 1880–1930." In Fox and Lears 1983, 1–38.

LeGrand, H. E., ed. 1990. *Experimental Inquiries: Historical, Philosophical and Social Studies of Experimentation in Science.* Dordrecht, Holland: Kluwer Academic Publishers.

Lens, Pierre de. 1818. "Liberté individuelle." In *Dictionnaire des sciences médicales,* 28: 95–121. Paris.

Levin, Kenneth. 1978. *Freud's Early Psychology of the Neuroses: A Historical Perspective.* Pittsburgh: Pittsburgh University Press.

Lombroso, Cesare, and William Ferrero. 1909. *The Female Offender.* Introduction by W. Douglas Morrison. New York: D. Appleton.

Longo, Lawrence D. 1979. "The Rise and Fall of Battey's Operation: A Fashion in Surgery." *Bulletin of the History of Medicine* 53: 244–67.

Lukacher, Ned. 1986. *Primal Scenes: Philosophy/Psychoanalysis/Literature.* Ithaca, N.Y.: Cornell University Press.

Lynch, Michael, and Steve Woolgar, eds. 1990. *Representation in Scientific Practice.* Cambridge, Mass.: MIT Press.

Macmillan, Malcolm. 1991. *Freud Evaluated: The Completed Arc.* Amsterdam: Elsevier Science.

Mantegazza, Paolo. 1886. *L'Amour dans l'humanité: Essai d'une ethnologie de l'amour.* Translated by Émilien Chesneau. Paris: F. Fetscherin & Chuit.

Marcus, Steven. 1985. "Freud and Dora: Story, History, Case History." In Bernheimer and Kahane 1985, 56–91.

Marshall, F. H. A. 1960 [1910]. *Marshall's Physiology of Reproduction.* Edited by A. S. Parkes. London: Longmans, Green.

Martin, Emily. 1994. *Flexible Bodies: Tracking Immunity in American Culture from the Days of Polio to the Age of AIDS.* Boston: Beacon Press.

Masson, Jeffrey Moussaieff. 1984. *The Assault on Truth: Freud's Suppression of the Seduction Theory.* New York: Farrar, Straus & Giroux.

Matus, Jill L. 1995. *Unstable Bodies: Victorian Representations of Sexuality and Maternity.* Manchester: Manchester University Press.

McGrath, William. 1986. *Freud's Discovery of Psychoanalysis: The Politics of Hysteria.* Ithaca, N.Y.: Cornell University Press.

McLaren, Angus. 1974–75. "Doctor in the House: Medicine and Private Morality in France, 1800–1850." *Feminist Studies,* 2.3: 39–54.

Micale, Mark S. 1985. "The Salpêtrière in the Age of Charcot: An Institutional

Perspective on Medical History in the Late Nineteenth Century." *Journal of Contemporary History* 20: 703–31.

———. 1989. "Hysteria and Its Historiography: A Review of Past and Present Writings." *History of Science* 27: 223–61.

———. 1990a. "Charcot and the Idea of Hysteria in the Male: Gender, Mental Science, and Medical Diagnosis in Late Nineteenth-Century France." *Medical History* 34: 363–411.

———. 1990b. "Hysteria and Its Historiography: The Future Perspective." *History of Psychiatry* 1: 33–124.

———. 1995. *Approaching Hysteria: Disease and Its Interpretations*. Princeton: Princeton University Press.

Miller, Nancy K. 1980. *The Heroine's Text: Readings in the French and English Novel, 1722–1782*. New York: Columbia University Press.

Mitchell, Juliet, and Jacqueline Rose, eds. and trans. 1982. *Feminine Sexuality: Jacques Lacan and the École freudienne*. New York: W. W. Norton.

Mitchell, S. Weir. 1875. "Rest in Nervous Diseases: Its Use and Abuse." In *A Series of American Clinical Lectures*, ed. E. C. Sequin, 1: 83–102. 3 vols. New York: G. P. Putnam's Sons.

———. 1877. *Fat and Blood, and How to Make Them*. Philadelphia: J. B. Lippincott.

———. 1885 [1881]. *Lectures on Diseases of the Nervous System, Especially in Women*. 2d ed. Philadelphia: Lea Brothers.

Moll, Albert. 1931 [1891]. *Perversions of the Sex Instinct: A Study of Sexual Inversion, Based on Clinical Data and Official Documents*. Translated by Maurice Popkin. Reprint. Newark, N.J.: Julian Press.

———. 1933 [1897]. *Libido Sexualis: Studies in the Psychosexual Laws of Love Verified by Clinical Sexual Case Histories*. New York: American Ethnological Press.

Moscucci, Ornella. 1990. *The Science of Woman: Gynaecology and Gender in England, 1800–1929*. Cambridge, Eng.: Cambridge University Press.

Mulvey, Laura. 1992. "Visual Pleasure and Narrative Cinema." In *The Sexual Subject: A Screen Reader in Sexuality*, 22–34. New York: Routledge.

Munthe, Axel. 1930 [1929]. *The Story of San Michele*. New York: E. P. Dutton.

Nayrac, Jean-Paul. 1906. *Physiologie et psychologie de l'attention: Evolution, dissolution, rééducation, education*. Paris: Félix Alcan.

Nordau, Max. 1895 [1892]. *Degeneracy*. Translated from the German. New York: D. Appleton.

Pateman, Carole. 1988. *The Sexual Contract*. Cambridge, Mass.: Polity Press.

Pinel, Philippe. 1806. *A Treatise on Insanity*. Translation by D. D. Davis of *Traité médico-philosophique sur l'aliénation mentale ou la manie* (1799–1800). London: Cadell & Davies.

Poirier, Suzanne. 1983. "The Weir Mitchell Rest Cure: Doctor and Patients." *Women's Studies* 10.1: 15–40.

Porter, Roy. 1993. "The Body and the Mind, the Doctor and the Patient: Negotiating Hysteria." In Gilman et al. 1993, 225–85.

Rabinbach, Anson. 1982. "The Body Without Fatigue: A Nineteenth-Century Utopia." In *Political Symbolism in Modern Europe: Essays in Honor of George L. Mosse*, ed. Seymour Drescher, David Sabean, and Allan Sharlin, 42–62. New Brunswick, N.J.: Transaction Books.

———. 1986. "The European Science of Work: The Economy of the Body at the End of the Nineteenth Century." In *Work in France: Representations, Meaning, Organization, and Practice*, ed. Steven Laurence Caplan and Cynthia J. Koepp, 475–513. Ithaca, N.Y.: Cornell University Press.

Reiser, Stanley Joel. 1978. *Medicine and the Reign of Technology*. Cambridge, Eng.: Cambridge University Press.

Renterghem, A. W. van. 1907. *La Psychothérapie dans ses différents modes*. Amsterdam: Imprimerie électrique, F. van Rossen.

Richards, Thomas. 1990. *The Commodity Culture of Victorian England: Advertising and Spectacle, 1851–1914*. Stanford: Stanford University Press.

Richer, Paul. 1885. *Étude cliniques sur la grande hystérie ou hystéro-epilepsie*. 12th ed. Paris: Adrien Delahaye & Émile Lecrosnier.

Ricoeur, Paul. 1970. *Freud and Philosophy: An Essay on Interpretation*. Translated by Denis Savage. New Haven: Yale University Press.

Ripa, Yannick. 1990. *Women and Madness: The Incarceration of Women in Nineteenth-Century France*. Translated by Catherine du Peloux Menagé. Minneapolis: University of Minnesota Press.

Robinson, Paul. 1993. *Freud and His Critics*. Berkeley and Los Angeles: University of California Press.

Rosenberg, Charles. 1985. "The Therapeutic Revolution: Medicine, Meaning, and Social Change in Nineteenth-Century America." In *Sickness and Health in America: Readings in the History of Medicine and Public Health*, ed. Judith Walzer Leavitt and Ronald L. Numbers, 39–52. Madison: University of Wisconsin Press.

Rothfield, Lawrence. 1992. *Vital Signs: Medical Realism in Nineteenth-Century Fiction*. Princeton: Princeton University Press.

Roudinesco, Elisabeth. 1986. *La Bataille de cent ans: Histoire de la psychoanalyse en France*. 2 vols. Paris: Seuil.

Rousseau, G. S. 1993. "'A Strange Pathology': Hysteria in the Early Modern World, 1500–1800." In Gilman et al. 1993, 91–221.

Roustang, François. 1982. *Dire Mastery: Discipleship from Freud to Lacan*. Translated by Ned Lukacher. Baltimore: Johns Hopkins University Press.

Rudnytsky, Peter. 1987. *Freud and Oedipus*. New York: Columbia University Press.

Safouan, Moustapha. 1980. "In Praise of Hysteria." In Schneiderman 1980, 55–60.

Schafer, Roy. 1980. "Narration in the Psychoanalytic Dialogue." In *On Narrative*, ed. W. J. T. Mitchell, 25–49. Chicago: University of Chicago Press.

Schneiderman, Stuart, ed. and trans. 1980. *Returning to Freud: Clinical Psychoanalysis in the School of Lacan*. New Haven: Yale University Press.

Schrenck-Notzing, Albert von. 1956 [1895]. *The Use of Hypnosis in Psychopathia Sexualis, with Especial Reference to Contrary Sexual Instinct*. Translated by Charles G. Chaddock. Reprint. New York: Institute for Research in Hypnosis Publication Society and Julian Press.

Sedgwick, Eve Kosofsky. 1990. *Epistemology of the Closet*. Berkeley and Los Angeles: University of California Press.

Shepherd, John A. 1980. *Lawson Tait: The Rebellious Surgeon (1845–1899)*. Lawrence, Kans.: Coronado Press.

Shorter, Edward. 1992. *From Paralysis to Fatigue: A History of Psychosomatic Illness in the Modern Era*. New York: Free Press.

Showalter, Elaine. 1985. *The Female Malady: Women, Madness, and English Culture, 1830–1980*. New York: Pantheon Books.

————. 1993. "Hysteria, Feminism, and Gender." In Gilman et al. 1993, 286–344.

Sicherman, Barbara. 1977. "The Uses of a Diagnosis: Doctors, Patients, and Neurasthenia." *Journal of the History of Medicine and Allied Sciences* 32: 33–54.

Sims, J. Marion. 1880. "Battey's Operation in Epileptoid Affections." *Medical Record* 17.23 (June 6): 622.

Skey, F. C. 1867. *Hysteria: Remote Causes of the Disease in General, Treatment of Disease by Tonic Agency, Local or Surgical Forms of Hysteria, etc.* London: Longmans, Green, Reader, & Dyer.

Slavney, Philip R. 1990. *Perspectives on "Hysteria."* Baltimore: Johns Hopkins University Press,.

Smith-Rosenberg, Carroll. 1985. "The Hysterical Woman: Sex Roles and Role Conflict in Nineteenth-Century America." In id., *Disorderly Conduct: Visions of Gender in Victorian America*, 197–216. New York: Knopf.

Soranus of Ephesus. 1956 [2d century a.d.]. *Soranus' Gynecology*. Translated and with an introduction by Owsei Temkin. Baltimore: Johns Hopkins Press.

Spence, Donald P. 1987. "The Sherlock Holmes Tradition." In id., *The Freudian Metaphor: Toward Paradigm Change in Psychoanalysis*, 112–59. New York: W. W. Norton.

Spillane, John D. 1981. *The Doctrine of the Nerves: Chapters in the History of Neurology*. London: Oxford University Press.

Spitzka, Edward C. 1878. "Reform in the Scientific Study of Psychiatry." *Journal of Nervous and Mental Diseases* 5.2: 201–29.

Sprengnether, Madelon. 1990. *The Spectral Mother: Freud, Feminism, and Psychoanalysis*. Ithaca, N.Y.: Cornell University Press.

Stallybrass, Peter, and Allon White. 1986. *The Politics and Poetics of Transgression*. Ithaca, N.Y.: Cornell University Press.

Star, Susan Leigh. 1989. *Regions of the Mind: Brain Research and the Quest for Scientific Certainty*. Stanford: Stanford University Press.

Steinach, Eugen. 1940. *Sex and Life: Forty Years of Biological and Medical Experiments*. New York: Viking Press.

Storer, Horatio R. 1972 [1871]. *The Causation, Course, and Treatment of Reflex Insanity in Women*. Reprint. New York: Arno Press.

Sulloway, Frank J. 1979. *Freud, Biologist of the Mind: Beyond the Psychoanalytic Legend*. New York: Basic Books.

Sydenham, Thomas. 1815. *The Works of Thomas Sydenham on Acute and Chronic Diseases with their Modes of Cure*. Translated and with an introduction by Benjamin Rush. Philadelphia: Johnson & Warner.

———. 1848–50. *The Works of Thomas Sydenham*. Translated by Dr. Greenhill. With a Life of the Author by R. G. Latham. 2 vols. London: Sydenham Society.

Thornton, E. M. 1976. *Hypnotism, Hysteria and Epilepsy: An Historical Synthesis*. London: Heinemann.

Trillat, Étienne. 1986. *Histoire de l'hystérie*. Paris: Seghers.

Veith, Ilza. 1965. *Hysteria: The History of a Disease*. Chicago: University of Chicago Press.

Vrettos, Athena. 1995. *Somatic Fictions: Imagining Illness in Victorian Culture*. Stanford: Stanford University Press.

Walkowitz, Judith R. 1980. *Prostitution and Victorian Society: Women, Class, and the State*. New York: Cambridge University Press.

Weber, Samuel. 1982. *The Legend of Freud*. Minneapolis: University of Minnesota Press.

Wells, Spencer. 1886. "Castration in Mental and Nervous Diseases." *American Journal of the Medical Sciences*, n.s., 82: 455–71.

White, Allon. 1993. *Carnival, Hysteria, and Writing: Collected Essays and Autobiography*. Oxford: Clarendon Press.

Williams, Linda. 1986. "Film Body: An Implantation of Perversions." In *Narrative, Apparatus, Ideology: A Film Theory Reader*, ed. Philip Rosen, 507–34. New York: Columbia University Press.

Wolf-Man. 1971. "My Recollections of Sigmund Freud, by the Wolf-Man." In *The Wolf-Man by the Wolf-Man*, ed. with introduction and chapters by Muriel Gardiner and foreword by Anna Freud, 135–52. New York: Basic Books.

Woolf, Virginia. 1929. *Orlando: A Biography*. New York: Harcourt, Brace.

Index

In this index an "f" after a number indicates a separate reference on the next page, and an "ff" indicates separate references on the next two pages. A continuous discussion over two or more pages is indicated by a span of page numbers, e.g., "57–59." *Passim* is used for a cluster of references in close but not consecutive sequence. In the absence of other attributions, works listed here are those of Sigmund Freud.

Library of Congress Cataloging-in-Publication Data

Sadoff, Dianne F.

  Sciences of the flesh : representing body and subject in
psychoanalysis / Dianne F. Sadoff.

    p.   cm.

  Includes bibliographical references and index.

  ISBN 0-8047-3084-9 (cl.)

  ISBN 0-8047-3508-5 (pbk.)

  1. Psychoanalysis—History.   2. Freud, Sigmund, 1856–1939.
I. Title.

BF173.S254   1998

150.19'52—dc21   98-16198

                                                        CIP

Last figure below indicates year of this printing:
07   06   05   04   03   02   01   00   99   98